God's Exiles and English Verse

In this critical study of the Exeter Anthology of Old English poetry, John Niles argues for approaching this unique collection as a shaped miscellany, one that is expressive of the devout yet cosmopolitan culture of English monasticism during the period of the tenth-century Benedictine Reform. Characterizing the authors of these poems as craft poets working in an innovative register, he argues that the Anthology draws on the time-honoured resources of Old English alliterative verse so as to express Christian verities in a manner designed to astonish and delight. In the course of his analysis of the codex as a whole, he offers new insights into many individual poems and problems of interpretation.

John D. Niles is Emeritus Professor at the University of Wisconsin, Madison, and the University of California, Berkeley.

'John Niles's book is premised on one of those simple, but foundational ideas that one can hardly believe has not been attempted before, so fundamentally important is the Exeter Anthology to our understanding of pre-Conquest English poetry. What has been previously lacking is intelligent, sensitive literary criticism of the whole codex: profound readings of the poems as poems. Niles's book is a carefully thought-out, elegantly written and critically incisive work that will be a landmark study for scholars and students of early English poetry.'
Chris Jones, Professor of English, University of St Andrews

'A well-written account of the manuscript and its many contents, containing detailed, insightful, and occasionally beautiful readings of the poems themselves.'
Elaine Treharne, Roberta Bowman Denning Professor of Humanities, Stanford University

'An excellent work that should be well received.'
Professor Bernard J. Muir, University of Melbourne

EXETER MEDIEVAL

God's Exiles and English Verse

*On the Exeter Anthology
of Old English Poetry*

John D. Niles

UNIVERSITY
of
EXETER
PRESS

First published in 2019 by
University of Exeter Press
Reed Hall, Streatham Drive
Exeter EX4 4QR
UK
www.exeterpress.co.uk

Emended second edition published in 2021.
Paperback edition published in 2022.

© John D. Niles 2019

The right of John D. Niles to be identified as author of this work has been asserted by him in accordance with the Copyright, Designs and Patents Act 1988.

British Library Cataloguing in Publication Data
A catalogue record for this book is available from the British Library.

ISBNs
978 1 905816 09 5 (Hbk)
978 1 804130 69 8 (Pbk)
978 1 905816 15 6 (epub)
978 1 905816 14 9 (pdf)

Cover image: Saint Cuthbert praying by the River Tyne.
London, British Library, Yates Thompson MS 26, fol. 10v
(© British Library Board, through Bridgeman Images)

Typeset in Gentium by BBR Design, Sheffield

Contents

Preface and Acknowledgements   vi
List of Abbreviations   x

PART ONE
READING THE ANTHOLOGY IN ITS HISTORICAL CONTEXT

1. Monastic Poetics   3
2. Scribes, Authors, Compilers and Readers   21
3. Exeter, Glastonbury and the Benedictine Reform   40

PART TWO
READING THE ANTHOLOGY AS A CODICOLOGICAL WHOLE

4. An Overview of the Book's Contents   65
5. Teaching the Tools of the Poet's Trade   145
6. The Enigmas—a Special Problem?   164
7. Poetry and World-View   180
8. Keywords   204
9. Intratextual Hermeneutics   223
10. Summary and Conclusions   238

Appendix 1: A Translation of *The Wanderer*   246
Appendix 2: Folio-by-Folio Contents of the Exeter Anthology   249
Appendix 3: Latin Genre Terms and the Poems of the Exeter Anthology   251

Bibliography of Works Cited   254
Index of Modern Authors Cited   276
Index of Old English Words Discussed   279
General Index   281

Preface and Acknowledgements

This book offers a codicologically based account of the Exeter Anthology of Old English poetry: its principles of design, its relationship of parts, its leading themes, its points of formal and stylistic interest, its probable makers and readers, and its possible uses in its time. While I make a point of the value of approaching the Anthology in a historically grounded manner, my main intention is to clarify what each poem brings to the ensemble and what the ensemble brings to each poem. By this means, issues pertaining to the interpretation of individual poems and passages can be resolved with greater confidence, while at the same time the contribution of verse to the culture of late Anglo-Saxon England will more readily be apparent.

It is a source of some wonderment to me that an integrative, book-length critical study of the Exeter Anthology has not been undertaken before. My study will be a success if it is forgotten in another generation or two—forgotten not because of neglect or indifference on the part of its prospective readers, I hope, but because my main argument about the Anthology's intellectual coherence in the context of late Anglo-Saxon monastic learning will by then be taken for granted, even if it encounters initial resistance on the part of those who are accustomed to reading certain of these poems in a different manner.

A word may be in order on the book's short title, 'God's Exiles and English Verse'. One reason why modern readers have been strongly attracted to certain poems of the Exeter Anthology, I suspect, has been their sympathetic response to the images of exile featured in that volume. They have felt the magnetism of persons who are outcast from society or alienated from society and who must fall back on their own resources for survival in a landscape that is desolate or wintry. Particularly in the middle decades of the war-torn twentieth century, the era of Eliot's *The Waste Land* and Camus's *L'Étranger*, the Wanderer's soliloquy must have seemed surprisingly contemporary, as it still does to many of us today.

The sympathetic portrayal of the condition of exile to be found in the Exeter Anthology is understandable given the likelihood that the book was made chiefly by and for 'God's exiles': that is to say, by and for monks and cloistered women, or by extension other Christians who took their religion seriously and strove to live by its tenets. Those people had a well-developed consciousness that they were exiles on this earth, strangers whose true happiness resided elsewhere. Orthodox doctrine confirmed them in that knowledge, elaborating on the matter in a vast intellectual system.

People who had opted for the monastic life were thus well situated to understand the existential situations of the solitary, exiled or destitute persons whose voices are heard in the pages of the Anthology. They may even have thought of those same imagined persons—the Wanderer, the Seafarer and others, including the hermit saint Guthlac and the speaker of *The Penitent's Prayer*—as God's exiles like themselves, in a meaningful sense. From their education and training they would have been aware that the Old Testament figure of Job, for example, a fortunate man before he was singled out for affliction and became in time a prophet, was one of God's exiles, whether or not he was aware of that fact or chose to be in that condition.

My study owes a great deal to the prior scholarship of others. Although no one else can be held responsible for the views expressed here, my debts to scholars who have written on individual poems of the Exeter Anthology are incalculable, as the notes to the book ought to testify. I am equally conscious of my debt to those scholars who have edited the Anthology as a whole, thereby giving sharp definition to its contents. The two most authoritative current editions are *The Exeter Book*, ed. George Philip Krapp and Elliott Van Kirk Dobbie (1936), and—supplanting it for most purposes—*The Exeter Anthology of Old English Poetry*, ed. Bernard J. Muir (2nd edn, 2000). I am fortunate to be in a position to build on Muir's insights as to how the poems of the codex speak to one another across textual boundaries, thereby constituting what he calls 'an anthology with a purpose' rather than a miscellaneous collection. I also owe a major debt to Patrick W. Conner's researches into the Anthology's origins, contents, intellectual context and transmission history, even when my own research has led me in different directions.

On palaeographical grounds the Exeter codex is ascribed a date between c.960 and c.990, with the compromise date 'c.975' being used by some. Muir (2000: 1: 1), expressing what may be a growing consensus, identifies c.965–75 as the apparent period when the Anthology was designed and copied out. I see no reason to differ from his judgement, though one should keep in mind that these dates are approximate. As for identifying the date of composition of the individual poems included in the codex, I likewise accept Muir's conclusion, which is based on the scholarship of others, that 'there is little reason to believe that any of the poems in the anthology dates from much before the Alfredian period, perhaps with the exception of the three lists embedded in *Widsith*' (2000: 1: 40). Confidence in this matter naturally stops short of certainty. This question of the origin of individual texts—one that I view as unanswerable in most instances—is not my chief concern. The possibility is now increasingly entertained, however, that certain poems or passages of the Exeter Anthology were composed close to the time when the book was compiled and written out, if not contemporaneously with those events. This line of thought directs attention to the period of c.965–75 as a crucial one of reception and shaping of the book's contents.

Two facsimiles of the manuscript are available in print or on DVD: *The Exeter Book of Old English Poetry*, with introductory chapters by R.W. Chambers, Max Förster and Robin Flower (1933), and *The Exeter Anthology of Old English Poetry*, an electronic edition prepared by Bernard J. Muir (2006). Another facsimile is available in *Exeter Manuscripts*, ed. Matthew T. Hussey, volume 22 of the series 'Anglo-Saxon Manuscripts in Microfiche Facsimile' (2014). Readers are encouraged to consult one or another of these resources while following along with the ensuing chapters.

Quotations from the poems of the Exeter Anthology are drawn from Muir's edition unless noted otherwise, with the difference that I capitalize the word 'God' when it occurs in passages of Old English while Muir adopts lower-case 'god'. The titles I adopt for individual poems, which are untitled in the manuscript, are normally the same as Muir's, which in turn are largely conventional ones, though in certain instances I have departed from Muir's practice as is set out in Appendix 2.

Translations of Old English passages, or of Latin texts other than the Vulgate Bible, are my own unless specified otherwise. When citing passages from the Bible, I rely on the Vulgate text and the Douay-Rheims translation as edited side by side in the Dumbarton Oaks Medieval Library (DOML). Psalms therefore have their Vulgate numbering. For the sake of accuracy, I have made a point of consulting the precise and perceptive prose translations of Old English verse offered by S.A.J. Bradley in his 1982 anthology *Anglo-Saxon Poetry*, whether or not my final choice of wording is the same as his. Bradley too is an advocate for a codicological approach to the poems of the Exeter Anthology, and his headnotes offer astute insights into the book's religious tenor. I have likewise consulted the DOML editions of Old English texts, with their clear facing-page translations.

When quoting Old English texts in inset passages, as well as when citing entries from the *Dictionary of Old English*, I follow the lead of my source texts and dispense with the diacritical marks that are sometimes used to mark long vowels. For the sake of philological precision, however, I employ diacritics when discussing individual Old English words or when incorporating short textual quotations into the body of my text, silently adding them when they are not in my source. I also silently add hyphens to separate the elements of compound words, following DOML editorial practice in that regard.

Appendix 1 is a translation of *The Wanderer* into modern English prose. Since those who have edited, translated or commented on this poem have often differed from one another in their understanding of its speech boundaries, its temporal shifts and aspects of its poetic syntax and metaphorical diction, the translation is meant to make clear how I stand on these philological issues. Appendix 2 lists the folio-by-folio contents of the Exeter Anthology. The list serves as a guide to my preferred titles for individual texts while also confirming the relative placement of poems within the codex. Appendix 3 lists a number of the poems of the Anthology with notes on their apparent genre, according to Latin generic terms familiar to educated Anglo-Saxons.

The book has its origins in a talk titled 'What Was the Exeter Book For?' that I presented at the 2009 biennial meeting of the International Society of Anglo-Saxonists. That talk evolved into an essay that turned out to be too unwieldy for publication in article form, hence my decision to develop it as a book. Reviews written by anonymous readers either of that long essay or of earlier drafts of the present book have helped me to ascertain where my arguments have needed strengthening, curtailing or modulating. I owe those readers heartfelt thanks for having taken time out of their own scholarly undertakings so as to provide those critiques. I also wish to thank Professor Brian O'Camb of Indiana University Northwest for some helpful comments on an early draft of the book. I am appreciative of the numerous exchanges that the two of us have had concerning the poems of the Exeter Anthology and what both he and I, going back to conversations preparatory to his 2009 University of Wisconsin PhD dissertation 'Toward a Monastic Poetics: *Exeter Maxims* and the Exeter Book of Old English Poetry', have come to regard as its underlying monastic poetics.

I am grateful to Peter Thomas, Librarian of Exeter Cathedral, and to his predecessor in that post, the late Michael Howarth, for courtesies extended over a number of years, whether to me personally or on behalf of certain of my former graduate students at the University of Wisconsin, Madison. Bernard J. Muir kindly provided the image of Exeter, Cathedral Library, MS 3501, fol. 78r that is reproduced as Fig. 2. Finally, I have reason to thank the members of the informal group known as the Saxon Circle of Berkeley, California, in the company of whom I set out some twenty-five years ago to read the whole contents of the Exeter Anthology in codicological order rather than reading certain of its poems in piecemeal fashion, as was (and still is) the norm. The present book, which would not otherwise have been written, is dedicated to that group of colleagues, former students, and friends.

Abbreviations

ACMRS	Arizona Center for Medieval and Renaissance Studies
ASE	*Anglo-Saxon England* (the journal)
ASPR	The Anglo-Saxon Poetic Records, ed. George Philip Krapp and Elliott Van Kirk Dobbie, 6 vols (New York: Columbia University Press, 1931–53)
Bjork, *Poems of Cynewulf*	*The Old English Poems of Cynewulf*, ed. and trans. Robert E. Bjork, DOML 23 (Cambridge, MA: Harvard University Press, 2013)
Bjork, *OE Shorter Poems*	*Old English Shorter Poems, Volume II: Wisdom and Lyric*, ed. and trans. Robert E. Bjork, DOML 32 (Cambridge, MA: Harvard University Press, 2014).
Blackwell Encyclopedia	*The Wiley-Blackwell Encyclopedia of Anglo-Saxon England*, ed. Michael Lapidge, John Blair, Simon Keynes and Donald Scragg, 2nd edn (Chichester: Wiley-Blackwell, 2014)
Bosworth & Toller	Joseph Bosworth and T. Northcote Toller, *An Anglo-Saxon Dictionary* (Oxford: Oxford University Press, 1898), with *Supplement* by T. Northcote Toller (1921) and *Enlarged Addenda and Corrigenda* by Alistair Campbell (1972)
Bradley	S.A.J. Bradley, *Anglo-Saxon Poetry* (London: Dent, 1982)
CCCC	Cambridge, Corpus Christi College
Clayton, *Poems of Christ*	*Old English Poems of Christ and His Saints*, ed. and trans. Mary Clayton, DOML 27 (Cambridge, MA: Harvard University Press, 2013)
d.	died
DOE	*Dictionary of Old English*, ed. Angus Cameron *et al.* (Toronto: Pontifical Institute, 1986–), letters A through I currently available online by subscription at https://www.doe.utoronto.ca

Abbreviations

DOML	Dumbarton Oaks Medieval Library
ed.	editor; editors; edited by
Edgar, *Poetical Books*	*The Vulgate Bible, Volume III: The Poetical Books*, ed. Swift Edgar with Angela M. Kinney, DOML 8 (Cambridge, MA: Harvard University Press, 2011)
edn	edition
ES	*English Studies*
et al.	and others
fol., fols	folio, folios
JEGP	*Journal of English and Germanic Philology*
Jones, *OE Shorter Poems*	*Old English Shorter Poems, Volume I: Religious and Didactic*, ed. and trans. Christopher A. Jones, DOML 15 (Cambridge, MA: Harvard University Press, 2012)
Kinney, *New Testament*	*The Vulgate Bible, Volume VI: The New Testament*, ed. Angela M. Kinney, DOML 21 (Cambridge, MA: Harvard University Press, 2013)
Klaeber's Beowulf	*Klaeber's Beowulf and the Fight at Finnsburg*, ed. R.D. Fulk, Robert E. Bjork and John D. Niles, 4th edn (Toronto: University of Toronto Press, 2008)
Muir	*The Exeter Anthology of Old English Poetry*, ed. Bernard J. Muir, 2nd edn, 2 vols (Exeter: Exeter University Press, 2000)
OE	Old English
PQ	*Philological Quarterly*
r.	reigned
RES	*Review of English Studies*
repr.	reprinted
s.v.	sub verbo
Venarde, *Rule of Benedict*	*The Rule of Saint Benedict*, ed. and trans. Bruce L. Venarde, DOML 6 (Cambridge, MA: Harvard University Press, 2011)
vol., vols	volume, volumes

Fig. 1. Oxford, Bodleian Library,
MS Auctarium F.4.32 ('Saint Dunstan's Classbook').
Frontispiece: Saint Dunstan kneeling at the foot of Christ.

Fig. 2. Exeter, Cathedral Library, MS 3501 (the Exeter Anthology). Fol. 78r: the end of *The Wanderer* and the beginning of *God's Gifts to Humankind*.

wundrum heah wyrmlicum fah. sohlsar popnoman ascahyr
þe paþþin pæl gefeun pyro reð mæsse. ⁊þær stan hleoþu stop
mæg cyssað hyið hyeorstros hyuse binoeð purcusse poma
son þon cemeð niþeð mlrt seua norþan on stroeð hyu
hæsl sane hælebum on aroan. eall is unpoðlic wiþ þan
pies on stroeð pyroa ge festips piþpulo uroði heoponu.
hsh bið reoh læsse. hsh bið fwoiro læsse. hsh bið mon læsse.
hsh bið mæg læsse. eal hir wiþ þan gesæal roæl pæmped.
Spa cpæð snotton on mode gesæt lum runðon æt
nune til bið rehelur cyþore gehæiloch nesæul næsene
lur toyn toyrcsus beyn of hur broscum acs þan non
þe heosi þa bote cunne. wyl mio elne ge spunman wel
bið þam þe him ane ræceð snoyne toyroyr on heoponu
þær us eal sæ sæstnung stonðeð :~ 7

F ELA BIÐ ONFOLD an.
foyð ge senna gecngsia gecrona. þa haganst
bshirð pegað Ingepresse spa hsh piopuða
god meoruð mealreum spið monnum oæleð þ.
leð runðon gsss stroeð pros agne sheðe þasn
æshyrle mot oiyrhr puwistroya oæl onron nebið

PART ONE

Reading the Anthology in its Historical Context

CHAPTER 1

Monastic Poetics

The Exeter Anthology (Exeter, Cathedral Library, MS 3501, fols 8–130), also known as the Exeter Book, is well known as 'the largest and most diverse single volume of Old English poetry'.[1] Among its contents are some of the most widely admired poems composed in English before the time of Chaucer. It is a volume that presents a sustained challenge to the intellect. This is not to say that the rest of the surviving literature of the Anglo-Saxons is without puzzles or mental challenges, for scarcely any work that has come down to us from the earliest period of English literature is free from interpretive problems. The Exeter Anthology, however, puts unusual demands on its readers almost from start to finish. It is not just that many of its constituent parts are of an oblique, metaphorical, allegorical or riddling kind. In addition, the reasons for anyone's assembling a volume of this character are hard to discern. Equally hard to fathom is the rationale for the arrangement of the book's parts, if such a rationale can be said to exist.

There is thus some justification for the present study. Despite the considerable critical interest that certain individual poems of the Exeter Anthology have inspired,[2] and despite the attention that has been given to Exeter, Cathedral Library, MS 3501 as a product of an Anglo-Saxon scriptorium,[3] I know of no book-length critical study that tries to account for this volume, in all its parts, as a product of the Anglo-Saxon literary imagination.

Leaving aside its seven extraneous initial folios and its fire- or water-damaged leaves, the Exeter codex comes down to us as a single object with a handsome and more or less uniform physical appearance. Whatever

---

1   Matthew Hussey's assessment (2014: 21) is an uncontroversial one. The only reason why the Anthology is not also acknowledged to be the most important single volume of Old English poetry is that the *Beowulf* manuscript too has survived the vicissitudes of time.
2   Critical studies published up to shortly before the year 2000 are listed in Muir 2: 756–882. Those published since 1972 can generally be located via the searchable online bibliography maintained by the *Old English Newsletter* at http://www.oenewsletter.org/OENDB/, or via other online bibliographies. Roberta Dewa (2002) reviews how the Exeter Anthology has been edited since 1842, when Benjamin Thorpe brought out its first modern edition.
3   See in particular Conner 1993a: 48–147, Gameson 1996 and R. Butler 2004.

the prehistory may have been of the individual poems that comprise the Anthology, and whatever the value of those poems is thought to be when viewed separately, the collection as a whole has a coherence that corresponds to the book's visual integrity and beauty, two qualities that ought to be self-evident to anyone who consults either the original manuscript or one of its facsimiles. Moreover, the poems of the Anthology are composed in a compatible style, even when one text can be distinguished from others through differences of genre, length, voice or subject. The book is best approached as a single literary site, one to which each poem and passage contributes a measure of eloquence.

Moreover, the book and its contents are not timeless creations of the muse or of the bookmaker's art. Rather, the Exeter Anthology can fruitfully be placed within the cultural landscape of late tenth-century England, and its contribution to that landscape can be assessed. In addition, I will explore the possibility that—as with certain archaeological sites—a single world-view animates the book as a whole, regardless of the question of when and where its constituent poems were made. In keeping with the manuscript's apparent point of origin in the south of England during the period of the Benedictine Reform, I see this world-view as coinciding with what Brian O'Camb has called a monastic poetics.

Since this term has only been introduced to Old English studies in the last few years, it deserves some explanation. Thinking of *Exeter Maxims* and *The Wonder of Creation* in particular, O'Camb has characterized monastic poetics as 'an innovative mode of poetry that adapted monastic rhetorical models to cultivate contemplative, visionary experiences in its readers'.[4] When speaking of the monastic poetics of the Exeter Anthology as a whole, I use that term in a similar yet somewhat broader way to refer to a self-conscious effort, made by the Anglo-Saxon regular clergy though not necessarily restricted to that group, to develop the medium of English vernacular poetry as a vehicle for intellectual stimulation, moral guidance, aesthetic pleasure and spiritual enlightenment, with all aspects of this endeavour taking place within the sustaining environment of Christian theology.

While the term 'poetics' implies a distinct engagement with matters of form, style and rhetoric on the part of the makers of these poems, the qualifying adjective 'monastic' implies that any experimentation along such lines did not occur for its own sake, but rather in the service of a religious

---

4   O'Camb 2014: 411. Elsewhere, with reference to art-historical as well as textual evidence, O'Camb defines monastic poetics as 'a style of poetry upon which Anglo-Saxon poets could draw so as to promote spiritual enlightenment, including a measure of visionary experience, through the calculated interplay of verbal and visual texts' (2016: 198).

calling. If the poems of the Exeter Anthology were to be read for the sake of their intellectual content alone, putting aside all thought of their formal properties and their literary artistry, then they could form a gateway to the theological, philosophical and moral dimensions of Insular Christianity as articulated by any persons in monastic orders, including such leading intellectuals as Bede, Alcuin and Ælfric. Inevitably, unconsciously perhaps, but also in a self-conscious manner, the poems also echo the liturgy, especially those prayers, blessings, hymns and psalms that were repeated on a regular basis in keeping with the rhythms of the year. The differences between the poems of the Exeter Anthology and the works of learned monastic authors who are known to us by name have little to do with the core intellectual content of these works. Instead, they stem from the fact that the poems of the Exeter Anthology are rhetorically venturesome works composed in the vernacular.

Monastic poetics is thus a hybrid poetics, based on Latinate and Germanic models yet striving to achieve expansive new forms of expression in the medium of Old English alliterative verse.[5] The chief purpose of this hybrid poetics was to glorify God. A concurrent aim was to astonish and delight. A third, dual purpose was to justify lives lived in accord with divine law, as expressed through the Scriptures and scriptural commentaries; and, for cloistered persons, to reinforce the value system embodied in the Rule of Saint Benedict.[6] In relation to that latter aim, monastic poetics is a tool of conversion aimed at those who were already in the fold, but who might not yet have fully experienced Christ's Advent in their hearts.

The question might well be asked: is the term 'monastic poetics' uniquely applicable to the poems of the Exeter Anthology? Or can it meaningfully be applied to other Old English verse texts too, given the likelihood that Anglo-Saxon writings in general were produced in one or another monastic setting?

---

5   Heather Maring (2017) maintains this thesis with particular application to *Advent Lyrics*, poems that merge art and prayer. Similarly, Emily Thornbury (2014b: 31–32) remarks on how the twelve *Advent Lyrics* expand upon their liturgical sources, transforming them in a manner that illustrates the workings of an Old English lyric mode.

6   The Rule of Saint Benedict was disseminated in several ways in late Anglo-Saxon England, both through copies of the Rule itself, in its prologue and seventy-three chapters, and through the customary known as the *Regularis Concordia* ('Agreement about the Rule') that was adopted at Winchester in c.973. Very similar in its specifications was the *Regula Canonicorum* ('Rule for Canons') written originally by Bishop Chrodegang of Metz, a document meant to regulate the communal life of canons in a manner consistent with the Benedictine Rule, including those canons who lived in monastic cathedrals of the kind promoted by leaders of the Benedictine Reform. Both the Rule of Saint Benedict and the *Regula Canonicorum* were in circulation in both Latin and Old English versions. See Fulk and Cain (2013: 185–88) for details.

The answer to this question is surely a qualified 'yes': the term is indeed meaningful when applied to certain examples of Old English verse that happen to be preserved in manuscripts other than Exeter, Cathedral Library, MS 3501. Indeed, certain poems of that codex are recorded elsewhere in alternate versions. One example is *The Soul's Address to the Body*, an expanded version of which is recorded in the Vercelli Book. Another instance is the fragmentary poem *The Canticles of the Three Youths* (also known as *Azarias*), which has a close relation to part of the Old Testament verse paraphrase *Daniel* recorded in the Junius Manuscript. Likewise, there are analogues in two other codices to the versified paraphrase of the Lord's Prayer that is written out at folio 122r of the Exeter Anthology. The passages containing Cynewulf's two runic 'signatures', as well, are paralleled in the two poems of the Vercelli Book (*Elene* and *Fates of the Apostles*) that are similarly 'signed' by that poet.

The defining issue, then, is whether or not a given poem is composed in a style similar to what we see in the Exeter Anthology, relies on similar learning, and is expressive of much the same world-view. While it goes beyond my present purposes to evaluate which poems of the Old English corpus are meaningfully grouped in this category, examples that come readily to mind are the pair of wisdom poems from CCCC MS 41 and CCCC MS 422 known as *Solomon and Saturn I* and *Solomon and Saturn II*. Each of these takes the form of an imagined contest of wits between representatives of the biblical tradition and of pagan learning. A poem of an analogous kind is *The Rune Poem*, with its short verse paragraphs based on the names of the Anglo-Saxon runic symbols. The Vercelli Book poem *The Dream of the Rood*, as well, includes bewilderment effects of a kind similar to what one finds in certain parts of the Exeter Anthology before settling into a more straightforward homiletic discourse. Each poem or set of poems of the Old English corpus merits study in its own terms, however, and nothing is gained by trying to reduce those works to a common denominator. *Beowulf*, in particular, strikes me as a fish—a large one—that has swum in from some other ocean, even though the fact of its being recorded in writing implies a monastic contribution at least as regards the transmission of its text.

The emergence of a monastic poetics in Anglo-Saxon England was not an overnight occurrence, nor did this development take place in isolation, without a close relation to social and religious history as well as to the pre-existing poetics of both Old English and Anglo-Latin verse. The process began soon after the Conversion, when the seventh-century poet Cædmon, most likely together with other poets not known to us by name, first used the medium of early English alliterative verse for Christian devotional purposes. The process by which the language of early English verse was redirected and augmented so as to become a sophisticated instrument for religious expression had clearly reached a point of mature development by the time that the poems of the Exeter Anthology were composed and were assembled into a single compilation. By this time, literacy and letters in England had reached a stage of development such that it had become thinkable that a complex, sophisticated, English-language verse collection of this kind could be made. One can safely infer as well that by this time, the leading teachers in the realm would have appreciated the potential value of such a volume as this in a programme of bilingual education.

The present book argues that while any given poem or passage from the Exeter Anthology is subject to being read in a number of different ways when read in isolation, its meaning is more likely to emerge with clarity and certainty when it is read in the context of the book as a whole. In turn, the ground that sustains the Anthology as a whole is the great cumulative body of lore that pertained to the early medieval church. Whether explicitly or implicitly, Christian doctrine infuses all parts of the Anthology and animates its contents, doing so in a sophisticated rhetorical fashion in the medium of the vernacular.

One aim of the people who made the book, I suggest, was to promote deep and sustained meditation upon the core elements of Christian doctrine, including the moral implications of Christian eschatology. Another aim, one that had a literary as well as a religious motivation, was to promote the study and practice of a vernacular poetics within the bilingual culture of late Anglo-Saxon England.

God's exiles and the heroic ethos

In addition to being specialists in the craft of bookmaking, monks and cloistered women constituted a special group who knew one thing about themselves with certainty: that they were God's chosen exiles. They had renounced wealth, sex, childbearing, and the comforts and pleasures of ordinary society, including fine food and drink when available, so as to participate in an ordered life in a special precinct where they could devote themselves to the *opus dei*—that is, to a regime of work and prayer in the penitential service of God. The main function of that regime was to offer up a constant stream of praise and thanksgiving to God for having offered human beings a path to lasting joy despite their having proven themselves, again and again, to be unworthy of such favour at His hands.[7]

---

7   In a valuable survey of early English monasticism, Sarah Foot, drawing on the writings of Erving Goffman, speaks of such 'total institutions' as prisons, hospitals, asylums, boarding

From a collective point of view, the purpose of this stream of praise and thanksgiving was to ensure the welfare of society as a whole, for the Bible offered numerous examples—ones that were reinforced in the annals of recent history—of the disasters that could afflict a people if God was offended because of the moral corruption of human beings and the neglect of divine worship. From the point of view of the individual monk or nun, the overriding purpose of the monastic way of life was to prepare for one's death: or, to be more precise, to prepare for the crucial journey of one's soul, once it was separated from its mortal body, to its eternal destination. This was a journey fraught with fears and anxieties, whether because of its radically unknown nature or its uncertain outcome.

Monks and cloistered women were constantly encouraged to view their life on earth as an effort to return 'home' from their present condition of exile, with its ineluctable hardships and sufferings, so as to enter into a blissful state of union with God and the whole company of the saved. Hugh Magennis has summarized as follows the Christian concept of exile, illustrating that key concept through excerpts drawn from Old English prose homilies that date from roughly the same period as the Exeter Anthology:

> According to this metaphorical concept, which is widely represented in Anglo-Saxon homiletic writings, the human race was put into exile by the fall of Adam and Eve and yearns to return to its true home, which is with God. The possibility of such a return, a journey home from exile, was opened up for members of the human race by the atonement of Christ. The great narratives of exile and journey in the Old Testament were seen in Christian tradition as figures of this universal human condition, to which Christianity itself offered the only remedy. According to this tradition, we are all in exile, and death is the solitary journey which may lead to salvation.[8]

While the whole human race was consigned to this state of exile, and while any man, woman or child could hope for salvation through Christ, members of the clergy were the technicians of the sacred who dedicated their lives to finding a remedy for this existential predicament.

---

schools, army camps and monasteries as 'characterised by their tendency to alter the nature of the personalities of those who reside within them' (2006: 38). The notion of a 'monastic poetics' comes into sharper focus when viewed from such a perspective.

8 Magennis 2011: 161. The three illustrative excerpts reproduced by Magennis in modern English translation (at 161-62) are from the anonymous Vercelli homily 11, from the anonymous Blickling homily 2, and from homily 7 of Ælfric's first series of *Catholic Homilies*. I discuss an excerpt from that same Blickling homily in both Old English and modern English translation in Chapter 9 below, in the section headed 'Intratextuality versus intertextuality'.

Monks and cloistered women thus formed a special 'society within the society' consisting of persons who chose, quite literally, to live by different rules from those observed by the rest of their countrymen. Importantly for our understanding of those Exeter Anthology poems that touch on the experience of the warrior aristocracy, the monastic code required renunciation of the weapons that male Anglo-Saxons routinely carried, whether in life or, in the early Anglo-Saxon period, into the grave, where the spear served as an emblem of masculine identity.[9] Among the members of the laity who routinely bore arms were the fathers, grandfathers, brothers and cousins of those who had taken monastic vows and who had thereby chosen to wage only spiritual warfare. These two groups—the actual warriors of Anglo-Saxon England and the much smaller set of spiritual warriors—remained kindred in spirit, while some of them were kindred in their lineage even while living separately according to different codes.

I dwell on these familiar matters so as to highlight one aspect of the world-view that animates the Exeter Anthology as a whole. This is a distinct zeal in the pursuit of the holy life. Old English *ellen* 'fearlessness' or 'courage' is the name for it. This quality, which readers of *Beowulf* will recall being evoked right from the start of that poem,[10] somewhat paradoxically aligned the class of monks, in their voluntary self-abasement, with the Anglo-Saxon warrior aristocracy, the class traditionally associated with martial pride and the zealous fulfilment of heroic ideals. Much as the authors of *Beowulf* and of the late tenth-century poem *The Battle of Maldon* speak of courageous, self-sacrificing loyalty on the field of battle in a manner that confirms the core values of the warrior class, the poems of the Exeter Anthology speak of the conduct of the Christian life with confident reference to values meant to strengthen believers' resolve in every aspect of their existence. The cure for a destitute exile's suffering, as the narrator of *The Wanderer* remarks at the end of that poem—not the main speaker of that poem, but the narrator—is therefore to act in the world *mid elne* 'with courage' (114a) while seeking for grace in the Christian sense. As people of exceptional courage in their chosen vocation, monastics saw how apt it was to adopt the vocabulary of heroism and exile to advance their calling through what Saint Benedict refers to as *zelus bonus*, or 'zeal of the good kind'.[11]

---

9   John Damon (2003) distinguishes the actual warriors of Anglo-Saxon England from the holy men and women who, as depicted in the saints' lives, appropriated the language of combat in their quest for spiritual perfection. Sam Lucy (2000: 87–88) offers summary remarks on the archaeology of the spear and the grave.

10 'Hwæt, wē ... gefrūnon,/hū ðā æþelingas ellen fremedon' ('Indeed, we ... have heard how those noblemen performed fearless deeds', *Beowulf* 1–3; *Klaeber's Beowulf*, p. 3.

11 In chapter 72 of his Rule, when summing up the virtues that ought to characterize the monastic vocation, Benedict speaks of the 'good zeal' that monks should have, the type that

The present book, with its title 'God's Exiles and English Verse', explores these links between the monastic way of life, the old heroic code, the theological concepts of exile and the return home, and the value that the Anglo-Saxons placed on sophisticated devotional poetry composed in the vernacular.

Paul, Benedict and others on spiritual warfare

Like almost any other early medieval book, the Exeter Anthology was doubtless thought by its original readers to be a compendium of knowledge and wisdom. Many of its poems or passages have a didactic or homiletic cast, often with an eye towards Judgement. The book's didactic character would have encouraged its readers to reform their daily lives in accord with whatever knowledge or wisdom they were able to glean from its pages. This is as much as to say that the book had a role in an educative process whose motivating purpose was the salvation of souls.

The situation is very different today. In keeping with the more secular spirit of our age, few present-day English-speaking readers are likely to approach the poems of the Exeter Anthology as serious vehicles of doctrine or moral instruction. Instead, most readers today are likely to appreciate these poems either for their perceived aesthetic value, which is recognized in certain cases to be considerable, or for the light that this verse sheds on aspects of early medieval social history, including hierarchical power relations and gender relations. As a consequence, persons of the present era who are perfectly familiar with certain individual poems of the Anthology may still have only a limited conception of the character of the codex as a whole. Such persons are unlikely to adhere to the opinion that a single coherent world-view underlies the collection, while relatively few, I imagine, will be inclined to adopt such a world-view as their own.

My own considered conclusion is that a single coherent world-view does animate the Exeter Anthology as a whole, infusing its parts with a harmonious spiritual vision. This mind-set could be called that of heroic Christianity.

What I mean to denote by this phrase is the compounding of two things: the theology of orthodox Christianity, as that religion had developed by the second half of the tenth century in England, and a certain monastic zeal. By referring to the book's religious perspective as 'heroic', what I mean to suggest is that it inverts, subverts or otherwise strongly challenges the more materialistic and 'realistic' view of life that was doubtless taken for granted

---

separates one from vice and that leads to God and eternal life. Venarde, *Rule of Benedict*, pp. 226–27.

by most persons of the Anglo-Saxon era, much as it is taken for granted by most persons living in developed societies today. Neither during the tenth century nor in more recent times has the strenuous Christian ethos that finds expression in the Exeter Anthology been embraced by more than a small minority of persons, for most people view it as impractical to an extreme. To advocate it and to seek to live by its dictates even unto death, as the early disciples of Christ are venerated for having done, can therefore justly be regarded as an act of courage and heroism, one that is analogous to what is expected of members of a warrior elite.

The leading members of the warrior elite who are honoured in the pages of the Exeter Anthology, of course, are persons living in monastic orders. These celibate warriors of Christ are the 'truth-fast' or 'righteous' ones (OE sōþ-fæste) who undertake a form of voluntary exile so as to devote their lives to the worship and service of God, trusting to God and not the world for their reward. By extension, the circle of the righteous can be taken to include any Christians who take their faith seriously and live by its dictates in hope of salvation.

The trope of which I speak—that of the *miles Christi*, the warrior of Christ—was a commonplace of medieval devotional literature. It is put on display in a fully developed form in Prudentius's allegorical poem the *Psychomachia* (c. AD 400), which tells of the defensive war waged by the Virtues, figured as armed virgin soldiers, against the Vices, which take on various monstrous shapes. The trope's wellspring is in the epistles of Saint Paul, who in his sixth letter to the Ephesians introduces a multifaceted metaphor of spiritual warfare while exhorting his Christian brethren to pursue a life of uncompromising dedication to the faith:

> Induite vos arma Dei, ut possitis stare adversus insidias diaboli ... State ergo, succincti lumbos vestros in veritate et induti loricam iustitiae et calciati pedes in praeparatione evangelii pacis, in omnibus sumentes scutum fidei, in quo possitis omnia tela nequissimi ignea extinguere. Et galeam salutis adsumite et gladium spiritus (quod est verbum Dei) per omnem orationem et obsecrationem.
>
> (Put you on the armour of God, that you may be able to stand against the deceits of the devil ... Stand therefore, having your loins girt about with truth and having on the breastplate of justice and your feet shod with the preparation of the gospel of peace, in all things taking the shield of faith, wherewith you may be able to extinguish all the fiery darts of the most wicked one. And take unto you the helmet of salvation and the sword of the spirit (which is the word of God) by all prayer and supplication.)[12]

---

12 Ephesians 6:11, 6:14–18; Kinney, *New Testament*, pp. 1032–35.

While the trope of spiritual warfare is associated with the genre of the saint's life in particular,[13] one meets with it in practically any devotional context, as John P. Hermann has charted in his 1989 book *Allegories of War: Language and Violence in Old English Poetry*. Hermann demonstrates the centrality of the metaphor of the Christian warrior over some few centuries in a number of historical contexts, including Anglo-Saxon England in particular.[14]

Like other aspects of early Christian thinking, the metaphor of the monk or nun as warrior represented an inversion of the language of the dominant society by a devout few who had renounced the use of arms. Christians of the Anglo-Saxon period drew on the rhetorical trope of warfare, as Paul and others had done, in order to encourage one another in a way of life that was based on prayer and that was to remain as immune as possible from feelings of anger or aggression. This system of belief naturally struck many outsiders as impractical or deviant, as indeed it does today, even to the point that hostility or scorn can be directed against those relatively few individuals who refuse to bear arms because of their religious convictions.

The figure of speech of the Christian warrior would have been familiar to educated persons of the late Anglo-Saxon period through any number of treatises, homilies and other devotional texts. One of these, Aldhelm's prose treatise *De virginitate*, which was studied intently in tenth-century England, was designed to confirm monks and nuns in their vows of chastity. In a manner reminiscent of Prudentius, its author makes pointed reference to the courage required of combatants in the monastic army.[15] Yet more influential was the use of this same martial metaphor in the Rule of Saint Benedict, where it is adopted at the start of the prologue to the Rule. Here monks, who were non-combatants in actual warfare, are admonished to take up the weapons of obedience so as 'to fight for the Lord Christ, the true king':

> Ad te ergo nunc mihi sermo dirigitur, quisquis abrenuntians propriis voluntatibus Domino Christo vero regi militaturus oboedientiae fortissima atque praeclara arma sumis.

---

13 Lisa Weston (2012) makes this point with particular reference to the Latin and Old English lives of Saint Guthlac. Hugh Magennis (2006) likewise emphasizes the manner in which Ælfric and other authors of saints' lives appropriated the heroic ethos, though not the elaborate diction by which that ethos found expression in heroic poems on secular themes.
14 Hermann 1989. Although the matter is a peripheral one, I would dispute Hermann's claim that the metaphor of spiritual warfare was complicit with actual social violence during the period before the Conquest. The crusading spirit of a later historical period is another matter. Joyce Hill (1981) surveys the figure of the *miles Christi* in Old English literature.
15 Lapidge and Herren 1979: 51–132, esp. chap. 11 (at p. 68). Scott Gwara (2001) has prepared an exemplary critical edition of Aldhelm's Latin text.

(To you, therefore, my word is now directed—to whoever, renouncing his own will in order to fight for the Lord Christ, the true king, takes up the brilliant and mighty weapons of obedience.)[16]

Paul's metaphors of truth, righteousness, peace, faith and salvation are here distilled into Benedict's single metaphor of obedience.[17] There was no text more foundational than this for the sponsors of the tenth-century Benedictine Reform. Among these sponsors was Æthelwold of Winchester (c.904–84), who translated the Rule into English prose that is a model of quiet eloquence as part of his programme of fostering a bilingual system of education.

The Exeter Anthology: a tool of acculturation?

A possibility worth exploring in light of the preceding remarks is that the Exeter Anthology was compiled not just as a vehicle for Christian instruction, but also as a means of acculturating high-ranking members of Anglo-Saxon society into the cenobitic way of life. Naturally, such persons would not have been the book's sole prospective readers, for any book can have multiple audiences and readerships. There is no reason why the Exeter Anthology could not speak, and cannot still speak, to the condition of anyone at all. Still, it is a distinct possibility that this narrower segment of society—one that consisted of persons born into the aristocracy who had answered a religious calling—was an important target group for the unknown compiler.

The Anglo-Saxon warrior aristocracy resembled the class of monks in that its importance in society was in inverse proportion to its numbers. Traditionally, going back to prehistoric times, the male aristocracy in Germanic-speaking parts of Eurasia consisted of persons whose prowess in arms constituted them as a ruling class. Many such warrior-thegns had personal ties to royalty or to other persons of very high rank. In the course of time, such ties extended to ecclesiastics of high status. In the mid-tenth century, as Alexander Rumble (2008) has documented, many persons born into the upper ranks of Anglo-Saxon society were sponsors of the Benedictine Reform, donating both lands and money for the foundation of monasteries. Certain pious laymen of high status took up the monastic life themselves, as

---

16 Venarde, Rule of Benedict, pp. 2–3 (Prologue, 3).
17 Katherine O'Brien O'Keeffe (2012) offers a wide-ranging study of how Benedict's prime virtue of obedience entered into the discourse of monasticism in Anglo-Saxon England, doing so through such Latin prose texts as Ælfric's Colloquy and the vitae of Saint Æthelwold and Saint Dunstan, always in an unspoken dialectic with notions of individual agency.

did Æthelstan Half-King, who retired to Glastonbury in c.957 and was buried there, following a tradition whereby persons of high birth ended their days in the cloister.[18] Although it is hard to estimate how many children born into the Anglo-Saxon nobility entered monastic life as oblates, this was a practical option for younger sons or for unmarried daughters born to parents of high status. It was likewise a significant means by which monasteries replenished their numbers. The ties between certain families of high rank and particular monasteries were thereby strengthened in a manner that calls to mind the ancient Germanic custom of fosterage.

Significantly, in the vernacular tract dating from c.970-84 known as 'King Edgar's Establishment of Monasteries', Æthelwold states that he undertook to translate the Rule of Saint Benedict from Latin into English for the sake of 'unlearned laymen ... who for fear of hell-torment and for love of Christ abandon this wretched life and turn to their Lord and choose the holy service of this rule'.[19] Lay converts to the monastic way of life were therefore an important target readership for the Rule, as was surely true of other contemporary writings in the vernacular. The birthright of pious laymen was not wholly effaced when they sought to save their souls and advance the welfare of the church by entering the cloister. Since part of this birthright was mental and pertained to the ethos of the warrior class, there was a place for modes of education that did not simply negate the heroic ethos, but rather channelled this ethos so as to bring aspects of it into alignment with monastic values. As an inversion of the warrior ethos that was couched in similarly idealistic terms, the trope of the *miles Christi* had an obvious utility in this regard. So too did the use of the vernacular language to express religious concepts in the medium of alliterative verse, with its powerful affective dimension.

The choice of vernacular poetry as a means of acculturating persons into a Christian world-view deserves closer attention, however, seeing that what was involved was both the conversion of individual men and women and a conversion of the verse medium itself.

---

18 Patrick Wormald (1978) explores this phenomenon in an attempt to ascertain a valid reading context for *Beowulf* and other Old English poetry. On the historical phenomenon of kings 'opting out', see also Langenfelt 1959 at 71-72, n. 4, and more fully Stancliffe 1983.
19 This excerpt quoted from Rumble (2008: 244); for the full document, with translation into modern English, see Whitelock 1981, part 1, no. 33 (pp. 142-54).

Mastering the craft of vernacular verse as a vehicle for conversion

Since the Exeter Anthology consists very nearly entirely of vernacular verse, some of which is of a challenging character, it throws a spotlight on verse-making as a craft, one that, like any other artisanal activity, required technical skills on the part of its makers. Whether one thinks of the book's parade of literary genres, its dazzling admixture of styles, its bursts of stylized diction, its arresting uses of alliteration, rhyme, the refrain and other aural linking devices, or its brassy or subtle deployment of such rhetorical tropes and schemes (taught routinely in the schools) as metaphor, allegory, litotes, anaphora, exclamatio and paronomasia, the Exeter Anthology is practically a handbook of the *ars poetica* of Old English verse, an art that is easily recognizable here not just as an analogue to its Latin counterpart but as a radically innovative medium in its own right.

Whoever compiled the Exeter Anthology would have been aware of the book's potential use as a resource for persons who had already mastered the elements of Latin grammar. By studying the poems of the Exeter Anthology in the same manner that texts of the Latinate tradition were studied, educated persons could have learned how to propagate Christian teachings through the elegant deployment of the vernacular. The value of verse as a means of training in eloquence had long been recognized. This value rested in part on its more demanding compositional techniques, hence its sharper challenges to the intellect. Also recognized was its stronger affective power: that is, its ability to arouse an emotional response on the part of its readers or listeners. This is particularly true of poetry in the lyric mode, as Katherine O'Brien O'Keeffe has persuasively remarked with reference to the use of the 'lyric I' in such poems as *The Seafarer* and *The Wife's Lament*.[20] Over the long history of literary criticism, poetry has traditionally been esteemed as a higher form of art than prose because it is more demanding to write, more challenging to understand, and more fully capable of engaging the emotions in conjunction with the intellect. The assembling of the Exeter Anthology is expressive of the conviction that only the best should be offered up to God.

In the Exeter Anthology poem *God's Gifts to Humankind*, appreciative notice is taken of the talents of both poets and instrumental musicians:

---

20 As O'Brien O'Keeffe remarks, 'The lyric *ic* ... offers the fiction of unmediated access to the voice of the poem, a voice demanding to be heard in the here and now.' Through this 'fiction of immediate presence', she adds, these lyric poems 'allow the irruption of affect—longing, mourning, regret, resignation—and invite the reader's or hearer's response' (2017: 13).

> Sum biþ woðbora,
> giedda giffæst ...
> Sum mid hondum mæg   hearpan gretan,
> ah he gleobeames   gearobrygda list.
>
> (One man is a poet gifted with visionary songs ... Another has the ability to play the harp with his hands; he has the art of dextrous flourishes upon the singing wood.)[21]

The same term *wōð-bora* 'visionary poet' that occurs in the first line of this passage is used somewhat later in the codex in line 2 of *The Wonder of Creation*, a poem that tells of divine wisdom as revealed through prophetic song. The word refers to persons gifted in prophecy or in philosophical insight. This unusual compound noun distinguishes the 'new poet' of inspired religious verse from old-style court poets such as the imagined scops Widsith and Deor, with their more worldly perspectives.

Since Anglo-Saxons of high rank had evidently long been patrons and connoisseurs of song, the recruitment of persons from wealthy families into the religious houses of late tenth-century England could well have stimulated the composition of Christian poetry in the vernacular. Oral poetry in the Anglo-Saxon context is widely believed to have had the function of giving expression to the ideals of loyalty, courage and self-sacrifice that largely constitute the military ethos, thus helping a society maintain stability over time in the face of real-world enemies.[22] By adapting that same medium to religious ends, the poets of the Exeter Anthology redirected the warrior ethos so as to promote a Christian way of life, doing so via the arts of literacy within what might metaphorically be called the *comitatus* (or, better, the *gedryht*) of the monastery.[23] Among the many researchers who have addressed this topic, Hugh Magennis has spoken of the 'conversion' of the older poetic tradition so as to express a Christian message, and of the concurrent Germanizing of Christian discourse so as to express religious concepts in heroic terms.[24]

---

21 *God's Gifts to Humankind* 35b–36a, 49–50; Muir 1: 221; translation based on Bradley, p. 327.
22 This is a thesis that many have argued and that I have taken up myself in Niles 1983 and elsewhere; it is pursued as well by John Hill 1995 and 2000.
23 The term *comitatus*, used by Tacitus to refer to a band of closely knit warriors centred about the figure of a chief, is used with some strain to refer to Anglo-Saxon social institutions. The native Old English term for a leader's retinue is *gedryht*, a derivative of the word *dryhten* 'lord'. In the Exeter Anthology poems *The Ascension*, *Christ in Judgement* and *The Phoenix*, the word *gedryht* is used to refer either to Christ's apostles or to a host of angels or of the righteous. See the *DOE*, s.v. *gedryht*, senses *a* and *c*.
24 Magennis 2011: 68; see further Cherniss 1972. Lesley Abrams (2008) reviews this shift in perception and sensibility from a historian's perspective.

The aim of this act of appropriation of the medium of heroic verse was much the same as the aim of such verse had always been: that is, to help a society maintain stability in a world whose agonistic and potentially violent character needs no exposition here.[25] The difference between the agonistic world centred on the great hall and the agonistic world centred on the cloister was that the monk's adversaries were not hostile human groups; rather, his opponents were Satan and his legion of diabolical allies. Depending on one's perspective, the monk's task might seem yet more heroic than that of the warrior-thegn, for Satan's assaults on humankind were believed to be omnipresent, ceaseless, terrifying, deadly, and without motive other than eternal malice.

While verse composed in the Latin language could have fulfilled this same role of promoting a heroic ethos, and while some of it did (such as Prudentius's *Psychomachia* and Aldhelm's *De virginitate*), it could not do so quite so readily in the context of late tenth-century England. By this time the linguistic situation had changed from what it had been in the years more closely following after the Conversion.[26] Although the native speech of the first Roman missionaries, Latin had become a foreign language to virtually all educated English-speakers. The conventions of Latin verse and prose composition had to be taught somewhat laboriously through textual examples. Native speakers of English were more likely to learn the corresponding elements of vernacular verse through a process of absorption, much as they had learned to speak their native tongue. As Joyce Hill has noted, 'Latin was so far removed from the Germanic vernacular that it had to be learnt and maintained in a situation of linguistic disjunction, always as a hard-won, bookish second language'.[27] Moreover, even well-educated persons living in Anglo-Saxon England did not necessarily master the art of metrical composition in Latin with ease, as can be inferred from the one rather inept poem composed in Latin that is included towards the end of the Exeter Anthology.[28]

---

25 I address the impact of this agonistic social world on the Anglo-Saxon psyche and literary imagination in Niles 1992. The reason why strife is endemic to human societies is addressed at lines 192–200 of *Exeter Maxims C* with reference to Cain's archetypal crime of violence.
26 Olga Timofeeva (2010) reviews this changing linguistic situation in some detail.
27 Joyce Hill 2003: 8. Among valuable accounts of the medieval curriculum in *grammatica* are M. Irvine 1994, Law 1997 and Orme 2006.
28 This is Riddle 89 (Muir 1: 375–76), a five-line puzzle composed in an irregular metre reminiscent of the Latin hexameter. The poem may have been garbled in the course of its textual transmission. The inclusion of this poem in the Exeter Anthology is one reminder that the book's readers would have been categorically bilingual. Other reminders are the macaronic ending of *The Phoenix*, with its alternating verses in Old English and Latin; the macaronic line 100 of *The Canticles of the Three Youths*, with its *a*-verse in the vernacular and

Poems composed in Latinate metres had to be conned, while the language of Old English alliterative poetry must have been like second nature to those who had grown up in environments where it was part of the cultural ecosystem.

Moreover, some high-ranking Anglo-Saxons may have composed or performed such verse themselves. Well known are Asser's remarks about King Alfred's fondness for vernacular poetry, which Alfred is said to have learned to read and recite when still a boy.[29] As Emily V. Thornbury has remarked, the scene described by Asser confirms that 'one significant similarity did exist between Latin and vernacular literary education', in that 'the absorption of large quantities of verse was obviously a prerequisite, in either language, for status as a cultured person' (2014a: 63).

In addition to their other functions, the poems of the Exeter Anthology could have served as models whereby native English-speakers learned how to compose poems of a comparable kind themselves. Any such fledgling poets would have been following the lead of Cynewulf: a man who, though known to us only by name, was evidently a member of the clergy, probably a monk, and correspondingly a poet of some learning. Cynewulf clearly took pride in his mastery of the native poetic idiom, and he is likely to have consolidated his skills both by listening to other singers and by studying prior written examples of both Latin and vernacular verse.

Writers of Latin verse had previously made comparable use of the poetic works of Aldhelm (d. c.710), the early West Saxon abbot, bishop and man of letters who pioneered the composition of Latin Christian verse in England. As a man who was descended from Wessex nobility and had connections with the royal court, Aldhelm exemplifies the class of men who turned away from a life of privilege in order to embrace a monastic vocation.[30] As Michael Lapidge has pointed out, Aldhelm made use of variable but metrically predetermined formulas when composing his Latin hexameters, doing so in a learned manner analogous to the method used by traditional poets composing along the lines of the Parry–Lord model of oral composition. In succeeding generations, it

---

b-verse in Latin; and the use of the title 'sanctus Paulus' at line 69 of The Panther, when the normal practice in vernacular writings was to refer to this saint as 'sē hāliga Paulus'.

29 For text and translation see Stevenson 1904, chap. 23 (p. 20).
30 For a capsule portrait see Lapidge, 'Aldhelm', in Blackwell Encyclopedia, pp. 27–29. As Lapidge elsewhere observes, 'Aldhelm's relationship with the West Saxon royal family provides the key to understanding his career; ... We will better understand Aldhelm's extraordinary achievement if we think of him as a well-connected prince-bishop rather than as a retiring monk whose only link to reality was expressed through deliciously difficult Latin prose and verse' (2007: 65–66).

was not unknown for other poets to compose Latin verses that were 'patently manufactured from formulas in Aldhelm's poetry'.[31]

In like manner, readers of the Exeter Anthology could have learned from the poems of that collection the kinds of formulaic system that helped to generate Old English alliterative verse on religious themes.[32] For an illustration of this process one can turn to the names of the Christian deity as they figure in *Advent Lyrics*, the sequence of poems with which the Anthology begins. In addition to the direct term *God*, these include *dryhten* 'lord', *fæder* 'father', *hælend* 'saviour', *meotod* 'maker', *scyppend* 'creator' and *waldend* 'ruler'. Names involving more complex elements include the formulaic verses *hælend God* 'God the saviour', *weoroda God* 'God of hosts' and *witig God* 'God the wise'. A formulaic system built on *dryhten* rather than *God* includes the nominal phrases *dryhta dryhten* 'lord of hosts', *ēce dryhten* 'eternal lord', *heofona dryhten* 'lord of the heavens' and *sige-dryhten* 'lord of victory'. The simple noun *fæder* is varied by *sōð-fæder* 'truth-father', *wuldor-fæder* 'father of glory' and *fæder ælmihtig* 'almighty father'. Yet other formulaic synonyms for the deity are the verses *hæleþa scyppend* 'creator of humankind', *milde scyppend* 'merciful creator' and the whole-verse epithets *hæleþa cyning* 'king of men', *heofones cyning* 'king of heaven', *heofones heah-cyning* 'high-king of heaven', *weoroda wuldor-cyning* 'glorious king of hosts' and *ealra cyninga cyning* 'king of all kings'. Also featured in *Advent Lyrics* are the whole-verse epithets *frēa ælmihtig* 'almighty lord', *folca neriend* 'saviour of peoples', *heofena hēah-frēa* 'high lord of the heavens', *meotod mancynnes* 'maker of humankind', *rodera weard* 'guardian of the skies' and *sigores weard* 'guardian of victory'. The preceding list does not pretend to completeness. The deployment of such a lavish vocabulary of praise is one aspect of the art of *amplificatio* as practised in these lyrics. While taking as their starting points the words of familiar Latin antiphons, the twelve Advent Lyrics develop those themes at length, in a manner that is at once familiar-sounding and original, doing so through a process of internalization and renewed expression in a time-honoured formulaic style.[33]

Much as the memorization of set passages from the Bible or from noted Christian authors such as Aldhelm formed a regular part of training in *grammatica*, medieval readers who made a close study of *Advent Lyrics* and other poems of the Exeter Anthology, including Cynewulf's two signed poems

---

31 Lapidge 1979: 230; see also Orchard 1994.
32 In Niles 1983: 121–37, I draw attention to the utility, in the Old English compositional context, of flexible formulaic systems one half-line in length, as opposed to the relatively fixed formulas that are characteristic of the Homeric model of oral composition.
33 See further Maring 2017, chap. 7: 'Signifying the Coming of Christ in *The Advent Lyrics*'.

The Ascension and *Juliana*, would have been well on the way towards becoming competent makers of English devotional verse. While committing to memory a number of religious epithets and other terms useful to poets composing on Christian themes, such persons would at the same time have been assimilating the special habits of an appositive syntax, geared to flexible modes of formulaic diction, that was the chief basis of composition in the alliterative form.

Through means like these, aspiring poets could have had a role in acculturating members of a monastic community—including those novices who were drawn from the upper ranks of society—to the rhythms of their vocation, with its call for a life committed to prayer, the daily recitation of the psalms, close study of the Bible amid a wide range of scriptural commentaries, the making of books, and other weapons of spiritual warfare.

CHAPTER 2

Scribes, Authors, Compilers and Readers

One's understanding of the poems of the Exeter Anthology is naturally affected by the knowledge that this codex was written out—almost surely by a monastic scribe—painstakingly, in a beautiful hand, evidently by a single person, as a manifest act of devotion.

The physical beauty of this volume puts one in mind of the labours of the so-called 'hero scribes' of the early Middle Ages—that is to say, of those learned persons, particularly in the Irish tradition though also in the English, who had mastered the art of calligraphy so well as to take pleasure in creating books that would please or astound the eye. Such persons sometimes copied an entire manuscript single-handedly as an act of love and as a contribution to the perennial struggle of God's champions against the infernal powers.[1] Saint Columba was one such scribe, to judge from an extant psalter that is taken to be the work of his hand. This is the late sixth- or early seventh-century Cathach (or 'Battler') of Columcille, now owned by the Royal Irish Academy, Dublin.[2] The theme of spiritual warfare is readily apparent in the title by which that manuscript is traditionally known.

The scribe who wrote out the Exeter Anthology would not have been acting alone, of course. He—or she?—would have been working under the direction of other ecclesiastics and with their guidance in the communal environment of a scriptorium. As with most matters having to do with the early Middle Ages, we should think in terms of collective efforts and anonymous achievements rather than seeking out named persons acting on individual initiative, even if certain master-scribes were revered in their own lifetimes and are known to us by name.[3]

---

1 Michelle Brown (2011: 53–54) offers illuminating discussion of this point.
2 M. Brown 2003: 69, 72 fig. 37. There is a tradition, perhaps apocryphal, that monks carried the 'Battler' up to the place of battle while singing psalms in their role as 'support troops' for Irish warriors.
3 M. Brown 2011: 44–55, with examples.

Craft-poets

A similar principle regarding anonymity and collective efforts ought to hold true when we think of the authors of these poems, though here we must venture into more speculative ground. The likelihood is great that these poets were multiple in number; that they were members of ecclesiastical communities; and that they were therefore also competent scribes who knew at least the rudiments of Latin grammar and rhetoric and sometimes much more. They are best viewed as craft-poets: that is, as educated persons who had made a close study of the technology of verse, but who did not necessarily have a sense that their verse-making abilities set them into a special class of human beings like the real or imagined bards of former times. Poetry, in this context, is best approached as a community-based activity rather than being thought of as the product of individual talent alone.

In her recent study *Becoming a Poet in Anglo-Saxon England*, Emily V. Thornbury takes up the question of the identity of actual Anglo-Saxon poets, scrutinizing the evidence for literate and Latinate contexts for poetic production in addition to oral contexts that must remain the subject of speculation. Thornbury arrives at a conclusion that may seem surprising but that need not be: that is, that there is little or no evidence for the existence of professional poets in Anglo-Saxon England. She finds this to be true despite the fact that a large amount of verse was composed by Insular poets whether in Latin or English. Instead, to judge from the information that is available, 'people whom we know were poets were very likely to also be teachers, scribes, musicians, or courtiers: some were more than one of these'. In short, Anglo-Saxon poets for whom we have documentary evidence, as opposed to the imagined bards of former times, 'practised their art as one aspect of their duties' (2014a: 4).

Writing about the composition of Old English religious verse in a manner that is not inconsistent with Thornbury's findings but that takes a different direction based on concepts of textual communities, Anya Adair conceives of the authors of *Advent Lyrics*—whom she envisions in the plural—as 'poet-priests, who worked to celebrate and define a liturgical and theological canon'.[4] Postulating that these poets lived either in the same monastic establishment or in similar ones and that they shared a unifying system of life and thought, she argues that 'the monastery, as a building, an institution and way of life was that fundamental physical and spiritual reality which defined their lives and within which they prepared for their deaths'. Adopting a critical approach to *Advent Lyrics* that departs from conventional author-based notions of unity and has no need to speak of individual poetic achievement, she posits that this

---

4   Adair 2011: 844; the subsequent quotations are from the same page.

shared monastic background and mental world 'may point the way towards the unity of the lyrics'.

Building on such insights as these, it is plausible to think that the whole contents of the Exeter Anthology came into being through the work of a number of craft-poets, all of them educated along similar lines and sharing a common outlook. The collaborative efforts of such persons helped to bring into existence a collection of verse whose parts reinforce one another's effects. Whether consciously or unconsciously, all such craft-poets would have drawn on the stock resources of an oral poetic tradition that evidently had long enjoyed high status in Anglo-Saxon society. In addition, craft-poets working in a tenth-century ecclesiastical milieu would have striven to emulate in English the finer effects of the Latin poetry that was available to them through their schooling. They also could have learned much of their technique through emulation of one another, at times through the reworking of vernacular verse that was in previous circulation. This kind of reworking is evidently what was involved, for example, when the Vercelli Book poem *The Dream of the Rood* was composed on the basis of a much shorter poem of earlier date of which a few lines are inscribed in runic characters on the Ruthwell Cross. Similar reworking can be observed when we compare the Exeter Anthology poem *The Soul's Address to the Body* with the slightly expanded Vercelli Book version of that same poem.[5]

To suggest an analogy, the Exeter Anthology poets, all of whom can reasonably be taken to have been active during the period c.880–970, can be likened to the largely anonymous early medieval stonemasons who carved the doorways, vaults, niches and sculptures that made up the facade of a great minster such as Exeter Cathedral. Looking farther afield geographically though not temporally, one could liken them to the anonymous Japanese woodworkers who crafted the elegant yet large and sturdy buildings of a temple complex such as those at the UNESCO World Heritage Sites of Nara or Ise. A certain few of these stonemasons or woodworkers are likely to have been admired in their own time as masters of their craft, even earning a name for themselves in recognition of their talents, as certain masons did at Exeter.[6] Other craftsmen would have worked in relative obscurity, perhaps only as apprentices. If several successive generations of workers were involved in

---

5   While there are different ways of postulating how these parallel texts came into being, Peter Orton (1979a, 1979b) has argued persuasively that the Exeter Anthology version, or an examplar of it, served as the basis of the version in the Vercelli Book.
6   Nicholas Orme (2009: 49) observes that the names of four master masons who helped build Exeter Cathedral are known. Other craftsmen who had a role in the Cathedral's thirteenth-century rebuilding included carpenters, sawyers, glaziers, smiths, roofers, plumbers, painters, carvers, plasterers, turners, goldsmiths, pavers and carters.

these projects, this did not prevent them from using equivalent tools and materials or from speaking the same craft-language. Nor did it prevent them from sharing a common vision, or from creating works based on a common aesthetics, all the while working under the direction of a central authority which itself was of a pluralistic and evolving kind.

Although use of the term 'craft-poet' may strike some readers as belittling when compared with the terms 'scop', 'bard' or simply 'poet' (in the Romantic sense of an author afire with inspiration), nothing could be farther from my intent. This is to locate a critical vocabulary adequate to its period-specific subject. In the corpus of Old English writings, the word *cræft* has a variety of meanings, including: (1) 'strength, power, might', (2) 'skill, ability, dexterity', (3) 'strength, merit, excellence, power', (4) 'skill, ability, faculty, talent', and (5) 'art'.[7] Old English compound nouns that build on the simplex noun *cræft* include *bōc-cræft* 'book learning', *glīw-cræft* 'musicianship', *leornung-cræft* 'scholarship', *lēoþ-cræft* 'the art of poetry', *rīm-cræft* 'arithmetic', *sang-cræft* 'the art of singing', *scōp-cræft* 'the art of composing verse', *stæf-cræft* 'skill in letters' or 'literacy', and *wōþ-cræft* 'the art of lofty song'. Use of this last word is specific to the poets represented in the Exeter Anthology, for its sole occurrences in Old English are twice in *The Phoenix* and once in *The Whale*.[8] The editors of the *DOE* add the following judicious note on the semantics of *cræft*:

> The most frequent Latin equivalent of *cræft* is *ars*, yet neither 'craft' nor 'art' adequately conveys the wide range of meanings of *cræft*. 'Skill' may be the single most useful translation for *cræft*, but the senses of the word reach out to 'strength', 'resources', 'virtue' and other meanings in such a way that it is often not possible to assign an occurrence to one sense in Modern English without arbitrariness and the attendant loss of semantic richness.

In the Exeter Anthology, *cræft* is used chiefly with reference to God's supreme strength, power and might. In *Advent Lyric 1*, Christ the carpenter is pointedly called *sē cræftga* 'the Craftsman' (12a) with reference to his ability to fix the broken 'house' of earth. The simplex *cræft* is used elsewhere in the Anthology to denote 'skill, ability, faculty, talent', as in that passage from *God's Gifts to Humankind* that refers to the talents of three different groups of clergy as singers, scholars and writers.[9]

---

7   See the *DOE*, s.v. *cræft*.
8   *The Phoenix* at 127a, with reference to the phoenix's enchanting song; *The Phoenix* at 548a, with reference to the composition of this same poem; and *The Whale* at 2a, with reference to the composition of *The Whale*.
9   I quote the passage in Chapter 6 below, in the section headed 'Composing riddles as a monastic pursuit'.

Moreover, ordinary craftsmen and their trades are mentioned in these poems with some frequency.[10] This is true not just of *God's Gifts to Humankind*, with its long catalogue of skills and talents, but also of the riddle collection, with its images pertaining to the art of the blacksmith, the horn-maker, the woodworker, the scribe, the bookbinder, the brewer, the glass-maker and so forth.[11] These were all respected craftsmen whose skills were essential to the maintenance of an early medieval estate, whether secular or monastic in kind. Ælfric, as well, provides some rather colourful 'self-portraits' of craftsmen among the imagined participants in his well-known *Colloquy*. This exercise was designed not just for the teaching of Latin vocabulary and to improve students' facility in conversational Latin, but also to confirm the validity of a social order in which all *hādas* 'vocations' were valued, that of the monk above all.[12] According to Kevin Leahy, certain Anglo-Saxon craftsmen were of relatively high status and enjoyed a correspondingly high wergild, though this would have been the exception. The story that Saint Dunstan himself was a skilled metalworker who once caught the devil's nose in his tongs is perhaps, alas, no more than wishful thinking.[13] Regional styles in the crafts are sometimes identifiable, and the poems of the Exeter Anthology, in the form in which we have them, are plausibly associated with a southern English literary style.

When I use the term 'craft-poets' to refer to those people who fashioned the *gieddas* 'songs' or *lēoð* 'poems' that are recorded in the Exeter Anthology, then, it is with value-neutral reference to persons with the ability to compose religious verse and to have that verse preserved on vellum. While the Old English term *scop*, sometimes misused by critics to refer to the entire category of Anglo-Saxon poets, is suggestive of inspiration, imagination and age-old oral tradition, a 'craft-poet' is someone capable of producing verse that can be appreciated for both its intellectual substance and its formal artistry. Although one can rest assured that not all craft-poets were equally capable, my use of the term is meant to call to mind the skills that were required to produce the high-end jewellery of this same period through the goldsmith's art, or high-end weaponry through the blacksmith's art, or illuminated manuscripts of a sumptuous quality through the collaborative labours of scribes, draughtsmen, colourists and artisans working with gold leaf.

---

10 As Nicholas Howe (1985: 126) remarks, crafts are represented in these poems as expressions of the orderly, benign life; they are part of the proper order of the world.
11 Dieter Bitterli (2009: 135–90), among others, calls attention to the prominent place occupied by crafts in the riddle collection.
12 Christina Jacobs (2001) discusses Ælfric's *Colloquy* in relation to the instructional purposes of the Exeter Anthology.
13 On these different matters see Leahy 2003: 169 and 172, respectively.

In a craft tradition, the work forgets its maker; the work alone remains as a testament to the maker's skill. This way of looking at the anonymous poetry of the Exeter Anthology remains valid even though there is one well-known exception to the rule. This is the poet Cynewulf, who was unusual in his desire to emulate the status of Latin poets known to posterity by name. As S.A.J. Bradley puts the matter:

> there is a natural plausibility in the idea that Cynewulf ... composed in writing, not strictly orally, and relied upon a written text of his poetry to preserve the authorial form of it and thus to achieve that identity between a poet's name and the stable corpus of his works that the Latin poets were seen to enjoy (218).

So Cynewulf stands apart in this regard, even though we might just as well refer to him as 'the Cynewulf poet' in the same manner that we speak of 'the *Beowulf* poet', for he remains little more than a name, a shadowy effect of his own verse signatures.

The compiler and the compilation

Given that so little can be known about the processes by which the Exeter Anthology was made, there is no reason to discount the possibility that the roles of poet, scribe and compiler may have overlapped to some extent in the volume's production, doing so in a manner that may be too complex for anyone now to discern.[14] It is chiefly as a matter of grammatical convenience, then, that we speak of 'the compiler' of the Exeter Anthology, for there is no way to tell what individual or what group is implied by that term. Even if there was just one compiler, then that person would still have been acting on behalf of a group and with the co-operation of others. Nor is there any way of ascertaining if the scribe, or a given poet, or the compiler was male or female, for both men and women had an active role in Anglo-Saxon textual communities and took part in the making of books.[15] Although more names of male scribes are recorded than of female, this is only to be expected since there were more monasteries than minsters that housed women.[16]

---

14 See Muir 2005 for possibilities along such lines.
15 For discussion of female scribes and female literacy see M. Brown (2011: 73–78), Horner (2001: *passim*) and Lees and Overing (2011). Orme (2006: 24) briefly reviews the place of women in education during the early Anglo-Saxon period.
16 Sarah Foot (2006: 175) nevertheless identifies no fewer than sixty-six minsters housing women up to the year 850. As for female scribes, Donald Scragg (2012) has set out the preliminary

As to whether the scribe who wrote out the poems of the Exeter Anthology was distinct from the authors of these works or from their compiler, I have no convictions, for a single person might have fulfilled more than one of these roles. The fact that the scribe made copying errors does not resolve this point, for when authors copy or rework their own compositions, their work is still potentially subject to the kinds of mistake made by scribes. By inference from the quality of the scribe's hand, we can be sure that this person was an experienced and capable member of the clergy. On the basis of the other work that has been ascribed to him, the scribe was equally capable writing in Latin or in English.[17] He—or she?—might thus have been of high standing in his textual community, hence also a person of learning and a sponsor of books. This, however, remains a matter for speculation.

While the stylistic resemblances and verbal echoes that can be traced among different poems of the Exeter Anthology might fuel the suspicion that a number of these poems are the work of the same author, judgements along such lines are tempered by the recognition that different authors may have had a common debt to a prior Anglo-Saxon oral poetic tradition. This is a long-standing assumption among specialists in Old English literature, and it is well founded in my view. In addition, however, these resemblances may result from different poets having read one another's work, or from their having heard noteworthy poems being performed aloud. These more immediate influences would have been natural enough in reformed monastic settings, where small groups of people were pursuing common ends under the governance of a single Rule. From their exposure to one another's work, whether via writing or via face-to-face encounters, aspiring poets could have emulated one another in expressing devotional themes in language capable of inspiring wonder and reverence.

Readers, constructed and otherwise

My use of the verb 'read' and the noun 'writing' in the course of the preceding remarks is meant to draw attention to an aspect of the poetry of the Exeter

---

results of a research project seeking to identify by name the scribes who contributed to the vernacular manuscripts of the late Anglo-Saxon period. These names are not all gender-specific, however, while a large number of writings cannot be attributed to named scribes.

17 Patrick W. Conner (1993a: 80–86) discusses the close palaeographical similarity between the script of the Exeter Anthology and that of London, Lambeth Palace Library, MS 149, which includes Bede's *Explanatio Apocalypsis* and Augustine's *De adulterinis coniugiis*, and of Oxford, Bodleian Library, MS Bodley 319, a copy of Isidore's *De fide catholica contra Iudaeos*. These three manuscripts, one written almost entirely in English and the other two entirely in Latin, are widely accepted to be the work of the same scribe (Muir 1: 25).

Anthology that has been undervalued in the past. This is its active participation in the mainstream of learning in its time as a book intended for reading.

It matters to our understanding of the poems of the Exeter Anthology that monks or, conceivably, cloistered women evidently made the book so that it might be read by other monastics. This is not to exclude other members of society as prospective readers of this book or as listeners. I wish to emphasize, however, what would surely have been the book's primary intended audience. This was the class of persons who not only had achieved a functional literacy in Latin through study of the trivium and the conduct of the liturgy, and especially through the singing, copying and memorizing of the psalms,[18] but who were also potentially engaged in higher studies involving texts of some difficulty composed in either Latin or English.

There should be no mistaking this matter. Despite what can be said about the literacy of the laity in late Anglo-Saxon England, and despite the fact that literacy of a functional kind was expected of all ecclesiastics, monks were the elite of early Christendom as regards the making and reading of books. And at point after point, the Exeter Anthology demands an alert, intelligent and well-informed readership. First and foremost, readers of such a description would have belonged to monastic foundations, whether a well-established one or one of the newer ones, including those communities of monks that, starting in the 960s, were being established in English cathedral centres as an aspect of the Reform. Although little is known about reading practices or literary production in such centres, we can be sure that cathedral schools, where they existed, would have been a means by which knowledge derived from a learned Latinate tradition was diffused more widely among members of the laity. Monastic cathedrals, generally referred to as priories, were relatively few in number during the Anglo-Saxon period, however, as well as being a uniquely English phenomenon. According to Stanford Lehmberg (2000), only four of them (at Christ Church Canterbury, Winchester, Worcester and Ely) were in existence during the Anglo-Saxon period, as opposed to the considerably greater number that came to be established after the Norman Conquest. To this number can be added the smaller monastic cathedral at Sherborne, which became monastic in about the year 998.[19]

In any event, to whatever type of ecclesiastical centre or centres one wishes to ascribe their origins, many poems of the Exeter Anthology

---

18 As George Hardin Brown (1995) has emphasized, the practical foundation of literacy during much of the Middle Ages was study of the psalms, which were recited daily and were regularly read and committed to memory.

19 Julia Barrow, 'Cathedral Clergy', in *Blackwell Encyclopedia*, pp. 87–89 (at 89).

practically cry out for a learned and ingenious readership.[20] This is true of Cynewulf's two poems *The Ascension* and *The Passion of Saint Juliana*, with their theological preoccupations, their dense patterns of allusion to Latinate sources and their cryptographic 'signature' passages. As Cynewulf states towards the end of his Vercelli Book poem *Fates of the Apostles* when introducing the version of his runic signature that is included there, the anticipated reader of his verse is a person who is 'clever at deduction' (*foreþances glēaw*) and who moreover 'takes pleasure in poetic compositions' (*sē ðe hine lysteð lēoð-giddunga*).[21] In order to construe Cynewulf's signature passages intelligibly, readers must switch between the roman and the runic alphabets while interpreting the runic symbols not just via the names traditionally ascribed to them, but also by means of some creative thinking within the parameters of the Old English alliterative verse form.[22] Intelligence, poetic sensibility, special knowledge and hermeneutic agility are thus all asked of the reader, who is indeed imagined to be a reader of texts on the page and a person habituated to the authority of books, not just a listener to verse voiced aloud.

This is one instance of a general principle. Even with its fondness for maxims and ancestral wisdom, the Exeter Anthology is the last thing from an easy read. Its constituent poems could scarcely have been the basis of entertainments in a chieftain's mead-hall, nor, to my mind, were they meant (at least primarily) for the edification of guildsmen at their feasting, even though such scenarios as these have been imagined and need not be ruled out.[23] It seems to me unlikely, however, that even an ordinary parish priest would have had anything much to do with a book of this kind, given its physical elegance as well as its sometimes esoteric contents. People who were not specialists in the Word and who had little or no training in the culture of

---

20 As Roberta Dewa remarks, 'to some extent the runic riddles already assume a learned audience, one familiar with both runic and roman alphabets, with the vernacular and ... with Latin' (1995: 26).
21 *Fates of the Apostles* 96–97, cited from Bjork, *Poems of Cynewulf*, pp. 136, 53; translation based on Bradley, p. 157.
22 I address this topic in Niles 2006c. As Bradley observes: 'The standard nouns for the runes ... do not always make good sense when mechanically applied to Cynewulf's signatures, and so the possibility must be considered that a given rune may be used for any word beginning with that letter which is appropriate in the given context of sense and metre. Thus the challenge of finding the right word becomes a riddle of the kind much favoured in Anglo-Saxon poetry' (218).
23 The idea that certain poems of the Exeter Anthology were once performed in the halls of chieftains was once a critical commonplace, though it is now seldom heard. Arguments for a guildhall setting have been advanced by Conner 2005, 2008 (at 270–71) and 2011.

literacy would have had considerable difficulty construing no few of the poems included here.

As regards the question of audience, it is helpful to distinguish the book's actual readers from its constructed ones. Concerning the book's actual readership we have no solid knowledge. To pretend otherwise is a sham. Concerning the book's constructed readership, however, a good deal can be said. The poems of the Anthology address their reader—normally in the singular, as in the rhetoric of preaching—as someone who is in need of spiritual and moral guidance and is willing to accept it;[24] as someone, still, who is fully literate and is sufficiently learned to recognize scriptural or liturgical allusions at a glance;[25] and as someone who is not just willing but even eager to rise to intellectual challenges, as in the book's cryptographic passages, its instances of hidden wordplay and other potentially enigmatic matters. These aspects of the book assume the reader's participatory presence as someone who is committed to the life of the mind and who therefore, whether through ingenuity or rumination, will be an avid decipherer of the book's verbal and spiritual mysteries.

The book's participatory character is most obvious in the riddle collection, with its frequently repeated clause 'saga hwæt ic hatte' ('say what I am called') and similar phrases. It is made equally clear at the start of *Exeter Maxims*, where the reader is asked to take part in an exchange of wise sayings, and at the start of *The Wonder of Creation*, with its query, 'Wilt þū, fūs hæle ... wīsne wōð-boran wordum grētan?' ('Wilt thou, eager man ... meet the wise inspired poet with words of welcome?', 1–2). A dialogue between two seekers for wisdom is even simulated in the short poem *Pharaoh*, which begins with the imperative phrase *Saga me* (1a), voiced by an initial imagined speaker, and continues with a response spoken by an imagined interlocutor (at 4–8).[26] As Elaine Tuttle Hansen has observed, *The Wonder of Creation* evokes a poetic tradition that 'demands the co-operative efforts of its audience' in the process

---

24 As in the repeated imperatives at the beginning of *A Father's Precepts*: 'Dō ... dēag ... wēne ... efn ... frēo' ('Do ... do good ... believe ... act ... love'), and so forth, or at the end of that same poem: 'Ne bēo ... ac bēo ... ber ... gemyne ... geheald' ('Be not ... but be ... bear ... remember ... hold fast').

25 Note the reiterated formula 'ūs secgaþ bēc' ('books tell us'), used by the authors of these poems at *The Ascension* 346b [785b] and *The Holy Death of Saint Guthlac* 60b [878b] and elsewhere in the Anthology in variant forms. (When citing line numbers from the three poems of the Christ cycle, I first give Muir's primary lineation, then his secondary lineation between square brackets. The second lineation is based on a continuous numbering of the three poems as a single text, as for example in Krapp and Dobbie 1936.) Examples of learned allusions are legion, especially in the poems at the start of the codex, including *Advent Lyrics* and *The Ascension*.

26 Joseph Trahern (1970–71) has called attention to the medieval genre of the 'dialogue poem' to which this poem pertains.

of creating and transmitting wisdom (1988: 83). Correspondingly, the reader of that same poem is characterized somewhat later as 'sē þe on elne lēofað,/ dēop-hydig mon' ('one who lives fearlessly, a deeply contemplative person', 17b–18). As Huppé comments on this latter passage: 'In view of the probable monastic provenance of such a poem as this, it is not surprising to find the monastic ideal of contemplation advocated through the striking association of contemplation with the virtue of fortitude' (1970: 38).

Unsurprisingly, the book's constructed reader is someone who can expect at any time, like any churchgoer, to be exhorted to think and act as a devout Christian living among others of the devout. This is the hortatory rhetoric of the passage with which *The Seafarer* draws to a close, the passage that begins: 'Uton wē hycgan hwær wē hām āgen' ('Let us now consider where we have a home', 117).[27] Attention shifts at this point from the poem's starting point, the monologue of a solitary *peregrinus* speaking of his personal experience, to a more generalized address directed to any Christian seeker.[28] The Old English term *gesīþas*, a staple of the heroic vocabulary and a term that signifies 'comrades, fellow travellers' (from the noun *sīþ*, meaning 'journey'), is worth recalling in this connection; for here as elsewhere in the Anthology, the imagined authors, speakers and readers of these poems are called to mind as if they were companions on a journey whose goals are enlightenment and eventual salvation. In their shared participation in this quest, the members of this Anglo-Saxon 'fellowship of the book' resemble those archetypal companions, Christ's disciples, who are the subject of Cynewulf's Vercelli Book poem *Fates of the Apostles* and who are designated by that same Old English term *gesīþas* near the start of *The Ascension*.[29]

A wise twenty-first-century critic will keep in mind that the ideal reader of the Exeter Anthology is not constructed as a twenty-first-century critic. Readers of our own era who hope to understand the Anthology in terms consistent with the culture that produced it should first of all conform themselves as much as possible to the image of the reader who is constructed by the text. Only then, in all humility, will it be time to assert other perspectives.

---

27 I quote the start of that passage in Chapter 8 below, in the section headed 'The journey home: the keyword *hām*'.
28 Magennis (2007) writes with characteristic insight about the rhetorical shift at the end of *The Seafarer* away from 'aloneness' and towards community-based homiletic address. A similar rhetorical shift occurs towards the end of other poems of the Anthology, e.g. *The Wanderer*, *The Rhyming Poem*, *The Fortunes of Men* and *Christ's Descent into Hell*.
29 'Hē him fægre þæs/lēofum gesīþum lēan æfter geaf' ('He afterwards generously rewarded them, his beloved companions, for that', 33b–34 [472b–73]). The reference is to Christ's rewarding his disciples with love, power and grace.

Script, intellectual character and purpose

For what purpose or purposes was the Exeter Anthology compiled, then?

If this question is not often posed in the scholarly literature, this is perhaps because questioning the underlying purpose of a poetic miscellany can be an exercise in futility in the absence of definitive statements on that topic by the book's maker or makers. Even then some questions may remain. Informed speculation can sometimes lead to insights in such matters, however, and it is in that spirit that I will take up the matter here.[30]

The assumption that the Exeter Anthology did have an underlying purpose or purposes is safe enough. The codex is a large and handsome one that would have been expensive to produce. Its 123 folios are inscribed in an elegant Insular square minuscule script that Robin Flower has called 'the noblest of Anglo-Saxon hands' (1933: 83). Most experts agree that there was but one scribe, as N.R. Ker concluded some while back.[31] Elaine Treharne too ascribes the manuscript to 'a single accomplished scribe, whose polished performance is noted for its aesthetic calligraphic appeal, its clarity and sustained regularity' (2009: 100). Jane Roberts phrases the matter yet more directly, characterizing the book's script as 'stately' and as 'among the most beautiful to be seen in Anglo-Saxon vernacular manuscripts'.[32]

The different parts of the book are very much of a kind in physical appearance. This would have been true at least before certain folios were lost, scored, stained, worn or partially burnt as a result of the hazards of time. The emblematic visual decorum of the scribe's work encourages the thought that someone, or some group, working in a southern English textual community in the 960s or 970s, wished to make a statement about the value of vernacular poetry in a bilingual cultural environment. In the much the same way, as Malcolm Parkes has discussed, Anglo-Saxon scribes working in an earlier century had adopted an emblematic version of uncial script for the copying of important Latin writings such as biblical texts, the works of Gregory the Great, the Rule of Saint Benedict and certain charters.[33]

Very likely the Exeter Anthology fulfilled functions in late tenth-century England that were analogous to the ones it fulfils today. While such a claim

---

30 As Thomas Shippey remarks, 'The problem of purpose is indeed the most baffling one in Old English poetic studies, and can only be considered speculatively' (1976: 18).
31 Ker 1957: 153: 'The hand is the same throughout.'
32 Roberts 2005: 60 and 39, respectively. Roberts includes a facsimile page from the MS, together with a diplomatic transcription of it and brief comments on the hand (2005: 60–61). In accord with an earlier consensus, she allows for a date for the MS within the period 970–90 while acknowledging that some experts favour a slightly earlier date.
33 Parkes 2008: 129–30, with references.

may at first seem so plausible as not to be worth making, it has not been voiced in such a direct manner before and seems to me worth pursuing. The main functions of the Exeter Anthology were—and still are—three in number.

First of all, quite obviously, the book served as an anthology of noteworthy poetic texts composed in the vernacular. Determining what the original compiler thought to be noteworthy deserves a moment's reflection, however. An anthologizer of the present day who had the whole extant corpus of Old English shorter poems available to choose from would be unlikely to come up with the same selection of poems as this, set in the same order, for certain favourites in the eyes of modern readers find no place here. On the other hand, the Anthology includes certain other poems and passages that are now generally thought to have a very limited literary value. Chiefly these are poems or passages of a didactic kind. In his survey *The Anglo-Saxon Literature Handbook*, for example, Mark C. Amodio writes in a disparaging tone about *A Father's Precepts*, in which 'the poet rarely rises above the platitudinous in his advice'; of *Vainglory*, where the poet's doctrinal purpose is approached 'in a conventional and largely undistinguished fashion'; and of *The Fortunes of Mortals*, whose closing moral regarding the thanks that people owe to God is said to be perfunctory.[34] In general, in a manner that has ample precedent in the criticism of medieval literature and is reflective of a widespread modern bias, Amodio flags those Christian didactic passages that occur in this codex as being artistically inferior to the book's other parts.

My own sense of the matter is that the poems written out in the Exeter Anthology were included there first and foremost because they were believed to be edifying in one way or another, in addition to whatever literary value they were thought to have. While this latter value may have been viewed as considerable, this was not necessarily the compiler's chief concern, nor was it necessarily that of the unknown authors of these works. Correspondingly, the book's didacticism was very likely held to be a virtue in a setting where book learning held a prime place in the quest for wisdom and salvation. A persuasive argument along such lines has been advanced by Rafal Boryslawski, who likens the character of the Exeter Anthology to that of a medieval cathedral, viewed as an artful compendium that is both 'a complex theological text' and 'a didactic instrument' (2002: 39).

A second function fulfilled by the Exeter Anthology, one that would have been more central to its tenth-century reception than it is today, was to confirm its readers in a particular world-view. This was the ethos of orthodox Christianity in its late Anglo-Saxon inflection as transmitted in the medium of native verse. There was no need to teach Christian doctrine directly, for

---

34   Amodio 2014: 234, 238 and 244, respectively.

the book's readers would already have been amply familiar with it. On the other hand, devotees of a faith often take pleasure in seeing its elements elaborated upon or encoded in one literary genre or another, much as they may appreciate seeing them dramatized through liturgy and religious drama. The Exeter Anthology offers such satisfactions as these in abundance.

A third function of the book was—and is—to facilitate study of the formal elements of Old English verse, including its versification and rhetoric. A programme of this kind would have supplemented the customary Latin curriculum in *grammatica*. The programme would have been practicable in mid- or late tenth-century Anglo-Saxon England, with its bilingualism, though evidently not elsewhere in Europe at this time, leaving Ireland aside. Tenth-century teachers, one can imagine, would have pursued this aim in a manner consistent with the Anthology's didactic orientation, asking their students not just 'What are the formal elements of Old English verse as shown by this passage?', as their counterparts in the classroom are apt to do today, but rather 'How are the formal elements of English verse being exploited here as an eloquent vehicle for religious doctrine?' Although this is an imagined scenario, it directs attention to how a tenth-century instructional setting might have differed from a present-day one in its aims and underlying assumptions.

So as to avoid possible misunderstanding, I should emphasize that I am not arguing that the Exeter Anthology was used as a somewhat high-end instructional text. My more modest claim is that the book appears to have been made with that thought in mind, particularly as regards instruction in vernacular poetics. The contents of the book make sense when approached from this perspective, regardless of how the book ended up actually being used, if it ever was used in any but an occasional way.

Likewise, I do not claim to know that the book was successfully used for the acculturation of novice monks, particularly ones of upper-class background, to a world-view consistent with the Rule of Saint Benedict. We do not know how the book was used; we do not know who read it, or if it was much read at all; we cannot say with any certainty what the intentions were of the people who made it, or what the mental or psychological effects were of anyone's reading it. My more modest aim is to point out that the book's contents would have made it eminently suited to such a purpose.

There are two reasons for my reluctance to push these aspects of my argument farther. First, the whole subject of what was or was not an instructional text in early medieval Europe is a fraught one that does not admit of definitive answers. As Patrizia Lendinara has noted, 'educational manuscripts are not a well defined category', whether in early medieval England or other parts of Europe. Moreover, Lendinara is surely justified in remarking that the educational strategies of this period are 'quite conjectural and in part unrecoverable'.³⁵

Second, the Exeter Anthology is a large, elegantly written codex that shows no overt signs of having been used in the schools. Unlike a number of identifiable school-texts, it is not glossed or annotated in a manner that suggests either preparation for classroom study or a history of such use. As far as one can tell, the dry-point drawings, patterns and letterforms that are to be found here and there in the edges of the manuscript are of no apparent educational function. The same can be said of the occasional runes that are either penned or written in dry point in the margins of the book or in the space between texts.³⁶ The fact that the book was never glossed or annotated in a systematic manner, however, does not rule out its having been conceived of with instruction in mind. After all, other medieval codices exist that have often been regarded as classbooks and yet are very sparsely glossed if at all. After reviewing the sparse English glosses in Cambridge, University Library, MS Gg.5.35—the 'Cambridge Songs' manuscript—R.I. Page shows characteristic circumspection when he observes that 'perhaps this was a schoolbook more in theory than in practice' (1982: 149). It is best to be cautious when using such labels.

A book that was meant for reading

During the Anglo-Saxon period, the most likely place where a book like the Exeter Anthology would have been housed was a monastic library, whether attached to an ordinary foundation or to a Reform-era cathedral with its attached monastic community. This is not to rule out other possibilities, since books by their nature are portable and have multiple potential owners and readers.³⁷ For the most part, Anglo-Saxon libraries were small affairs by modern standards. Their holdings consisted very largely of books written in Latin, while books written wholly or even partly in English were relatively few in number. The number of literate persons with access to these libraries and their holdings is impossible to know, but it could never have been great. The number of persons who ever had access to any one particular manuscript such as the Exeter Anthology must therefore have been small indeed. Copies

---

35 Lendinara 2007: 71 and 61, respectively.
36 On these miscellaneous marginalia see Muir 1: 15–16 and Conner 1993a (chap. 5 *passim*).
37 Much more is now known about Anglo-Saxon libraries than was known in former years, particularly as regards regions outside the main centres of book production. See especially Gneuss 1996 and Lapidge 2006a.

of manuscripts could be made, at some trouble and expense and with the risk that a manuscript, once loaned out, might not be returned. But there are no extant copies of the Exeter Anthology, nor need we assume that it is a copy of a pre-existing codex, though its pages represent fair copies of something. As a result, the book would have been available to a small number of 'insiders' alone.

As needs no emphasis, the situation today is different. Thanks to the powers of both mechanical and electronic reproduction, no one with an interest in the poetry of the Exeter Anthology need venture farther than their own office or the nearest university or public library to be able to access that volume's texts, whether through collective editions, specialized editions or facsimiles of the manuscript. Through various and sundry translations, as well, versions of many of the poems of the Anthology have become available in one form or another to an enormously larger readership than was conceivable at the time of its making. All these persons, however, are 'outsiders' to the culture from which the book arose; it is impossible for anyone today to be an 'insider'.

Early medieval reading practices, too, differed greatly from our own.[38] Reading had a place in the *opus dei* that was part of a monastic's daily regime. The particular regime to be followed during Lent is set out in principle in chapter 48 of the Rule of Saint Benedict, 'De Opera Manuum Cotidiana' ('On the Regime of Daily Manual Labour'):

> In Quadragesimae vero diebus a mane usque tertia plena vacent lectionibus suis ... In quibus diebus Quadragesimae accipiant omnes singulos codices de biblyotheca, quos per ordinem ex integro legant; qui codices in caput Quadragesime dandi sunt.
>
> (In the days of Lent, they [the brothers] should be free for their reading in the morning until the end of the third hour ... In these days of Lent, let each brother receive his own book from the library and read it through, in its entirety; the books are to be given out at the beginning of Lent.)[39]

Here it is specified that each book taken by a brother from a monastic library should be read through from front to back in regular increments. Other scenarios than this were possible. Particularly if a reader of the Exeter Anthology were already familiar with some of its contents, then that

---

38 See Nicholas Howe (1993), M.B. Parkes (1997). While Howe adopts a cultural and historical perspective with emphasis on the oral/aural dimension of all reading in the Anglo-Saxon context, Parkes is concerned with minute aspects of the legibility of texts, including the systems of scribal punctuation that were once in use.
39 Venarde, *Rule of Benedict*, pp. 162–63.

person could fairly easily have turned to a known page so as to single out an individual passage, whether for private reading or for group study.

The singling out of individual poems or passages for attention would not necessarily have been a routine or facile task, however, for the book's constituent parts, which are all written out like prose, are not distinguished from one another by being set out on separate pages. Nor are the poems given titles, headers or footnotes as in modern editions; nor, as it has come down to us, is the Anthology equipped with a list of contents. Apart from the scribe's occasional use of ornamental initials—a few of them eye-catching, as on the folio reproduced at the start of the present volume (Fig. 2)—one unit of reading has the outward appearance of just about any other. Especially problematic are sectional divisions (or the lack of them) involving *Advent Lyrics*, *Doomsday*, *The Husband's Message* and enigmas 1-3, 44, 48, 68 and 75.[40] Moreover, the scribe's practice is scarcely systematic as regards the use of ornamental initials and end punctuation. While discussing these features of the physical manuscript, Muir has made clear that they do not serve as a reliable guide for modern editors, whose concepts of sectional divisions and of the boundaries between poems may differ from the notions apparently held by the scribe. Medieval readers would thus have encountered the Exeter Anthology as a single large codex with many divisions, some of which are of uncertain significance. These divisions vary considerably in length, from the briefest of riddles to poems or clusters of poems that carry on over several pages without a visible break. Particularly for a reader coming across the volume cold, the separate integrity of its parts might have mattered less than their participation in a single complex whole.

The situation today is again quite different. Thanks to the existence of modern editions with their titles, lineation and calculated *mise en page*, each of the book's constituent parts can now readily be studied in isolation from the others.[41] This fact is reflected in the modern critical literature, where certain individual poems of the Anthology have been given exquisite attention while others have been relatively ignored.

One of my guiding assumptions as to the poems of the Exeter Anthology, then, is that they were written out so that they could be read, and read (where time permitted) as a group. This is not to deny the possibility that individual poems were also voiced aloud at one time or another so as to be

---

40 The book's division into sections is discussed by Muir at 1: 16-20; the scribe's use of ornamental initials and different kinds of final punctuation at 1: 27-29. See Muir's textual notes (vol. 1) and his commentary (vol. 2) for discussion of individual problems relating to the interpretation of these signs.
41 Roy M. Liuzza (2006) provides an exemplary analysis of problems associated with the modern editorial treatment of early medieval texts.

received aurally, but I do not assume that song or speech was the primary medium of this verse. Rather, ink and vellum were.[42] My perspective on this point therefore differs from that of R.D. Fulk and Christopher M. Cain in their 2003 *History of Old English Literature*, for what Fulk and Cain emphasize is the orality of the medium of the native alliterative verse form. In those authors' view, all Old English poems 'were sung, or capable of being sung, to the accompaniment of a stringed instrument, a lyre or harp' (2013: 29). While this observation is undeniable since words by their nature can be sung, especially when versified, I find it more productive to think of the poems of the Exeter Anthology as being meant first of all for the eyes of readers. In this regard they resemble the Latin Christian verse of this same period.

More on the book's potential readers and uses

The Exeter Anthology was very likely written out, then, for the benefit of one or more bilingual textual communities of mid- to late tenth-century England. Ecclesiastics who had been born into the upper ranks of society had leading roles in such communities. Such persons in particular are likely to have been receptive to the redirection of the heroic ethos to confirm values associated with the cenobitic way of life. One of the effects of the poetry of the Exeter Anthology would have been to reassure its readers that a decision to become one of 'God's exiles' was both courageous and rational, given the precarious nature of life on earth and the certainty of Judgement, not to mention the potential spiritual comforts of a communal way of life.

Poetry of this kind would have strengthened members of the regular clergy in their resolve, teaching them doctrinal truths that were already familiar to them but that, through verse of this expressive kind, they could see in a new light and take fully to heart.[43] The book would thus have been a tool of conversion, in the root sense of that word: a conscious and willing change of course from one path to another, hence personal transformation.

---

42 Peter Orton points out that the riddles that involve runic characters imply 'not just a literate target-audience, but more specifically a readership' (2014: 161). He likewise concludes that Cynewulf's runic signatures require learned readers ('he wrote for the solitary monastic', 128) and observes that Riddle 60 ('Reed') speaks of reader and pen enclosed in 'a private world of literate communication' (171), thus encouraging contemplation of the paradox of silent speech.

43 Michael Drout comments on the educational value of the Exeter Anthology in similar fashion: 'The wisdom poems are instructional: they teach novice monks and reform monks ways to think, helping monks to understand their entire culture in relation to monastic life, demonstrating that every aspect of that culture fits into a larger whole' (2007: 465).

A book can have many purposes and uses, though, just as it can have multiple real or potential readers. However one envisions the readership of the Exeter Anthology, once this book was made, its contents could have served much the same purposes as the polished Latin *carmina* that had a long history of use as models in the schools.

What is special about the Exeter Anthology is that it is composed almost entirely in English, a language with a well-established native verse tradition of its own. One reader of the book—someone with an interest in eloquence—could readily have learned to compose religious poetry of a similar kind by studying these examples. Another reader might have approached these poems chiefly as focal points for spiritual contemplation, responding to their challenges to the intellect while drawing on them for moral guidance. Yet other readers might have been content to test their wit solving some riddles while also savouring the book's portraits of saints, sinners, exiles, bards, tyrants, abandoned or threatened women, and other exemplars of the struggling human race.

CHAPTER 3

Exeter, Glastonbury and the Benedictine Reform

The existence of the Exeter Anthology is one of many factors that point to the achievement, in the second half of the tenth century, of an English cultural renaissance. This can be accounted for in part as an aspect of the making of a united English nation. It can also be seen as a response by the organized church, with its Continental affiliations, to the Viking wars that had devastated the land before, during and after the reign of King Alfred the Great (r.871–99). At the heart of this renaissance was a significant increase in the number of monasteries and other ecclesiastical centres, together with a surge in the number of schools and in the production of manuscripts written in Latin, the vernacular or both tongues. Concurrently, the Reform entailed changes to the liturgy through specification of an elaborate set of ritual observances.[1] By the end of the century, about forty religious houses of men and about twelve of women had been founded or refounded, and many of these had their own school.[2] The contrast is great with the situation at the start of the tenth century, before the period of nation-building, when there had been only 'a handful of schools at most', in Michael Lapidge's estimate (1991: 3).

This period of renewal is summed up in the phrase 'the Benedictine Reform', also known as 'the Benedictine Revival'.[3] While the emphasis on

---

1 The liturgical reforms are spelled out in the *Regularis Concordia* (for which see Symons 1953), the customary sanctioned by the Council of Winchester in c.973. This agreement rewards close reading in conjunction with the poems of the Exeter Anthology, with their liturgical echoes.
2 Orme 2006: 32–46 (at 36). See further Lapidge 1991.
3 Two starting points for the extensive literature on the Reform are Knowles (1963: 31–69) and Stenton (1971: 433–69). Lapidge, 'Monasticism', in *Blackwell Encyclopedia*, pp. 327–29, provides a succinct review of the historical processes involved. See further Stafford 1978, G. Brown 1984, Cubitt 1997 and Blair 2005, with a select bibliography at 350 n. 281. Gretsch 1999 addresses the Reform's impact on English schools and on the development of a specialized Winchester vocabulary.

Benedictinism in those phrases is to some extent justified, it runs the risk of obscuring the extent to which the major factor in this process was the growth of well-organized monasticism under royal patronage, together with the extension of Continental-style monastic discipline into English cathedrals and cathedral schools. The change in question was very much a matter of stones, towers, endowments, classrooms, book production and church ornaments, with this building programme proceeding hand in hand with reforms in ecclesiastical organization and in the forms of the liturgy. The effects of these changes were to increase the power of monks and their establishments within the ecclesiastical hierarchy; to align the whole of the church, as thus reorganized, with the power and patronage of the monarchy; and to ensure that the English church, with its augmented liturgy and iconography, was in alignment with the whole of Western Christendom, under the ultimate jurisdiction of the Pope. The involvement of scholars from Ireland, Wales and the Continent was a key factor in these developments, as was the role of the laity in the founding of monasteries and in the progress of learning.[4] Very little did these changes have to do with doctrine, and only incidentally with ecclesiastical infighting, even though this latter factor too was a real one, as is to be expected during periods of social change involving shifts in power and privilege.[5]

The Reform and its bilingual character

Literary production underwent significant transformation during this period. Five codices containing an appreciable amount of Old English verse were produced within a period of not much more than half a century, from c.950 to the first decade of the eleventh century—five that we know of, since others may have been lost. The manuscripts in question are the Exeter Anthology, the Vercelli Book, the main part of the Junius Manuscript, the earlier of the two medieval copies of *The Old English Boethius*, and the *Beowulf* manuscript.[6] While not every poem included in these volumes is overtly

---

4 Note Lapidge 1991: 3-4 and Rumble 2008.
5 Offering a corrective to the recent trend of publications engaged with the Benedictine Reform, Christopher A. Jones (2009) has sought to loosen the binary opposition of 'reformed' versus 'unreformed' monasticism, one that is sometimes invoked without much reflection as to its explanatory power.
6 Gunhild Zimmermann (1995) analyses four of these manuscripts as conscious products of the Benedictine Reform. The set of poems known as *The Metres of Boethius* remains outside the scope of her discussion, perhaps on the assumption that the Old English translation of the poems that make up a good part Boethius's *De consolatione philosophiae* is to be

religious in content, and while the date of original composition of individual poems remains uncertain, the medium of vernacular verse was clearly being exploited as a means of propagating the ideals that animated the Reform. Poetry composed in the native verse form of the Anglo-Saxons had come into its own by this time as a means of reinforcing the Christian ideology that underpinned the governance of England.

A number of scholars working largely independently of one another, but following a precedent set by Patrick W. Conner in this regard,[7] have found reason to view the Exeter Anthology as a product of the same historical forces that shaped the tenth-century Benedictine Reform. Among these specialists are Mercedes Salvador Bello, Michael D.C. Drout, María José Sánchez de Nieva and Lenore Abraham.[8] Of special interest is that links have been traced between the Anthology and other manuscripts known to have been produced in a tenth-century Reform milieu and that share the project of using the vernacular to express typological and exegetical ideas, as Matthew Hussey has pointed out; while in a complementary study, Brian O'Camb has called attention to direct verbal links between *Exeter Maxims* and Æthelwold's Old English translation of the Benedictine Rule.[9] The cumulative force of this recent surge of scholarship is to suggest that one function of the Exeter Anthology was to acculturate its readers to a world-view consistent with English reformed monasticism.

Events taking place in the south-west of England during the period when the volume was very likely being compiled and written out (c.965–75) point to a shift in social relations whereby monastic ideals were being propagated through public displays backed by the most powerful members of West Saxon society. A merging of two worlds—that of the high-ranking laity and that of the clerical elite—was confirmed by the grand ceremonial re-enactment of the coronation of King Edgar the Peaceable (r.959–75) at the feast of Pentecost, at the city of Bath, Somerset, in May of the year 973. According to *The Coronation of Edgar* (as the vernacular Chronicle poem that commemorates this event is known), this was an impressive spectacle, for 'gathered there was a multitude of priests, a great throng of monks, of people of wisdom, as I

---

    dated to the late ninth century or thereabouts. If, however, as seems possible, this translation was completed not long before the earliest manuscript containing the *Metres* was made (one dating from about 950), then this verse can be ascribed to the early years of the Reform. For informed discussion of the dating of both the prose and the verse parts of the *Old English Boethius*, see Godden and Irvine 2009: 1: 140–51.

7   Note in particular Conner 1993b and more generally Conner 1993a.

8   Salvador Bello 2006, 2015; Drout 2006, esp. chap. 8: 'The Exeter Book Wisdom Poems and the Benedictine Reform' (pp. 219–86); Drout 2007; Sánchez de Nieva 2009; Abraham 2011.

9   Hussey 2009; O'Camb 2009.

have heard tell'.[10] In a recent analysis of this event, Simon Keynes finds that 'there is no mistaking' the contemporary tenth-century perception of it as 'a symbolic event of the utmost significance in its day'.[11] The church gathered its forces for a display at Bath in 973 so as to demonstrate its solidarity with the king who was the backbone of the Reform. Immediately after this event, Edgar held another major assembly at Chester, one that is remembered in the annals as having been attended by all the kings of the island. In Simon Keynes's view, 'it is difficult to see in the events of 973 very much less than the ceremonial reaffirmation and public celebration of Edgar's rule throughout Britain' (2008: 50–51).

England's security, wealth and power during most of the remainder of the tenth century, up to the time of renewed Viking attacks beginning in the year 991, can be ascribed in part to the success of this alliance of the king and other members of the nobility with abbots, bishops and other leading representatives of the church. Such an alliance represented the culmination of a process that had been evolving for some while, for leaders of the clerical establishment had long been drawn from the ranks of the aristocracy. This is a point that Patrick Wormald (1978) has emphasized, arguing that such a merging of interests and perspectives would have stimulated the production of vernacular poetry in a heroic mode tempered by Christian teachings. Although the focus of Wormald's discussion is northern Britain during the Age of Bede—a place and time to which he ascribes the making of *Beowulf*, though that point is subject to dispute—an alliance between church and state gained yet sharper definition in southern Britain during the era of the Reform. As Roberta Frank has observed, 'the aristocratic nature of the early English church is, if anything, more pronounced with the passage of time, reaching a kind of culmination under the successors of Alfred'.[12]

The making of such a high-end codex as the Exeter Anthology, with its West Saxon affiliations and its potential appeal both to the clergy and to pious members of the aristocracy, was a natural development in this context.

---

10 'Þær wæs prēosta heap,/micel muneca ðrēat, mīne gefrēge,/glēawra gegaderod.' Lines 8b-10a of *The Coronation of Edgar* (Dobbie 1942: 21). Salvador Bello (2008) analyses this poem and its companion piece, *The Death of Edgar* (the Chronicle entry for the year 975), as works meant to propagate the ideology of the Reform, while Scott Thompson Smith argues that *The Coronation of Edgar* celebrates Edgar as a 'holy king' whose consecration represents 'the confluence of royal and ecclesiastical authority in a single figure' (2011: 106).

11 Keynes 2008: 49. Keynes approaches the Reform as a dimension of English nation-building during the reign of Edgar. In a complementary study (1999) Keynes emphasizes Edgar's role in strengthening the institutions of royal government through his patronage of Dunstan and the monastic party.

12 Frank 1982: 58.

English bookmaking, bilingualism and the iconography of the Reform

In a phenomenon that corresponds to the ones just mentioned, several English books produced during the decades of the 960s and 970s feature a hieratic iconography showing King Edgar as simultaneously vicar of Christ and head of the English church. The leading example of this development in the visual arts is the frontispiece to the New Minster Charter, an impressive document produced in Winchester in 966 to commemorate the refoundation of the New Minster, Winchester, by King Edward with the assistance of his new bishop Æthelwold.[13] Julia Barrow has called attention to 'the detail, comprehensiveness, and vim of the elaborate theological programme worked out by Æthelwold' in this document, particularly in its opening part.[14]

The frontispiece to the Charter is divided into two unequal levels, the upper one being devoted to Christ in Majesty and the lower one to King Edgar flanked by the Virgin Mary and Saint Peter, the patron saints of the New Minster. As Catherine E. Karkov has observed,[15] while Edgar, with outstretched arms, offers Christ the golden charter, Mary and Peter are grouped with Edgar rather than with Christ, thus being depicted 'as representatives of the church rather than members of the kingdom of heaven to whom the church is being offered'. Such an arrangement of the figures underscores the alliance of king and church that was at the heart of the Reform. A point of special interest for readers of the Exeter Anthology, whose first set of poems, *Advent Lyrics*, features imagery relating to Mary and the Celestial Jerusalem, is that 'the palm held by Mary and the key held by Peter are *adventus* symbols: the palm of Palm Sunday, the Entry into Jerusalem, and the entry into paradise; and the key the entry into heaven'. As Karkov notes, 'it is also possible to understand the two figures [Peter and Mary] as symbols of the larger Church: Peter as the rock upon which the Church was built, and Mary as Ecclesia'. Members of the New Minster congregation looking at the King Edgar frontispiece, in her view, would have conceived of that king as visually and symbolically 'a type of ecclesiastical body', a corporate body representing this particular church in which all were united 'as living stones built up, a spiritual house, a holy priesthood, to offer up spiritual sacrifices' (1 Peter 2:5).

---

13 For a facsimile image see M. Brown 2007: 114 (plate 84). The minster had been refounded in 964, two years prior to this.

14 Barrow 2009: 148, building on the research of others.

15 Karkov 2008; the following quotations are from pp. 225, 226, 226 and 240–41, respectively. Robert Deshman (1995, 2010a and 2010b) writes with particular insight on the iconography of manuscripts produced in conjunction with the Reform.

The Exeter Anthology achieves effects analogous to this in its own genre of a miscellany of poems composed in the vernacular. This is so especially at its beginning, with its poems on the theme of Advent, its passages in honour of the Virgin Mary, and a great homage to Christ in Majesty in the juxtaposed poems *The Ascension* and *Christ in Judgement*. Moreover, a thread of architectural imagery, running from the start of the volume to close to its end, features the steadfast rock of the church, with individual Christians seen as the living stones that make up a congregation and the church as a whole likened to a great building founded on Christ as the original living stone.[16] In these regards as in others, the Exeter Anthology is expressive of the same historical impulses that motivated the rededication of the New Minster, Winchester, in 964, and the making of the New Minster Charter.

A corresponding shift in the Anglo-Saxon educational tradition was under way during these same years, as has been charted in landmark studies by Donald Bullough and Michael Lapidge and has been traced more recently by Gernot Wieland and Patrizia Lendinara.[17] Although Lendinara organizes her discussion around a distinction between 'popular learning' (in the medium of Old English) versus 'formal schooling' (in the medium of Latin), such a distinction loses much of its force when applied to the second half of the tenth century, when the simultaneous employment of England's two languages of literacy resulted in potential interchanges between the popular and the learned domains. This merging of two worlds finds expression in the contents of the Exeter Anthology, where elements of native Germanic lore and 'common stock' wisdom cohabit the same space as learning derived from Latinate sources, particularly in such poems as *Widsith* and *Exeter Maxims*.

One effect of the development of a bilingual system of education in tenth- and eleventh-century England was that the English language, used side by side with Latin, was gaining an increasingly important place in monastic schools and in literary production. As literacy in general became more widespread, the literacy of the laity, in addition to that of the clergy, increasingly becomes a factor for historians and literary scholars to reckon with.[18] Roy M. Liuzza has emphasized the 'fundamental cultural shift' that occurred between the age of Bede and the late ninth and tenth centuries in this regard, for only in this later period did the English language begin to serve as the basis of literature in the Mediterranean sense (2012: 104–05). Although it would be a mistake to think

---

16   I discuss this architectural thread in Chapter 9 below, in the section headed 'The Christian sojourner and the two cities'.
17   Bullough 1972; Lapidge 1991; Wieland 2011; Lendinara 2013.
18   Gretsch 2013; Liuzza 2012. For different perspectives on the topic of the literacy of the laity, see S. Kelly 1990 and Keynes 1990, supplementing Wormald 1977.

that works composed in English were made either by or chiefly for the laity, certain members of the laity could have made use of them.

The role of verse in the schools

In tandem with these developments, room was evidently being found for the study and exhibit of Old English verse as an aspect of the educational mission. While any such use of native poetry would have been an innovative turn, an interest in verse was based on Latinate precedent. As Lapidge has emphasized, verse composed by Latin masters had long been the primary medium of instruction in grammar and rhetoric, taking precedence over the study of prose.[19] Although the Bible remained 'the fundamental and defining text of Latin Christendom during the Middle Ages', study of the Bible was chiefly undertaken through poetic paraphrases of Scripture made by the early medieval poets Juvencus, Sedulius, Avitus and Arator. Another poet whose Latin works were part of the core curriculum in tenth-century England was Venantius Fortunatus; yet another was Aldhelm, an adept stylist in both verse and prose. Still it was the works of Juvencus, Sedulius, Avitus and Arator that, in Lapidge's words, 'came to form a canon of texts for study by devout Christians with a taste for the higher registers of poetic expression'. Moreover, since these poets were studied 'day in day out, line by line and word by word', their compositions were bound to have had an effect on 'the mental perception of a young Anglo-Saxon scholar'.

It is in this context that versified Old English paraphrases of scriptural texts came to be written down and preserved in monastic settings. The leading extant examples of such works are the poems of the Junius Manuscript, with their apparent precedents, now lost, in the poetry of Cædmon. Once scriptural paraphrases like these were recorded in writing, the way was open for the preservation, in monastic settings, of religious poems composed on a wide variety of topics, as were the Latin poems of Venantius Fortunatus and Aldhelm. English poems of this kind, such as are preserved in the Exeter Anthology, would then have been available as models for those who wished to explore the higher registers of poetic expression in their native tongue, whether or not Latin poems too served as models for such verse.

---

19 Lapidge 2006b; the following quotations are from pp. 11, 23, 24, and 24, respectively. As M.L.W. Laistner (1957: 215) observed in his classic study of learning in the early medieval West, much of what we speak of today as rhetoric was taught in the Middle Ages under the rubric of *grammatica*, which for Alcuin and other authorities encompassed the study of figures of speech, metre, stories (*fabulae*) and history.

In England by the middle decades of the tenth century, then, the formal study of vernacular poetry side by side with its Latin counterpart was entering the realm of the practical. We know of nowhere else in Europe, with the exception of Ireland and Anglo-Saxon religious foundations on the Continent, where this was the case.

The Exeter Anthology is likely to have had a role in these developments. By the time that this book was inscribed, a fairly substantial body of vernacular prose texts was in circulation. There were precedents for the recording of Old English verse texts as well, including a set of verse paraphrases of psalms 51–150, verse paraphrases of the thirty-one metrical parts of Boethius's *De consolatione philosophiae*, and at least the two earliest of the poems on historical subjects that were incorporated into the *Anglo-Saxon Chronicle*. Only thanks to the survival of the Exeter Anthology, however, do we have evidence that at least one ecclesiastical centre wished to preserve a diverse collection of poems, composed in English, that drew on Latin learning in original ways while promoting the ethos of heroic Christianity. The organization and contents of the Exeter codex are such as to suggest that, like certain books of the Latin tradition that have been called 'classbooks' whether or not they show consistent signs of classroom use, it was made with the prospect of its educational use in mind.

Arguing along similar lines, Seth Lerer has seen the Exeter Anthology as constituting a book that was didactic in conception and that may have served as an instructional manual.[20] Concentrating his attention on the riddles that comprise much of the second half of the Anthology, Lerer emphasizes their bookishness while at the same time pointing out the self-reflexivity of the Exeter Anthology as a whole as regards its didactic and educational functions. Moreover, he sees in the Exeter Anthology 'a rough, but ... illuminating homology' (1991: 105) with Cambridge, University Library, MS Gg.5.35, the central part of which, known as 'The Cambridge Songs', is a late eleventh-century anthology of Latin lyric poetry produced at Saint Augustine's Abbey, Canterbury. This manuscript as a whole includes a number of classroom texts, including the poem *De ave phoenice*, a century of Latin enigmas composed by Aldhelm, and a copy of Boethius's *De consolatione philosophiae*.[21] Even though this manuscript post-dates the Conquest, one can see at a glance that it bears a resemblance to the tenth-century Exeter Anthology, which likewise

---

20 Lerer 1991, esp. chap. 3, 'The Riddle and the Book' (pp. 97–125). Lerer's argument is briefly seconded by Martin Irvine (1994: 360), while Christina Jacobs (2001) develops it in a new direction with reference to *A Father's Precepts* and Ælfric's *Colloquy*.
21 On this manuscript see further Rigg and Wieland 1975 and M. Irvine 1994: 358–64. Jan Ziolkowski (1994) has edited that part of the manuscript that consists of 'The Cambridge Songs'.

includes a paraphrase of *De ave phoenice*, a near-century of enigmas and some passages that are of Boethian inspiration. The resemblances are strong even though the Exeter Anthology is composed almost entirely in English. Elizabeth Tyler has recently explored the affinities between the 'Cambridge Songs' manuscript and the Exeter Anthology in close detail, arguing for 'the integral place of "The Cambridge Songs" within English literary culture' (2016: 185) in a continuum extending from the late tenth century to the late eleventh and beyond.

Much of the groundwork for understanding the Exeter Anthology along lines like these was established by Milton McC. Gatch more than fifty years ago in his judicious book *Loyalties and Traditions: Man and his World in Old English Literature*. Gatch succeeded in demonstrating that, far from being the expression of a 'folk' or 'primitive' muse, a good deal of Old English poetry was anchored in the institution of monasticism and to the corresponding Latinate educational tradition, with its systems of exegesis.[22] Gatch's arguments, in turn, were anchored in part by James Cross's prior achievement in documenting widespread and specific parallels, in earlier Latin Christian writings, to certain themes featured in the Exeter Anthology. A well-known example is Cross's identification of Latinate precedents for the phrasing of those lines from the Wanderer's monologue (92–93) that begin with the reiterated query *Hwǣr cwōm?*[23] Cross's analysis of this elegiac passage leaves no doubt that the author of *The Wanderer* was converting to new purposes the *ubi sunt* figure of speech that was a commonplace of the medieval educational tradition through the influence of Isidore of Seville and other canonical authors.

What ought to be increasingly clear is that the Exeter Anthology as a whole, and not just certain of its parts, had a potential role in a thriving Insular tradition of literary education. Much is gained, at least in the tenth-century context, by thinking of this tradition as 'Anglo-Saxon' rather than trying to separate it out into Latin versus vernacular linguistic streams. As Lapidge has observed:

> We should always remember that works in Latin and the vernacular were copied together in Anglo-Saxon scriptoria, and were arguably composed together in Anglo-Saxon schools. What is needed, therefore, is an

---

22 Gatch 1971, esp. 61–100.
23 Note especially Cross 1956 (with particular reference to *The Wanderer*) and Cross 1963 (with reference to *The Seafarer*, *The Rhyming Poem* and *The Life of Saint Guthlac*). Muir (2: 522–23) cites passages from the homilies of Gregory the Great that help to establish a reading context for the *ubi sunt* motif within the broad tradition of Christian pessimism as to the stability of the things of this world.

integrated literary history which treats Latin and vernacular productions together as two facets of the one culture, not as isolated phenomena.[24]

So as to ascertain more clearly how the Exeter Anthology fits into an integrated literary history of this kind, it will be helpful to turn to the question of where the Exeter Anthology was composed, as far as one can tell.

Interpreting Leofric's donation to Exeter Cathedral

Most experts agree that the Exeter Anthology was written out somewhere in the south of England between the years 960 and 990. Equally uncontroversial is that it was among the books given to the monastic church of Saint Peter in Exeter—that is, to Exeter Cathedral—by Leofric, bishop of Cornwall and Devon, sometime after 1050, when the see of Cornwall and Devon was moved from Crediton to Exeter, and probably close to the time of Leofric's death in the year 1072.[25] Famously, a list of Leofric's donations to the cathedral chapter includes mention of a codex that is almost certainly the one we know as the Exeter Anthology.[26] Opinions differ, however, as to where this manuscript was first made and where it was housed for approximately the first hundred years of its existence.

In an argument that he has mounted with some vigour, Patrick W. Conner has maintained that the Exeter Anthology very likely originated at Exeter itself.[27] In a rejoinder to that argument, Richard Gameson has discounted the evidence for an Exeter origin and has drawn attention to several other places where the book might have been made and kept initially, including Glastonbury, Crediton and Christ Church, Canterbury. Gameson's cautious conclusion, which I endorse, is that the book's place of origin 'is best considered unknown'.[28]

---

24 Lapidge 1991: 2, n. 1 (in the reprinted edition).
25 Orme (2009) discusses in colourful detail the medieval history of Exeter Cathedral, including Leofric's place in that story.
26 See Scragg, 'Exeter Book', in *Blackwell Encyclopedia*, pp. 183-84, for a balanced sifting of current knowledge. Förster (1933) provides details pertaining to Leofric's donation list. R.W. Chambers's essay (1933b) introducing the facsimile volume to which Förster too contributed is profitably read alongside Lapidge's succinct entry on 'Leofric' in *Blackwell Encyclopedia*, pp. 287-88. Joyce Hill (2005) suggests that Leofric's book collection was a purposeful one, an expression of his ideology. Tyler (2016: 193-201) likewise analyses Leofric's book list in the light of that bishop's training on the Continent, as well as his literary ambitions as a sponsor of 'works of dignity' composed in English as well as Latin.
27 Conner 1993a, chap. 4, 'The Palaeographical Context of the Exeter Book' (pp. 48-94).
28 Gameson 1996: 179. Frederick Biggs (1998) comes to similar conclusions.

One reason why Conner's thesis has met with fairly wide scepticism is that it is hard to reconcile with Bishop Leofric's list of his benefactions to Saint Peter's. A close look at that list, together with Conner's interpretation of it, is therefore necessary before further conclusions can be drawn.

Leofric's list of donations is a legal document that has also been called a grant, a will and a catalogue. The part of the document that is relevant to the present discussion is its list of books bequeathed to Saint Peter's.[29] The document begins with an introductory statement making clear its purpose and occasion: 'Hēr swutulað on ðissere bēc hwæt Lēofric bisceop hæfð gedōn intō Sancte Petres mynstre on Exanceastre þær his bisceop-stōl is.'[30] The key Old English phrase here is *hæfð gedōn intō*. Since what this phrase literally means is 'has put into',[31] the sentence as a whole would seem to present no problems of interpretation: 'Here in this document[32] is made clear what Bishop Leofric has put into [that is to say, has bestowed upon] the church of Saint Peter's in Exeter, where his episcopal see is located.' This construction of the document's initial sentence is consistent with the remainder of the text, which itemizes the lands and furnishings that are to remain in the monastery's possession, whether as part of its earlier holdings or as bequeathed by Leofric. This construction is also in accord with the document's close, with its reference in the last sentence to 'ðās gyfu & þisne unnan' ('this gift and this grant'), a phrase that can be taken to denote the sum total of what Leofric established as the minster's property. As with many Anglo-Saxon charters and wills, the document ends with an anathema calling for damnation for anyone so bold as to contravene it.

---

29 For an edition of one of the two extant Old English versions of Leofric's list (from Oxford, Bodleian Library, MS Auctarium D.2.16), see Robertson 1939: 226–31. For an edition of the other version (from the first two of the seven initial folios of the Exeter Anthology, which were bound together with it at a later date), see Conner 1993a: 226–35 (his appendix 5). Förster (1933: 18–30) has edited that same text, while Lapidge (1985: 64–69) provides a partial edition, with variants from the Bodleian manuscript, concentrating on the identification of the books that Leofric names. Conner titles the document 'Bishop Leofric's Inventory of Lands and Books', departing from the custom of other scholars, including Robertson, to treat the document as having a legal status like that of a will or charter rather than that of an inventory.

30 I cite the text from Conner's edition (1993a: 230).

31 See the *DOE*, s.v. *dōn*, sense I.B: 'with preposition (or adverb of place): to place, set, put'; also s.v. *gedōn*, sense 3: 'to place, set, put' and sense 4 'to give'. This same passage from Leofric's bequest is cited as an illustrative quotation (s.v. 'Rec. 10.1') under the headword *ge-dōn* (past part.), sense 2, 'with preposition (or adv. of place): placed, set, put'. Robertson likewise translates the phrase as meaning 'what [he] has bestowed upon' (1939: 227).

32 *Bēc*, dative singular of *bōc*. See the *DOE*, s.v. *bōc*[1], sense D: 'legal document'. In the copy of Leofric's bequest that is edited by Robertson, the word refers specifically to the Gospel book (*Crīstes bōc*) in which this text is written out.

Conner, however, translates the document's initial sentence as follows: 'At this place in this book is set out what Bishop Leofric *has brought about* at Saint Peter's minster at Exeter where his episcopal see is.'[33] Correspondingly, instead of seeing this document as a legal record of Leofric's donations to the cathedral church at Exeter, Conner maintains that Leofric's purpose in drawing up the document was to call attention to his achievement in having gathered together a good number of treasures that already belonged to the minster. In Conner's view, 'the furnishings for the church, the service books, and probably other books as well, are described as an *accumulation*, and not as a catalogue of Leofric's personal collection' (1993a: 226). This argument, however, rests on an untenable interpretation of the Old English verb *gedōn*.

The same problem undermines Conner's analysis of a key part of the document's third section, which itemizes the crosses, vestments, liturgical vessels, other ecclesiastical accoutrements, liturgical books and other books with which Leofric has endowed the church of Saint Peter's. This section begins as follows (1993a: 230):

> Ðonne is seo oncnawennis þe he hæfð God mid gecnawen & Sanctum Petrum into þam halgan mynstre on cyrclicum madmum, þæt is þæt he hæfð þiderinn gedon .ii. bisceoproda, & .ii. mycele gebonede roda ...

The sentence carries on for some while as the list of individual items continues. While its first part is less than transparent, what the statement evidently means is as follows:

> This, then, is a declaration of what he has dedicated to God and Saint Peter within that holy church in the form of ecclesiastical treasures; that is, that he has bestowed upon it [*hē hæfð þiderinn gedōn*] two episcopal crosses and two large ornamented crosses ...

And so on through the list. Conner, however, construes this passage as follows: 'Then here is the recognition that he has honoured God and St Peter in churchly treasures at the holy minster, that is that *he has therein acquired* two episcopal crosses and two great ornamented crosses.' The plain meaning of Leofric's statement, namely that he has donated certain items to the church, is converted into its near opposite, namely that he has acquired these items *from* the church.

It is of incidental interest that a later version of this same document, one that dates from the fifteenth century and is preserved as Exeter Cathedral

---

33 Conner 1993a: 231. Both here and elsewhere, I single out key terms in Conner's translations through the use of italics. Förster (1933: 15) had previously offered 'done therein' as a modern English equivalent to what he calls the 'rather indefinite' Old English phrase *þider-inn gedōn*.

Library, Charter 2570, reads as follows: 'þat he haþ þider-yn y-yeue .ii. busschopys crossys', and so forth.[34] This corresponds to the Old English clause 'þæt hē hæfð þider-inn gedōn .ii. bisceop-rōda'. Whoever wrote this version of the document understood OE *hæfð ... gedōn* to mean *haþ ... y-yeue* 'has given'. This is very likely how the Old English phrase was always construed.[35]

The conclusion to be drawn from the foregoing discussion is that the Exeter Anthology was one of the treasures given to the cathedral community at Exeter by its new bishop after he had consolidated his episcopacy there. The manner in which the book came into Leofric's hands remains undetermined, as does the place where it originated.

In any event, there is no doubt that the Exeter Anthology is the one designated by the following entry in Leofric's list of donations: '.i. mycel Englisc bōc be gehwilcum þingum on lēoð-wīsan geworht'. What this entry means is not 'one great English book with everything made in verse', as Conner translates it here, nor yet 'i great English book about all things, composed in verse' as Alexander Rumble would have it, nor 'one large English book in which everything is wrought in verse' as Michael Drout translates the phrase.[36] Rather, what Leofric is specifying is that he has given the minster many gifts 'and one large book, written in English, on various subjects [*be gehwilcum þingum*],[37] composed in verse'. By specifying that this item is a large vernacular verse miscellany, Leofric ensured that there would be no problem identifying it. No other Anglo-Saxon codex that fits this description survives, and it is possible that none was ever made.

Dunstan, Glastonbury and Benedictine cosmopolitanism

Where might the Exeter Anthology have been made, then, if other possibilities than Exeter are to be entertained?

Robert M. Butler (2004) has argued that, like two other manuscripts written out by the same scribe that were part of Leofric's eleventh-century

---

34 Förster 1933: 15, with an edition of this text at pp. 30–32.
35 Conner interprets this document differently, taking '*haþ ... y-yeue*' to be a mistranslation of the corresponding OE phrase (1993a: 239–42). As we have seen, however, one phrase is the equivalent of the other. Conner also posits that the fifteenth-century translator was working directly from an eleventh-century original rather than from an intermediary text, but of this matter we have no knowledge.
36 Rumble 1998: 285; Drout 2006: 225, respectively.
37 See the *DOE*, s.v. *gehwilc*, sense A.2: 'in plural: some, certain, many, various'. This same passage from Leofric's document is cited as one of the Dictionary's illustrative quotations for this sense of the word (s.v. 'Rec 10.1').

donation, the Exeter Anthology was once owned by Saint Mary's monastery, Glastonbury. These other books, which are written in Latin throughout, are Oxford, Bodleian Library, MS Bodley 319 and London, Lambeth Palace Library, MS 149. It is of interest that the Exeter Anthology was by no means the poor stepsister of these two Latin manuscripts. On the basis of a careful comparison of scribal errors and corrections, Bernard J. Muir has found that 'the scribe has taken more care in the preparation of the vernacular texts in the Exeter Book than he has with the two manuscripts containing Latin patristic texts'. Muir takes this as a sign that 'doctrinally sound religious poetry in the vernacular was held in high regard' in England by the time the Exeter Anthology was written out (1991: 12).

Certain features of the Anthology gain interest in the light of Butler's hypothesis regarding the book's origins at Glastonbury. Four of the sequence of poems with which the volume begins, *Advent Lyrics*, are composed in honour of the Virgin Mary, as would suit a book written at a monastery dedicated to her. Moreover, as Jackson J. Campbell has noted, the whole set of *Advent Lyrics* has a liturgical link to the veneration of the Virgin, for the Latin antiphons on which these lyrics were based were used at the hour of Vespers in conjunction with the Magnificat, the hymn recited by the Virgin in response to the announcement that she is to bear the Messiah. As Campbell has pointed out (1959: 6), those antiphons were sung once before and once after Mary's hymn of praise. On the other hand, one possible rejoinder to Butler's suggestion is that the Marian emphasis at the start of the Exeter Anthology can be accounted for perfectly well on thematic grounds alone. A second rejoinder is that the dedication of an Anglo-Saxon minster to the Virgin Mary was scarcely unique to Glastonbury.

Of interest, still, is the prominent place awarded to the East Anglian saint Guthlac towards the beginning of the volume.[38] Before the Anthology was made, certain of Guthlac's relics had come to be housed at Glastonbury. One of the early abbots of Glastonbury happened to have this same name 'Guthlac', and this onomastic coincidence seems to have contributed to the cult of this saint at this West Saxon minster. Again, however, a sceptic might reply that it is possible to account for Guthlac's prominent place in the Exeter Anthology on thematic grounds alone, seeing that Guthlac was a native English saint who embodied the ideal of the spiritual warrior.

Butler also points out that it was apparently at an ecclesiastical centre in the region of Glastonbury that a number of substantial marginalia were added to CCCC MS 41, another of Leofric's later donations to the monastic church at Exeter. Among the texts written out in this book's margins is a

---

38 See R. Butler 2004: 200–04.

direct address by Christ to the individual sinner beginning with the words 'Ego te, O homo'. This speech parallels the one in the Exeter Anthology poem *Christ in Judgement* that begins with the equivalent Old English words 'Hwæt ic þec, mon'.[39] Counting against Butler's hypothesis of a link between the Exeter Anthology and Glastonbury, however, is that the ascription of the CCCC MS 41 marginalia to that region is by no means certain. Since versions of this same address by Christ to those who have rejected him are found in sundry early medieval settings, there is no need to posit the direct influence of one of these two texts on the other, though there is no doubt of their origins in a common culture.

A fourth factor that could be thought to point to Glastonbury as the place where the Exeter Anthology was made is that Æthelnoth, abbot of Glastonbury from 1053 to 1077, sold off a number of church treasures at about the same time that Bishop Leofric was building up a collection of church ornaments and books for his new foundation at Exeter. As Butler remarks, 'Glastonbury was selling when Exeter was buying' (2004: 210). The Exeter Anthology might have been among the books obtained by Leofric at this time, though this thought remains a speculative one.

In sum, none of the factors mentioned by Butler confirms a connection between Glastonbury and the Exeter Anthology. Each of them, however, stimulates thought about this possibility. What adds to the interest of Butler's argument is that Glastonbury was not just the starting point for the Benedictine Reform. As the place where three tenth- or eleventh-century West Saxon kings were buried, it was a wealthy, prestigious and influential ecclesiastical centre up to the time of the Conquest. The three kings buried at Glastonbury were Edmund (d.946), Edgar the Peaceable (d.975) and, somewhat after the period of the Reform, Edmund Ironside (d.1016). The second of these was one of the staunchest supporters of the Reform.[40]

Perhaps it is best, then, to leave aside the thorny question of the exact geographical origins of the Exeter Anthology so as to direct attention instead to what is potentially a more productive question. What is a plausible reading context for that volume? The strands of evidence that can be brought to bear on this matter point fairly uniformly to the cluster of monasteries that were established or re-established in the south of England during the period *c.*950–90. Certainly Glastonbury itself was an intellectual hub where an eclectic and visually beautiful codex such as the Exeter Anthology might have

---

39 *Christ in Judgement* 513 [1379].
40 Nicole Marafioti (2014: 65–80 and 84–98) discusses these burials and their significance in relation to contemporary royal politics.

found both sponsors and receptive readers,⁴¹ but the same is likely to have been true of other monasteries that had close ties to Glastonbury and, hence, to Dunstan (*c*.910–88), the leading figure in the initial stages of the Reform.

Dunstan received his early education at Glastonbury Abbey and was appointed abbot of that foundation during the 940s. Both he and his brother Wulfric, who became a very wealthy landowner, were apparently well born. Both men were well connected with the court, and when Dunstan was a young man he served at the court of King Æthelstan (r.925–39). After Dunstan was made Archbishop of Canterbury (959–88), he evidently still served as abbot of Glastonbury, perhaps until the mid-970s.⁴² As is widely recognized, Dunstan was not just a teacher and an educational reformer; he was also a scholar of note and a poet.⁴³ One of the two verse compositions of his that have survived is an accomplished Latin acrostic poem composed in what has come to be known as the hermeneutic style.⁴⁴ 'Accomplished' is one way of putting the matter. Gernot Wieland, echoing Lapidge's assessment, has characterized the poem as 'fiercely difficult', adding that 'Dunstan, it appears, enjoyed writing the poem in a code which only great skill and knowledge can unravel' (2011: 50). Whether deployed in verse or prose, the hermeneutic style offered an intellectual challenge to its readers through the use of arcane vocabulary and other refined effects.⁴⁵ No few Old English poems of the Exeter Anthology show traces of the influence of this style, with their rare compound words, their cryptographic elements, their sometimes violently compressed syntax, their extreme formal innovations (as in such a work as *The Rhyming Poem*) and other kinds of deliberate obscurantism.

---

41 Michael Winterbottom and Michael Lapidge (2012: xxiii–xxix) discuss the convergence of influences that led to Glastonbury's exceptional wealth and standing by the time of the Norman Conquest.
42 Nicholas Brooks (1992) reviews the evidence bearing on Dunstan's life, as do Winterbottom and Lapidge (2012: xiii–li).
43 Dunstan's early biographers, writing in the eleventh and twelfth centuries, comment on his accomplishments as a harper and a singer of vernacular songs on religious subjects, as Jeff Opland (1980: 178–80) observes. It is impossible to say if these stories have a basis in fact. Comparable accounts enhanced the posthumous reputations of Aldhelm and of Alfred the Great, to cite two well-known examples.
44 See Lapidge 1975 for discussion. In later years Lapidge has refined his assessment of this style, speaking less of the exploitation of arcane vocabulary than of 'a high stylistic register' to be achieved in the medium of prose (2005: 336). Elizabeth Tyler has recently characterized the hermeneutic style as cultivated in England as 'a difficult style, unintended to communicate beyond elite Benedictine reformed circles' although paralleled in certain works written on the Continent (2016: 177).
45 Michael Lapidge, 'Dunstan', in *Blackwell Encyclopedia*, pp. 150–51; Winterbottom and Lapidge 2012: li–lxiii. The two extant poems that can be attributed to Dunstan are presented in an appendix to Lapidge 1975. See also Lapidge 1980 for discussion.

Dunstan was the teacher to whom Æthelwold, the second great leader of the Reform, went for instruction after serving in Æthelstan's royal household when a young man. Æthelwold too was of high birth, evidently higher than Dunstan's. As abbot of Abingdon (c.954–63) and bishop of Winchester (c.963–84), he established a school at the Old Minster at Winchester that was the premier seat of learning in the realm. In the view of Mechthild Gretsch, instruction in Latin and instruction in Old English were 'the two pillars on which Æthelwold's school rested' (1999: 2). Tellingly, in four separate Anglo-Saxon copies of the Rule of Saint Benedict, the Latin text of that document and its Old English translation alternate chapter by chapter, an indication that the two versions of the Rule were to be studied side by side, as Joyce Hill has remarked (2001: 154). Although known chiefly for his straightforward English prose style, as is seen to advantage in his translation into Old English of the Rule of Saint Benedict, Æthelwold also cultivated what Lapidge has described as a 'flamboyant' example of the hermeneutic style favoured by certain authors writing in Latin.[46] Taking the works of both Dunstan and Æthelwold into account, Lapidge favours the view that 'this style was cultivated at Glastonbury where the reform movement effectively began'.[47]

Glastonbury by the 970s, then, the approximate time when the Exeter Anthology was written out, could take pride in having a thriving school where highly sophisticated literature was both appreciated and, apparently, composed. Lapidge infers that already by the 930s 'there was an active and skilled scriptorium at Glastonbury', and he posits that the minster there was 'owned and used by the royal family' (1991: 23). Situated in the main axis of the Reform—an axis that extended from Wessex to Canterbury and beyond that to Fleury, Cluny and Rome—Glastonbury was subject to multiple cosmopolitan influences. Its Insular connections were enhanced through its proximity to centres of learning in Wales and Ireland, two regions that, in turn, had long benefited from ties to centres of learning on the Continent.

Books whose origins have been traced to Glastonbury reflect these influences.[48] A striking example is Oxford, Bodleian Library, MS Auctarium F.4.32, a tenth-century composite codex commonly known as 'Saint Dunstan's Classbook'.[49] This is remarkable for its diversity of languages, all of which contributed to the textual ferment at Glastonbury. The works included in this miscellany at the time of its original compilation include: (1) a glossed

---

46 Lapidge, 'Æthelwold', in *Blackwell Encyclopedia*, p. 21. See further Lapidge and Winterbottom 1991, including their detailed introduction.
47 Lapidge 1975: 96–97.
48 Donald Bullough (1972: 302, 306–07) provides bibliographical details.
49 A facsimile of the MS is available (Hunt 1961). Mildred Budny (1992) offers a more recent and more detailed description, with select images.

copy of Eutyches's *Ars de verbo*, a sixth-century Latin grammatical treatise; (2) the *Liber commonei*, a miscellany of computistical, exegetical and liturgical materials incorporating an unusual set of lessons and canticles in parallel columns of Greek and Latin; (3) a runiform version of the cryptic alphabet known as 'the alphabet of Nemnivus';[50] and (4) the first book of Ovid's *Ars amatoria*, written in what seems to be a ninth-century hand and glossed in both Latin and Old Welsh. The manuscript is thus remarkable for what Ralph Hexter has called its 'wide range of interests' and its 'mixture of theoretical and practical concerns, as well as of Latin and vernaculars' (1986: 27).

The Exeter Anthology, 'Saint Dunstan's Classbook' and *timor domini*

'Saint Dunstan's Classbook' is well known to art historians on account of its frontispiece.[51] This page, which is reproduced near the front of the present volume (Fig. 1), consists of a full-page illustration of Dunstan kneeling at the feet of Christ. An inscription at the top, added at a later date, states that the drawing is by Dunstan's own hand, a statement that has been neither proven nor disproven. Summing up her response to the frontispiece portrait of Dunstan at the feet of his Saviour, Mildred Budny remarks that it 'conveys a poignant, intimate and enigmatic aspect of an active, visionary, many-faceted and controversial figure who possessed a marked taste for the arts and a lifelong dedication to books' (1992: 142).

Certain details of the frontispiece deserve close attention. Since Christ is shown holding a *virga* 'rod' that plausibly signifies both a royal sceptre and a teacher's corrective rod,[52] the image is expressive of the fear of the Lord's awful power that was at the heart of medieval spirituality.[53] In addition, as Budny points out, Christ is shown holding a book on which verse 12 of Psalm 33 is written: 'Venite, filii; audite me; timorem Domini docebo vos' ('Come, children; hearken to me; I will teach you the fear of the Lord').[54] Fear of the

---

50 Ramsay *et al*. 1992, black and white plate 6 (top).
51 A full-page colour photograph is available in M. Brown 2007: 112 (plate 82).
52 Thomas D. Hill (1980) offers a deft explication of the symbolism of the *virga* in the Anglo-Saxon context.
53 See Stanley 2006 and 2009 for discussion of the theme of *timor domini* and its associated diction. Bahr (2014) points out that in *Beowulf* the word *egsa* 'fear' is regularly used in a worldly sense, to refer for example to the fear inspired by Grendel's ravages, rather than in the religious sense favoured in Old English devotional works.
54 Edgar, *Poetical Books*, pp. 234–35. The Old English prose translation of this verse reads as follows: 'Cumað nū, bearn, and gehȳrað mē; ic ēow lǣre Godes ege.' O'Neill 2016: 112 (verse 11).

Lord had its counterparts in the king's relation to his people and the *magister*'s relation to his students. Its complement was fearlessness in carrying out one's duties and one's sworn word in defiance of all temptations to do otherwise.

The theme of *timor domini* or *timor dei*—in Old English, *Godes ege* or *Godes egesa*—is a recurrent one in Anglo-Saxon art and literature, as it is in the early medieval world more generally. In his characteristically gentle way, Saint Benedict speaks of the need for monastic brothers to 'fear God in love' (*amore Deum timeant*).[55] The theme figures importantly in the early eleventh-century book known as the Eadui Psalter (London, British Library, MS Arundel 155) as part of a full-page illustration depicting Saint Benedict receiving the gift of a book, a copy of his own Rule, from the monks of Christ Church, Canterbury.[56] A prominent feature of this image is a white band that encircles the saint's head just below his tonsure. The band is inscribed *timor dei*. Other inscriptions on this page confirm Saint Benedict's dignity and reinforce the authority of his Rule.

The same theme of *timor dei* recurs with some frequency in the Exeter Anthology. In the poems of the Christ cycle, it is linked to the Day of Judgement, with its apocalyptic imagery and its terrors not just for humankind but even for the ranks of angels.[57] In *The Phoenix*, the mythological bird that is the subject of that allegorical poem is likened to a warrior of the Lord who maintains God's commandments and flees from every sin *for Godes egsan* 'on account of the fear of God' (461b).[58] In *The Life of Saint Guthlac*, the saint's fear of God's awful majesty is what leads him to embrace an eremitic way of life, for 'fear of God had a greater place in his heart than his desire to obtain worldly honour for his gratification'.[59] In *The Passion of*

---

55 Venarde, *Rule of Benedict*, pp. 226–27 (chap. 72).
56 Barbara Raw (2004: 112–13) offers close discussion of this page. Katherine O'Brien O'Keeffe (2012: 144–49) provides a yet more detailed analysis in the light of her analysis of monastic self-fashioning in Anglo-Saxon England. A full-page colour reproduction is available in M. Brown 2007: 154 (plate 120), and another one (slightly less legible) as the frontispiece to O'Brien O'Keeffe 2012. Although Brown interprets the scene as one in which Saint Benedict presents his Rule to the community, an alternative way of construing the scene, one favoured by Raw, O'Brien O'Keeffe and myself, is that the brethren are presenting the book to the saint (that is, to a lifelike *figura* of the saint). By presenting him with their own copy of the Rule, they signify their obedience and zeal.
57 See *The Ascension* 399–401a [838–40a]; *Christ in Judgement* 57b [923b], 80a [946a], 108b [974b], 148b [1014b], 153b [1019b], 197b [1063b], 498a [1364a], 503b [1369b], 680b [1546b] and 697a [1563a]; and *Doomsday* 52a.
58 Although Jones, *OE Shorter Poems*, p. 49, translates this verse as 'for the sake of God's love', this looks to be a rare slip.
59 'Him wæs Godes egsa/māra in gemyndum þonne hē menniscum/þrymme æfter þonce þegan wolde.' *The Life of Saint Guthlac* 167b–69; Muir 1: 114. See Muir 2: 448 for a note on the biblical sources and analogues of 167b, *Godes egsa*. These include Psalms, Proverbs and Job.

Saint Juliana, similarly, we are told that 'fear of God had a greater place' in Juliana's heart 'than the entire fortune that this nobleman [her prospective husband] had in his possession'.[60] The similar phrasing in these two saints' lives is a possible sign of the direct influence of one of the two on the other. The same phrase *for Godes egsan* that is used at verse 461b of *The Phoenix* with reference to God's warriors is used towards the end of *The Seafarer* at verse 101b with reference to the fear that should be felt by sinners who hoard their wealth while on earth. With characteristic precision, G.V. Smithers translates the phrase as used here as meaning 'in face of the awe inspired by God [on the Day of Judgement]'.[61] The theme of *timor dei* is reiterated as the speaker of this same poem observes, 'Great is the awful majesty of God ... A fool is he who fears not his Lord.'[62]

In giving sustained voice to this theme, which rests on the authority of numerous passages of Scripture including Psalm 110:10, 'Initium sapientiae timor Domini' ('the fear of the Lord is the beginning of wisdom'),[63] the Exeter Anthology reinforces the ideology of the Reform as articulated by Dunstan and others at Glastonbury. Whether the book was made there or elsewhere in the south of England, it is expressive of the piety and the urbanity that are characteristic of the early stages of the Reform period.

Influences from Ireland and elsewhere

Certain of the manuscripts associated with Dunstan's Glastonbury point to influences emanating from Ireland, Brittany and Carolingian France. As Butler has remarked, the legendary founder of Glastonbury was Saint Patrick, the patron saint of Ireland. If medieval sources can be trusted, among Dunstan's teachers were Irish masters, though this matter remains conjectural.[64] In any event, the number of Irish pilgrims on the monastery's staff

---

60 'Hire wæs godes egsa/māra in gemyndum, þonne eall þæt maþþum-gesteald/þe in þæs æþelinges æhtum wunade.' *The Passion of Saint Juliana* 35–37; Muir 1: 189.
61 Smithers 1957: 142 (his brackets).
62 'Micel biþ sē meotudes egsa ... Dol biþ sē þe him his dryhten ne ondrædeþ.' *The Seafarer* 103a, 106a; Muir 1: 233.
63 Edgar, *Poetical Books*, pp. 458–59. The author of the Old English poetic paraphrase recorded in the Paris Psalter makes the same point in the style of homily: 'Þæt byð secga gehwām snytru on frymðe/þæt hē Godes egesan glēawe healde' ('For each human being the essence of wisdom in the first instance is to carefully maintain a fear of the Lord'). O'Neill 2016: 452–53 (verse 7).
64 Orme 1991. Although Orme concentrates his attention on later medieval Glastonbury (from the thirteenth century to the Dissolution), some of his remarks have a bearing on the pre-Conquest period, for which very little documentary evidence survives.

led to its being known as 'Little Ireland'.⁶⁵ Long before this time, probably as early as the seventh century, Irish scribes had taken the bold step of making copies of vernacular works in addition to Latin ones, thereby setting an example that was imitated in English-speaking parts of Britain from the reign of King Alfred on.

Irish, Welsh or more broadly Celtic influences have been inferred in several poems of the Exeter Anthology, though in none of these apart from *The Seafarer* does the influence extend to more than mood or detail.⁶⁶ One point of interest in *The Husband's Message* as well as in *The Seafarer* is the characterization of the cuckoo's cry as one of sadness or foreboding, for the cuckoo as a bird of lament is a commonplace of Welsh lyric but not of the poetry of other language areas.⁶⁷ More substantial in their implications are coded allusions in *The Seafarer* to the kind of austere *peregrinatio pro amore dei* ('pilgrimage for the love of God') for which Irish monks were famed.⁶⁸ Linking the theme of penance—one that figures importantly in the second half of the Exeter Anthology—to the harshness of the wintry sea as evoked in *The Seafarer*, Mark Atherton has called attention to an analogous passage in Muirchú's *Life of Saint Patrick*. In this late seventh-century hagiography, Patrick imposes as penance on a wicked disbeliever that he should bind his feet with an iron fetter and throw its key into the sea, 'then get into a one-hide boat and put to sea without a rudder or an oar' so as to travel at the will of God and at God's mercy.⁶⁹ The combined notions of binding and seafaring as aspects of a penitential journey are prominent in both the Irish *vita* and the Old English poem.

Whatever one makes of the possible Irish or Welsh affinities of certain poems of the Exeter Anthology, conditions were favourable at mid-tenth-century Glastonbury for the making and copying of books that offered their readers linguistic and stylistic challenges. As Daniel Anlezark has argued in the introduction to his edition of the Old English dialogues known as *Solomon and Saturn* (2009), the circle of educated persons who produced these works may have been located at Glastonbury in or about the 930s. This group could

---

65 R. Butler 2004: 196.
66 Roy F. Leslie (1985: 34–37) discusses this mix of cultural elements, some of which point to Ireland as a centre of influence.
67 Ida Gordon (1960: 17) raises this point as part of a more extended discussion of Celtic influences in *The Seafarer*.
68 Dorothy Whitelock (1950) touches on this matter. Colin Ireland (1991) offers additional remarks on that poem's possible Irish affinities. Orton (2001) takes a more sceptical view of these Hibernian connections.
69 Atherton 2002: 92–93, with reference to chap. 26 of 'The Life of Patrick by Muirchú', trans. Thomas O'Loughlin, in Davies 1999: 108.

have included the young Dunstan. One of the two manuscripts in which a poetic version of *Solomon and Saturn* has been preserved, CCCC MS 41, was among Leofric's donations to Exeter Cathedral. In Anlezark's view, 'many of the idiosyncrasies of style and intellectual interest' in these dialogues 'reflect the strong influence of Hiberno-Latin literature, symptomatic of a close contact between the circle which produced these texts and the world of Irish learning' (2009: ix). Certain of the more challenging aspects of the Exeter Anthology may reflect this same direction of influence, including riddles that play upon the letters of the alphabet and poems (such as *The Rhyming Poem*) that experiment with the formal resources available to poets composing in the vernacular. Such effects lend parts of the Exeter Anthology an arcane character when compared with most other vernacular works produced in mid- or late tenth-century England.

Summary: a plausible reading context for the Anthology

The period of the Benedictine Reform, then, was marked by a dramatic increase in the number of monasteries in the south of England, with their attendant scriptoria, libraries and schools and their links to cathedral complexes and to patrons among the high-ranking laity. Bilingual literacy was becoming the norm. The literary arts and book production thrived in this context, whether in Latin or in the vernacular. Certain details of the Exeter Anthology are suggestive of its indebtedness to books that were central to the Reform, including the Rule of Saint Benedict itself, while other details point to a variety of cosmopolitan influences.

One important centre of book production during this period was Dunstan's Glastonbury, a monastery at the vanguard of the Reform. Here works of an arresting literary quality were produced in a milieu subject to influences emanating from many different directions, from Ireland to the Continent. In view of the date and approximate locale that can be ascribed to the Exeter Anthology on palaeographical grounds, and taking account as well of its cosmopolitan range of themes and its quasi-hermeneutic stylistic elements, it is not unreasonable to approach this volume as a product of a literary culture that, emanating from Glastonbury Abbey itself, was characteristic of a number of monastic foundations located in the south of England during the earlier years of the Reform. This is true even if the precise origins of the volume must remain in doubt.

PART TWO

Reading the Anthology as a Codicological Whole

CHAPTER 4

An Overview of the Book's Contents

The Exeter Anthology has long been characterized as a miscellany, one whose selection of parts and whose principles of organization are obscure. Writing in the 1930s, Kenneth Sisam lent his authority to the view that the book is a miscellany whose order of contents, though falling into two broad groups whose fulcrum is *The Wanderer*, is 'generally haphazard'.[1] N.F. Blake, likewise, has referred to the book as 'a poetic miscellany in which there does not appear to have been a recognisable principle of selection' (1964: 2). Similarly, R.D. Fulk and Christopher Cain have characterized the book as 'an anthology of diverse poetic types'. Like the Vercelli Book, in their view, it is 'a jumbled collection of seemingly mismatched genres' (2013: 27–28). Although Anne Klinck has discerned principles of coherence in the codex, her view is that 'if there was an overall plan for the Exeter Book, it must have been rather vague' (1992: 24).

On the other hand, the book's chief recent editor, Bernard J. Muir, has envisioned the compiler as a self-conscious anthologizer, one who arranged his material in a meaningful way. As he writes at the start of his edition:

> I was prompted to undertake this new edition by a feeling that it was time to focus attention on the collection as an anthology. I have found in my own study of the texts that there is much to be gained by reading the manuscript from beginning to end (Muir 1: ix).

In particular, Muir discerns thematic connections linking the first eight poems in the collection, from *Advent Lyrics* to *The Passion of Saint Juliana*, seeing these as knit together by 'their concern with different models for Christian living' (1: 23). This is in addition to other examples of careful deliberation that he and other critics have found in the choice and arrangement of the book's parts, such as the juxtaposition at folios 122v–123v of the two first-person narratives known as Riddle 60 and *The Husband's Message*, both of

---

1   Sisam 1953: 97, in an essay first published in 1934.

which feature an inanimate object—first a reed, then something made out of wood—that 'speaks' in riddling fashion.

Others have affirmed the validity of such an approach. Mary Clayton, who has recently re-edited four of the book's overtly religious poems, finds that 'the contents of the manuscript were very deliberately ordered'.[2] Elaine Treharne discerns coherence in the manuscript's collection of parts and emphasizes the 'deliberate crafting of textual items' positions and relationships' (2009: 100). Frances McCormack remarks in passing upon an intellectual coherence in the Anthology's parts, for in her cautiously stated view, 'a certain theological unity seems to underpin much of the Exeter Book' (2015: 144). Moreover, Roy M. Liuzza has advanced the plausible suggestion that attempts were made to enhance the book's coherence at the time when it was written out. Liuzza postulates the existence of creative scribes and/or compilers, asking us to contemplate a form of poetic unity 'that can only be called codicological or scribal' (1990: 11).

Writing along comparable lines, S.A.J. Bradley has made a sweeping case for a codicological approach to the poems of the Exeter Anthology as well as to Old English poetry more generally. Bradley justifies as follows his sensible decision to group his translations of Old English poems according to the codex in which they are written, as opposed to trying to organize them according to genre, thematic content or putative date:[3]

> The codices are, after all, evidence as palpable as any that serves to illuminate the crucial association between the poetry and its patrons ... Whatever life the poems may have enjoyed before they were collected into the codex, we are in most cases allowed to know only this fact of their existence, that they are uniquely recorded in this codex and met the purposes of this patron.

Moreover, as Bradley points out, there is a reciprocal relationship between one's reading of the contents of a whole poetic codex from the Anglo-Saxon period and one's insights into the meaning of any one poem from that codex, for these two hermeneutic processes depend on one other:

> For each one of the four main codices as for the lesser poetic manuscripts, it is both practical and proper to investigate the organizational principles governing their compilation—a procedure involving examination of the

2   Clayton, *Poems of Christ*, p. ix. The four poems from the Exeter Anthology included in Clayton's edition are *Advent Lyrics*, *Christ in Judgement*, *The Life of Saint Guthlac* and *Christ's Descent into Hell* (all titled somewhat differently in this edition).
3   Both quotations that follow are from Bradley, p. xxiii, disregarding his use of italics for emphasis.

reciprocal relationships of theme, emphasis, imagery, verbal formulations, sometimes of editing in the process of compilation, between the component poems (and prose pieces, in some cases), and the context of the whole collection. The best interpretation of a poem will take into account the implications of its context in the collection, while any attempt to define the organizational principles of a codex must depend partly upon the interpretation given to individual poems.

In like manner, Donald Scragg suggests that there are linguistic reasons for concluding that the Exeter Anthology was arranged by a shaping hand: 'The linguistic uniformity of the collection (in contrast to that of the other poetic codices) suggests that someone (perhaps the anthologist or perhaps a later copyist) imposed his own forms on the material he collected.'[4] If Scragg's supposition is justified, then the integrative work of such a person at the level of diction and spelling could be compared to the work of the scribe who wrote out the whole of the Exeter Anthology in a uniformly elegant Insular square minuscule hand. Indeed, these two persons could have been co-workers in a single scriptorium, if indeed we are talking about two persons rather than one.

In the light of these last comments, one can discern a turn away from the view that the grouping of Old English poems codex by codex is a matter of little or no concern to their interpretation. Similarly, scholarly opinion has shifted away from the notion that the contents of the Exeter Anthology represent a miscellany whose arrangement is fairly much at random. My own critical judgements are in accord with these trends.

Principles of order

A guiding theme of the present study is that the Exeter Anthology as a whole provides a reading context to which each of its constituent poems contributes and within which each poem makes sense, even though the same poem might seem enigmatic, or might seem to lead to a different interpretation, or might simply be discounted as having little value when read as a separate 'object', as is the modern habit. The Anthology is therefore more like an edifice than it is like the stones out of which an edifice is made.

Research in archaeology offers an analogy to this principle. A current field archaeologist who wants his research to be respected will set out to 'read' an archaeological site—a funerary complex, for example—as an interconnected

---

4   Scragg, 'The Exeter Book', in *Blackwell Encyclopedia*, p. 183.

cultural system rather than singling out its constituent objects for individual display, as was common practice in the past. What matters from the archaeologist's perspective is not just the figure inscribed on the pot or on the decorative brooch, nor just the pot or brooch itself as a discrete material object, but also the ensemble of site-specific finds, their stylistic or functional affinities with one another, and their location in the ground relative to one another, regardless of what can be ascertained about the ultimate origin of any of the objects found at the site. In addition, the site's relation to a larger topographical and cultural landscape will be taken into account. In like manner, a literary scholar approaching the poems of the Exeter Anthology will do well to study that codex in all its parts, investigating it as a complex web of affinities while also placing it within a larger social and intellectual horizon.

The medieval category of instructional miscellanies offers a framework within which we can fruitfully evaluate not just the coherence of the Exeter Anthology, but also its apparent randomness, doing so without anachronistic expectations about what constitutes structural unity. If differences of opinion exist as to whether or not the arrangement of parts in the Exeter Anthology is governed by principles of order, the same is true of scholarly responses to medieval miscellanies more generally. Summing up recent research in this area with an eye to Anglo-Saxon England, Patrizia Lendinara has pointed out that the making of the miscellaneous manuscript, as opposed to the unitary book, was a characteristic feature of the early Middle Ages though not of classical antiquity. She concludes: 'The early Middle Ages were characterized by a large use of miscellaneous manuscripts, containing the works of different writers, as well as different genres of texts.'[5] Moreover, as she emphasizes, the varied contents of these works often served an instructional purpose. While certain miscellanies were compiled more or less at random, others were relatively coherent in their arrangement of parts and in their pedagogical aims.

Lendinara takes note of the hierarchical structure that is characteristic of certain of these miscellanies, observing that a manuscript might include a diverse set of contents including liturgical, patristic, medical, historical or grammatical texts, not all of which had equal status or pedagogical potential. Among the authors featured with some frequency in medieval miscellanies were canonical fourth- and fifth-century poets such as Sedulius, Martianus Capella, Prudentius and Prosper of Aquitaine. Also included with some frequency were sets of enigmas. Yet more popular were works of a sententious

---

5 Lendinara 2007: 60. See Nichols and Wenzel 1996 for discussion of an assortment of miscellanies dating from the later Middle Ages.

nature, including the third- or fourth-century work known as the *Disticha Catonis*, a ubiquitous compendium of proverbial wisdom to which some of the sententious contents of the Exeter Anthology can be compared.⁶ Lendinara's main conclusion has implications for one's approach to the Exeter Anthology: 'Miscellaneous compilations embraced the entire spectrum of monastic culture and were the teaching instruments of the Middle Ages' (2007: 61).

The Exeter Anthology is best viewed as a miscellany of this kind, one whose aims were not just didactic but also in part instructional. As with such a work as Ælfric's *Grammar*, the volume's chief originality resides in its use of English, not in its type of contents. The compiler of the Anthology is likely to have had some freedom to negotiate its contents, seeing that as far as is known there was no precedent for an English-language poetic compendium of this kind, nor did an obvious niche in the classroom await it. While its parts are varied, and while the order of these parts relative to one another may at times reflect the happenstances of compilation rather than the fulfilment of a design, still the book's intellectual coherence should be apparent to a reader who approaches it as a whole and who approaches it, moreover, without preconceptions of the kind that have sometimes biased the modern reception of Anglo-Saxon literature.

Among the principles of order that can be discerned in the Exeter Anthology, five seem to me to stand out. Before I discuss them, however, several of my guiding assumptions should be made explicit.

First of all, I see no reason to doubt that the codex is essentially complete as it stands despite the loss of at least seven folios and probably more.⁷ What I mean by 'essentially complete' is that the surviving 123 folios suffice to give a modern reader a firm conception of the book's character even when one experiences the frustration of coming across fragmentary or imperfect texts. Among the missing leaves is at least one initial folio that would have contained the first part of *Advent Lyrics*. Leaves might possibly have gone missing at the end, where additional enigmas might once have been included,

---

6   Jill Mann analyses the role of works akin to the *Disticha Catonis* in medieval English education; that is, of 'works that impart moral instruction by means of proverbs or exemplary anecdotes' (2006: 41).

7   At least one leaf is missing at the start of the codex; another is lost after line 117 [556] of *The Ascension*; another after line 368 of *The Life of Saint Guthlac*; another that would have contained the end of *The Holy Death of Saint Guthlac*; another two leaves after line 288 of *The Passion of Saint Juliana* and between lines 558 and 559 of that same poem; another between line 2 of *The Partridge* and the first surviving lines of *Christ's Pledge of Grace*; another, most likely, between the enigmas numbered 40 and 41; and, evidently, another between what are now thought to be the two fragmentary poems *Contrition* and *The Penitent's Prayer* (as will be discussed later). More than one leaf might have been lost at certain of these places.

though this is no more than speculation. As for the prose documents recorded in what are now the manuscript's seven initial folios, they were probably bound into the book in the sixteenth century, as has long been recognized (Muir 1: 3), so that they can be ignored in the present study despite their interest for social historians.

The question should be addressed as to whether or not the order of parts in the manuscript as it stands can form the basis of a critical response to the book as a whole. Arguing otherwise on the basis of a close examination of the physical manuscript, Patrick W. Conner has maintained the controversial thesis that the contents of the Exeter Anthology were originally written out in three distinct sections, or booklets; that these were composed in a different sequence than their order in the present manuscript would suggest (that is, 2-3-1 rather than 1-2-3); and that the three booklets were only later combined into the present sequence.[8] Conner's booklet theory was sharply challenged, however, by Fiona and Richard Gameson (1995) on the grounds that the details of the codicological analysis on which it rests are scarcely secure. Muir too takes a sceptical view of Conner's argument and the conclusions to which it leads. His summary remarks on the topic are worth citing, in conjunction with what he has to say elsewhere on the interrelationships of the Anthology's parts:

> I have expressed reservations about accepting his [Conner's] theory, since codicological data suggest to me that the texts in the manuscript were copied out from start to finish in the order in which they are found today (allowing for the loss of folios and gatherings ...). During the course of preparing this edition, supplementary data—codicological, literary, and linguistic—have come to my attention which confirm my reservations about Conner's booklet theory ... It is my contention that the anthologist who compiled the present collection drew his material from other collections available to him and arranged it in a meaningful manner. There is evidence (codicological and literary) to suggest that the anthologist at times adapted his material to give the collection cohesion. If this manipulation of the material was not carried out during the preparation of the present manuscript ... then it is to be attributed to the anthologist of the exemplar(s) (Muir 1: 6-7).

If I am in full agreement with Muir on this point, it is because my own independent study of the Exeter Anthology has led me to see the workings of a controlling intelligence in the shaping of that book's contents in their overall trajectory from start to finish. The manner in which certain poems

---

8   Conner 1986 and 1993a: 95-147.

or passages from the early part of the volume (as it stands) anticipate poems or passages that come later (again, as the book stands) is particularly evident when one takes account of the poem *The Ascension*, with its anticipatory details, as I shall do in the next section of the present chapter. One of my guiding assumptions is therefore that any comprehensive study of the poetry of the Anthology must needs rest on the shape of the volume as we have it, regardless of the question of when any of its constituent poems, passages or sets of poems were originally composed.

Let me then turn to what I discern to be the volume's five main principles of order:

1. The Exeter Anthology is *hierarchical* in its arrangement of parts. That is to say, there is a directional quality to it, as tended to be true of other miscellanies of the early Middle Ages, ones dealing with grammar in particular. If the Exeter Anthology were a moving vehicle, we could speak of works perceived to be of high importance, seriousness and prestige being front-loaded, while lighter or lesser works are put in the back. Although this is not a hard-and-fast rule, it is a distinct tendency. Admittedly, determining the relative 'weight' of a literary work is not necessarily a self-evident matter. As Bernard F. Huppé (1959: 8–9) has noted, however, a rough guide for determining 'weight' is provided by Saint Augustine's distinction between the eloquence of Scripture, which is 'solid' (*solidum*), versus pagan eloquence, which is 'inflated' or empty by nature, even though it may be a model of charm or sweetness.

2. While the principle of randomness may enter into the book's scheme to some extent (for it is an accepted feature of medieval miscellanies), it does so within an overall structure that is comprehensive to the point of being *quasi-cosmological*. The codex as a whole was arguably meant to be encyclopedic in scope, as Mercedes Salvador Bello has found to be true of the Exeter enigmas when taken as a group, in much the same manner as earlier riddle collections composed in Latin were grounded on the medieval encyclopedic tradition codified by Isidore of Seville.[9] When read in its entirety, the Exeter Anthology goes far to encompass the whole of creation: God, angels, demons, saints, human beings and their different characters and works, and created nature.

---

9   Salvador Bello (2015) characterizes the Exeter riddle collection as mini-encyclopedic in scope, as saturated with monastic learning, and as organized roughly along the lines of Isidore's classification of knowledge into the four categories of cosmology, zoology, tools and prodigies. In a complementary study, Claudia Di Sciacca (2008: 138–43) discusses Isidore's influence on the poems of the Exeter Anthology with particular reference to those elegiac poems that feature the *ubi sunt* motif.

While these components can potentially interact at any time, the divine elements are introduced first. They gradually give way to the quotidian ones. Within this scheme, poems of similar genre alternate with poems that, though different in genre, offer linguistic and thematic parallels to the works in their codicological vicinity. Variety within unity is thus the rule, just as in the cosmos itself, which from an Isidorean perspective is a network of similitudes linked through principles of analogy and difference.

3. The compiler's refusal to consistently group 'like with like' enhances the volume's *intratextuality*. So as not to be mistaken, I should perhaps reiterate that what I am speaking of is horizontal intratextuality rather than vertical intertextuality: that is to say, the book's constituent parts speak to one another in a polyphonic conversation regardless of their possible sources, antecedents or parallels outwith the codex. For example, it may matter more to one's understanding of the Exeter Anthology to know that *The Phoenix* is juxtaposed with certain other poems on folios 32v–76r of the codex (these are *The Life of Saint Guthlac, The Holy Death of Saint Guthlac, The Canticles of the Three Youths* and *The Passion of Saint Juliana*) than to know that the main body of *The Phoenix* is a creative adaptation of a fourth-century Latin poem ascribed to Lactantius. More will be said later about these codicological interrelations, certain of which may result from the fresh composition of lines, linking passages or whole poems at the time when the Anthology was compiled.[10]

4. Not all the book's parts weigh in equally as regards the importance of their thematic content, as opposed to their technique or literary type. Certain poems noteworthy for their enigmatic nature or their unusual formal properties, for instance, may have been included chiefly for their value for the practice of intellectual exercises thought to be appropriate to Christian education. As Huppé has remarked while summing up the Augustinian view of the value of intellectual challenges in the study of rhetoric: 'Obscurity, allegory, symbol are pleasurable means of revealing Christian beauty' (1959: 10–11). The chief rationale for the inclusion of certain other poems may have been that works of their kind had a customary place in Latin literary miscellanies. The Exeter Anthology is thus *self-referential* as regards the art of Old English verse: it was then and is now a major resource as regards vernacular poetics. An attempt to discover why a particular

---

10   Colin Chase (1974), Roy M. Liuzza (1990) and Brian O'Camb (2009, 2014) all raise this possibility in different ways.

work was included in the Anthology may prove frustrating unless what one focuses on is its status as a literary text. This is especially true of the Exeter enigmas. What these hyperliterary texts often represent are textbook examples of particular rhetorical schemes or tropes such as metaphor, paradox, prosopopoeia and paronomasia. They provide pleasure by stimulating the intellect. Patrizia Lendinara (2013: 307–09), among many others, has emphasized this aspect of both Anglo-Latin and Old English educational literature (including riddles), calling particular attention to texts that involve acrostics, cryptography or other play on the letters of the alphabet.

5. The Anthology is ordered in part, though not throughout, according to the *shape of the liturgical year*. The poems on Advent that initiate the collection (at fols 8r–14r) celebrate the first of the great mysteries of the Christian faith. This is the union of God and man that was achieved at the Incarnation—the event known in Old English as *Crīstes geflǣscnes*—through the miraculous mediation of the Virgin Mary. With its initial paraphrases of Latin antiphons sung during or just after the season of Advent, the Anthology is anchored at the start in that part of the liturgical year that centres on Christmas. Located towards the end of the book (at fols 115v–122v), correspondingly, is a series of poems with a close relation to the liturgy of Easter Week, the time of Christ's triumph over death. This series runs from *Doomsday* to the short liturgical paraphrase that I call *One Faith One God* (otherwise known as *Homiletic Fragment II*). The theme of penance that is addressed in the paired poems *Contrition* and *The Penitent's Prayer*, which are written out near the start of this sequence (at fols 117v–119v),[11] have a direct relation to Lent as a season of reflection, penance and renewal. The poem *Christ's Descent into Hell* that follows just after *The Penitent's Prayer* (at fols 119v–121v)[12] has an equally direct relation to

---

11 I take these to be two related poems rather than two parts of a single one. A leaf (or perhaps more) seems to have gone missing between fols 118v and 119r. While Muir treats the two poems as fragments A and B of a single poem that he titles *Contrition*, others postulate that what A and B represent are fragments of two different poems on complementary themes. See Muir 2: 670–71 for a review of critical opinion and Malmberg (1979) for an edition of this pair of texts under the title *Resignation*. In adopting the title *The Penitent's Prayer* for fragment B, I am in accord with Stanley 1955, though he uses that title to refer to both poems. The potential sources for confusion here are unfortunate but unavoidable, given the condition of the manuscript and changing scholarly perceptions.

12 M.R. Rambaran-Olm (2014) has prepared an edition of *Christ's Descent into Hell* under the title *John the Baptist's Prayer or The Descent into Hell from the Exeter Book*, advancing an argument for titling this poem *John the Baptist's Prayer* in acknowledgement of John's prominent role as speaker of much of this text. Others, including Muir, have preferred the title *The Descent into*

the liturgy of Holy Saturday. This was the day traditionally ascribed to the Harrowing of Hell and dedicated to the rite of baptism, two typologically related phenomena.[13] The Resurrection—the second of the two great mysteries of the faith and the guiding theme of Easter—is thereby associated with rebirth through baptism. As for the riddle-like dialogue poem *Pharaoh* that is included on the next folio (122r), it calls to mind the Christian exegetical tradition that associates the drowning of Pharaoh's army in the Red Sea with the fate of the damned at Doomsday. Correspondingly, this short poem calls to mind the rite of baptism seen as a means of salvation.

While it is only certain poems of the Exeter Anthology that have a relation to this progression from the Nativity to Eastertide, the two major poems composed in celebration of Christ in Majesty that follow directly upon *Advent Lyrics* at the volume's start (these are *The Ascension* and *Christ in Judgement*, at fols 14r–32v) confirm the theological significance of Christ's Incarnation as a means of restoring a paradise otherwise lost to humankind.[14] Grouped in the 'Eastertide' section of the volume (at fols 115v–117v) is *Doomsday*, a poem whose eschatological theme brings out the ultimate significance of Christ's Resurrection. The figure of Christ in Majesty, *ealra cyninga cyning* ('king of all kings', 95a), is featured prominently here. Also included in the 'Eastertide' section, with its liturgical associations, are two poems of obvious application to the liturgy and personal devotion: *A Versified Lord's Prayer* (a verse paraphrase of the Pater Noster) and *One Faith One God* (a verse paraphrase of the Creed).

The poem written out directly after these two prayers (at fol. 122v) is Riddle 30b. This enigma, which has the solution 'tree' or 'wood' (OE *trēow*),[15] might seem to have been included here by accident or oversight since a nearly identical version of this same text is written out earlier in the codex (at

---

Hell, while Thorpe ascribed the poem the title *The Harrowing of Hell* in his 1842 *editio princeps*. The title *Christ's Descent into Hell*, which I borrow from Chambers 1933a, has the advantage of being immediately expressive of the poem's core subject, which was a favourite one in medieval iconography. The poem does not, however, tell the full story of the Harrowing.

13   As Rambaran-Olm observes (and as she demonstrates in detail) the poem 'is inextricably linked to the Easter liturgy' (2014: 54), while like other poems nearby it in the codex, it 'draws on the metaphor of the soul's journey, the path to salvation through baptism' (57).

14   I discuss the use made of the image of Christ in Majesty in the iconography of the frontispiece to the New Minster Charter in Chapter 3 above, in the section headed 'English bookmaking, bilingualism and the iconography of the Reform'.

15   I discuss this poem's imagery and the wordplay involved in its solution in Niles 2006a: 130, with references there to prior scholarship. Arnold V. Talentino (1981) relates the imagery and diction of Riddle 30 to the Christological imagery of *The Phoenix* and of *The Dream of the Rood*, including the concept of the Cross as a spiritual vehicle.

fol. 108r).¹⁶ There is no error here, however. The inclusion of this poem right at the close of the 'Eastertide' sequence serves a programmatic purpose, for what the poem features at its end is the fundamental symbol of Christendom, the Rood, speaking in its own voice as an object of awe and veneration:¹⁷

> Þonne ic mec onhæbbe,   hi onhnigaþ to me,
> modge miltsum,   swa ic mongum sceal
> ycan upcyme   eadignesse.
>
> (When I raise myself high, they bow down to me with reverence, those courageous ones, much as I add to the happiness that arises among a multitude.)

The centrality of the Rood in the iconography of the Crucifixion and of Doomsday needs no labouring, especially to readers familiar with either the Vercelli Book poem *The Dream of the Rood* or, from this same Exeter Anthology, *Christ in Judgement*. Not to be overlooked is the ambiguity of the Old English word that is the exact solution to Riddle 30b; for the noun *trēow* can mean either 'tree' or 'truth' (or 'faith'), with the word often used in the latter of these two senses in religious contexts. This potential wordplay is activated at verse 145b [584b] of *The Ascension*, as well, where Cynewulf uses the phrase *gǣst-hālig trēow* ('a sacred pledge', or alternatively 'a sacred tree') with double reference to Christ's holy covenant with humankind and the Rood on which Christ died. Comparable in its wordplay is line 22 [159] of *Exeter Maxims C*, where we start with foliage and end with truth: 'Trēo sceolon brǣden ond trēow weaxan' ('Trees put forth branches and truth flourishes').¹⁸ So truth too, or the faith, is likened here to a green and growing thing even if potentially subject to the axe of lies.

In the Anthology's overall design, then, it is evidently no matter of chance that images of Christ's Incarnation, with attendant wonder at the supreme mystery of the fusion of God with man, yield place later on to passages and images relating to the Resurrection, with attendant joy at Christ's sacrificial

---

16 Sisam (1953: 36), for example, expresses conventional wisdom when referring to the 'exceptional chance' by which two versions of this same riddle are included in the Anthology.
17 Riddle 30b, lines 7-9; Muir 1: 352. See Muir 1: 306-07 for the earlier version, Riddle 30a, whose wording differs slightly, as Roy M. Liuzza (1988) has discussed in close detail. Given the association of courage (*ellen*) with the monastic vocation, it is tempting to construe the plural noun *mōdige* 'courageous ones', unique to the second version (at 8a), as a coded reference to monks and cloistered women.
18 When citing lines from *Exeter Maxims*, I first give Muir's primary lineation, then his secondary lineation between square brackets. The secondary number is based on a continuous lineation of parts A, B and C.

redemption of humankind through the Cross and awe at the prospect of Doomsday.

Later sections of the present study will offer support for the claims about the organization of the Exeter Anthology that are advanced here in preliminary form. I am aware that the amount of attention that I will devote to certain individual poems may strike some readers as disproportionately high, while other poems may seem to be slighted despite their significant interest or appeal. Disparities of such a kind are virtually inescapable, however, given the Anthology's wide scope and an author's need to establish focal points for an argument. Among my recurrent points of reference will be certain texts that are widely read and are frequently singled out for critical attention, including *The Wanderer* and *The Seafarer*. Other points of reference will be certain poems whose inclusion in a volume that is essentially religious in character might strike a modern reader as anomalous, though I shall argue that this is a misapprehension based on an untenable 'sacred versus secular' binarism. Among these poems are *Widsith*, *Wulf and Eadwacer*, *The Wife's Lament* and *The Ruin*, as well as those enigmas that play on the theme of human sexuality.

The book's opening parts: *Advent Lyrics* to *Juliana*

The overall plan of the Exeter Anthology begins to come into focus when one takes account of the book's opening parts, especially when these are considered in relation to certain poems near the volume's close.[19]

The codex begins with *Advent Lyrics*, twelve songlike praise-poems that are divine, radiant and quasi-liturgical in nature. They form a unified composition even when approached as separate lyrics, each with a separate character.[20] The elevated rhetoric of each lyric is proclaimed straight away through use of the opening exclamation *Ēalā!*, the vernacular equivalent of

---

19 When speaking of the manuscript's parts, I am referring to sets of poems that are meaningfully discussed as a group. The manuscript is not organized into subdivisions, nor are there markers for breaks between poems other than occasional end punctuation, the inclusion of a line of space after end punctuation, and/or the use of ornamental capitals at the start of a number of items. These signposts are not always used in a predictable fashion, while some may be the result of a scribe's misunderstanding. Editors and commentators are therefore justified in speaking of the miscellany's individual poems, or its parts, on the basis of their own critical judgements as to where to posit textual divisions.

20 Clayton, *Poems of Christ*, presents *Advent* as a single poem. Muir, following general custom, treats the twelve Advent lyrics as separate poems in a sequence. I follow that latter practice here while also respecting the poems' effect when read continuously.

Latin *O!* This same Old English exclamation serves as a devotional equivalent to the *Hwæt!* of native heroic discourse. Since the scribe has regularly written the initial letters of *Ēalā!* in ornamental capitals, the book begins with an eye-catching visual display, one that corresponds to the exalted style of its initial contents.

After another eighty-five folios occupied by poems on a wide range of topics, the Exeter Anthology winds towards its close with a sequence of texts that chiefly have to do with the sweat, tears, small joys, and ruins of the everyday world (at fols 100r–130v). This series extends from *Deor* and *Wulf and Eadwacer* through the whole sequence of enigmas. Interspersed here are nine poems on devotional themes and three poems of an elegiac character. Among these last is *The Ruin*, a poem strategically placed towards the end of the codex. Lighting the way (at fol. 122r) is a versified paraphrase of the Lord's Prayer, a text to comfort any *viator* 'pilgrim'. The Exeter Anthology has no cadences of closure, though. While it begins in an exalted fashion, it comes to an end at the bottom of fol. 130v without fanfare, as does many another medieval work or compilation.

Between these opening and closing parts, what one finds is a roughly graded descent down Parnassus. Texts that deal with the most sacred and awesome mysteries of existence—these are the three poems of the Christ cycle—are followed by texts that either present models of saintly action in the world (*The Life of Saint Guthlac* and *The Passion of Saint Juliana*) or feature the theme of the salvation of God's chosen ones (*The Holy Death of Saint Guthlac*, *The Canticles of the Three Youths* and *The Phoenix*). Following these, in turn, are poems illustrative of what is generally known as the 'wisdom' genre.[21]

The initial poem of the tripartite Christ cycle, *Advent Lyrics*, is strategically chosen for this position so that the Anthology begins in the voice of prayer, worship and thanksgiving. In Mary Clayton's words, the Advent sequence 'is almost certainly the work of a monk who saw the Bible through the lens of the liturgy and of patristic exegesis and who had deep experience of the liturgy'.[22] The book begins with the first of the great mysteries of the faith, the mystery of the Incarnation, 'the doctrine that in Christ, God himself

---

21 The term 'wisdom poetry' has been given broad currency by Thomas Shippey (1976, 1994). Shippey's studies in turn owe a debt to Morton Bloomfield (1968) on the value of reading Old English poetry with an eye to the large category of wisdom literature in the ancient world. One advantage of the term is its capaciousness. The term has its drawbacks as well, as will be discussed later in this chapter in the section headed 'The voice of the sage'. Fulk and Cain (2013: 33–34, 241–56) offer an overview of what they prefer to call 'sententious lore' in Old English verse and prose; see also Hansen 1988 and T. Hill 2005.

22 Clayton, *Poems of Christ*, p. xi. Greenfield and Calder (1986: 183–88) offer a perceptive reading of *Advent Lyrics* with reference to the poems' sources, contents and critical reception.

had entered the world's pain in love'.²³ Elaborating greatly on antiphons sung during the season of the Nativity and organizing those elements in an original way,²⁴ these poems are lyric effusions addressed first and foremost to Christ, who is addressed successively as King (lyric 1), as Saviour (lyric 2), as the Light of the World (lyric 5), as Emmanuel, hence both King and law-giver (lyric 6), as Creator as well as Son (lyric 8), and as King of the Heavens (lyric 10). Correspondingly, the Virgin Mary is adored as Mother of Christ (lyric 4) and as Queen of the Universe (lyric 9). Lyric 3 is a hymn to the Heavenly Jerusalem conceived of as Christ's citadel, while lyric 11, based in part on the Sanctus of the mass, is a hymn in praise of the Trinity. In keeping with the liturgy of the Advent season, lyric 7 consists of a quasi-dramatic dialogue between the Virgin and Joseph. In addition to taking its cue from an antiphon sung in that season, the dialogue is based on a sermon once erroneously attributed to Saint Augustine.²⁵ The sequence concludes with lyric 12, where the mystery of the Incarnation is reiterated and where the mode of address changes from one of personal devotion to one of moral exhortation. Here all those who are *dōm-hwæte* 'eager for salvation' (429a) are urged to worship Christ always, in words and deeds, so as to gain an eternal reward in God's own homeland (*in þām ēðle*, 436a), 'in the joy of the land of the living' ('in lifgendra londes wynne', 437).²⁶

Advent Lyrics thus establishes Christ as the cornerstone (*weall-stān*, 2a) on which the Christian religion rests, just as Christ is the cornerstone on which the Exeter Anthology itself is built both in this preliminary part of the volume and in the pages that follow. Among the Old English terms introduced

---

Edward B. Irving (1996) celebrates these lyrics as poetry, powerful in their emotional effect even if approached largely in isolation from the world of learning that they inhabit.

23 The phrasing is that of Ron Ferguson (1991: 16), paraphrasing teachings on the subject by George MacLeod, the founder of the Iona Community in Scotland.

24 Albert S. Cook (1900: xxv–xliii) took a leading role in identifying the liturgical sources for *Advent Lyrics*; his research has been supplemented and refined by Campbell 1959 and Burlin 1968. Verses from individual Latin antiphons that are cues for the twelve Old English lyrics are reproduced by Muir at the head of each lyric, with modern English translations. Susan Rankin discusses the relation of each of the twelve poems to the sequence of liturgical services from Advent (lyrics 1–10) to Christmas (the exultant lyric 11) to the week after Christmas (lyric 12), emphasizing that the synthesis of these materials involved some creativity on the part of the poet: 'it has become apparent that, far from writing a group of lyrics based on those Advent antiphons known by his community, the poet made deliberate choices and selections' (1985: 336).

25 See Allen and Calder (1976: 74–76) for a modern English translation of Pseudo-Augustine, Sermon 193.

26 This same whole-line phrase 'on lifgendra londes wynne' is used as the last line of *The Life of Saint Guthlac* (at line 818), where the citadel of heaven, the holy city of Jerusalem, is figured as a joyful land where blessed souls dwell forever.

here that play a key role in the rest of the Anthology are *sīþ* 'journey', as, for example, the speaker of lyric 1 alludes in verse 21a to the *wlitigan wil-sīþ* ('glorious longed-for journey') whose destination is heaven; *ēðel* 'homeland', in the sense of a home that was lost to humankind through the Fall but that can be regained through Christ (as at 32b and 436a); and *gerȳne* 'mystery', a key term used here (at 41b, 74a, 95a and 423a) with repeated reference to the Incarnation.

The next two poems of the Christ trilogy (*The Ascension* and *Christ in Judgement*, also known as *Christ II* and *Christ III*, respectively) address the aftermath and consequences of God's union with humankind. While the theme of the Crucifixion is addressed in only one extended passage of *Christ in Judgement* (lines 241–324), both these poems celebrate Christ's victory over death and his exalted majesty, and each one warns of Christ's impending return at Doomsday.

The Ascension—the first of the two 'signed' poems by Cynewulf included in the Anthology—begins by recapitulating the story of the Nativity, thus building a bridge back to *Advent Lyrics*. As the poem approaches its end, the poet tells of Christ's last words to his disciples, his ascent to heaven and his abundant gifts to humankind. Featured in the last third of the poem is an account of the six 'leaps' of Christ, a term that likens the major stages of the Saviour's life to a stag's beautiful leaps on the mountainside. The 'leaps' begin with the ineffable mystery of Christ's leap from his eternal throne into the womb of a mortal woman. The next leap is his birth in the form of a helpless infant, while the next is his willing acceptance of the agony of the Cross. The leaps that follow are his Entombment, his triumphant Harrowing of Hell, and his ascent into glory in the heavens from which he came. The poem concludes with an evocation of that fearful time when, shaking the firmament, Christ will return to earth as King and Judge so as to judge the living and the dead. The last part of *The Ascension* thus forms a bridge looking forward to *Christ in Judgement*.

To approach *The Ascension* as a versified paraphrase of the story of Christ's triumph over death, however, would be to mistake both the guiding concept of this work and the compiler's probable intention in placing the poem here. The poem serves as a compendium of Christian doctrine. It addresses all the main tenets of the faith, from the Incarnation to Judgement, while touching on incidental points of doctrine as well. Its form is that of a versified sermon addressed by a person who is steeped in the mysteries of the faith to one who is in greater need of instruction. When the speaker tells of the Nativity, for example, the audience's knowledge of the story is taken for granted. What is focused on straight away (at 447–58) is the question of why the angels who appeared on earth at the time of the Nativity were not clad in white garments, though they were clad in this manner at a later time, when Christ went with his disciples to Bethany. While this question might not seem of the first importance to present-day readers, Gregory the Great took it up in his twenty-ninth homily, Cynewulf's primary source.[27] The question would have had practical implications for the book's readers if those persons were accustomed to acting out aspects of the drama of the Nativity as part of the annual liturgical cycle, as they may well have been.[28]

Among the other themes touched on in this poem, many are reiterated in other poems of the Exeter Anthology. Indeed, the degree to which this is true leaves one wondering which came first, *The Ascension* or the rest of the volume.[29] An account of the most significant of these parallels follows:

- Featured early on, at lines 37–51 [476–90] of the poem, is a paraphrase of Christ's pledge to his disciples that he will never turn away from them, no matter what sufferings and perils their apostolic mission may entail. Echoing this pledge in a later part of the Anthology is *Christ's Pledge of Grace* (also known as *Homiletic Fragment III*), a short poem that offers the same assurance to all Christians who are steadfast in the faith.
- Somewhat later on, at 161–72a [600–11a], Cynewulf introduces the theme of the miraculous nature of the divinely ordained universe, with its sun and moon, its dew and rain, and its sustenance for humankind, for all of which we owe the Lord thanks. This theme is taken up later in the Anthology as the subject of *The Wonder of Creation*.
- What might at first reading seem to be an odd reference to Christ as an ascending bird, at 194–219 [633–58], comes into focus when one sees that the allegory that is developed at sustained length in *The Phoenix*, which follows thirty-five folios later, relies centrally on similar avian imagery.
- The theme of God's manifold gifts to human beings, introduced at 225–46 [664–85], is later developed at some length as the subject of the

---

27 See Allen and Calder (1976: 79–81) for a translation of the relevant parts of Gregory's sermon into modern English.
28 The presence of liturgical drama in England at about the time when the Exeter Anthology was written out is evidenced by the *Regularis Concordia*, which served as the constitution, as it were, of the Benedictine Reform in England. Included in this text is the *quem quaeritis* trope, which marks the beginnings of English liturgical drama. The leaders of the Reform were evidently interested in the affective potential of drama, as well as of poetry, as a means of promoting the faith.
29 Colin Chase (1974) has advanced a provocative argument that *The Ascension* unites the thematically related poems that precede and follow it and may have been composed as a bridge between the two. Dolores Warwick Frese (1975: 327–34) has independently made a similar suggestion based on her study of the runic 'signature' section of *The Ascension*.

poem *God's Gifts to Humankind*. Since the same theme is introduced at lines 64–96 of *The Fortunes of Mortals* and at lines 70–74a of *The Panther*, as well as briefly in *Widsith*, it can be considered one of the leitmotifs of the volume, first stated here in anticipatory form.

- The theme of God as the author of light and the sun's light that is introduced at 252b–62a [691b–701a] anticipates the full development of that concept in that part of *The Wonder of Creation* that consists of an exalted hymn to the sun and to Christ as the light of lights (57–81). *The Phoenix* likewise consists in part of a hymnlike song in praise of the sun and to Christ as *sēo sōþ-fæste sunne* ('the true sun', 587). While the equation of God and light is a Christian commonplace, the manner in which this theme is elaborated upon in these passages is nothing short of breath-taking. *Advent Lyric 5*, as well, has the form of a comparably exalted hymn addressed to 'Earendel' (the equivalent of Latin *Oriens*), conceived of as the rising sun, hence the light of Christ entering the world.[30] The lines from *The Ascension* are thus Janus-like in looking both forward to the main contents of the Anthology as they unfold, and backward to *Advent Lyrics* seen as a prelude to what follows.

- While the theme of the six 'leaps' of Christ that is introduced in *The Ascension* is taken up nowhere else in the Anthology, the six incidents of the life of Christ that are metaphorically called 'leaps'— that is, Christ's conception in the Virgin's womb, the Nativity, the Crucifixion, the Entombment, the Descent into Hell to bind Satan, and the Ascension—are treated as well at other points of the Anthology. Such repetitions are only to be expected; but significantly, as Patrick Conner and Karl Tamburr have pointed out, Cynewulf adds one 'leap' that is not in his source.[31] This is the fifth one, the Descent into Hell. It is hard to understand why he did so if not to anticipate the use of that same theme as the subject of the poem *Christ's Descent into Hell* that is included at folios 119v–121v, thus forging a link between the first part of the Anthology and the later 'Eastertide' sequence.

- Cynewulf's development of the Prudentian motif of the deadly arrow-attacks of fiends, at lines 320b–38a [759b–77a] of *The Ascension*, should come as no surprise given that this imagery is a commonplace of the homiletic literature of the Middle Ages. Still, worthy of note is the manner in which the image-cluster is used here compared with its use in poems included later in the Anthology, notably in the saints'

---

30   Cook (1900: 89–91) offers apt discussion of this coded reference to Christ.
31   Conner 1980: 186; Tamburr 2007: 44–83 (the chapter headed 'Providential View and Penitential Mode in the Old English Harrowing of Hell'), at 59–60.

lives *The Life of Saint Guthlac* (at 88b–92 and 177–91a) and *The Passion of Saint Juliana* (at 364–76a and 647–52a), as well as in the versified homily *Vainglory* (at 26–44a). While the theme is treated in an allusive fashion in all three of these last-named texts, Cynewulf develops it in a paradigmatic manner, emphasizing that the Trinity will shield us from the devil's assaults when we pray to God for refuge.

- The theme of the need for personal contrition and prayer is introduced with some poignancy, at lines 350b–57 [789b–96], within an eschatological context. While this too is a medieval commonplace, a penitential theme takes on increasing significance as the Anthology progresses, starting with *The Seafarer* and proceeding to the paired poems *Contrition* and *The Penitent's Prayer*. The passage from *The Ascension* anticipates this later shift of mood and theme.

- The theme of Doomsday, which is interwoven into Cynewulf's 'signature' passage in short and allusive form at lines 358–65a [797–804a] of *The Ascension*, is taken up *in extenso* in the succeeding poem *Christ in Judgement*, as it is in the poem *Doomsday* that figures later in the Anthology as part of the 'Eastertide' sequence. The same theme contributes to the typological dimension of *Christ's Descent into Hell*, where the release from hell of those who died before the Crucifixion anticipates the rising of all the dead from their graves at Doomsday.

- The trope of life on earth as a kind of seafaring, taken up in the closing lines of *The Ascension* (at 411–27 [850–66]), anticipates the extended semi-dramatic development of that same nautical metaphor in *The Seafarer*, a poem that occupies a noteworthy place in the Anthology's 'wisdom' section. A reader of this passage from *The Ascension* should be in no doubt as to how that later enigmatic poem is to be construed; it is as if Cynewulf were offering a preliminary versified exegesis of it.

While certain parallels of the kind just mentioned are inevitable in a large poetic miscellany like the Exeter Anthology, this is not true of all of them. Taken together, they point to a self-conscious effort to bring the prospective contents of the volume into communication with one another. The simplest way to account for the fact that this group of briefly stated themes is packed into the single poem *The Ascension* is through the hypothesis that the author of this poem, who identifies himself as 'Cynewulf', wished to anticipate the contents of much of the rest of the volume by offering a versified precis of many of its leading themes and patterns of imagery, with a glance back to themes introduced in the prefatory sequence *Advent Lyrics* as well. According to this scenario, Cynewulf must have been not just an accomplished poet, but also someone who took a keen, well-informed interest in the volume's prospective contents and arrangement.

Anyone reluctant to embrace the idea that an author whose own works figure so prominently in the Anthology was also involved in the volume's making is free either to ignore the parallels to which I have drawn attention or to develop a more complex way of accounting for them through one or another theory of interventions on the part of scribes, authors or the compiler. Bradley, for instance, calling attention to certain of these echoes and anticipations, draws the cautious conclusion that 'the compiler of the Exeter Book ... valued the poem [*The Ascension*] for its highly prescriptive content, the topics, interpretations and idiom it shares with other pieces of the compiler's choosing' (217). His delicate wording implies that certain poems written out on subsequent folios were favoured for inclusion on account of their harmonious relation to the 'highly prescriptive content' of *The Ascension*. Perhaps. Such a view is consistent with Bradley's understanding that Cynewulf probably lived during the eighth century, long before the Exeter Anthology was compiled. Such an assumption has been cast into doubt by more recent research, however. The scholar who is perhaps the leading current authority on Cynewulf, Robert E. Bjork, accepts a range of possible dates for that author that extends up to the time when the Exeter Anthology and the Vercelli Book were compiled, 'some time in the second half of the tenth century'.[32]

To sum up my main point (leaving aside the vexed questions of Cynewulf's dates, identity and possible role in the making of the Anthology), it would seem wilful to attribute the concentration of these anticipatory or 'echo' passages in this one poem to no more than the workings of chance. Here as elsewhere, one suspects the presence of one or more shaping hands.

The third and last poem of the Christ cycle is the long, didactic one known as *Christ in Judgement*. This tells of the rising of the dead from their graves and of Christ's impending admonishment of humankind, with words of praise for the just and a blistering castigation of those who have rejected him. Drawing on a number of sources including Revelations, Isaiah and a large medieval sermon literature on the subject of Doomsday,[33] the author dwells on the terror that the Second Coming will inspire as Christ manifests himself in his true and glorious form, 'brighter than the sun' (*sunnan lēohtra*, 785b), at midnight of 'the Great Day' (*sē micla dæg*, 2a).[34] A masterpiece of Anglo-Saxon

---

32 Bjork, *Poems of Cynewulf*, p. x. Bjork takes into account arguments concerning Cynewulf's dates that have been advanced by Fulk 1996 and Conner 1996.
33 For a convenient assembly of a number of these sources in modern English translation, see Allen and Calder 1976: 84–107. Graham D. Caie (1976) offers a rewarding analysis of the Doomsday theme and related topics in Old English literature.
34 Line numbers given for textual citations in the present paragraph are Muir's primary ones. The secondary numbers, based on continuous numeration from *Advent Lyrics* on, are respectively 1651b, 868a, 914b, 878–81a, 934–35a, 964–70a, 977–78a, 1043a and 1085.

spirituality, the poem is composed from start to finish with an emotional intensity that takes one's breath away and with mastery of the poetics of the alliterative line. Standing out amid the poem's darker tones is the figure of Christ in his shining beauty (in his *scīnan wlite*, 48b) as he will appear to the souls of the blessed, in contrast to the dread countenance he will turn to the guilty. Trumpets will resound from the four corners of the earth (12-15a); the sun will turn blood red (68-69a); seas, earth and sky will burn (98-104a); mountains and cliffs will melt away (111b-12a); the stars of heaven will fall from the sky (177a). The cross on which Christ suffered his Passion will then shine in the presence of all nations, 'bēacna beorhtast, blōde bistemed' ('the brightest of symbols, drenched with blood', 219), just as in the Vercelli Book poem *The Dream of the Rood*.[35]

The poems that follow after the Christ trilogy highlight models of saintly conduct on earth and the theme of the resurrection of the blessed. The first of these recounts the devout life of Saint Guthlac (*The Life of Saint Guthlac*), while the next is a shorter poem on that saint's exemplary death (*The Holy Death of Saint Guthlac*). This latter poem is now tentatively attributed to Cynewulf after having been excised for some years from modern notions of the Cynewulfian canon.[36]

The prominent place awarded to Guthlac in the Exeter Anthology can be attributed to several factors in addition to that saint's veneration at Glastonbury and elsewhere. One is that Guthlac was a native English saint, as befits this collection of verse composed in the vernacular. Moreover, the fact that this saint lived in a relatively recent period of history adds to the truth-value of his story; for as the author makes a point of noting, repeating this point from Felix's earlier Latin *vita* of this saint, 'eall þās geēodon in ūssera/ tīda tīman': 'all these things took place in our own age' (*The Life of Saint Guthlac* 753-54a). The phrase 'ūssera tīda tīman' evidently refers to post-conversion Anglo-Saxon England. There is no need to conclude, as some have done, that the author of this Old English version of the saint's life lived very soon after Guthlac's death in the year 715.

Another possible reason for the prominent place occupied by this saint in the Anthology is that the shape of Guthlac's life so clearly exemplifies the theme of conversion that is crucial to the book's design. As a scion of the Mercian royal line, the young Guthlac takes up the weapons of physical

---

35   Compare, from *The Dream of the Rood*, the verses *bēama beorhtost* (6a), *þæt fūse bēacen* (21b) and *mid wǣtan bestēmed* (22b). There is evidence here of poets working in the same 'school'.
36   A number of scholars have posited Cynewulf's authorship of *The Holy Death of Saint Guthlac* on the basis of similarities of style between that poem and his four 'signed' poems. Bjork, *Poems of Cynewulf*, p. xi, cautiously endorses this suggestion, with references.

combat only to renounce those weapons not long thereafter, when he adopts a life of physical austerities and prayer as a voluntary exile from society. That Guthlac was scarcely an exemplary youth, for there are hints of sinful or even criminal behaviour on his part,[37] does not detract from the moral value of his conversion story. On the contrary, this factor enhances the *vita*'s moral dimension by showing how God's grace and love can penetrate with special power into the hearts of those who have sinned, a theme made familiar through accounts of the conversion of Mary Magdalene, among others. As Alaric Hall observes, the manner in which the author of *The Life of Saint Guthlac* reworks his source material 'puts a new emphasis on conversion and redemption' (2007: 212).

A third reason why the choice of Guthlac as the leading male saint featured in the Exeter Anthology was a felicitous one is that the narrative of his life was so amenable to the heroic motif of spiritual warfare, with its monastic associations. This military motif is first introduced in that passage where the saint takes up his solitary abode in a wilderness. Here he prepares himself for his upcoming struggles against satanic enemies and establishes a sacred precinct, or battleground, by erecting a Rood at that spot:

> Gyrede hine georne   mid gæstlicum wæpnum;
> wong bletsade,
> him to ætstælle   ærest arærde
> Cristes rode.
>
> (Zealously he armed himself with spiritual weapons; he sanctified the place, and as his first act he raised up the Rood of Christ as his rallying-point.)[38]

As Jane Roberts has pointed out (1979: 3), Guthlac's very name (in its original signification) denotes 'battle-play', from OE *gūþ* 'warfare' plus *lāc* 'play'. Correspondingly, the saint remains an *oretta* 'combatant' (344a) for the rest of his life, dedicating himself to weapons of the spirit so as to fight for God, the King of kings, rather than for any earthly king (*Gode compian*, 345a). As

---

37 Guthlac is said to have undertaken savage deeds in his youth (108–10a), while later in the poem, devils chide him and threaten him with damnation for his sins of the flesh (579–89).
38 *The Life of Saint Guthlac* 177–80a; Muir 1: 114, with lineation slightly modified and the deletion of an editorial addition made by Muir *metri causa* in line 178. The resulting text appears to lack a half-line, though in reality there is a kind of metrical continuity here if one takes 'mid gæstlicum wæpnum' as functioning both as a *b*-verse in relation to 'Gyrede hine georne' and as an *a*-verse in relation to the following phrase, 'wong bletsade'. This is not the only half-line in the Exeter Anthology that is technically anomalous but that is best left unemended.

the leading exemplar of the figure of the *miles Christi* to be honoured in the Exeter Anthology,[39] he is variously referred to as *sē cempa* 'the warrior' (180b; cf. 438b), *Crīstes cempa* (153a), *hālig cempa* 'the holy warrior' (513b), *meotudes cempa* 'the Lord's warrior' (576a) and *dryhtnes cempa* 'the Lord's warrior' (727b).[40] The noun *cempa* that is used here with such frequency, derived from Latin *campio* 'judicial fighter',[41] is one of a number of lexical items that were adapted from the vocabulary of the war band so as to characterize the right conduct of the Christian life. Guthlac fulfils the definition of the warrior of Christ as offered at lines 451–65a of *The Phoenix*, where such a soldier is characterized by his charity, his offerings of prayer, his observance of God's law, his cheerfulness in devoting himself to good works, and his resolute courage in resisting every vice. It is in such terms as these that Guthlac wages battle for Christ 'þurh monigfealdra mægna gerȳnu'—that is, 'by means of the mysteries of manifold powers' (644), a line that is exactly paralleled at line 164 [603] of *The Ascension*. The poet's reference is to the whole marvellous array of divine powers that are manifest in the universe and that are potentially available to God's chosen ones in their struggle against the devil and his wiles.

The poem that follows, *The Holy Death of Saint Guthlac*, whether best attributed to Cynewulf or to another author of his 'school', was composed as a free versified periphrasis of that part of Felix's *Vita Guthlaci* that tells of that saint's death. In a manner that recalls the contents of *The Ascension*, this poem engages with the saint's death from a sweeping perspective, one that takes in the whole course of redemption history from the pivotal moment of the Fall to the moment of the salvation of an individual soul through steadfast belief in Christ. As Daniel G. Calder has remarked, 'the poet's purpose is not so much to retell the holy life of an Anglo-Saxon saint as to elucidate how that saint's life re-enacts major events within the whole context and scope of Christian history' (1972: 235). Like *The Passion of Saint Juliana*, the poem is more compelling as a lesson in doctrine than as a study in human psychology or character.

Rather than being conceived of as an ending, death is presented here in terms of the separation of the soul from the body,[42] as is characteristic of

---

39 David F. Johnson (2008) demonstrates the key role of the *miles Christi* topos in *The Life of Saint Guthlac*.
40 Dorothy Whitelock (1951: 80) has commented on how prominently the metaphor of spiritual warfare is also put on display in Felix's Latin *Vita Guthlaci*, where mention is made of the saint's shield of faith, his breastplate of hope, his helmet of chastity, his bow of patience and his arrows of psalmody, and where the arrows of the devil are mentioned as well. See in particular Felix's chap. 27 (Colgrave 1956: 90–93). The metaphor is used in a less elaborate way in the Old English Guthlac poems.
41 For discussion see D.H. Green 1998: 73–74.
42 Stephen D. Powell (1998) points to the prominence of the theme of separation in this poem.

medieval religious thought in general. The Old English word used for this parting is *gǣst-gedāl* (320b [1138b]), a term best translated as 'the release of the soul'.[43] Guthlac's main task in the poem, besides exemplifying a holy death, is to convince his one companion at this time to refrain from grief at the loss of his master. The companion, who is left unnamed perhaps so as to present him more as an ideal monastic type than as an individual person, is a thoughtful and caring attendant whom Guthlac comforts as his 'dear son' ('mīn þæt swǣse bearn', 348a [1166a]). In turn, the attendant addresses his master in devout terms as his *fæder* 'father' (393a [1211a]). The relationship between the two men thus recalls that between the speaker of *A Father's Precepts* and his assumed interlocutor. As for Guthlac himself, he is serene at the prospect of his passing, repeatedly declaring himself 'eager for the journey forth'.[44] The word *sīþ* that recurs with some regularity in this context is the same one that is used in *Advent Lyrics* and elsewhere in the Anthology to denote the soul's journey from the time of its union with the body on earth to its attainment of its final resting place.

The main point of *The Holy Death of Saint Guthlac* is thus to reinforce the doctrine that the story of one's life on earth is the prelude to a story of transfiguration, one that takes place in a realm invisible to mortal sight. In Guthlac's deathbed scene, correspondingly, the saint's spirit is absorbed into a body of radiant light (*wuldres scīma*, 468b [1286b]). A radiance hovers about him during the whole of the night preceding his death; and after his soul departs from his body, a similar brilliance surrounds his whole house, rising to the zenith with brightness greater than that of the sun (*sunnan beorhtra*, 495b [1313b]).[45] The imagery of light in this passage recalls that in *Advent Lyric 5*, with its hymn to Christ in the form of 'Earendel, engla beorhtast' ('Earendel, brightest of angels', 104–08): that is, to Christ as the true radiance of the rising sun and the source of illumination for every age.

The two poems on the life and holy death of Guthlac are followed by *The Canticles of the Three Youths*, a fragmentary poem featuring the songs of praise voiced by the three devout youths who, in the biblical book of Daniel, are thrust into Nebuchadnezzar's furnace to be tortured and burnt to death, but who remain miraculously unscathed. The poem has a close relation to the story of the three youths as paraphrased in lines 279–439 of the Old English

---

43 The first line number given in my citations to *The Holy Death of Saint Guthlac* is Muir's primary one; the one in square brackets is his secondary number, which is based on continuous lineation starting with *The Life of Saint Guthlac*. Bjork, *Poems of Cynewulf*, uses the continuous lineation, as do Krapp and Dobbie 1936.
44 Note *sīþes georn*, 227a [1045a]; *sīþes fūs*, 259b [1077b]; and cf. *þā hē wæs sīþes fūs*, 557b [1375b].
45 Compare the reference in *Christ in Judgement* to Christ's manifestation in his true form at Doomsday *sunnan lēohtra* (785b [1651b]).

poem *Daniel*, from the Junius Manuscript, although the relationship between these two texts is a complex one. Sometimes the parallel between the two poems is word for word and sometimes phrase for phrase, while at other times the readings of the two poems are entirely independent of one another.⁴⁶ Both of these reworkings of Scripture into the language of vernacular poetry have strong liturgical associations, as Conner points out (1993a: 154), for the *Benedicite*, the Latin canticle that in turn is based on this part of the book of Daniel, was regularly sung as a song of deliverance as part of the Easter liturgy. Educated persons might also have encountered the main substance of *The Canticles of the Three Youths* through Walahfrid Strabo's mid-ninth-century Latin poem *De ymno trium puerorum*, a verse paraphrase of the *Benedicite*. Still, the Exeter Anthology version of the story of the three youths is striking for its occasional independence from these other texts. The second of the poem's two sets of blessings, for example, is a magnificent eighty-eight-line paean to the Deity (lines 73–160), whereas the corresponding passage in *Daniel*, though equally exalted in tone, numbers only forty-seven lines (lines 362–408). The author of *The Canticles of the Three Youths* significantly expands upon his theme, for he not only calls on the heavens, the angels, the stars, the sun, the moon, the birds of the air, the fish of the sea and all manner of other features of the natural world to bless the Lord their Creator, but also exhorts priests and other members of the clergy to do so as well, making particular allusion to persons in monastic orders:

> Bletsien þe þine sacerdas,   soðfæst cyning,
> milde mæsseras,   mærne dryhten,
> ond þine þeowas,   ðeoda hyrde;
> swylce haligra   hluttre saule,
> ond, ece God,   eaðmodheorte.
>
> (May your priests, your gracious mass-priests, and your servants bless you, righteous King, glorious Lord, Shepherd of the peoples; likewise the pure souls of the saints and, eternal God, those who are humble in disposition.)⁴⁷

---

46 Texts and translations of *Daniel* and *The Canticles of the Three Youths* (here titled *Azarias*) are conveniently published together in the DOML edition edited by Daniel Anlezark (2011: 248–99 and 302–15). Paul G. Remley (2002) offers a close analysis of the textual relations between the two poems, positing a chain of transmission among multiple exemplars that are now lost. One of his chief conclusions is that 'a single redactor who was also a competent alliterative poet', one whom he calls 'the Canticle-Poet', was responsible for creating *The Canticles of the Three Youths* in the form in which we have it during the period c.960–80, or at roughly the same time as when the Exeter Anthology was written out (2002: 137).
47 *The Canticles of the Three Youths* 148–52; Muir 1: 162.

The poet's inclusion of the *ēað-mōd-heorte* in this list, directly after mention of the saints and God's *þēowas* (an evident allusion to men and women in monastic orders), seems specially designed to acknowledge the duty of those who live by the Benedictine Rule to send up to God a never-ceasing stream of praise and thanksgiving, as indeed monks did each day as the main part of the *opus dei*.[48]

Taking the three devout youths of this poem as representative of those persons of pure spirit who lived before Christ, Muir speculates that *The Canticles of the Three Youths* was included in the Exeter Anthology in order to demonstrate 'that salvation was possible for the Just under the Old Dispensation' (Muir 2: 461-62). Perhaps so. Self-evidently, however, the poem praises God as the source of all blessings, a theme with a timeless bearing on the salvation of humankind. The deliverance of the three youths from the fiery furnace illustrates God's power to preserve his chosen ones, body and soul, whether in the midst of earthly afflictions or beyond the apocalyptic fires of Judgement. Departing from the biblical book of Daniel in that it speaks explicitly of Christ (103a, 165b) and of the Triune Deity (155-57), *The Canticles of the Three Youths* relies on eschatological symbolism of the same kind as is featured in *The Phoenix*, the poem that immediately follows.

While most of *The Phoenix* (lines 1-380) represents a free paraphrase of the poem *De ave phoenice* attributed to the early Christian poet Lactantius, its substantial remainder (lines 381-677) consists of a versified exegesis of the symbolism ascribed to that same work.[49] The Old English poem features paradisiacal imagery and dwells on an image of resurrection: the rebirth of the phoenix from its own ashes despite being consumed by flames. The poem's fiery imagery recalls that of *The Canticles of the Three Youths*, while the manner in which the phoenix survives its immolation whole so as to be purified and made new, we are told, signifies the resurrection of the reunited body and soul even through the fires of Judgement. There is no need to labour the relevance of this theme to other poems of the Anthology, including *Christ in Judgement* and *Doomsday*.

The allegorical content of *The Phoenix* is deeply invested in the figure of the sun, imaged as the phoenix's consort. The array of poetic synonyms for the sun that the poet puts on display makes for a dazzling demonstration of what was involved in a mature Old English monastic poetics, for these synonyms

---

48 See Bosworth & Toller, s.v. *þeów*. Here the phrase 'gif ōðer wyle Godes þēow bēon' is glossed 'if one wishes to enter a monastery'. Hugh Magennis (1998) discusses phrases of the type '*þēow* of the Lord' or '*þegn* of the Lord' and notes their customary use with reference to monks, nuns or the saints.

49 For close discussion see N.F. Blake's introduction to his edition of *The Phoenix* (1964). The section of his introduction titled 'The Form' was later reprinted as Blake 1968.

have no parallel in the source poem attributed to Lactantius.⁵⁰ The solitary phoenix in its terrestrial paradise is first of all said to watch for the glorious rising of the sun, which is called here in succession *Godes condel* 'God's candle' (91b), *æþelast tungla* 'the noblest of heavenly bodies' (93b), *torht tācen Godes* 'the bright symbol of God' (96a) and *swegles lēoma* 'the radiance of the sky' (103b). After bathing itself twelve times in the pure welling streams of its tranquil homeland, the phoenix then enjoys an unobstructed vision of that same *bēacen* 'beacon' (107b), the sun, with that name now varied by the metaphoric terms *swegl-condel* 'sky-candle' (108a) and *swegles tapur* 'the sky's taper' (114b), as well as by the more literal term *lēohtes lēoma* 'the radiance of light' (116a). The sun in its glory, shining from on high above earth and seas, is then called by the terms *wuldres gim* 'jewel of glory' (117b), *mǣrost tungla* 'the most splendid of heavenly bodies' (119b), *hluttor heofones gim* 'the brilliant gem of heaven' (183a), *weder-condel wearm* 'the warm candle of the air' (187a) and *swegles gim* 'jewel of the sky' (208b). Significantly, none of the periphrastic terms used in this 110-line passage duplicates another. While rooted in a formulaic verse-making technique, these verbal pyrotechnics have the appearance of being a triumphant creation of this poet and his school.

At the end of the poem, in a manner that confirms its symbolism, the sun that is so fulgently praised in the lines just cited is brought into relation to the true and abiding sun (*sēo sōþ-fæste sunne*, 587), Christ himself, who will cast his light on righteous souls gathered in the citadel of heaven, with those souls figured metaphorically as beautiful birds (*fuglas scīne*, 591b). Earlier in the poem, as well, the narrator has likened the phoenix to 'the chosen servants of Christ', who are seen as maintaining their faith and composure even in the midst of earthly trials:

> Þisses fugles gecynd   fela gelices
> bi þam gecornum   Cristes þegnum
> beacnaþ in burgum,   hu hi beorhtne gefean
> þurh fæder fultum   on þas frecnan tid
> healdaþ under heofonum,   ond him heanne blæd
> in þam uplican   eðle gestrynaþ.

> (This bird's nature very closely resembles the chosen servants of Christ, in their enclosures, how through the Father's help they maintain their shining joy in this savage era and strive for exalted glory in the homeland above.)⁵¹

---

50   Cook (1919) edits the Latin source in tandem with the Old English text. For a convenient modern English translation of the poem attributed to Lactantius, together with ancillary source materials, see Allen and Calder 1976: 113–20.
51   *The Phoenix* 387–92; Muir 1: 177.

Here as elsewhere in the Exeter Anthology, the relevance of the phrase 'chosen servants of Christ' to the monastic vocation seems clear, especially when reference to monasteries is encoded into the adjoining phrase *in burgum* (389a). While this latter phrase might look like a throw-away alliterative 'filler' meaning no more than 'in the towns', in this context it is best understood as an allusion to monastic minsters, conceived of here as sacred grounds that anticipate the Celestial Jerusalem.⁵²

Much of the appeal of *The Phoenix* rests in its delightful initial evocation of the earthly paradise, seen here as a place of the utmost gentleness and tranquillity. In this regard the terrestrial paradise of *The Phoenix* serves as a counterpart to 'the land of the living' of *Advent Lyrics*. Moreover, the delightful topography of the phoenix's homeland, where no storms or torrents are known and where no hills, mountains or cliffs mar the evenness of the terrain, has its counterpart in the holy precinct to which, in *The Life of Saint Guthlac*, Guthlac is borne by miraculous means just prior to his death. This too is characterized as a green and tranquil land, a fragrant *locus amoenus* that resounds with birdsong (726b-48a). Here again we see possible evidence of a shaping hand in the compilation, for it is tempting to read this brief scene from *The Life of Saint Guthlac* as a self-conscious prelude to the sustained depiction of a *locus amoenus* with which *The Phoenix* begins.

The poem that follows directly after *The Phoenix* is *The Passion of Saint Juliana*, Cynewulf's versified saint's life recounting the life and death of a virgin martyr of the early church. Technically this *vita* too is an example of periphrasis, for what the poem represents is a free versified adaptation of a prior Latin anonymous *vita* of Juliana that had enjoyed fairly wide circulation in the medieval West.⁵³ The choice of this poem for inclusion in the Anthology was an auspicious one, for Juliana is an apt counterpart to the English male saint Guthlac. Both saints are paragons of chastity. Each one renounces the prospect of earthly wealth and comforts in favour of a life devoted to the worship of Christ.⁵⁴ Much as the courageous Guthlac wages spiritual warfare

---

52 See the *DOE*, s.v. *burh*, sense B.4.b, 'for the Heavenly Jerusalem, the City of God'. The word is often used in this sense in the poems of the Exeter Anthology from *Advent Lyrics* to *The Phoenix*. *Burh* is also sometimes used in Old English as a synonym for the earthly Jerusalem (sense B.4.a); it was also a name for the *minster-burh* once called *Medeshamstede* and now called Peterborough (sense B.5.d.i). Carolyn M. Heighway (1984: 40) observes that in the tenth century, Gloucester was organized along the lines of a royal *burh*, though it was never listed as such.

53 See Muir 2: 486. Allen and Calder (1976: 121-32) present a Latin *vita* of Juliana in modern English translation, while Lapidge (2003) discusses what he believes to have been Cynewulf's closest source while also presenting an edition of that Latin text (at 156-65).

54 Much as Juliana chooses to be the bride of Christ rather than of any earthly suitor, Guthlac too, in *The Life of Saint Guthlac*, is devoted to Christ above all others, as he declares himself to

against demons in his mountainous stronghold, causing them to flee in disarray, the fearless Juliana physically grasps the devil in order to force him to confess the nature of his evil. In like manner, though not so frequently since she is not literally of the warrior class, she is called one of *Godes cempan* 'God's soldiers' (17a).[55] She is one of those stalwart warriors of God who have taken up Saint Paul's shield and armour of righteousness, as the devil makes clear in one of his confessional moments in this poem:

> 'Gif ic ænigne   ellenrofne
> gemete modigne   metodes cempan
> wið flanþræce,   nele feor þonan
> bugan from beaduwe,   ac he bord ongean
> hefeð hygesnottor,   haligne scyld,
> gæstlic guðreaf ...   ic sceal feor þonan
> heanmod hweorfan,   hroþra bidæled'.

('If I ever meet with a courageous champion of God, one who is zealous in his courageous stand against a storm of darts, he will not flee from there shirking battle but will rather, astute in his thinking, raise his defence against me, his holy shield and his spiritual armour ... I must retreat far away from there, humiliated, deprived of comforts.')[56]

Here as in *The Life of Saint Guthlac*, the vocabulary of worldly heroism is converted to Christian ends. Of additional interest in *The Passion of Saint Juliana* is that the formulaic language of the war band is associated not with the heroine's devoted followers, as one might anticipate, but rather with her persecutors.[57] In a passage of high drama, the pagans who have tortured and killed Juliana are drowned when a storm engulfs the ship on which they had embarked in hope of fleeing God's wrath. Their souls are then swept into the depths of hell, there to remain eternally:

> Ne þorftan þa þegnas   in þam þystran ham,
> seo geneatscolu   in þam neolan scræfe,

---

be when speaking to a throng of devils: 'Eom ic ēað-mōd his ombieht-hēra,/þēow geþyldig' ('I am his humble obedient attendant, his patient servant', 599–600a). Indeed, the whole of the saint's speech at 593–684a is expressive of his passionate love for Christ as his King and Saviour.

55 Cf. *cempan sænran* ('weaker warriors', 395b), with reference to those whose courage is less than Juliana's, and *metodes cempan* 'the Lord's warriors' (382b). For discussion of the poet's use of this term, see Morrison 1979.

56 *Juliana* 382–87a, 389b–90; Muir 1: 201.

57 Claude Schneider (1978) draws pointed attention to the subversion of secular heroic values in *Juliana*, as does Magennis (2004: 171).

> to þam frumgare feohgestealde
> witedra wenan, þæt hy in winsele
> ofer beorsetle beagas þegon
> æpplede gold.
>
> (Those thegns, that band of comrades, had no need in that dark homeland, in that strait place of confinement, to expect from that leader their allotted riches, that they might partake of gifts of rings, of gold with its brilliant sheen, in the wine-hall over the drinking benches.)[58]

Imagery of the kind that in the world of *Beowulf* celebrates a gracious lord and his retainers is here used to discredit a corrupt, sadistic band of infidels. These enemies of Christ are depicted in such a manner as to call to mind the drunken, hell-bound carouser portrayed in *Vainglory*, a poem featured somewhat later in the Anthology. Positive counterparts to these damned souls are the three young men in *The Canticles of the Three Youths* whose steadfast faith in God permits them to survive being consumed by flames, much as Juliana herself survives, unscathed, being immersed in a clay vessel filled with boiling lead (*Juliana* 573b–94a).

In the succeeding twenty-five folios of the Anthology (76v–101r), narratives of the saintly life give way to models of heroic endurance in the face of earthly adversity. The fate of those who succumb to a corrupt way of life is brought to mind as well, as it does in the inset passage just quoted. This becomes a leading theme in later parts of the Anthology, as does the related theme of the need for penitence on the part of those who hope to be redeemed.

Voices of wisdom: *The Wanderer* and related poems

The first of the poems to succeed those on overtly religious topics is *The Wanderer*, a tribute to stoic fortitude in a world characterized by adversity and pain. This poem's role in the Anthology is a pivotal one, for it initiates a series of meditations on the human condition, with its endemic sufferings as well as its undenied sources of joy. While critics sometimes approach these meditative poems as examples of 'secular' Old English verse, one can scarcely think of an adjective that is as deceptive as this in offering an entry to their meaning,[59]

---

58 *Juliana* 683–88a; Muir 1: 212.
59 To cite one example of this tendency, Fred C. Robinson (2001) discusses the so-called elegies of the Exeter Anthology, along with *Widsith*, *The Rhyming Poem*, *Exeter Maxims* and *The Rune Poem*, in a chapter titled 'Secular Poetry' written for a companion to Anglo-Saxon literature.

for in the medieval Christian world-view that was reinforced by the psalms in particular, 'The earth is the Lord's and the fulness thereof, the world and all they that dwell therein.'[60] The Latinate genre term *planctus* might fruitfully be invoked when thinking of *The Wanderer* and two other Exeter Anthology poems, *Wulf and Eadwacer* and *The Wife's Lament*.[61] While set in an ancestral Germanic past, each of these poems replicates the conventions of that Latinate genre in that it is a fictive poetic lament (a 'staged discourse') that is set in the voice of a first-person persona (or, as one might say, that creates the phenomenon of the 'poetic I').[62] Two other poems included in the Anthology, *The Soul's Address to the Body* and *The Penitent's Prayer*, could perhaps be approached as adaptations of the *planctus* genre so as to express overtly Christian themes. In *The Soul's Address*, this theme is the bitterness caused by the loss of salvation, while the subject of *The Penitent's Prayer* is the speaker's anxious hope for salvation.

However we think of its genre, the main part of *The Wanderer* is put into the voice of a man who seems to dwell in a wintry northland of the Anglo-Saxons' historical imagination. Although presented as a member of the warrior aristocracy, this persona is not presented as either being or having been active in battle himself. While it is the habit of modern critics to speak of this man as 'the Wanderer', the Old English word used at the very start of the poem to refer to people of his condition is *ān-haga* 'lone-dweller' (1a). This term calls to mind the figure of the Christian recluse: a man like Guthlac,

---

While this chapter title may have resulted from editorial directive, Robinson's main point is that the authors of these works 'showed a pervasive awareness of their Germanic cultural heritage' (2001: 281). While this is true enough, an alternative perspective is that these poems systematically draw on that Germanic heritage so as to promote themes consistent with a Christian world-view.

60 Psalm 23:1: 'Domini est terra et plenitudo eius, orbis terrarum et universi qui habitant in eo.' In Old English: 'Drihtnes ys eorðe and eall þæt hēo mid gefyld is, and eall mancynn, þe þær-on earda ð, is Dryhtnes' (O'Neill 2016: 74).
61 Rosemary Woolf (1975) has advanced this suggestion. In searching for Latinate genre terms that have a degree of explanatory power when used with reference to poems of the Exeter Anthology (as I attempt to do systematically in Appendix 3), I follow a path taken by Patrick Conner (1993a: 152). Conner's research, however, has taken him in different directions, in keeping with his identification of what he finds to be 'clerical' elements in what he calls 'Booklet II' of the Anthology.
62 I borrow these terms from Ursula Schaefer's (1991) account of the rise of fictionality in Old English poetry. It will be evident that I do not approach the so-called elegies of the Exeter Anthology as 'intensely personal' poems, as does Stacy Klein (2006: 115), in keeping with a strong tendency in the critical literature. Instead, I view them as crafted poems that simulate the voices of men or women who are separated from others and who experience pain, loneliness, bitterness, anxiety or other strong emotions. As Stanley B. Greenfield (1955) has emphasized, the poetic language in which these emotions are expressed is governed by convention, though it is no less effective on that account.

another *ān-hoga* (179a [997a]) and a man whose isolated existence in the wilderness is self-willed rather than being imposed by blind fate. The speaker of *The Wanderer*, though evidently a man with no knowledge of Christ, is thus implicitly linked to persons of an anchoritic resolve.[63] We might perhaps more properly speak of him as 'the Lone-Dweller' rather than 'the Wanderer', though there is a weather-beaten mystique to that conventional name that one would not want to do without.

Bereft of companions, the Wanderer expresses wisdom that only those who have experienced life's bitterest misfortunes can grasp. He speaks with some urgency when lamenting the demise of prior civilizations (73–105). This extended passage features repeated use of the exclamation *ēalā!* (at 94a, 94b and 95a) in the inset speech of a seer of some future age. The use of that exclamation in this bleak context offers a sharp contrast to the prominent use of that same exclamation to celebrate Christ's Incarnation in *Advent Lyrics* and, in a later part of the Anthology, to salute Christ's triumph over death in *Christ's Descent into Hell*.

Since speech divisions within *The Wanderer* are unmarked in the manuscript and are the subject of critical debate, I should make clear what my own view is in this regard. In brief, I see the poem as divided between three speakers. The first of these is the narrator, himself a persona ('the poet-philosopher', Muir 2: 503–04). The narrator introduces the poem in lines 1–7 and brings it to a close in lines 111–15. The second speaker is the Wanderer himself, an imagined figure whose monologue extends from line 8 to line 110. The third speaker inhabits an undefined future age; he is a wise man (*glēaw hæle*, 73a) whose imagined words the Wanderer calls to mind at lines 92–110.[64] As Carol Pasternack (1995: 47–48) has emphasized, the three voices featured in *The Wanderer* coincide with one another in a manner that defies clear resolution, so that the effect is more like that of a single polyphonic meditation than of a drama divided into different parts for different actors.[65]

---

63 The same word *ān-haga* is used of the penitential sojourner who is the speaker of *The Penitent's Prayer* (at 20b). Since this term is also used twice of the blissful solitary bird the phoenix (at 87a and 346b of *The Phoenix*), one might be misled into thinking that it had auspicious associations; and yet elsewhere in Old English, in *Cotton Maxims* 19a, the word is used of the wolf, characterized as an *earm ān-haga* 'wretched lone-dweller'. The situation of the Wanderer is therefore an ambivalent one. While his present state is one of wretchedness, it can also be regarded as a prelude to a more blessed condition.

64 Muir 1: 218, and Bjork, *OE Shorter Poems*, pp. 8–9, interpret the poem's speech divisions this same way.

65 Likewise Gerald Richman (1982) and Lois Bragg (1991: 128–35) discern elements of ambiguity or indeterminacy in regard to speech boundaries in *The Wanderer*; while Shippey remarks that in general, the voices of different personae are often hard to distinguish from

I shall have more to say later about *The Wanderer*. It is the first of the poems of the Exeter Anthology that affirm that as the religion of Jesus, who experienced doubt and temptation and knew excruciating pain, Christianity speaks above all to those who have suffered adversity or are in present distress. This message is implicit in all the Exeter Anthology poems (including most of the so-called elegies) that are set in the voice of an anguished person, whether or not that person is in a position to hear this message or to respond to it with an appropriate change of heart.[66]

The next of the 'wisdom poems', following directly after *The Wanderer*, is *God's Gifts to Humankind*. This is also the first of the Anthology's so-called 'catalogue poems', to use a super-generic term that has gained some currency in the critical literature despite its limited explanatory power.[67] The poem enumerates the marvellous variety of gifts or talents with which, by God's grace, humanity has been blessed. The sources of this theme in the Gospels and in the Epistles of Saint Paul has been well charted by Muir, and its handling in the sermon literature of the early Middle Ages is likewise well documented.[68] E.G. Stanley (2015) has recently re-edited the poem with characteristically discerning insights into its unusual poetic diction, its theocentric orientation, its potent touches of humanity and its chief didactic purpose of teaching humility, among other special qualities. His study goes far towards establishing a frame of reference within which the Exeter Anthology as a whole can be well understood.

In keeping with the character of the Exeter Anthology as a volume directed to persons who are not just literate but who are also striving for enlightenment, many of the gifts named in *God's Gifts to Humankind* contribute to the exercise of intellectual powers. Some pertain to the martial equipment with which members of the clergy and other zealous Christians are endowed, according to the trope of the *miles Christi*:

---

one another in Old English wisdom poetry, this being an aspect of these poems' art rather than being a failing of some kind (1976: 1–2).

66 The genre term 'elegy', a modern one, has been used in different ways by different critics with reference to up to ten poems of the Exeter Anthology. Among those specialists who have found the term a useful one, within certain limits, are Stanley B. Greenfield (1955, 1966) and Anne Klinck (1992: 221–51). Greenfield and Calder distance themselves from the genre term 'elegy' but still favour the adjective 'elegiac' when speaking of these poems (1966: 280–302). Other critics have questioned the term's value in the Anglo-Saxon context. Fulk and Cain, in particular, see the vogue for 'elegy' in Old English literary criticism as having arisen from 'a projection of the sensibilities of the Romantic age back onto the early Middle Ages' (2013: 259).

67 Nicholas Howe (1985) has given the term 'catalogue poem' a certain currency, arguing that it is aligned with the medieval temperament though not so often with the modern one.

68 Muir 2: 514–15; Allen and Calder 1976: 154–55.

> Sum bið deormod   deofles gewinnes,
> bið a wið firenum   in gefeoht gearo.
>
> (Another person is fierce in combat against the devil; he is always prepared for battle in the fight against sins.)[69]

Among other gifts to humankind mentioned in this poem are a number of skills or crafts, including carpentry, metalwork, musicianship, singing, reading and writing. The application of such skills as these to a well-run monastic estate should need no emphasis. Likewise mentioned are such skills as falconry, hunting, equestrianism, seamanship and the warrior's arts, thus reinforcing the point that God's gifts to his favoured species are indeed manifold. Noteworthy is this poem's even-handed acknowledgement that both worldly gifts, including material wealth and physical beauty, and religious ones, including a talent for singing hymns or psalms of praise (91–94a), are expressions of God's munificence.[70]

This poem is followed by *A Father's Precepts* (fols 80r–81v), a poem set in the voice of a wise Father who counsels his son against a nest of vices. This persona enunciates the principles of moral choice that apply to each and every person, whatever his status or gifts may be. The values expressed here, as Bradley has remarked, 'often interestingly gloss conduct described in other poems' of the Anthology (328–29). In addition, certain of the Father's precepts bear a close resemblance to the monastic instructions offered in chapter 4 of the Rule of Saint Benedict.[71] Two examples among others that could be cited are the admonitions 'Druncen beorg gē ond dollīc word' ('Guard yourself against drunkenness and foolish words', 34) and 'Yrre ne læt þē æfre gewealdan,/hēah in hreþre' ('Never let anger overcome you, rising up high in your breast', 83–84a). With these precepts can be compared not just the 'courageous prudence' that is held up as a behavioural model in such other Exeter Anthology poems as *The Wanderer* and *The Seafarer*,[72] but also Saint Benedict's call for equanimity and moderation in all things: 'Iram non

---

69 *God's Gifts to Humankind* 89–90; Muir 1: 223.

70 Speaking of the section of this poem that enumerates spiritual gifts (lines 84b–96), Howe remarks: 'It would not be inaccurate to describe this last series of gifts as monastic, or if that seems too limited, as characteristic of Christian culture at its highest' (1985: 114).

71 Sandra McEntyre (1990) calls attention to these points of resemblance.

72 I borrow this term from Eugene Green in his study of *Deor*, *The Wanderer* and *The Seafarer* as three poems that respond in comparable ways to a spirit of widespread apprehension that he sees as having been characteristic of tenth-century England in the aftermath of Viking attacks (2001: 157–75, at 175). Still, apprehension and its adjunct, mutability, are common aspects of the human condition, amplified in the Christian writings of the Middle Ages during almost any historical period.

perficere ... veritatem ex corde et ore proferre ... non esse superbum, non vinolentum' ('Do not give in to anger ... speak truth with heart and tongue ... do not be proud, nor overly fond of wine').[73] In the light of parallels between this poem, other poems of the Anthology and outside sources or analogues, Michael Drout has argued that the compiler of at least four poems from this part of the Anthology, the ones that I call *God's Gifts to Humankind*, *A Father's Precepts*, *The Fortunes of Mortals* and *Exeter Maxims*, 'had wholeheartedly adopted the beliefs and traditions of the Benedictine Reform', so that these poems 'transmit monastic ideas and traditions' in a rhetorically heightened form.[74]

Following after *Precepts* is *The Seafarer*, a monologue set in the voice of a man who scorns domestic comforts and camaraderie so as to pursue a life of the most stringent austerity. Since the poem's temporal setting is left indeterminate, one can equally well imagine this persona as an inhabitant of some former era or of the contemporary world. As his monologue unfolds, alert readers will become aware that the Seafarer is not deranged or masochistic, nor is he simply misanthropic, nor (contrary to some early twentieth-century views) is he a Jack London-like character who is so thrilled by the rigours of wintry sailing that he rejects all lesser pursuits. Rather, through his life of exile, he puts himself into spiritual alignment with the small minority of dedicated persons who choose to endure physical hardship so as to live their lives in accord with the ideal of *peregrinatio pro amore dei*: that is, who undertake a self-imposed penitential journey for the sake of the love of God. During the early Middle Ages, as Dorothy Whitelock has emphasized, such real-life journeys were regarded as an extension of the monastic way of life.[75] In addition, as has been documented by G.V. Smithers (1957) among others, the notion of human life on earth as itself constituting a kind of exile from Paradise was a commonplace of medieval homiletic literature, one that was firmly rooted in patristic thought. This is true whether Paradise was conceived of as the originary home of Adam and Eve or as our final home in heaven.

---

73 Venarde, *Rule of Benedict*, pp. 32–35. Similar precepts find expression in the Enlarged Rule of Chrodegang, a set of canons whose Old English translation is thought to have been produced in Dunstan's and Æthelwold's circle of scholars. Aaron Ralby (2010) traces a connection between *A Father's Precepts* and the Christian tradition of penitentials.

74 Drout 2006: 264. Following Conner, Drout sees the resulting programme of education as having taken place at Exeter, though I see no good grounds for such a specific localization. In like manner, Shippey points out the 'strong monastic flavour' of the word *þēod-scipe* 'discipline' that is used at verse 69b of *A Father's Precepts*, where its apparent reference is to 'a form of community life bound by strict rules' (1976: 128 n. 8).

75 Whitelock 1950. For related discussion see Dyas 2001: 67–124 and Mullins 2014.

The Wanderer and *The Seafarer* are thus rightly read as companion pieces. While they resemble one another in regard to their monologic form, their reliance on wintry imagery and their common theme of exile, they differ sharply in terms of the speaker's awareness of the need for salvation and the means by which it can be achieved. The Wanderer's stoicism and despair give way to the Seafarer's knowledge of the consolation brought by Christ's redemption of humankind. While this latter theme is present in *The Wanderer* as well, where it is introduced through the narrator's voice in the poem's initial and closing lines, it finds direct expression in *The Seafarer*'s homiletic close. Here the speaker makes clear that the remedy for earthly afflictions is to be found through spiritual warfare, by which a good man 'should bring it about before dying, by actions on earth against the hostility of enemies, by valiant deeds against the devil' that he should win the praise of those who come after 'and his glory live then with the angels'.[76]

Significantly, the poem that immediately follows *The Seafarer* is *Vainglory*, the main part of which is a monologue excoriating an arrogant city-dweller who swills wine and revels in the path of vice. This is just the type of person the Seafarer regards with contempt (at lines 27-30 of that poem) and from whom he chooses to distance himself. When the author of *Vainglory* speaks of the impending damnation of sinners of this kind (46b-50a), one is reminded of the group of infidels who are drowned at sea at lines 671b-82 of *The Passion of Saint Juliana* for having mocked and tortured the faithful bride of Christ, for these persecutors too, as we have seen, are likened to drunken carousers in the hall.

The trajectory of the Exeter Anthology up to this point thus takes us from the world of Christ, his angels and his saints to that of ordinary human beings. While at first what is most vividly dramatized is the path that leads to bliss, later it is the path that leads to damnation. While, we are told, some people live by high moral standards in our harsh and transitory world, others indulge their pride and wallow in sensuality even at the cost of their eternal souls. The fact that this theme is a devotional commonplace did not prevent the poets of this period from exploiting it in original ways, 'consciously practicing the rhetoric of the difficult in order to intensify the reader's intellectual excitement', as Bernard Huppé has written of the author of *Vainglory* (1970: 26).

Noteworthy among the 'wisdom' poems of this part of the codex are those that take the form of dramatic monologues. The equivalent term in the Latinate rhetorical lexicon is ethopoeia (literally 'character drawing'). What this Latin term denotes is an exercise by which an author adopts the voice of

---

76 'Þæt hē gewyrce, ǣr he on weg scyle,/fremum on foldan wið fēonda nīþ,/dēorum dǣdum dēofle togēanes,/... ond his lof siþþan lifge mid englum.' *The Seafarer* 74-78; Muir 1: 231-32.

an absent person so as to characterize the ethos, or character, of that speaker through the style of his or her speech.[77] The early medieval writer's task in composing such an exercise, as Ivan Drpić has remarked, was 'to imagine what a particular person would say in a given situation, typically a critical moment in his or her life' (2014: 907).

Anglo-Saxon poets excelled in this mode of composition, which in the Exeter Anthology takes on a moralistic cast and alternates with the figure of prosopopoeia by which an inanimate object is ascribed a first-person speaking voice.[78] At one point in the Wanderer's monologue, as we have seen, ethopoeia is nested within ethopoeia as the imagined speaker of this poem calls up to his mind's eye the imagined sage of some future era. Speaking amid an imagined scene of universal desolation, this future person laments the demise of any number of prior civilizations (lines 92–96). With its apocalyptic overtones, this passage introduces the theme of earthly transience that has a leading role elsewhere in the volume, as it does in Anglo-Saxon literature more generally.[79]

A place is next found in the Exeter Anthology for *Widsith*, a poem that presents a complex attitude towards the glories of past civilizations through the poet's introduction of two voices representing two different perspectives. One voice is that of Widsith himself, an imagined bard of pagan times, while the other is that of a Christian narrator whose discourse frames that of the central persona. Given the complexities of this framing device as well as other aspects of its art, this poem will be discussed in a later section of the present chapter.

The series of 'wisdom' poems resumes with *The Fortunes of Mortals*, a catalogue poem whose main subject is the myriad ways by which death comes to humankind. This versified *memento mori* sounds more grisly than it is, for the poem is practically devoid of sentimentalism even when alluding to the fearful, hungry flames of a funeral pyre (43–48) or when referring in wry fashion to a young tree-climber who plunges 'featherless' to his death (*fiþer-lēas*, 22a). In its own medium of English alliterative verse, the poem

---

77 Isidore of Seville, in book 2, chap. 14 of his *Etymologiae*, defines ethopoeia as that rhetorical feature whereby, through direct speech, 'we represent the character of a person in such a way as to express traits related to age, occupation, fortune, happiness, gender, grief, boldness', so that the speech fits the speaker: 'One caught up in joy speaks one way, one wounded, another' (Barney *et al.* 2006: 74).
78 Christine Fell (2002) comments on this alternation in the Exeter Anthology between the elegies (as examples of ethopoeia) and certain of the enigmas (as examples of prosopopoeia), while noting as well that in Isidore's *Etymologiae*, the definition of prosopopoeia comes immediately before that of ethopoeia.
79 Fell (1991) discusses a wide range of Old English texts that foreground the theme of mutability, including this passage.

responds to Saint Benedict's dictum in chapter 4, verse 47, of his Rule to 'keep the prospect of death before your eyes every day'.[80]

Readers who approach *The Fortunes of Mortals* within the context of the Exeter Anthology as a whole are encouraged to face the prospect of death with a degree of equanimity, knowing that death comes when God wills, while what death consists of when understood from a Christian perspective is a separation of the soul from the body rather than the end of life. Still the future state of one's soul can be a source of grave potential anxiety, as is dramatized another ten folios later through the poem *The Soul's Address to the Body*, with its speaker's excoriation of the mute body of an unrepentant sinner. The need for conversion before death is implied at lines 33–57 of *The Fortunes of Mortals* through references to death by the gallows and to sudden deaths incurred either by violence in the mead-hall or through the quasi-suicidal madness of uncontrolled drinking.

In addition to enumerating causes of death, *The Fortunes of Mortals* tells of the state of the material body after death has taken place. In passages that are reminiscent of *The Soul's Address to the Body* and of that grim part of *The Wanderer* that tells of the devouring of a corpse by wolves (82b–83a), this poem alludes to a man who is eaten by wolves (12b–14) and of another whose body rots on the gallows while a raven plucks out his eyes (33–42a). As both Stefan Jurasinski and Heather Maring have observed, such passages as these reflect the horror with which the Anglo-Saxons viewed the dismemberment of the material body, a dread that was reinforced by the Christian literature of late antiquity.[81] Correspondingly, especially in Anglo-Saxon monastic settings, care for the material body of the deceased was the object of elaborate devotional practices, as is made clear in a passage of the *Regularis Concordia* that offers a sharp contrast to those passages from the Exeter Anthology that tell of the devouring, rotting or dismemberment of corpses:

> When the brother has departed this life, his body shall be washed by those appointed to do so; when washed it is clothed in clean garments, namely in shirt, cowl, stockings, and shoes, no matter what his rank. But if he is a priest a stole may be placed about him over his cowl, if such be the rule. The body shall then be borne into the church with the chanting of psalms and the tolling of bells. And if the brother died before dawn, in the night, or after the dark hours, in the early morning, let him be buried before the brethren have their meal, when the Masses have been celebrated, provided that those things necessary for a burial can be prepared; otherwise let the brethren be appointed by turns to chant psalms unceasingly by the body

---

80 'Mortem cottidiae ante oculos suspectam habere': Venarde, *Rule of Benedict*, pp. 34–35.
81 Jurasinski 2007; Maring 2017, chap. 2.

throughout that day and the following night until early morning when it shall be committed to the earth.[82]

For seven successive days after a burial, as is specified in the same chapter of the *Regularis Concordia*, the Office of the Dead was recited in full, while up to the thirtieth day after burial each priest was to say a special mass daily for the dead brother. Meanwhile, word was sent to neighbouring monasteries telling of the death of the man 'whom the Lord has deigned to call forth from the prison-house of this world' ('quem Dominus de ergastulo huis saeculi vocare dignatus est'). Fear of bodily dismemberment lent urgency to the doctrine of the ultimate unity of body and soul. At the end of *The Ascension*, Cynewulf urges that we who are on earth turn our hearts to salvation, so that each of us may believe in our souls that the living God will ascend from here *mid ūsse līc-homan* 'with our body' (316a [755a]).

With its uninhibited didacticism, *The Fortunes of Mortals* is yet another poem of the Exeter Anthology that expresses the mind-set of the cloister even when it treats of the world of ordinary affairs. Although the poem begins by calling up an image of parents who have the satisfaction of seeing their children grow up into adulthood (lines 1–8a), this narrative quickly shifts into a tale of woe as the catalogue of deaths begins (8b–57), with its images of lamenting women. This sudden shift of theme from the prospect of domestic happiness to the reality of loss and grief could well have confirmed those who were committed to celibacy that their choice was a wise one.

The poem's catalogue of deaths does not continue as far as the poem's end, for at lines 64–96 the related theme is introduced of God's gifts to humankind. God's gifts are shown to be remarkable for their variety, as in the other passages on this theme that are included in the Anthology, for they include skills essential to the goldsmith's art, musicianship, table-games and falconry, as well as the wisdom that pertains to book learning. A reader of *The Fortunes of Mortals* in its entirety is thus guided towards an understanding that death, like God's blessings, is part of an ordained order.[83]

After *The Fortunes of Mortals* comes the tripartite gnomic poem known as *Exeter Maxims*, a loosely didactic set of reflections pertaining chiefly to proper behaviour. While often printed and discussed as if it were a single poem, *Exeter Maxims* is perhaps best regarded as three sets of versified gnomic statements that were conjoined in the Exeter Anthology on account of their compatible

---

82 *Regularis Concordia* 12: 66; Symons 1953: 65, punctuation slightly adjusted.
83 As Howe remarks, both *God's Gifts to Humankind* and *The Fortunes of Mortals*, when read together, 'illustrate the omnipotence and omniscience of God as they are made known in the lives of human beings' (1985: 115).

content and rhetoric. When referring to these as separate parts, I will call them *Exeter Maxims A*, *Exeter Maxims B* and *Exeter Maxims C*. The differences of style and subject between them are noticeable, even if inessential to one's understanding of the poems as a group.[84]

Exeter Maxims A begins with an imagined speaker's exhortation to the reader to engage in an intellectual exchange, as if both persons were in one another's physical presence: 'Frīge mec frōdum wordum ... Glēawe men sceolon gieddum wrixlan' ('Ask me questions with words of deep understanding ... Wise people should exchange sententious sayings', 1–4a). The speaker then makes no secret of what kind of *gieddas* he has in mind: 'God sceal mon ǣrest hergan' ('One should first of all praise God', 4b). The next dozen lines develop the reasons why such praise of God is justified, while the remainder of the poem consists largely of maxims that reinforce both the dictates of good sense and the teachings of the Rule of Saint Benedict. Special value is put on the monk's virtues of wisdom, deliberation, peacemaking, generosity, and the kind and nurturing education of youth. The emphasis on reciprocity at the poem's start is evidently meant to encourage readers to rise to the challenge of composing additional versified maxims along similar lines.

The emphasis of *Exeter Maxims B* is on the order of life on earth. God's supreme power in maintaining this order is acknowledged, most emphatically in those lines where the Christian God, the saviour of souls (*sāwla nergend*, 134b), is compared favourably with the old Germanic god Woden and his useless shrines (*Wōden worhte wēos*, 'Woden made idols', 132a).[85] The cumulative effect of the poem's aphorisms is to confirm the rightness of the order of the world as the Anglo-Saxons knew it: the cycle of the seasons, the proper conduct of trade, the regular provision of food, good manners at court and proper relations between men and their wives, whether the couples be cottagers or royalty. The role of armed warriors in defending a land from its enemies goes unquestioned, as is typical of Anglo-Saxon monastic discourse even though monks themselves were non-combatants. No *hād* is despised. 'Books befit a student' (*bēc [sculon] leornere*, 130b), we are told in a manner that is meant to reassure any doubters, just as treasure befits a queen or the Eucharist the priest. There is no hint here of apocalyptic

---

84 Since maxims are fairly ubiquitous in Old English poetry as in medieval writings more generally, and since as well they serve a variety of purposes, it seems to me a formidable task to try to formulate a general theory of their use, though Paul Cavill (1999) has made an ambitious attempt at such a synthesis.

85 When citing words or passages from *Exeter Maxims B* and *Exeter Maxims C*, I use Muir's secondary line numbering for the sake of consistency with other editions. This lineation is based on continuous numbering through all three poems of the sequence, a practice adhered to by Krapp and Dobbie 1936 and Bjork, *OE Shorter Poems*.

fears or concerns; rather, as in the Old Icelandic gnomic poem *Hávamál*, the sententiae that are the substance of *Exeter Maxims B* could be likened to a body of common law ruling both nature and human affairs. The fact that Woden is even mentioned here, when the strong tendency among Anglo-Saxon ecclesiastical writers was to expunge memory of the old Germanic gods, is one of many indications that the author of this poem had an unusually capacious notion of the role of poetry as a vehicle for knowledge and wisdom.

Exeter Maxims C consists of a loosely organized set of reflections on the ways of the world. The mentality underlying this section of the tripartite work is closely aligned to ordinary experience: the proper management of horses, the pleasures of music or table-games, the need for regularity in the preparation of meals, the ubiquity of conflict among members of the fallen human race, the need for wariness on the part of warriors, the variety of lifeways among different groups of people. To say that this poet's attitude towards his craft of verse-making is a lax one would be an understatement, for in no other part of the Exeter Anthology is such little heed paid to regular observance of the requirements of the four-stress alliterative line. The results, though regularly lineated in modern editions, are sometimes almost indistinguishable from prose. To say that certain of this poem's sententiae are truisms would be another understatement. What should one make, for example, of the declaration that 'a tree that lies on the ground grows least' ('licgende bēam læsest grōweð', 158)? If the statement was meant to be taken in a metaphorical sense and was based on common parlance, then it could perhaps be admired as a proverb; but one fears that it is meant literally, as is a neighbouring reference to the need to bandage a wound.

If there is a dominant theme in this section of *Exeter Maxims*, it is the value of companionship. This theme is announced early on: 'Wel mon sceal wine healdan on wega gehwylcum' ('One should be true to one's friend on every path', 144). In the lines that follow, similar wisdom is reiterated with reference to the friendless man who has only wolves for companions, the lone-dweller whom fate has forced to live on his own, and the hunter who would be mad to attack wild beasts by himself. Although none of these observations is news, the emphasis that this poet puts on the value of a trusted support group might have been comforting to readers who themselves were living in tight-knit ecclesiastical communities where horses were well cared for, wounds were promptly bandaged, wild beasts were left alone and meals arrived punctually.

As others have pointed out, certain distinct verbal parallels link *Exeter Maxims* to other poems in this same part of the Exeter Anthology, *The Seafarer* in particular.[86] Three of these parallels are worth citing here.

---

86 For discussion see O'Camb 2011.

First of all is the near-verbatim repetition of a verse that figures both early in *Exeter Maxims* and, half a dozen folios earlier in the manuscript, towards the end of *The Seafarer*:[87]

> Styran sceal mon strongum mōde.   (*Exeter Maxims A* 50a)
>
> Stieran mon sceal strongum mōde.   (*The Seafarer* 109a)

The interpretation of this pair of verses is subject to debate. To base one's reading on Benedictine parallels, the primary meaning ought to be 'One must restrain a headstrong spirit.' An alternative possibility, equally plausible syntactically, is 'One must steer [one's course in life] with a resolute mind.'[88] A third option is to embrace both of these alternatives, taking the nominal phrase *strongum mōde* as an example of intentional grammatical ambiguity: 'One must restrain a headstrong spirit with a resolute mind.' Whichever interpretation one favours, both poems deliver a message about the need for firm self-control.

A second pair of parallels provides another link between these same two poems. The lines occur at *Exeter Maxims A* 35 and *The Seafarer* 106, respectively:

> Dol biþ sē þe his dryhten nāt—   tō þæs oft cymeð dēað unþinged.
>
> (A fool is he who knows not his Lord; to such a one death often comes unappointed.)
>
> Dol biþ sē þe him his dryhten ne ondrǣdeþ—   cymeð him sē dēað unþinged.
>
> (A fool is he who fears not his Lord; death often comes to him unappointed.)

The theme of *timor domini*, one of the hallmarks of Benedictine thought, is reiterated here with specific reference to the unpredictable nature of human mortality.

A third pair of parallels links the first two of the three parts of *Exeter Maxims* to one another. The repeated phrasing is restricted to the *b*-verse, while the *a*-verse introduces two variations on the theme that a woman's behavioural indiscretions can cause tongues to wag. The first instance is at *Exeter Maxims A* 63, the second at *Exeter Maxims B* 100:

---

87   For discussion see Muir 2: 556 (his note on *Exeter Maxims A* 50a) and Muir 2: 502 (his note on *Juliana* 647–52).

88   Cf. Bjork, *OE Shorter Poems*, p. 69: 'One must steer with a strong mind.'

> Wīdgongel wīf word gespringeð— oft hȳ mon wommum bilihð.
>
> (A roving woman invites gossip; people often blacken her character.)
>
> Wīf sceal wiþ wer wǣre gehealdan. Oft hī mon wommum belihð.
>
> (A wife must keep faith with her husband. People often blacken her character.)

The three pairs of verbal parallels just cited are most likely to result not from 'tradition' but rather from direct textual influence. There are several ways of accounting for them. One possibility is that they result from the shaping work of persons who had exemplars of these poems right at hand.[89] Another is that they are the work of a single poet: someone who liked to vary his phrasing to a greater or lesser extent, or sometimes not at all, while composing works of a similar kind. A third possibility is that different craft-poets working within the same textual community, or perhaps within related communities, were aware of one another's work and chose to imitate it on occasion. Given our present state of knowledge, I see no way to choose between these alternatives. I find it tempting to surmise, however, that the author of *Exeter Maxims C*—evidently an apprentice poet rather than a master—had *Exeter Maxims A* before him at some point and answered the call, at the start of that poem, to respond to this body of gnomic verse with more verse of the same kind. While this is no more than a guess in the dark, such a possibility is worth entertaining as a way of stimulating thought about the Anthology's interactive qualities.[90]

A loose but distinct progression can be seen, then, in the 'wisdom' sequence that runs through the central folios of the Exeter Anthology. Dignified reflections set in a heroic world of the imagination (as in *The Wanderer*) are followed by more humble comments pertaining to life on earth as the great mass of people experience it (as in *Exeter Maxims* and, as well, in *The Fortunes of Mortals*, with its catalogues of deaths and talents). The progression takes us from 'What has become of the steed? ... What has become of the treasure-giver?' to 'Every man needs food; meals should arrive on time.'[91]

---

89 O'Camb (2011) favours this scenario.
90 Emily Thornbury (2014a: 101) has likewise entertained the possibility that both *Exeter Maxims B* and *Exeter Maxims C* represent responses, on the part of the scribe, to the challenge issued to the reader at the start of *Exeter Maxims A* to devise more aphorisms of the same kind.
91 'Hwǣr cwōm mearg? ... Hwǣr cwōm maþþum-gyfa?' (*The Wanderer* 92); 'Mūþa gehwylc mete þearf—mǣl sceolon tīdum gongan' (*Exeter Maxims B* 54).

In a shift of tone to a higher register, directly after *Exeter Maxims* come two poems that identify verse itself as a fit vehicle for both wisdom and worship. The first of these is *The Wonder of Creation*, a dramatic monologue set in the voice of a *wōð-bora* 'inspired speaker'.[92] As someone who speaks as both poet and prophet, this persona can fittingly be called the Seer: someone whose vision is so unclouded that he freely celebrates the Deity as creator of the universe and all of its marvels, including the sun in its majesty, day and night, the sky's magnificent canopy, land and sea, and the rivers and streams of the earth.

Much of this poem (at lines 57–81) consists of an extended hymn to the sun, seen as the brightest of the celestial bodies and hence the one that most closely resembles its Maker. As Alvin A. Lee points out, writing of this passage in particular, 'Clearly the poet is not describing the world of actual human experience ... but rather the ideal world whose lasting form is in heaven and to which all human endeavor ideally turns' (1972: 135). Hovering in the background of this poem are Jesus' words in the Gospel of John: 'Ego sum lux mundi; qui sequitur me non ambulat in tenebris sed habebit lucem vitae' ('I am the light of the world; he that followeth me walketh not in darkness but shall have the light of life').[93] While magnifying the Lord as the light that illumines all light, *The Wonder of Creation* at the same time identifies human beings as creatures of reason who are capable of gaining salvation by meditating on nature's divine order.

Significantly, the speaker of this poem calls upon his audience to 'harken to this war-song' ('gehȳr nū þis here-spel', 37a). This verse is easily misunderstood, for the compound noun *here-spel* 'war-song', unique to this passage, is indeed a surprising term to use with reference to contemplation of the divine nature of the universe. Where is there warfare here? When the word is taken in a metaphorical sense that is central to the Exeter Anthology as a whole, however, its meaning is clear enough. The poem is a call to arms for every *miles Christi* 'warrior of Christ' to make use of Pauline weapons of faith and righteousness in the very medium of exultant verse in which this song is composed. The pen itself, from this perspective, is a weapon in the hand of a zealous Christian scribe and poet. The same metaphor is deployed in Riddle 51, whose solution is 'quill pen'. As Dieter Bitterli has remarked, the pen that is the speaker of this riddle is presented as a 'struggling warrior' (*winnende wiga*, 6a). The act of writing thus takes on the aspect of an act of spiritual warfare in a figure of speech that has been traced back to Cassiodorus, who

---

92 While Muir and others adopt the title *The Order of the World* for this poem, I follow Huppé 1970 and Stanley 2012 in preferring *The Wonder of Creation*.
93 John 8:12; Kinney, *New Testament*, pp. 524–25.

spoke of the role of the scribe as being 'to fight with pen and ink against the unlawful snares of the devil'.[94] Aldhelm drew on the same metaphor in his verse treatise *De virginitate* in lines where he likens himself to a warrior who has donned the helmet of verse and a breastplate of prose. Speaking of the whole category of such authors, Aldhelm adds: 'May a sword arm his right hand as a shield arms his left.'[95] *The Wonder of Creation* plays on this same metaphor. Bernard Huppé was therefore justified in taking *here-spel* in this passage as denoting 'military tale' or 'tale of war', despite the coolness with which his interpretation has been greeted by even the best authorities.[96] That a martial metaphor is deployed here is confirmed by a neighbouring allusion to the angels as 'the greatest of hosts' (*herga mæst*, 91b), with an echo of that same noun *here* and its military associations.

Robert DiNapoli has characterized *The Wonder of Creation* as 'the manifesto for a school of poetry, esoteric and visionary, whose very existence ... has hitherto received scant notice'.[97] This seems an apt assessment. The terms 'esoteric and visionary' that are rightly used with reference to *The Wonder of Creation* apply with nearly equal force, however, to such other poems in the Anthology as *Advent Lyrics*, *The Holy Death of Saint Guthlac* and *The Phoenix*, each of which, too, treats religious themes in a manner that is at times so elevated as to verge on the sublime. The equation of life with light that is made explicit in *The Wonder of Creation*, particularly through reference to the Lord 'þe ūs þis līf gescōp, ond þis lēohte beorht' ('who created this life for us, and this brightness of light', 59), finds cogent expression in these other poems as well, as in the hymn to Earendel featured in *Advent Lyric 5*, in the account of the 'heavenly radiance ... brighter than the sun' that ascends to the roof of the skies from the house where Guthlac has given up his spirit, and the paean

---

94 Cassiodorus, *Institutiones* 1.30.1, as cited by Bitterli (2009: 149). As Michelle Brown (2011: 52) likewise points out, by speaking of each word penned as 'a wound on Satan's body', Cassiodorus ascribed to the monastic writer the role of *miles Christi*.
95 Lapidge and Rosier 1985: 166.
96 Huppé 1970: 40; and see the *DOE*, s.v. *here-spell*. The dictionary entry for this word reads as follows: 'laudatory speech, eulogy, panegyric; glorious discourse; the first element of the word has been less plausibly associated with *here* "military", in support of an interpretation "military tale, tale of war; adventurous song"'. Despite this caution on the part of the dictionary's editors, a look at the long list of other *here-* compounds attested in Old English encourages one's confidence that the meaning 'military' does indeed apply here. Among these compounds are *here-beacen* 'battle-signal', *here-broga* 'fear of war', *here-byme* 'battle-trumpet', *here-byrne* 'battle-corselet', *here-cirm* 'battle-cry' and *here-cumbol* 'battle standard'—and this only takes us as far in the list of *here-* compounds as the letter C.
97 DiNapoli 1998: 97; cf. O'Camb 2014: 411, as cited in Chapter 1 above, n. 4. Similarly, Jacob Riyeff analyses *The Wonder of Creation* as 'a means of access to contemplative vision so central to the religious life of early medieval Christianity' (2015: 20).

to the sun, the celestial consort of the phoenix, that is a prominent feature of *The Phoenix*.[98] If *The Wonder of Creation* is rightly approached as a manifesto for a new kind of religious poetry composed in a heightened register in the vernacular, then other Exeter Anthology poems respond to this same call.

As if in a different response to this call, the poem that follows *The Wonder of Creation*, the one known rather colourlessly as *The Rhyming Poem*, stands out for its elevated register as well as its theme of conversion. This poem too repays close attention despite the scorn that was once fashionable to heap on its boldly experimental 'non-Germanic' style. The speaker of this monologue, a persona whom I will call the Convert, tells first of all of the life of wealth and ease he once enjoyed as a man of the highest rank in society; for, as we are told, he was once a chieftain or king in possession of all the benefits of nobility including horses, a ship and a retinue of men-at-arms. In his old age, however, he has chosen to adopt the austere life of a religious person.

In the first part of his monologue, the Convert tells of the delights of his previous opulent life in the hall, where music and song were a memorable source of joy. Rather than castigating its vanities, he looks back on this period of his life as a happy one:

> Scealcas wæron scearpe, scyl wæs hearpe,
> hlude hlynede, hleoþor dynede,
> sweglrad swinsade ...
>
> (Keen-hearted were the hall-thegns, clear was the harp; loudly it resounded, sounds of merriment were heard, the music sounded out delightfully ...)[99]

To think of such images as these as anomalous in a book that is of an essentially religious character would be a mistake, for the pleasures of which the Convert speaks are in no way indecorous. Indeed, the Scriptures make frequent mention of the joys of music and song in a communal setting, a prime example being the psalms—the songs of King David—with their allusions to the music not just of the harp but also the lute, the lyre, the tambourine and the trumpet. In the Augustinian and Boethian perspectives that permeate the Exeter Anthology, the appeal of such joys is not denied. As for poetry and music, they function 'as *specula* reflecting the universal order'.[100] The problem from an early medieval Christian standpoint lies in

---

98 *Advent Lyric 5*, 104–18; *The Holy Death of Saint Guthlac* 490b–96a [1308b–14a]; *The Phoenix* 106–19.
99 *The Rhyming Poem* 27–29; Muir 1: 263.
100 Bjork 1985: 93–94, with reference to Augustine's *De musica* and Boethius's *De institutione musica*.

the transitory nature of worldly delight. The Convert does not despise the privileged life he has led; it is just that he realizes that the joys of earth are fleeting, and now he desires lasting ones.

Moreover, the pleasures of song and music had a key role not just in royal courts but also in the observances of religious communities. This was particularly so when the psalms were sung as part of the liturgy of festive occasions. The passage just quoted from *The Rhyming Poem* calls to mind the corresponding passage in *God's Gifts to Humankind* where mention is made of inspired singers and skilled harpists.[101] As any reader of *The Rhyming Poem* should know, convivial scenes of the kind that the Convert calls to mind have long had their counterparts in churches, where joy can be enhanced by music and by a kind of spiritual inebriation.

Only in the second half of *The Rhyming Poem* does the speaker reveal that he is now an aged man whose thoughts have turned towards eternity. He calls to mind the grim image of a grave where his corpse will be food for worms (lines 75–79), a theme that finds sustained expression in the Anthology just three folios later in *The Soul's Address to the Body*. Although the Convert's existential change from a life of ease to one of austerities may remind one of the Wanderer's exile from his former happiness, there is a difference in the social status of those two men. While the Wanderer represents the *hād* of the retainer, the Convert represents that of the lord or king. Also distinguishing these two speakers are matters of fate and volition. While the Wanderer is driven from society by implacable circumstance, the Convert's exile is self-chosen. The relationship of these two poems is thus complementary. *The Rhyming Poem* identifies the reasons why a person of deep understanding might want to embrace the very austerities that the Wanderer is capable of viewing only as afflictions.

I shall defer to Chapter 5 a discussion of the esoteric diction and unparalleled verse form that add formal lustre to *The Rhyming Poem*, thereby promoting its devotional message though at some cost to its intelligibility at the level of word and phrase. Worth emphasis here is the poem's relation to its prospective audience. To the extent that the Exeter Anthology was meant to speak to the condition of persons of high rank who 'opted out' of their worldly responsibilities so as to take on a cloistered life, then *The Rhyming Poem* would have reinforced the wisdom of their choice.[102] By extension, the poem speaks to the condition of anyone contemplating *ta eschata*, or 'final things'.

---

101 I quote the text of this passage (lines 35b–36a, 49–50) in Chapter 1 above, in the section headed 'Mastering the craft of vernacular verse as a vehicle for conversion'.
102 Karl P. Wentersdorf (1985) offers a reading of this poem with attention to a number of historical Anglo-Saxon rulers who retired to a monastery, citing in this connection Æthelred of Mercia, Cenred, Offa of Wessex, Ceolwulf, and Æthelwulf of Wessex.

The voice of the sage: *A Father's Precepts* and related poems

When referring to certain poems of the Exeter Anthology as pertaining to the category of 'wisdom literature', I have used a blanket term that is of some advantage because of the number of unruly objects it can cover. Use of the term 'wisdom' in this loose manner, however, can encourage the false supposition that wisdom resembles a heirloom that is handed down from one generation to the next. With their allusions to participatory exchange between an imagined reader and an imagined speaker, however, the poems of the Exeter Anthology often present wisdom as something to be won in the course of a dialogic quest. Moreover, a broadly capacious use of the term 'wisdom literature' with reference to both the ancient world and the medieval era runs the risk of effacing the purpose of acquiring wisdom in the tenth-century ecclesiastical milieu in which the volume was evidently produced.[103] In such circles, the pursuit of wisdom was undertaken along lines established by Scripture, scriptural commentaries and the Rule of Saint Benedict, and was synonymous with the quest for salvation. A monk's or nun's quest for enlightenment during the early Middle Ages was not undertaken as an autonomous enterprise, but rather in conjunction with the practice of the *opus dei* and a life lived *in imitatione Christi*; that is, in imitation of the life of Christ, conceived of as the source of all wisdom.[104]

There is another potential drawback to the use of the term 'wisdom literature' without close attention to its application to the poems of the Exeter Anthology. This is that it can obscure the presence of a particular thread that runs through the Anthology, lending the contents of that book a special value in the monastic context in which it was evidently meant to be read. This thread features not wisdom in the abstract, but rather the idealized figure of the sage. By this term I mean to denote a speaker who has gained such insight into the world, whether through inspiration or reflection, as to have the authority to speak truth of an inspirational kind. Models for such speakers were readily available to the Anglo-Saxons through those books of the Bible that feature the voices of Job, David the psalmist, Ecclesiastes,

---

103 To cite one example: while Elaine Tuttle Hansen (1988) pays rewarding attention to the Near Eastern antecedents of Old English wisdom literature, she does so at the cost of somewhat neglecting a large body of early medieval Christian literature that was readily available to the Anglo-Saxons.

104 James W. Earl develops the notion of *imitatio Christi* as the fundamental concept around which the Christian life is organized, taking that term as denoting 'the ordering of the life of the individual in harmony with the typological relations which define the movement of history from beginning to end' (1975: 17). The lives of the saints are the supreme examples of this aspiration; the life of any cloistered person was ordered along compatible lines.

Solomon the son of David, Isaiah, Jeremiah, Ezekiel and other revered and authoritative figures. The philosopher-poet Boethius provided Anglo-Saxons with a model of a comparable kind drawn from the early Christian era. The choice of a monastic vocation in the days of Dunstan and Æthelwold would have offered not just the prospect of ultimate salvation, but also unparalleled opportunities here and now to pursue the quest for learning and wisdom that had the potential of leading to a sage-like status on earth.

When we first hear the voice of a sage in the Exeter Anthology, it is in that part of *The Ascension* where Cynewulf's account of Christ's redemption of humankind is amplified through allusions to four ancient seers. The first of these is Job, figured as a visionary prophet who tells of having seen his soul ascend in the form of a bird (at lines 194 [633] and following). This image prepares the way for the avian imagery of *The Phoenix*, where Job is introduced again, as we will shortly see. The second sage to be introduced in *The Ascension* is an unnamed *witga* 'visionary' who is perhaps best taken to be a projection of David the psalmist (at 211b [650b] and following). The third is an unnamed *witga* who has the character of an ancient stargazer or astronomer (at 252b [691b] and following). The fourth is Solomon, the son of David, presented as the singer and prophet who proclaimed Christ's 'leaps'. These are then expounded to the reader (at 273 [712] and following). Oliver J.H. Grosz has demonstrated the importance of all four of these passages in advancing Cynewulf's announced programme of revealing, through the gift of visionary poetry, the fundamental spiritual mysteries (*gǣst-gerȳne*, 1b [440b]) of the Christian faith.[105]

Cynewulf's reference to Job as visionary prophet is taken up in that part of *The Phoenix* (at lines 552–69) where the narrator of that poem paraphrases certain verses of Job 29 in order to confirm the eschatological significance of the phoenix.[106] As an ambassador of God (*Godes spel-boda*, 571b) as well as in his character as a prefiguration of Christ and an exemplar to all humanity because of his ability to endure pain and suffering. Job is characterized here as a *frōd guma* 'old and wise man' (570a). Endowed with deep wisdom (*glēaw-mōd*, 571a), he gave voice to spiritual mysteries in former days through the medium of song (he *gieddade* 'gave voice to inspired words', 571a). One chief source of Job's wisdom, as we are told in lines that glance back to the corresponding passage in *The Ascension*, is that he was granted a vision of his soul arising from his grave after his death 'just like the phoenix' ('swā sē fugel fenix', 558a).

---

105 Grosz 1996, at 104–07 in particular.
106 Bjork (2005) analyses the place of Job in an exegetical discourse that owed much to Gregory the Great and was carried on by Ælfric.

Language much like that used to characterize Job in *The Phoenix* is introduced towards the end of *The Wanderer* with reference to the unnamed sage (*glēaw hæle* or 'wise man', 73a) who, we are told, will know how appalling it will be (*hū gæstlīc bið*, 73b) at an unspecified future time when the whole world will lie waste, in accord with Christian teachings about the approach of Doomsday. This sage's rhetorically heightened speech (at 92–110) takes the form first of all of a sequence of questions that make arresting use of the figure of anaphora in the service of the *ubi sunt* trope: 'Hwǣr cwōm ... hwǣr cwōm ... hwǣr cwōm ... hwǣr cwōm ... hwǣr sindon'? These rhetorical questions are followed by threefold repetition of the exclamation *Ēalā!* In a voice that is scarcely to be distinguished from the Wanderer's own, the unnamed sage who is ascribed these lines then speaks of the transience of all earthly things, again making striking use of anaphora in a manner that confirms his authority:

> 'Her bið feoh læne; her bið freond læne;
> her bið mon læne; her bið mæg læne—
> eal þis eorþan gesteal   idel weorþeð.'

> ('Here wealth is fleeting; here friends are fleeting; here retainers are fleeting; here kinsfolk are fleeting; this whole framework of earth is turning to nothingness.')[107]

By the end of the poem, having expressed this stark wisdom through the voice of an imagined future seer, the Wanderer too is revealed to be *snottor on mōde* ('wise in spirit', 111a), having attained this state through both personal suffering and philosophical reflection.

Just two folios later, at the start of *A Father's Precepts*, we are introduced to another sage, a man who is identified as *mōd-snottor* 'wise in mind' (2a), *þonc-snottor* 'sharp in intellect' (21b), and, repeated three times, *frōd* 'wise by virtue of experience' (1a, 15b, 53a). As an embodiment of wisdom that transcends the paternal, he is even called an *eald ūð-wita* 'an aged philosopher' (66a), an epithet that connotes exceptional learning. His precepts can be interpreted either literally as being offered by a father to his natural son or, by allegorical extension, as the words of an abbot—OE *abbod*, a word derived from Greek and Syriac *abba* 'father'—to an oblate who is the abbot's spiritual son; for as Thomas Symons remarks, the abbot of an Anglo-Saxon monastery 'held the place of Christ and was the *pater spiritualis* of his monks' (1953: xxx). The Father concludes his address with moral precepts designed to help the younger man live to a happy old age:

---

107 *The Wanderer* 108–10; Muir 1: 218.

> Hæle sceal wisfæst
> ond gemetlice,   modes snottor,
> gleaw in gehygdum,   georn wisdomes,
> swa he wið ælda mæg   eades hleotan.

(A man must be firm in wisdom and temperate in demeanour, wise in spirit, sagacious in his thoughts, keen on acquiring wisdom, so that he can attain a state of blessedness in his old age.)[108]

The Father's precepts are thus not just prescriptive in a moral sense; their purpose is not just to enable others to lead a virtuous life. In addition to this, his words suggest that by observing what in essence are the tenets of the Rule of Saint Benedict, a young man can mature into an embodiment of mature wisdom.

Of interest in this regard is a parallel in the visual arts. As need not be laboured, Saint Benedict was revered in late Anglo-Saxon England as the father of Western monasticism. Correspondingly, a full-page illustration in the Eadui Psalter—the same one that was discussed earlier with regard to the theme of *timor dei*—depicts an enthroned Saint Benedict with a halo-like headband on which is written PATER MONACHORUM ET DUX ('father of monks, and their head'). Such a characterization of Benedict as *pater spiritualis* coincides with his own words at the very start of the Prologue to his Rule in a passage that begins as follows:

> Obsculta, o fili, praecepta magistri et inclina aurem cordis tui et admonitionem pii patris libenter excipe et efficaciter comple ...
>
> (Listen carefully, my son, to the teachings of a master and incline the ear of your heart. Gladly accept and effectively fulfil the admonition of a loving father ...)[109]

In that same illustration, the monks of Canterbury are shown presenting the enthroned Benedict with a book on which are inscribed the first five words of the passage just quoted: 'Obsculta, o fili, praecepta magistri.' The Exeter Anthology, the Rule of Saint Benedict and the iconography of reformed monasticism in England thus take on the appearance of three aspects of a single programme of religious revival.

Another representation of the idealized figure of the sage is introduced in *Vainglory*, the poem that follows two folios after *A Father's Precepts* and directly after *The Seafarer*. As Catharine A. Regan (1970) has pointed out,

---

108 *A Father's Precepts* 86b–89; Muir 1: 228.
109 Venarde, *Rule of Benedict*, pp. 2–3.

Vainglory is a sustained versified exposition of patristic writings on the state and actions of the mind or soul, with close attention to the psychology of sin. The poem takes the form of a set of wise observations that, as we are told, were communicated at some prior time to the poem's speaker. Taking up a suggestion made by Jane Roberts (2008), I will call this speaker 'the Man of Wisdom'. The poet refers to the prior source of the speaker's wisdom, in turn, as a *frōd wita* 'a man wise with the wisdom of experience' (1a), a *snottor ār* 'a wise messenger' (2a) and, in a phrase that echoes an Old English term that is used to introduce the philosopher Boethius, a *beorn bōca glēaw* 'a man wise through book learning' (4a).[110] In a later passage of *Vainglory*, this same person of a prior time is called a *witega* 'prophet' (81b), although no single biblical prophet has been identified as the poet's model. By telling of the archetypal instance of rebellion in heaven that came about through Lucifer's *ofer-hygd* 'excessive pride' (58b), this prophet of former days reinforces the tenor of the didactic address voiced by the Man of Wisdom, and the latter's address then carries on uninterrupted to the poem's end.

By calling attention to two antithetical types of human being, the humble and the arrogant, the Man of Wisdom gives voice to teachings much like those expressed in *A Father's Precepts*. The humble man lives in favour as *Godes āgen bearn* 'God's own son' (*Vainglory* 6b, a verse repeated verbatim at 80b). The most animated part of the speaker's discourse, however, concerns the arrogant man: the one who, significantly, is the 'weaker' one (*þone wācran*, 7b), for he lacks the courage of the *miles Christi*. This is the vainglorious, drunken carouser whose violent temperament shows him to be a son of the devil in human form ('fēondes bearn/flǣsce bifongen', 47b–48a). The vainglorious man is a city-dweller, hence a spiritual descendant of Cain, the first founder of cities.[111] In the poet's chief source, indeed, the man of arrogant disposition is called a citizen of Babylon.[112] When we are told that the carouser dwells among 'proud war-smiths' (*wlonce wīg-smiþas*, 14a) who sit at the feast 'in wine-citadels' (*wīn-burgum in*, 14b), an alert reader will be aware of two examples of thematically significant paronomasia, the first on *wīg* 'warfare'

---

110 'Hē wæs for weorulde wīs, weorð-mynða georn,/beorn bōca glēaw; Bōītius/sē hæle hatte' ('He was wise in respect of the world, eager for honours, a man wise through book learning: Boethius was his name'). Metre 1 of *The Old English Boethius*, lines 51–53a; Irvine and Godden 2012: 8, my translation.
111 In *The City of God* 15:1 (trans. Bettenson 2003: 596), Augustine calls attention to Cain as the founder of earthly cities, as in Genesis 4:17.
112 Joseph B. Trahern (1975) has identified the chief source of *Vainglory* as Sermon 233 by Caesarius of Arles. Caesarius draws a sharp contrast between the two ancient cities of Jerusalem and Babylon, taking them as types of the City of God and the City of Man, respectively, the one built by Christ on humility, the other built by the devil on pride.

and the other on *wīn* 'wine'. The first of these nouns, *wīg*, is a variant spelling (or homophone) of *wīh* or *weoh*, a word denoting 'pagan shrine' or 'idol'. The second, *wīn*, involves a play on *wynn*, denoting 'joy'. The morally corrupt and potentially idolatrous *wīn-burh* of 14b is thus the antithesis of the land of the blessed that later in this same poem is called *wuldres wyn-lond* 'a joyful land of glory' (65a).[113] While the 'humble man' of *Vainglory* has evidently absorbed the wisdom expressed in the preceding poem *A Father's Precepts*, the carouser has not. The humble person can therefore expect to find *wuldres drēam* 'the joy of salvation' (72b) at the end of his life, while, by the law of antithesis that governs homiletic discourse, the carouser will meet with eternal torment.

A reader of the Exeter Anthology who turns back just one folio at this point so as to reread *The Seafarer* in the light of these other poems will discern here too the voice of a sage. Speaking as a man grown wise through experience, the Seafarer has embraced a life of physical austerities as a means of mortifying the flesh. Aware of the moral order of God's universe, he avoids the sensual pleasures associated with a comfortable life in town (12b–13, 27–29a, 55b–56a). Like the Wanderer but from a superior vantage point, he has meditated deeply on the vanity of earthly things. In the entire last half of his monologue (lines 58–124) he speaks with the authority of a prophet, uttering truths about fundamental aspects of the human condition. He thus fulfils his initial pledge to utter a *sōð-gied* or 'true song' rather than an idle one (1b). His observations touch on the inevitability of death, the fleeting nature of earthly glory, the emptiness of sensual pleasures, and the need for steadfast vigilance in the face of the devil's machinations. Towards the end of his monologue, taking on a role like that of the wise Father in *A Father's Precepts* or the Man of Wisdom in *Vainglory*, the Seafarer exhorts the members of his audience to fear the Lord, to practise humility, to restrain their violent impulses and to fix their minds on their true home in heaven. Although his monologue has puzzled critics who have sought to understand it in isolation from the rest of the Anthology, often with reference to modern secular perspectives, it comes into sharp focus when received as the wisdom of yet another sage, this one a dedicated *peregrinus*.

The Rhyming Poem, too, features the direct address of a wise man or sage. Although difficult to construe on the verbal level and hence relatively neglected in the critical literature, this poem forms a fitting companion to neighbouring poems that critics have greatly esteemed, *The Wanderer* in particular. While the Wanderer speaks as a former member of a *gedryht*

---

113 Bernard Huppé (1970: 12–14) comments on these instances of paronomasia while calling attention to additional verbal and thematic correspondences between *Vainglory* and other Old English poems.

'warrior band' who, in his exiled state, is uncertain where to turn for solace, the Convert speaks as a former chieftain or king who is aware of his need for salvation and who looks to Christ for comfort. Each of these monologues, as well as that of the Seafarer, contributes to a single discourse on the subject of transience and conversion.

The figure of the sage can be traced in yet one more poem of the 'wisdom' series. This is *The Wonder of Creation*, the poem that follows directly after *Exeter Maxims*. This poem too is best approached not as a disembodied example of wisdom literature, but rather as the speech of a distinct persona, one whom I have called the Seer, capitalizing that name so as to distinguish this speaker from other authoritative ones introduced elsewhere in the Anthology. The Seer of *The Wonder of Creation* is a spokesman for the wisdom of the psalmist: 'Tuus est dies, et tua est nox; tu fabricatus es auroram et solem. Tu fecesti omnes terminos terrae; aestatem et ver tu plasmasti ea.'[114] As a poet, a natural scientist, an astronomer, a philosopher and a moral teacher, the Seer is an exotic figure meant to provoke fascination. He introduces himself as a 'stranger' (*fremde monnan*, 1b) and as someone who, like Widsith, is 'much travelled' (*fela-geongne*, 3a). Importantly, he is also a *wīs wōð-bora* (2a)—that is, a 'wise poet or prophet'. Unlike Widsith, he therefore has access to the deep mysteries of Creation. Like the semi-animated speaker of *Exeter Maxims*, he urges his imagined listener to interact with him as an informed interlocutor. Like the wise Father of *A Father's Precepts*, he exhorts that same listener to internalize his wisdom: 'Leorna þās lāre!' ('Take this lore to heart!', 23a). The Seer's address encapsulates an argument that is implicit in the rest of the Anthology from start to finish: namely, that through contemplation of the Incarnation and the marvels of God's universe, all humanity should be filled with wonder while aspiring to a state of permanent bliss.

In this way the figure of the sage is one of several threads running through the pages of the Exeter Anthology, giving forceful expression to its leading themes while lending the volume greater coherence than is generally acknowledged. The thread recurs in the poems set in the voices of the Wanderer, the Seafarer, the Father of *A Father's Precepts*, the Man of Wisdom who is the main speaker in *Vainglory*, the Convert who gives voice to *The Rhyming Poem*, and the Seer who is the inspired speaker of *The Wonder of Creation*. Through the device of inset speech, the same thread is introduced via the prophets or figures of prophetic wisdom whose voices are heard in various parts of *The Ascension*, *The Phoenix* and *The Wanderer*, and in that

---

114 Psalm 73:16–17: 'Thine is the day, and thine is the night; thou hast made the morning light and the sun. Thou hast made all the borders of the earth; the summer and the spring were formed by thee.' Edgar, *Poetical Books*, pp. 346–47; cf. O'Neill 2016: 280–81.

passage of *Vainglory* where an unnamed prophet of earlier times tells of the fall of the rebellious angels as a warning against pride. The inset passages featuring inspired speakers in these four last-named poems reinforce points of Christian doctrine in much the same way as quotations culled from respected authorities add to the persuasiveness of any claim.

Voices from the Germanic past: *Widsith* and related poems

A turn towards verse and verse-making as the subject of the poetry of the Exeter Anthology is evident in two poems included in the second half of the codex, *Widsith* (at fols 84v–87r) and *Deor* (at fols 100r–v). Although separated by twelve folios containing other materials, these two dramatic monologues serve as a kind of diptych, for each is set in the voice of an imagined bard of the Heroic Age of the Germanic peoples.

The two poems are linked by principles of contrast as well as similarity. While the itinerant singer Widsith—the Scop, as I shall call him—reels off the names of the great kings of olden days and tells of their wealth and fame, the more melancholic Deor—the Court Poet, as I shall call him so as to distinguish him from the itinerant Widsith—alludes to the legendary past with cryptic brevity while lamenting the turn of fate that has bereft him of his former position. Correspondingly, while the Scop's cup of praise is overflowing, the Court Poet makes laconic allusions to a world of crimes and misery that can only with great latitude be called 'heroic'.

The similarities between these two poems and their respective personae calls to mind such other Exeter Anthology non-identical twins as *The Ascension* and *Christ in Judgement*, the two hagiographic poems *The Life of Saint Guthlac* and *The Passion of Saint Juliana*, and the two meditative monologues *The Wanderer* and *The Seafarer*. Certain thematic pairings in the riddle collection might also be called to mind, for example Riddle 76 'oyster' and Riddle 77 'crab', which form a duo;[115] or Riddle 41 'water' and Riddle 50 'fire'; or Riddle 73 (solved in Old English as *æsc*, denoting 'ash tree' or 'ash-wood spear') and Riddle 74 (solved in Old English as *āc*, denoting 'oak tree' with the implication of 'oak-wood boat'). Much like these pairings is the juxtaposition of Riddle 60, which features a speaking reed that is also a pen, and *The Husband's Message*, with its speaking wooden object inscribed with runes. A universal feature of order—the pairing of items via principles of similarity and antithesis, as with the Old Testament and the New—is thus exploited in the organization of

---

115 Mercedes Salvador Bello (2004, 2015: 402–13) calls attention to this riddle pair as one of a number of such duos featured in the Anthology.

the Exeter Anthology. Pairing, however, is just one of the many principles by which like and unlike elements are linked both within the riddle collection and in the Exeter Anthology as a whole. In this regard the Anthology calls to mind Aldhelm's *Enigmata*, a work that, in the view of Michael Lapidge, depicts a universe that 'is characterized by subtle correspondences and relationships' rather than by simple binarisms;[116] for the parts of the universe itself, in the medieval Christian view, are knit together by a complex web of similitudes.

The main part of *Widsith* consists of the Scop's recitation of the names of a number of rulers and peoples of recorded history with passing comments on certain of them. While some of these historical figures are well known, others are so obscure as to make one wonder if they are the poet's invention.[117] In any event, what Hugh Magennis has aptly termed this poet's 'virtuoso display of arcane knowledge' (2010: 92) would have been of interest to tenth-century readers for its encyclopedic scope. The speaker's monologue has the effect of compressing northern and Mediterranean history into a single vision of the past, doing so in a manner that is likely to have appealed to persons of West Saxon ethnicity or sympathies during the tenth-century period of English nation-building.[118] Towards the end of his monologue, the Scop gives a pseudo-historical account of his having been offered lavish hospitality by the fourth-century Gothic king Eormanric (known to Latin chroniclers as Ermanaricus, d.376), thereby evoking the splendour of a legendary Age of Gold.

In pointed contrast, *Deor* uses the same device of a fictive first-person narrator to allude not to the magnificence of the Heroic Age, but rather to a series of misfortunes associated with famous figures of Germanic antiquity. One king who receives special mention is Theodoric the Ostrogoth, the early sixth-century ruler of northern Italy.[119] Best known today as the killer of

---

116 Lapidge and Rosier 1995: 65.
117 Joyce Hill (1984) points out the evident novelty of some of these names, arguing on this basis that *Widsith* as we have it could not be much older than the manuscript in which it is preserved, even if certain of its elements are archaic.
118 See Niles 1999b. On the dating of *Widsith* (in the form that we have it) to the tenth century or thereabouts as opposed to the much earlier date that was formerly attributed to it, see also Langenfelt 1959. Not all specialists concur with this revisionist approach to the dating of *Widsith*; see in particular Neidorf 2013, arguing on the basis of metre and onomastics for a date of composition early in the Anglo-Saxon period. Eric Weiskott in turn disputes Neidorf's arguments, maintaining that *Widsith* 'is not an ancient poem from a pan-Germanic distant past, but an encyclopedic Old English poem that turns inherited vocabulary to its own rhetorical purposes' (2015: 143).
119 I adopt the consensus view that the 'Þēodric' mentioned in line 18 is the same man as the historical king Theodoric the Great (d.526). Klinck (1992: 164–65) reviews scholarly opinions on this point.

his chief rival, Odoacer, and the sponsor of buildings of exceptional beauty in his capital city of Ravenna, Theodoric was familiar to readers of the Old English versions of Boethius's *De consolatione philosophiae* as the tyrant who imprisoned the philosopher-poet Boethius and put him to death. As an Arian Christian, Theodoric was widely regarded as a heretic.

Another notorious figure mentioned by Deor, as he is by Widsith as well, is the Gothic king Eormanric, viewed here as a cruel tyrant rather than a king of magnificent generosity. He figures in this poem as a *grim cyning* ('fierce king', 23b) known for his *wylfenne geþoht* 'she-wolf's disposition' (22a). More of his story may be implied than is stated outright, for in Old Norse tradition the great king Jǫrmunrekr (OE Eormanric) earned undying notoriety by having horses trample to death his young bride Svanhildr (OE Sunilda) as punishment for her supposed infidelity.

These two related poems thus offer readers of the Exeter Anthology two different perspectives on the Germanic past. While the Scop's evocation of that era is ostensibly celebratory, the Court Poet's is scarcely so.[120] Towards the end of *Deor*, moreover, the speaker expresses the commonplace idea that good fortune, just like bad, is the gift of the Lord:

> Mæg þonne geþencan   þæt geond þas woruld
> witig dryhten   wendeþ geneahhe,
> eorle monegum   are gesceawað
> wislicne blæd,   sumum weana dæl.

> (He [the dejected one] can then keep in mind that throughout the world, the wise Lord frequently alters his disposition. To many a man he shows favour, a just reward; to others a heap of sorrows.)[121]

Readers of the Exeter Anthology will recognize this as very nearly the same message of consolation that finds expression in *God's Gifts to Humankind*, a poem written out some twenty folios earlier in the codex:

> Sumum her ofer eorþan   æhta onlihð,
> woruldgestreona;   sum bið wonspedig,
> heardsælig hæle,   biþ hwæþre gleaw
> modes cræfta.

---

120 In *Widsith* too, even though the Scop praises Eormanric's generosity, the narrator to whom the poem's first lines are attributed identifies that same king as a *wrāþ wǣr-loga* 'a cruel troth-breaker' (9a). We are thus invited to see Eormanric from two perspectives, one of them adulatory—this is the Scop's—and the other one sharply critical, as both the Court Poet and the narrator of *Widsith* see him.

121 *Deor* 31–34; Muir 1: 282.

>   (To some here on earth he grants material possessions, worldly treasures; but another man is destitute, down on his luck, even though he is well endowed in intellectual capabilities.)[122]

Taken together, *God's Gifts to Humankind*, *Widsith* and *Deor* illustrate the contrasting conditions of wealth and poverty that are perennial aspects of the human condition. While the Scop exults in the favours he so successfully both grants and receives, the resigned Court Poet recounts a series of misfortunes culminating in his own.

The inclusion of quasi-historical texts of the character of *Widsith* and *Deor* in the Exeter Anthology should occasion no surprise. Texts dealing with human history often figure in early medieval miscellanies, and this volume is no exception. To call these two poems an expression of a 'secular' mentality, however, would distort one's conception of them, for such a characterization of *Widsith* and *Deor*, though familiar enough in the critical literature, mistakes the place of history in the medieval Christian world-view. From an Augustinian perspective, as Bernard Huppé has remarked, 'human history, like natural history, is worth studying, because the history of the world is in itself a symbolic book written by God and to be understood through the Bible' (1959: 21). In particular, the punishment of tyrants through their fall from power was a favourite topos of medieval historiography, which tended to take a God's-eye view of human affairs.

A third poem written out in this part of the Anthology can plausibly be grouped in the category of historical or quasi-historical verse, though this point is subject to debate. This is the enigmatic poem *Wulf and Eadwacer*. This lyric monologue, which begins immediately after *Deor* on folio 100v, is composed in the voice of an unnamed woman who is in an evident state of distress. I shall refer to this persona as the Young Lover, or simply the Lover, so as to distinguish her from the Wife of *The Wife's Lament*, a female persona of a somewhat different type, one who is perhaps best visualized as a somewhat older woman whose sufferings are of a marital kind.

Wulf and Eadwacer is so brief and allusive as to have invited numerous surmises as to the speaker's exact situation. The poem is technically an *enigma*, as early editors of poems of the Exeter Anthology took it to be,[123] in the sense that Isidore of Seville, writing in the early seventh century, defined that type of composition in Book I of his treatise the *Etymologiae*: 'an obscure

---

122 *God's Gifts to Humankind* 30–33a; Muir 1: 221.
123 For example, Frederick Tupper (1910: 1–2) presents *Wulf and Eadwacer* as the first of the riddles. At the same time, he acknowledges that the poem is 'unquestionably a lyrical monologue' (liv).

question that is difficult to solve unless it is explained'.[124] An example cited by Isidore is Judges 14:14: 'Out of the eater came forth food, and out of the strong came forth sweetness.' This is an enigma that the Philistines could never have solved if Samson's wife had not tipped them off. Lacking a native informant of this kind, no reader of the Exeter Anthology is well situated to answer the question 'Who is the Young Lover of *Wulf and Eadwacer*, and what is her exact predicament?' All the same, I will attempt to clarify how this poem fits into the design of the Exeter Anthology while suggesting that it too alludes to a prominent figure of the Heroic Age of the Germanic-speaking peoples.[125]

The Lover longs to be reunited with a man whom she addresses not just by the name 'Wulf', but as *Wulf, mīn Wulf* (13a), passionate phrasing that confirms their intimacy. The dual pronouns that occur later in the poem (*uncerne*, 16b; *uncer*, 19a) can best be taken as referring to this pair of lovers, who are joined (at least on the woman's side) by a consuming passion. As for Wulf's identity, I see him—though only provisionally, for reasons that will become clear—as the person who is referred to at first simply by the pronouns 'he' or 'him' (in line 2, repeated verbatim as line 8). The reference is to someone of male sex who is in grave danger. The drama's topographical setting is sketched in, even if only briefly: Wulf is on an island, surrounded by marshes or fens, while the Lover dwells on a different island (4–5). Bloodthirsty men threaten to kill Wulf—taking that latter identification provisionally, again—if he should fall into their hands (6–7). The epithet *beadu-cafa* (11a), a unique compound noun that can be taken to mean either 'one active in battle' or simply 'a man of the warrior class', is also best construed with reference to Wulf, for it refers to a man with whom the Lover has evidently had intimate sexual relations, as we are told in coded fashion. As for the name 'Wulf', it is most likely a meaningful pseudonym, analogous to 'Mr Fox' in the English folktale of that name, for the words 'wolf' and 'wolf's head' are associated with outlaws in early Germanic tradition.[126]

Whether or not he is legally an outlaw, Wulf is a fugitive whose life is in danger. Correspondingly, he journeys on distant paths (*wīd-lāstum*, 9a), and

---

124 Barney 2006: 63; *The Etymologies of Isidore of Seville*, book 1, chap. 27.
125 For summaries of critical responses to *Wulf and Eadwacer* see Aertsen 1994 and Klinck 1992: 47–49 (introduction), 168–77 (notes), and 372–76 (bibliography), along with the supplementary bibliography included in the 2001 reissue of her book. I depart from Klinck in my understanding of the character of Eadwacer, the identity of the *beadu-cafa* of verse 11a, and certain minor points of interpretation. Lindy Brady (2016) has recently reviewed the state of scholarship on this poem, advancing an argument of her own regarding its basis in an English local legend.
126 See Klinck (1992: 171, her note on verse 4a) with reference to that provision in the *Leges Edwardi Confessoris* that specifies that if captured, an outlaw's head could immediately be struck off like a wolf's.

his visits to the Lover are few and far between (we hear of his *seld-cymas* 'rare visits', 14b). These extended periods of separation have made the Lover ill with longing (13-15), and she recalls Wulf's embraces as having caused her both joy and pain (12). What I take this enigmatic statement to mean, though others have read it differently, is that while she has savoured her trysts with Wulf, she likewise hates the pain that his visits have occasioned because of their inherent danger and her consequent anxieties.

Only late in the poem (at lines 16-17) are two additional characters introduced, each one in what is again an allusive fashion. The first of these is a man with the unusual name 'Eadwacer'. He is in the woman's immediate vicinity, to judge from her question, 'Gehȳrest þū, Ēadwacer?' ('Do you hear, Eadwacer?', 16a). It is natural to infer that this man is in a state of hostility with Wulf and may have been responsible for Wulf's outlawry. If so, then Eadwacer is a figure of some standing in his community, very likely the leader of the 'bloodthirsty men' who will kill Wulf if they find him.

As for the other character newly introduced to the drama towards its end, the speaker refers to him in coded fashion as 'uncerne earmne hwelp' ('our poor whelp', 16b, using the dual form of the personal pronoun). It is natural to see a reference here to a boy child, very likely a love child born to the Lover and Wulf. All that we are told of the 'whelp' is that Wulf is now taking him to the woods. What is implied here is that the child is now old enough for Wulf to take him away with him to share his life as a fugitive.

Turning back now to the poem's beginning, as one normally has to do when reading enigmas, one can see that the male pronouns 'hē' and 'hine' in lines 2 and 7—pronouns that seemed at first to refer to Wulf, in his danger—can be read as referring to the boy, in his even greater vulnerability. The fear that a young mother might feel for the safety of her young child, in these conditions, could well exceed her fear for the safety of a mature man who might well have a long history of taking care of himself.

As with the Exeter Anthology riddles, which tend to reveal their answers only when one reads them through and then circles back again to their start, we are now in a position to understand most of the story that underlies the speaker's anxiety in *Wulf and Eadwacer*. The woman's monologue is imagined to well up not just out of her frustrations in love, but also out of her fear that her young son may be hunted down in a wilderness, slaughtered like a wolf cub, perhaps alongside her beloved Wulf.

Still, who is Eadwacer? Departing from how this text has regularly been received in the critical literature,[127] I offer as a period-specific answer to this

---

127 Magennis summarizes received opinion as follows: 'The most widely accepted interpretation of *Wulf and Eadwacer* is as a poem of love, in which the female speaker expresses

question that Eadwacer is the young woman's *father*.[128] Wulf, in this scenario, is plausibly viewed as the woman's betrothed, most likely through their having exchanged vows in private.[129] Such an inference is supported by the allusion in the poem's very last lines to Christ's words in Matthew 19:6, 'Quod ergo Deus coniunxit homo non separet' ('What therefore God hath joined together let not man put asunder'), with its liturgical echoes pertaining to the Christian sacrament of marriage.[130] A sexual liaison between the Lover and Wulf would not necessarily have been viewed as anomalous or even sinful as long as the couple had pledged their troth.[131] Any children resulting from the couple's sexual union could even have had a claim to legitimacy, although such a claim would have had to be asserted in defiance of the woman's father. This is true unless the father were to undergo a change of heart, of course, as sometimes happens in such scenarios, especially if a worthy heir is involved. The poem's plot is almost hopeless to disentangle, however, so that whatever line of interpretation one favours must remain speculative.

What is at stake in this analysis of *Wulf and Eadwacer*, one may ask? The answer is this. If the poem is interpreted along the lines that I suggest, then in no way does it either lament or celebrate an adulterous relationship, as has often been assumed in the critical literature.[132] There is nothing necessarily anomalous, therefore, about a text like this being included in a dominantly religious collection of verse. No matter what the authors of later medieval romances may have written about love triangles involving such figures as Queen Isolde, her husband King Mark and her lover Tristan, or their later

---

her longing for the absent Wulf ... It is generally accepted that the speaker is, unhappily, with a second man, Eadwacer, her husband, and that she has a child, of whom Eadwacer is understood to be the father. The large majority of critics find this general scenario to be the most likely and the most convincing one, though others have been put forward' (2011: 157).

128 I have been pleased to notice that my suggestion has been anticipated in the critical literature first, very briefly, by Israel Gollancz (1893) and then by P.J. Frankis (1962).

129 In seeing Wulf as, most likely, the woman's banished husband, I follow this aspect of a careful reading of the poem undertaken by Peter S. Baker (1981). I differ from Baker, however, in my understanding of the character and role of Eadwacer.

130 Kinney, *New Testament*, pp. 104–05; see Klinck 1992: 176–77 (her note on line 18).

131 In Anglo-Saxon society 'there were two parts to a marriage: the "wedding", that is, the pledging or betrothal ... and the "gift", the bridal itself, when the bride was given to the bridegroom, with feasting and ceremony' (Whitelock 1952: 153).

132 This assumption is so commonplace in the criticism as hardly to require documentation. To cite one example, Stacy S. Klein finds that 'the female speaker, abandoned by one man, finds temporary pleasure in the arms of another' (2006: 131). In her feminist-oriented reading, the female speaker is willing to see her child killed in an effort to disrupt the heroic world represented by the two male protagonists, either one of whom might be the father of the child. Although such a reading of the poem is as plausible as others that have been proposed, its modern tenor is noticeable.

counterparts Queen Guinevere, King Arthur and Sir Lancelot, this poem from pre-Norman England evidently tells of the sufferings of two lovers whose union is thwarted because of paternal opposition to the man whom the woman loves.

Such a reading of the poem's central drama has period-specific plausibility, for in the ancient Germanic world the fundamental and recurring love triangle did not involve an adulterous relationship. Rather, it hinged on the tense and emotionally charged relations between a woman, her beloved and her father—a figure who, along with the woman's oldest brother, had the responsibility of shielding her honour against unworthy suitors, including a suitor from a kin group that was anathema to the family.[133] In Anglo-Saxon society, as Dorothy Whitelock has observed, 'close kinsmen ... arranged marriages and settled the terms of marriage agreements for their members', while 'a woman's kindred continued to watch over her interests after her marriage' (1952: 45). The same principle holds true in the world of traditional Scottish ballads;[134] while, for better or worse, it can be traced in certain tradition-bound societies up to the present day. A conflict involving custodial relations of the kind referred to by Whitelock is therefore likely to be at the heart of *Wulf and Eadwacer*.[135] A special factor here is that the woman has given birth to a child. Here too, though, medieval attitudes to the birth of children out of wedlock may have differed from modern ones. For all we know, the child may have been destined for greatness, as in other stories of sons born to outlaws,[136] though no such stories relating to *Wulf and Eadwacer* are known.

This brings us to the matter of history. A point of interest in *Wulf and Eadwacer* is the name of the young woman's father, 'Eadwacer'. Such an unusual name as this is unlikely to have been the poet's invention.[137] Robert

---

133 Worth comparison is the plot of *Kristin Lavransdatter*, a novel by the Norwegian Nobel Prize-winning author Sigrid Undset that is set in early fourteenth-century Norway. This features a conflict between the young Kristin; her lover, Erlend, an older man to whom she has pledged her troth; and her father, a man of good standing in his community who has reason to oppose this relationship. The plot involves a passionate sexual relationship, the forced separation of the lovers and heart-wrenching longing on the part of the young woman. It is not unreasonable to construe *Wulf and Eadwacer* along similar lines.
134 See for example Child 7, 'Earl Brand' (Child 1882-98: 1: 88–105). In his headnote to the ballad Child comments on its many European parallels.
135 Jane-Marie Luecke (1983) advances an argument, fanciful in parts, construing Eadwacer to be the speaker's older brother rather than her father.
136 The Weland who is mentioned in *Deor*, for example, was famed in medieval tradition as the father of Widia, also known as Wudia or Old Norse Viðga, among other versions of the name. He in turn was a well-known hero, one who is named at lines 124 and 130 of *Widsith*.
137 For discussion see Klinck 1992: 175. A search of the *Prosopography of Anglo-Saxon England* online database (http://www.pase.ac.uk) reveals that a moneyer named 'Eadwacer' was

L. Reynolds and Robert S. Lopez have made the plausible suggestion that what it represents is an English equivalent of 'Odoacer'—that is to say, of the name of the historical figure known to medieval Latin chroniclers as Flavius Odovacer (d.493), the barbarian ruler, evidently part Hunnic, part Scirian and part Gothic in descent, who dethroned the last Roman emperor in the West and vied with Theodoric the Ostrogoth for control of northern Italy.[138] Odoacer is remembered as a ruler of the warlike Germanic-speaking people the Heruli, as well as for having formed a short-lived alliance with Childeric, the founder of the Merovingian dynasty, and his prominence in early medieval legendry rests in part on these associations. Although Klinck is cool about the inference that the Eadwacer of this Exeter Anthology poem is a literary reflex of the Odoacer of history, Magennis accepts the possibility of this connection, while Fulk and Cain find it 'not implausible'.[139]

An equation along such lines has much to recommend it. While the phonological mismatch between *Odo-* and *Ēad-* might be disconcerting to some present-day philologists, it is typical of the onomastic flux of the early medieval period, when proper names—like rocks turning to liquid when subjected to strong pressure—tended to undergo unpredictable metamorphoses when slipping from one spoken language to another.[140] Relevant to this point is that *Ēad-* was a prominent Anglo-Saxon name-initial element, particularly during the tenth-century period when the Exeter Anthology was compiled, while initial *Odo-* is very nearly unattested in the Anglo-Saxon onomastic records.[141] It is plausible to suppose that the historical ruler's name was naturalized on that account.

---

active in Cambridge and Norwich during the mid- to late eleventh century; this is the only attestation of the name given there.

138 Reynolds and Lopez 1946. These authors also note that the historical Odoacer had a brother whose name, though recorded as 'Hunoulphus', would have been formed of the initial onomastic element 'Hun' plus the very common element 'Wulf'. This raises the possibility that the Wulf of *Wulf and Eadwacer* represents a reflex of the 'Hunwulf' of history, though such a connection remains highly speculative.

139 See Klinck 1992: 174–75, with references; Magennis 2010: 90; and Fulk and Cain 2003: 271. Ruth P.M. Lehmann (1969) is a persuasive advocate for the connection.

140 As Gösta Langenfelt has remarked, 'it is well-known that foreign words and names imported into a certain country are adapted to certain declensions and patterns of the same language', so that 'personal names and place-names often become garbled when wandering from one people to another' (1959: 95, 107).

141 Note for example *Eadred*, son of Edward the Elder and king of the English (946–55); his nephew *Eadwig*, king of the English (955–59); and, somewhat after the date of the Exeter Anthology, *Eadric Streona*, the Mercian ealdorman who played a leading role in affairs of state during the reign of Æthelred 'the Unready'. Female names beginning with *Ead-* are also common during this period. A leading example is *Eadgifu*, queen of Edward the Elder and mother of kings Edmund and Eadred.

If memories of Odoacer and his seventeen-year rule in northern Italy do underlie *Wulf and Eadwacer*, then the islands and fens that are mentioned near the start of that poem may be a literary reflex of the topography near Ravenna, the leading seat of late Roman power in northern Italy. Relevant to this observation is that the immediately preceding poem *Deor* makes prominent mention of Theodoric, king of the Ostrogoths, whose capital city was Ravenna. In each of these poems, the Heroic Age of the Germanic peoples is called to mind in part, if not chiefly, because legends dating from that era so brilliantly illustrate the sufferings attendant on the human condition.

Before concluding this section, I wish to redirect attention to *Widsith* and its interpretation, doing so with reference to the phenomenon of 'voices within voices' in the poems of the Exeter Anthology.

What I am referring to is the device whereby a monologue attributed to a particular persona is nested within someone else's speech. This procedure can be thought of as a framing device whereby a speaker who has no strong individual character ('the narrator') introduces a second speaker who, as someone more colourful or memorable, then takes over the main discourse. The strategy is used to good effect not just in *Widsith*, but also in *The Wanderer* and *The Soul's Address to the Body*, though the following discussion will focus on *Widsith* alone.

The confidence with which Widsith, the professional merchant of fame, speaks of the value of the goods he circulates from court to court is undercut by several factors.[142] One of these is the prominent position granted to Attila the Hun (d.453) and Eormanric the Goth (d.376) at the head of the poet's list of famous kings: 'Ætla wēold Hūnum, Eormanric Gotum' ('Attila ruled over the Huns, Eormanric the Goths', 18). One need scarcely be reminded that Attila was the most ruthless ravager that the peoples of early medieval Europe had ever known, while Eormanric was the most famous suicide of the early Middle Ages as well as being a tyrant famed for his cruelty.

A second factor undercutting the upbeat tone struck by Widsith in his monologue is this poem's placement in the codex relative to others. *Widsith* directly follows *Vainglory*, a poem castigating the drunken and bellicose excesses of the mead-hall. Directly following *Widsith* in turn is *The Fortunes of Mortals*, with its catalogue of deaths and its warnings about the hazards of violence in the mead-hall and overindulgence in drink. These juxtapositions arguably serve to impress upon readers that the glorious courts of

---

142 My analysis of *Widsith* differs from that of Conner (1993a: 155), who identifies the poem as an encomium whose purpose is to promote the fame of Eormanric and his queen, Ealhild. While such a view coincides with the perspective of the fictive bard Widsith, its applicability to the poem as a whole can be questioned.

old were known to nourish the vices of sensuality, arrogance, greed and acts of impetuous violence, just their realms were subject to mutability and their kings to the same mortality that impacts us all. These are themes that resonate with many other passages in the Exeter Anthology, casting a dark shadow on the gilded past.

A third factor undercutting confidence in the lasting value of earthly fame is introduced in the poem's last nine lines. Like the first six lines of *Widsith*, they are set in the voice of the narrator rather than that of the Scop. With their reference to the transience of worldly things, they call to mind a realm that transcends earth and its real or imagined glories. Heroes can win fame and bards can celebrate those heroes' memory, the narrator implies, but all this lasts only for a time:

> ... oþþæt eal scæceð,
> leoht ond lif somod;   lof se gewyrceð,
> hafað under heofonum   heahfæstne dom.
>
> (... until everything passes away, light and life together. Those who achieve praiseworthy deeds will win lofty and secure renown under the heavens.)[143]

As Donald K. Fry (1980) has pointed out, this is the second of the two voices that are at work in *Widsith*. It is a sobering one. The Christian perspective that informs the narrator's closing remarks nurses doubts in the final validity of the heroic code that animates the Scop's boastful monologue. When one recalls the famous kings and courts that the Scop has called to mind, one is tempted to ask, like the imagined future sage whose voice is nested in *The Wanderer*, '*ubi sunt?*' Moreover, the ultimate value of earthly fame—here called *lof* (142b) and *dōm* (143b)—is called into question through the closing phrase *under heofonum*. While this phrase might at first be taken to mean 'under the heavens', that is, 'in the whole world', the same phrase is used elsewhere in Old English poetry to mean 'under heaven' with reference to the abode of God and the afterlife of Christian belief.[144]

While the only kind of *lof* or *dōm* that the bard Widsith knows is the kind gained by kings or heroes, then, what the narrator calls to mind in these closing lines is the God-given *lof* of which the Seafarer speaks in the homiletic second half of his monologue (at 78–80a). Here those people who battle the powers of hell while in residence on earth are said to win *lof* 'salvation' among the hosts

---

143 *Widsith* 141b–43; Muir 1: 243.
144 See the *DOE*, s.v. *heofon*, sense I.A.2.c, 'under heaven; in the (whole) world', and cf. sense IV, 'the abode of God, his angels, and holy people after death'.

of angels. Likewise, as Guthlac approaches his end, he is said to be about to receive *dōm* as his portion or reward (*dōmes hlēotan*, 154b [972b]): that is, he is about to win eternal glory. In chapter 27 of Felix's *Vita Guthlaci*, a corresponding distinction is made between earthly fame and heavenly glory. Here Guthlac is said to be rewarded by God *not only* with fame in this world, *but also* with perennial glory: 'et non solum praesentis saeculi famosa venerantia beavit, sed in gaudio perennis gloriae aeterna beatitudine constituit'.[145] A saintly hero is thus clearly distinguished from a Germanic-style one.

Through the device of narrative framing, the bard Widsith is shown to be yet another representative of an era whose uncertain intellectual foundations have been superseded through the light of Christian doctrine. In this regard the Scop resembles such other inhabitants of a pre-Christian northern world as the Wanderer, the Court Poet of *Deor*, the Young Lover of *Wulf and Eadwacer* (evidently), and the Wife of *The Wife's Lament*, not to mention the kings and heroes who people the world of *Beowulf*. While the people of that former era can be admired or pitied, and while certain of them may represent models of selfless heroic behaviour, still, like the patriarchs of the Old Dispensation, they cannot well serve as ultimate moral exempla, nor is any wisdom that they express necessarily to be regarded as final.

Implicit both in the narrator's framing comments in *Widsith* and in the main body of *Deor*, then, is the orthodox doctrine that God's will is manifest in history, while only God's grace offers release from the alluring but potentially vicious cycle of human rivalries and ambitions. The same moral can readily be inferred from the tragic situation called to mind in *Wulf and Eadwacer*. These three poems, each of which is evidently grounded in legends pertaining to the Heroic Age of the Germanic-speaking peoples, can therefore be understood in the same sense in which the three poems of the Christ cycle are to be read, as Bradley has observed: 'according to a Christian philosophy of history which accepts the premise that earthly reality, including time itself, is a transient construct subordinate to the creating Deity's purpose' (203).

Diversity within unity: the role of simulated speech

Although one thesis of the present book is that the Exeter Anthology has appreciable unity—unity when measured by medieval rather than neoclassical standards, that is—a feature of the Anthology that is equally noteworthy

---

[145] 'And not only did He reward him with fame and veneration in this present world, but He also established him in the joy and eternal blessedness of perennial glory.' Colgrave 1956: 92–93, his translation.

is its capacity for diversity. In this dual regard the volume mirrors the macrocosm, according to the Isidorean view of the universe that was one of the foundations of early medieval learning.

From an Isidorean perspective, the physical world in its nearly infinite parts is all of God's making and design. It is a world of diversity in unity, unity in diversity. This perspective informs the medieval *Physiologus*, with its account of the multiple creatures inhabiting the natural world, each of which is a sign of things invisible to human sight. The Exeter Anthology poem *God's Gifts to Humankind* reinforces this concept of diversity within unity with its expansive catalogue of the gifts that come to human beings from God. In a comparable manner, the compiler of the Exeter Anthology created a kind of microcosm of the human condition. A recapitulation of those parts of the book that feature the rhetorical figure of ethopoeia will help to clarify how this is so.

The list of personae whose voices figure prominently in the Exeter Anthology includes the noble but tragic figure of the Wanderer; the wise Father of *A Father's Precepts*; the fiercely devout Seafarer; the Man of Wisdom who is the speaker of *Vainglory*; the itinerant Scop of *Widsith*; the Seer of *The Wonder of Creation*; the wealthy Convert who, nearing his death, gives voice to *The Rhyming Poem*; the taciturn Court Poet of *Deor*; the Young Lover who gives voice to her fears and longing in *Wulf and Eadwacer*; the embittered Wife of *The Wife's Lament*; and the fearful but cheerful Penitent of *The Penitent's Prayer*. To this initial list, which is presented according to the order in which these personae are introduced, can be added the indignant Damned Soul of *The Soul's Address to the Body* and the enigmatic Messenger who represents the husband's interests in *The Husband's Message*. A few additional speakers, including Guthlac and Juliana, call for attention in this same light. It will be helpful to take a fresh look at the characters just mentioned, taking them up in thematic order rather than in order of their appearance, so as to determine their points of likeness and dissimilarity and their role in the book's design.

As an *ān-haga* 'lone-dweller', the Wanderer calls to mind the hermits of the Christian era even while being characterized as living in pre-Christian times.[146] A strong and stoic exemplar of the warrior class, he can be construed as a virtuous pagan of the kind that is put on display in *Beowulf* in the form of the hero of that poem, or the aged King Hrothgar, or the brave young retainer Wiglaf. Such men, and such women as Queen Wealhtheow as well, were arguably meant to represent as high a stage of enlightenment as is likely to be attained on earth in the absence of knowledge of Christ. In keeping

---

146 Worth keeping in mind is that English *munuc* and Latin *monachos* are derived from the Greek root *mono*, 'one' or 'sole'. In etymological terms, a monk is someone who lives a solitary life.

An Overview of the Book's Contents 131

with the Christian tenor of the Exeter Anthology as a whole, the Wanderer is presented as a tragic figure deserving of sympathy and respect rather than as a heroic one meriting esteem for his deeds.

A wanderer and lone-dweller of a different sort is the Seafarer, a man with an unclouded knowledge of God. The Seafarer speaks in the tones of a stern and self-reliant evangelist. Rather than being exiled by blind fate or bitter circumstances, he has chosen his austere way of life, which recalls that of the desert fathers but is confined to the wintry north. He scorns people of the *seft-ēadig* sort: that is, those who are content with a comfortable existence and who indulge the pleasures of the senses. The severe self-discipline embraced by the Seafarer might put one in mind of the unnamed Irish monk who was assigned to be bishop over the early seventh-century Northumbrians but whose regime, according to Bede, was so harsh that King Oswald sent him back to Iona with the request that he be sent a more moderate replacement.[147] Be this as it may, the Seafarer's understanding of the nature of earthly transience leads him to a course of action, not just despair. He has the theological understanding and the ascetic zeal that, one can assume, will gain him a place in the land of the living after his 'dead life' on land comes to an end (his *dēade līf*, 65b).

Two other characters round out the initial list of male exiles. One of these is the speaker of the fragmentary poem *The Penitent's Prayer*. Scarcely a picture of strength, painfully aware of his own sinful condition, the Penitent tries to summon up a cheerful smile even when, exiled from his homeland, he undertakes a penitential journey (*sīþ*, 4a), one that offers the prospect of physical hardships or even death. The term 'homeland' (*ēþel*, 20a) that he employs with reference to the land from which he is exiled can be understood equally well as a literal place of origins or as the originary paradise. As a counterpart to the heroic figure of the Seafarer, the Penitent stands in for the ordinary Christian who must atone for his sins, like it or not.

Yet another pilgrim-exile, one whose story is told close to the book's start, is Guthlac. Although not presented via a dramatic monologue, hence not technically a creation of ethopoeia, he is attributed long speeches in both of the poems that feature him. Robert E. Bjork has rightly regarded these passages as having a crucial role in confirming the poem's Christian themes and helping to shape readers' responses to the story.[148] Guthlac's speeches establish the precise nature of his virtue. As one who gets the best of demons

---

147 Bede, *Historia ecclesiastica* 3: 5.
148 Bjork 1985, chap. 1, 'Old English Words as Deeds and the Struggle towards Light in *Guthlac A*' (pp. 28–44) and chap. 4, 'The Artist of the Beautiful: Immutable Discourse in *Guthlac B*' (pp. 90–109).

in a face-to-face debate, he is an embodiment of *ellen*, the hero's virtue as well as that of the monk or nun. His admirable qualities go well beyond self-confidence and strength of will, however, for his speeches likewise show him to be a model of graciousness and good cheer in his latter days. He is beloved for his gentleness: birds fly fearlessly to his hands for sustenance. When nearing death, accompanied now by a devoted servant, he becomes an exemplar of the *ars moriendi*, and his speeches to this attendant confirm his authority as a blessed teacher even up to the time when his soul departs from his body.

The Wanderer, the Seafarer, the Penitent and Guthlac, then: these are not just four portraits included for the sake of their individual interest. They typify four distinct types of human being. Each embodies a different response to the challenge of a life lived in exile from settled society, regardless of whether this exile is self-chosen or not or is Christian or not in its motivation.

The cast of characters from the imagined past is filled out by two poets: the Scop and the Court Poet. There is the big-voiced Widsith, an imagined bard of ancient times whose prodigious memory and whose boasts about the gifts he has received at the hands of famous men make him a figure larger than life. Standing in sharp contrast to Widsith is the small-voiced Deor, a poet of philosophical reserve. The bitterness of his personal experience, for he too is a kind of exile, contributes to the sardonic cast of his words. Deor likes to assume that his listeners have read their Boethius, and he prefers innuendo to forthright speech: 'We've heard of Theodoric. Enough said.' One can imagine him as a former courtier whose taciturn manner may have contributed to his being ousted from his place.

There are three poets, however, and not just two, who have an important part to play in the book and whose character is revealed through the figure of ethopoeia. There is Widsith, there is Deor, and there is also the Seer—the *wōð-bora*—who speaks the whole of *The Wonder of Creation*. Rather than being depicted as a scop or court poet of ancient times, this man speaks as an inspired religious teacher, much as the Old Testament prophets were of old. As if speaking from the pulpit, he directly addresses 'you' (singular *þū*) as his audience, locating that audience in a transitory world whose counterpart is the 'better kingdom' of heaven. Poetry that is afire with spiritual insight, he implies, can unveil the mysteries of the faith. By developing new models of eloquence—that is, by heralding a monastic poetics—*The Wonder of Creation* offers an implied critique of the older Germanic school of heroic verse.

Among the anguished voices heard in the Exeter Anthology are those of two women. The Wife of *The Wife's Lament* speaks as an outcast from society nursing her misery and her rage. Her man, whether imagined as her husband or her lover, has betrayed the vows of love that once united the two of them.

Despairing of her lot (as I construe the poem's last lines), she curses him and all men of his type. Very different is the female Lover who is the speaker of *Wulf and Eadwacer*. If the reading that I have offered of this even more obscure poem is accepted, then this is a young woman whose anguish arises from her father's hostility towards her betrothed, by whom she has evidently given birth to a child. Both the Lover of this poem and the Wife of *The Wife's Lament* evidently inhabit a world where Christianity has no place. No remedy is therefore available to them for the suffering that they endure—suffering that one is free to regard from a Boethian or Benedictine perspective as the outcome of ungoverned human passions.

Significantly, a third female speaker is given a prominent place in the Anthology as well. This is the virgin saint Juliana. Although, like her male counterpart Guthlac, she is not offered a monologue of her own that could be called an instance of ethopoeia, her long speeches characterize her as a brave young woman—she is still in her teens—who has the courage to hold true to her convictions even when threatened with torture and death.[149] In addition, in a triumph of art over verisimilitude, her speeches reveal her to be a superbly confident speaker with a mastery of the arts of rhetoric. The scene of her interrogation of the devil, whom she has bound, has been singled out by Allen J. Frantzen as an example of the quasi-dramatic interactions that are an occasional feature of Old English narrative verse.[150] As a bride of Christ who testifies to the true faith and is willing to die for it if necessary, she is a model of constancy for cloistered women. She is likewise a paragon for all those, regardless of gender, who aspire to be *sōð-fæste*, or superbly resolved in their faith.

The anxious Lover of *Wulf and Eadwacer*, the unhappy Wife of *The Wife's Lament* and the virgin saint of *The Passion of Saint Juliana* thus represent three complementary types of female character. Each responds in a different way to the male-inflicted traumas that attend her actual or prospective marriage. There is diversity here, but also at work are principles of likeness and contrast.

Ethopoeia is a rhetorical figure that resists being circumscribed by firm lines. On one hand it resembles prosopopoeia, the rhetorical device by which an inanimate object such as a key or a ship is imagined to speak in its own

---

149 This is a point developed in different ways by Bjork 1985, chap. 2, 'Saintly Discourse and the Distancing of Evil in Cynewulf's *Juliana*' (pp. 45–61), as well as by Jill Frederick (2005).

150 Frantzen 2007. One need not follow Frantzen in his understanding that *Juliana* exemplifies the kind of 'public poetry' that was performed by the Anglo-Saxon scop in the hall. On the contrary, as I have argued earlier, that poem seems intended first and foremost for a well-informed literate readership, though it could have been read aloud as well, most likely in religious settings.

voice. This is the art of more than half of the Exeter enigmas,[151] as it is of *The Husband's Message*, a poem of a different type that is set in the voice of a speaking object. On another hand, ethopoeia shades into drama, where two or more characters are ascribed interactive speaking roles. A degree of ethopoeia can likewise be said to be present wherever a literary character is ascribed a sustained passage of direct speech that brings out the speaker's individuality. Properly speaking, however, ethopoeia refers to a whole poem, or nearly a whole poem, set in the voice of a single character.

The additional speeches of some substance that are embedded in the Exeter Anthology fill out its cast of characters, making the book yet more of a simulacrum of the human condition. One of these speakers is the historical Mary, the mother of Jesus, who speaks confidently in her own voice in *Advent Lyric 4* and in poignant dialogue with Joseph in *Advent Lyric 7*. Her tones in that latter poem are those of a vulnerable bride and mother-to-be, one who is pained by her husband's failure to comprehend the sublime mystery of her pregnancy. Mary too has marital problems, it seems, even though they will be assuaged through the man's love and understanding.

Mary is just one of the biblical characters, or what might be called cosmological personae, who are ascribed passages of direct speech as they enter and exit the pages of the Anthology. In order of their appearance, these other characters are Isaiah, a chorus of angels, Solomon, Christ himself, Job, an unnamed angel, the devil, an unnamed prophet and the soul of a deceased sinner. There are thus nine such speakers in addition to Mary, as will be evident from the following summary:

1. In *Advent Lyric 9* the prophet Isaiah foretells the coming of Christ in exalted tones.
2. In *Advent Lyric 11* a chorus of angels sings praises to God in verses that paraphrase the Sanctus and the Gloria of the mass.
3. In *The Ascension* the biblical king Solomon speaks in spiritual enigmas, anticipating the birth of Christ, who will come to earth like a stag that 'leaps upon the high uplands' (*gehlēapeð hēa dūne*, 278a [717a]).
4. In *Christ in Judgement*, Christ as judge of humankind speaks from on high in a pair of thematically central speeches. In the first of these (at 478-95 [1344-61]) he blesses a group of virtuous souls for their acts of mercy while on earth, while in the second (at 513-657b [1379-1523]) he castigates the race of human beings for having betrayed and scorned their Lord.[152]

---

151 Frederick Tupper (1910: lxxxix) enumerates fifty examples of prosopopoeia among the enigmas.
152 Bradley finds that the language of Christ's reproaches in this poem 'is not excelled in any of the later treatments of this popular theme in Middle English lyric, narrative and drama'

5. In *The Phoenix* the biblical Job expresses his hope of being resurrected through Christ 'just like the bird the phoenix' (*swā se fugel fenix*, 558a).
6. At the beginning of *The Life of Saint Guthlac*, an unnamed angel proclaims God's message of peace to a blessed soul that has just arrived in heaven, assuring the new arrival that the souls of all the righteous (*sōð-fæstra sāwla*, 22) will find salvation.[153]
7. In *The Passion of Saint Juliana* the devil is ascribed long speeches in which he recounts his former misdeeds and reveals his true character as a corrupter of humankind.
8. In *Vainglory* an unnamed prophet sings of the fall of the rebellious angels on account of their sin of arrogance (*ofer-hygd*, 58b).
9. In the main part of *The Soul's Address to the Body*, the soul of a deceased sinner reviles its erstwhile body for having condemned it to a wretched fate.

The primary effect of these speeches, set into the mouths of speakers of such diverse types, should be clear enough when one takes account of them as a group. It is to arouse the emotions of joy and compunction that properly pertain to the revelation of divine mysteries.[154] A second effect of the presence of such a gallery of speakers in this one volume is to enhance one's appreciation of the power of poetry to create a simulacrum of the universe. A sound reading of the Exeter Anthology will take into account the contributions made by all its inset voices to a universal drama. In a manner that puts one in mind of the Corpus Christi cycle of plays of the later medieval tradition, room is found in a single interactive space for both prophets and saints, both angels and devils, both holy men and sinners, both historical persons and imagined ones, and both the Divine Family and the risen Christ, in a literary drama that is as colourful as it is rich in doctrine and moral teachings.

Modern preconceptions as to what constitutes aesthetic unity, propriety or excellence are likely to be no more than impediments to the understanding of a book of this kind. Much as one cannot have *Juliana* without also accepting the devil as her chief interlocutor, a place in the reader's experience must be found for the divinely inspired poet of *The Wonder of Creation* in proximity to

---

(229). He calls attention to analogues in the Old English poems *Doomsday*, *Judgement Day II*, *The Soul's Address to the Body* and *Resignation* (that is, the pair of poems that I call *Contrition* and *The Penitent's Prayer*), in addition to certain prose homilies.

153 Although Muir takes this angel's speech to occupy verses 6–10a of the poem, I follow Bradley in taking it to extend to line 29.

154 The relevance of the term 'compunction' to the Exeter Anthology poem *Christ in Judgement* is argued persuasively by Frances McCormack (2015), building on Scott DeGregorio's (2005) research into the Anglo-Saxon antecedents of late medieval affective spirituality.

the grandiose bard Widsith and the stoic Deor. Likewise, no reading of *The Seafarer* should be tolerated that is blind to the fate of a group of morally corrupt seafarers at the end of *The Passion of Saint Juliana*, or the passage at the end of *The Ascension* where seafaring is explicated as a trope for the soul's journey through life and death to its final destination. Readers who are alert to such relationships as these will be in a position to see the Exeter Anthology as sustained throughout by a consciousness of the interface of the human and the divine, in all times and at all places.

The book's closing parts: *The Panther* to the end

A few poems included in the last quarter or so of the Anthology remain to be discussed, though no more than a few. The term 'miscellany' is an apt one when one turns to this closing part of the codex. One should not look for neat architectural symmetry here, nor for consistent groupings of poems of a similar genre; nor, indeed, should one look for such things elsewhere in the volume. As is the rule with medieval poetic miscellanies, what matters is that the book's constituent parts are grounded in a common culture and contribute to a common educational purpose.

Three Exeter Anthology poems that represent free versified paraphrases of chapters of the Latin Physiologus are included on folios 95v–97v directly after *The Rhyming Poem*.[155] These are *The Panther*, *The Whale* and the bare one-and-a-half-line shard that remains of *The Partridge*. The remainder of *The Partridge* is lacking because of the loss of at least one leaf in the codex.

The point of the medieval Physiologus was to call attention to the role of each creature of the natural world in the divine order of creation. The Physiologus is thus the last thing from a contribution to natural history; rather, it is a guide to a system of allegorical interpretation by which the true nature of the world is revealed. As the poet of *The Wonder of Creation* remarks, each of the wonders of the natural world, including its celestial bodies, is 'a well-known sign' (*orgeate tācen*, 8b) to a person who is competent in Christian modes of exegesis. The mythologized Panther of the Physiologus thus signifies Christ, we are told, while the mythologized whale-like creature signifies his eternal adversary the devil.[156] The subject of the third of these poems, the one that survives only as a fragment, is plausibly thought to have

---

[155] For source texts in modern English translation, see Allen and Calder 1976: 156–61.
[156] As Carolin Esser-Miles (2014) emphasizes, what the Old English term *hwæl* denotes in the poem that by convention is called *The Whale* is a sea-monster, not what today we would call a whale.

been the partridge, a creature of scant size and might compared with the panther or the whale. If the partridge is rightly construed as a figure for the human soul (Muir 2: 581-82), then these three poems taken together were meant to tell allegorically of the dangers faced by the individual soul as it pursues its quest for salvation, threatened by demonic malice yet given wings by God's sustaining love.

Important to note is that *The Panther*, *The Whale* and *The Partridge* are far from being a kind of 'mini-Physiologus' of which only these poems happen to survive. Most likely the three poems were meant to form a single work, one that would be complete were it not for the missing leaf or leaves. Although in a sense they represent a continuation of the theme taken up in *The Wonder of Creation*, the approach they take to their subject is homiletic rather than descriptive or analytic, as Ann Squires has pointed out.[157] The metaphor of seafaring, familiar from elsewhere in the Anthology, is taken up again here so as to explore how, in the pilgrimage of life, an individual Christian is to distinguish between the true beauty of Christ, as signified by the Panther, and the false allure of the devil's temptations. *The Whale* thus relies on a large body of theological and homiletic writings that strategize how to avoid sin.[158]

Included next in the Anthology are two additional poems of a homiletic character. The first of these, *Christ's Pledge of Grace* (a poem known more anaemically as *Homiletic Fragment III*), is a short piece of moral encouragement, set chiefly in Christ's own voice, to the effect that God's saving grace is always available to humankind. The message is particularly relevant to the condition of the soul, figured as a timid bird, in the fragment of a poem (*The Partridge*) that directly precedes this one.

The second of these two adjacent poems, *The Soul's Address to the Body*, is a substantial verse monologue set into the mouth of a Damned Soul.[159] As a versified paraphrase of a prior Latin source, the poem reiterates the theme of the soul's quest for salvation but gives that theme a negative twist, for the Damned Soul returns to earth at regular intervals to berate its own erstwhile body for having lived in gluttony and lust, thereby condemning them both to punishment in the afterlife. The blistering terms of the Damned Soul's recriminations call to mind the Man of Wisdom's castigation of the insolent carouser who is the central figure of *Vainglory*—a man who, correspondingly,

---

157 Squires 1988. Moreover, as Squires observes, 'the significance of each poem is only to be fully understood in the context of the other two' (22).
158 Jeremy Deangelo (2013) offers detailed support for this claim.
159 The poem is extant in two versions, one in the Exeter Anthology and another in the Vercelli Book; see Muir 2: 592. Moffat (1990) provides an edition of both texts. Jones, *OE Shorter Poems*, prints a composite version (at 192-203), supplementing it with ancillary materials. I follow Moffat in calling the poem's main speaker the 'Damned Soul'.

is said to be *grund-fūs*, or 'hastening to hell' (49a). In *The Soul's Address to the Body*, the body is condemned to torment as a consequence of its pursuit of hedonistic pleasures even though what the soul hungered for was the bread and wine of the Eucharist:

> Wære þu þe wiste wlonc   ond wines sæd,
> þrymful þunedest,   ond ic ofþyrsted wæs
> Godes lichoman,   gæstes drinces.
>
> (You were proud at the feast and sated with wine, you raved in your power; and I was thirsty for God's body, the soul's drink.)[160]

The passage brings home the theme of damnation, one that recurs elsewhere in the Anthology starting with the paired poems *The Ascension* and *Christ in Judgement*, with their images of sinners fleeing the judgement of an angry God. The theme recurs, with typological overtones, towards the end of *The Passion of Saint Juliana* with reference to the drowning of Juliana's tormentors. In *Doomsday* too the theme is raised, here again with reference to those who indulge their appetites at the feast without regard for the state of their soul in the afterlife.[161] The governing perspective in all these poems is Augustinian, in the sense that earthly pleasures are not denied. The problem is that such pleasures are inherently dangerous to the state of the eternal soul, and in the end they come to nothing. As the Damned Soul observes to its decaying fleshly counterpart, 'Eart þū dumb ond dēaf, ne syndan þīne drēamas wiht ('Now you are dumb and deaf; your pleasures are nothing', 60).

Dominating the last third of the codex are approximately ninety-five enigmas divided into two main sets (fols 101r–115r and 124v–130v). They form an encyclopedia-like compilation that has justly attracted much critical attention. When read as a group, these ninety-five or so riddles are knit together by numerous verbal and rhetorical parallels, regardless of the origins of an individual text. In Liuzza's view, these parallels include 'repetitive openings and closings whose homogeneity suggests a long series of revisions, as a group, in manuscript' (1990: 9).

This suggestion is a plausible one. Another possible inference, however, is that any Anglo-Saxon craft-poet with a claim to technical skill could have composed a new poem along such lines as these upon short notice, especially when a Latin exemplar was at hand. In general, poetry is an art form that values innovation yet is governed by convention, whether as regards its

---

160 *The Soul's Address to the Body* 36–38; Muir 1: 277.
161 I quote the passage from *Doomsday* (lines 77b–80) in Chapter 5 below, in the section headed 'Tropes'.

formal properties or its intellectual content. While the conventions that govern a particular verse tradition may require generations to take hold, once they are in place, even poets with no more than superficial talent can readily mimic them.

In any event, a good deal of the interest of the Exeter riddles resides in their rhetorical technique. The apparently scandalous content of some of them has attracted much attention as well. In the next two chapters I will have more to say about both of these matters, taking up first the special literary qualities of the riddles as a group and then the erotic content of a certain few of them.

Since certain of the poems that are written out in the last thirty or so folios of the codex, including *Deor, Wulf and Eadwacer, The Wife's Lament, The Penitent's Prayer* and Riddle 30b, have been discussed in preceding sections of this chapter, there is no need to introduce them here again. Most will be discussed in one or more later chapters as well.

Previous mention has also been made of the role of a series of eight poems, running from folio 117v to 122v, in establishing an 'Eastertide' sequence towards the back of the book, one that provides a counterpart to the 'Christmastide' sequence with which the volume begins. To take them up in order, these poems are *Doomsday, Contrition, The Penitent's Prayer, Christ's Descent into Hell, Almsgiving, Pharaoh, A Versified Lord's Prayer* and the poem that I call *One Faith One God*. The series carries over to the poem that is rather colourlessly known as Riddle 30b (solved as *trēow*, with a play on that word and with prominent allusion to the Rood), though a more expressive modern English title for that poem would be *The Tree*.

The emphasis in these folios thus falls on themes that recur with some frequency in the homiletic literature of the Middle Ages. None of these texts—up to Riddle 30b, at least, with its brilliant imagery and wordplay—has been thought to merit much attention in the critical literature.[162] *Doomsday*, for example, strikes one as a fairly routine treatment of its theme when compared with either *Christ in Judgement*, from an earlier part of the Anthology, or *Judgement Day II*, which is preserved in CCCC MS 201. There is nothing surprising about this observation, however, especially seeing that *Judgement Day II* is based on a Latin poem by Bede that is a model of deep

---

162 An exception is James E. Anderson in his book *Two Literary Riddles in the Exeter Book* (1986). What Anderson means by 'riddle' is not an enigma as conventionally understood, but rather a thematically linked group of enigmatic poems. He finds two such 'riddles' in the Exeter Anthology, one of which extends from *The Soul's Address to the Body* to *Wulf and Eadwacer* (fols 98r–101r), while the other runs from *The Wife's Lament* through to *The Ruin* (fols 115r–124v). Within each of these groups, he identifies thematic echoes or collocations that are suggestive of purposeful organization.

and refined religious expression. As a group, the poems from this part of the Exeter Anthology strike a penitential note. They draw attention to the place that all Christians ought to find in their hearts for fear of the awful majesty of God and for cognizance of their own sinful nature, hence their need for deliverance through Christ's saving grace.

The pairing of *Contrition* and *The Penitent's Prayer* has an undisguised significance in this penitential context. The first of these poems is an extended versified prayer addressed to the Almighty God on the part of a speaker who recognizes his own inadequacy and sinfulness, yet who also hopes to find mercy as he prepares for his soul's fateful separation from the body. *The Penitent's Prayer*, a dramatic monologue, is set in the voice of a person who is conscious both of his own sinfulness and of his long-lasting worldly afflictions. Exiled from his homeland, planning to set out by sea for an unknown destination and yet hampered by poverty, he resolves to endure his troubles with patience.

One poem in the 'Eastertide' sequence that is of special interest is *Christ's Descent into Hell*, with its relation to the iconography of Easter and to the Passion plays that have long been associated with the celebrations of Holy Week.[163] The poem has a dramatic quality about it that recalls the small drama in *Advent Lyric 7* featuring an exchange of speeches between Mary and Joseph. One wonders if *Christ's Descent into Hell* was ever read out loud in a minster setting. The simplicity of its style would suit that purpose, as would its exclamatory passages and its closing prayer.

The poem begins somewhat mysteriously with reference to a group of women who lament the death of a nobleman, but who then meet with a group of men who are rejoicing at the prince's tomb. The leader of the women is revealed to be Mary, while the nobleman is the Saviour, who by this time has already departed on his *hin-sīð* 'journey forth' (7a). As angels look on, we are told, 'the denizens of hell laughed' (*hlōgan hel-waran*, 21a)—that is, laughter wells up in the hearts of the Ancient Just who are imprisoned in the lower world. The reason for this outburst of joy is then made clear as the scene changes to the gates of hell, where John the Baptist laughs as he informs the Ancient Just that Christ himself, the *sīge-bearn Godes* 'victorious Son of God' (32b), will straight away release them from captivity. As Christ then arrives in triumph at the gates of hell, the locks of the gates fly off and the patriarchs, prophets and holy women of the Old Dispensation throng forward to greet their Saviour.

---

163 Maria Elena Ruggerini (2011) emphasizes the typological and liturgical aspects of *Christ's Descent into Hell*, arguing that Christ is described as a 'rider' in a manner that recalls the processional part of the Palm Sunday ritual, as that ritual was performed in Anglo-Saxon England and in recent times as well.

The remainder of the poem, which at least initially is set in John's voice, consists of words of thanks and praise directed first of all to John's kinsman Christ, then to the archangel Gabriel for his role in bringing about Christ's Incarnation, then to the Virgin Mary for having given birth to her son, then to Jerusalem and the River Jordan in Judea. Much as in *Advent Lyrics*, each of the passages addressed to Mary, Gabriel, Jerusalem and Judea takes the form of an apostrophe beginning with the exclamation *Ēalā!* The last part of John's address (at 107–37) consists of a first-person prayer of thanksgiving to the Lord of Hosts. While set at first in John's own voice, the prayer later modulates into the voice of one of the clergy, or perhaps of any believer, thus taking on tones reminiscent of *Advent Lyric 12*. As elsewhere in the Exeter Anthology, the demands of naturalistic representation yield place to the aesthetics of devotion. The poem concludes with a call for 'all dwellers in the settlement' (*ealle burg-waran*, 134b) to be baptized. There is double reference here to the baptism of Christ by John in the River Jordan and to the baptisms imagined to be taking place forthwith in a minster where, plausibly, this same poem has been read aloud.

A point of thematic interest in *Christ's Descent into Hell* is John's reference to the sword, byrnie, helmet and battle gear that the Lord formerly gave him and that he has kept in his possession ever since (lines 71b–75). While the manifest allusion in this passage is to the Pauline trope of the weapons of spiritual combat that plays a prominent role in earlier parts of the Anthology, there is also an arcane reference here to the infant John having seized weapons while still in the womb.[164] Another echo from an earlier part of the Anthology is the poet's characterization of the Old Testament denizens of hell as 'exiles' (*wræccan*, 42b, 63a) living in 'bonds' (*bendum*, 68a) until their deliverance by Christ, who effortlessly breaks the 'locks' (*locu*, 39b) of their prison. The speaker of *Advent Lyric 2*, similarly, refers to all Christians as living 'in prison' (*in carcerne*, 25b), 'deprived of our homeland' (*ēðle bescyrede*, 32b), as they wait for Christ 'who holds the locks' (*sē þe locan healdeð*, 19a) to release them from their incarceration. Rather than being fortuitous, these echoes point to an effort on the part of the compiler to create antiphonal patterns spanning large sections of the volume.

Rounding out the contents of the Exeter Anthology (at fols 122v–124v), just before the second group of riddles, is a trio of self-consciously enigmatic poems. Although the first of these is known rather colourlessly as Riddle 60 (solved as 'reed' or, better, as the Old English word *hrēod* meaning either

---

164 Thomas N. Hall (2008) calls attention to this additional allusion, one that points to the conclusion that the poems of the Exeter Anthology are aimed at highly learned readers as well as ones less advanced in their studies.

'reed', 'reed flute' or 'reed pen'), the title that would do better justice to this very artful composition would be *The Reed*. The second and third of the poems are *The Husband's Message* and *The Ruin*, two compositions that likewise are widely admired for their artistry. *The Husband's Message* is overtly riddle-like in incorporating in its concluding lines a set of five runes whose meaning must be guessed, while *The Ruin* is enigmatic in that it describes an ancient city that is perhaps deliberately left unnamed, thus allowing readers to make guesses about its identity.

The first two poems of this triad, *The Reed* and *The Husband's Message*, have in common that one must guess who (or what) is the speaker of each poem. In each case, the answer to this puzzle is an object made of a natural substance, one that, once it is transformed by human hands, is capable of communicating a 'message' to human beings. The object 'speaks' first of all through the medium of sound: this is the reed flute of *The Reed* or the mysterious speaking Messenger of *The Husband's Message*. It also 'speaks' through the medium of inscription: this is the reed pen of *The Reed* or the rune-inscribed object of *The Husband's Message*. I take this object to be the ship's personified mast, though other possibilities have been entertained.[165] Fittingly, a second riddle that is written out separately in this part of the manuscript, Riddle 30b (solved as *trēow*), features a set of objects that are made of a natural substance, wood, the last of which, the Rood, likewise 'speaks' to readers as part of the symbolic vocabulary of Christendom. As all Anglo-Saxonists will know, the Rood too, an object whose resemblance to a ship's mast needs no pointing out, was sometimes used as a medium for epigraphy. The collocation of these four poems one after another at folios 122v–124v of the Exeter Anthology—*The Tree*, *The Reed*, *The Husband's Message* and *The Ruin*—illustrates once again that some care was put into the book's design. Moreover, when these deliberately enigmatic poems, plus *Wulf and Eadwacer* and *Pharaoh*, are added to the total of ninety-five riddles (by Muir's count) that are included in the Exeter Anthology, then the sum total comes very close to one hundred, the same number of riddles as are included in Aldhelm's *Enigmata*. It is difficult to come up with a final number in this regard, however, given not just the uncertainties of generic definition that are involved but also some uncertain textual boundaries and the 'double count' of Riddle 30.

As has sometimes been discussed in the critical literature, *The Husband's Message* and *The Wife's Lament*, which is written out eight folios earlier, are so similar in their basic storyline as to make up a kind of a diptych.[166] The

---

165 I advance this argument in Niles 2003b.
166 David Howlett (1978) has made a brief but persuasive case for this connection. Klinck (1992: 58–59) remains sceptical as to such claims, however. See further Chapter 9 below, n. 30.

Husband's Message likewise complements certain other Exeter Anthology poems that dramatize the painful situation of a person who is cut off from his home community. *The Wanderer* presents the leading example of this type, while *The Seafarer* and *The Penitent's Prayer* play variations on the theme. What is unique about *The Husband's Message* is that the poem's central character has done quite well during his period of exile. Rather than bemoaning the blows of an inexorable fate, the Husband, through the mediation of the mysterious Messenger, tells of how he has overcome the adversities that had beset him at an earlier time, when enemies—his wife's kinsmen, evidently—drove him out from his native land. It is a fair surmise that one reason why this poem is included in the Exeter Anthology is that it offers an upbeat perspective on a theme treated elsewhere in bleak tones, thus contributing to the Anthology's comprehensiveness as a microcosm of human experience.

To turn finally to *The Ruin*, this poem takes as its subject an unnamed city that the passage of time has made desolate, thus recalling the scenes of ruination that are so memorably evoked in *The Wanderer* and *The Seafarer*. In terms of genre the poem is best approached as a meditation on the topic known in Latin as *excidium urbis*, or 'the city's ruination'. Since, with its theme of mutability, this poem plays a significant role in the Anthology's design, and since it has also been a lightning-rod for critical responses to the Exeter Anthology as a whole, I shall single it out for discussion in later chapters.

Since the preceding review of the contents of the Exeter Anthology involves many poems of a diverse kind, ones whose relationships are complex, multifaceted and hard to keep in mind, a summary of my reading of the volume as a whole may be welcome at this point.

Anyone who sets out to read the Anthology from cover to cover will soon gather that the volume is capacious in its contents: capacious enough to find a place for both the divine and the human, the eternal and the transitory, life and death, the proud and the humble, and salvation and damnation, with attention to the past, the present and the future as well as the natural world with its living creatures. Although a similar claim might be advanced about practically any literary compilation of its length that has ever been made, the Exeter Anthology is exceptionally ambitious in its scope when one compares it with other codices of the Anglo-Saxon period that have survived, whether written in Latin, the vernacular or both tongues. None of the other major manuscripts containing Old English verse are so nearly encyclopedic in scope.

The result of this capaciousness is not a mere miscellany, however. Rather, the volume's parts form an intellectually coherent whole, and those parts speak back and forth to one another in a manner that is both frequent and thematically significant. Readers who are alert to these relationships will recognize that it is not just here and there that the book's contents are expressive of a religious world-view. Rather, such an outlook permeates all the book's parts, speaking in particular to the existential situation of those persons who led cloistered lives, though also addressed to anyone committed to the Christian faith. The Anthology reinforces a value system that would have been cherished by those 'soldiers of Christ' whose vocation was prayer and whose daily life was structured in part upon book learning. Just such an equation between God's chosen ones and the readers and makers of books is made in lines 15–17 of *The Passion of Saint Juliana* where, speaking of the early Christian martyrs, Cynewulf uses the epithet *bōc-cræftge*—literally 'those who are knowledgeable about books'—as a synonym for *hālge* 'the holy ones', *gecorene* 'the chosen ones', and *Godes cempan* 'God's warriors'. Although it is hardly the case that either literacy or piety has ever been restricted to persons of a monastic vocation, this small but dedicated group is undoubtedly encompassed in those terms. In short, persons living in monasteries governed by the Benedictine Rule, or perhaps by an alternative rule that was based on it, would have constituted the primary textual communities by which and for which the Exeter Anthology was made.

Finally, a discerning reader of the Exeter Anthology will perceive that the value of many of its constituent poems rests on their stimulus to the intellect and their reinforcement of the craft skills involved in the composition of verse. This is especially true of certain of the contents of the volume's last forty folios or so, from *The Wonder of Creation* to the last of the riddles, with their strikingly self-conscious displays of formal artistry. This aspect of the Anthology will be the subject of the next chapter.

CHAPTER 5

Teaching the Tools of the Poet's Trade

In principle, the formal and technical aspects of Old English poetry can be mastered through study of almost any surviving example of that verse, for the basic structure of the four-stress alliterative metre differs little from one passage to the next. Still, an indiscriminate approach to this body of verse would be insensitive to the variations in style that distinguish one poem or passage from another. What Allen J. Frantzen and other leading authorities have emphasized in recent years, accordingly, is the variety of Old English verse rather than its uniformity.[1] On display in the Exeter Anthology is a scintillating mix of poetic forms, styles and strategies, far more so than in any other extant manuscript containing Old English. What Tiffany Beechy refers to as the 'extraordinary poetics' of certain poems or passages from the Exeter Anthology is especially evident at the book's start and in roughly its last quarter, which features poems conspicuous for their intellectual challenges and rhetorical effects.[2]

It will be useful to distinguish four categories of these effects—*cryptography, poetic form, tropes* and *rhetorical figures*—and to discuss each type in turn.

Cryptography

While cryptography formed no part of formal training in *grammatica*, it figures importantly in the Exeter Anthology, as it does here and there elsewhere in the extant records of Old English and Anglo-Latin literature. Its appeal to well-educated persons of the early Middle Ages seems to have been considerable, particularly in Insular contexts, where social and linguistic conditions stimulated interest in variant forms of the alphabet per se. One factor contributing to this interest was the linguistic diversity of different

---

1 See Frantzen 1994. Elizabeth M. Tyler likewise emphasizes 'the extraordinary diversity which exists within a poetic corpus which is tightly unified by shared poetic conventions and shared aesthetic values' (2006: 172).
2 Beechy 2010, with particular attention to *Advent Lyrics*.

regions of the British Isles, including not just lowland Britain but also Ireland, Cornwall, Wales, the lands of the Picts, and areas where there was substantial Scandinavian settlement.

As R.I. Page has remarked while commenting on the uses to which English runes were put, 'it is interesting to see the runic script preserved in miscellanies of scientific knowledge, among computistical or mathematical lore, in company with etymological and grammatical treatises, or with lists of exotic alphabets, cryptograms and puzzles' (1999: 60). This is in addition to the literary use of runes in parts of the Exeter Anthology, in parts of the Vercelli Book, in the manuscript (destroyed by fire in 1731) that once contained the unique poetic exercise known as *The Rune Poem*, and in the version of the poetic dialogue of *Solomon and Saturn* included in CCCC MS 422, where individual runes spelling out most of the word 'PATERNOSTER' are written alongside the equivalent roman letters.

Of special interest is the use made of runic cryptography in the group of ninety-five or so enigmas, written out chiefly in two sets that occupy much of the last thirty folios of the Exeter Anthology (at 101r–115r and 124v–130v). As we have seen, intermingled with these riddles are other poems of an enigmatic character, including *Wulf and Eadwacer* (at 100v–101r), *Pharaoh* (at 122r), *The Husband's Message* (at 123r–v) and *The Ruin* (at 123v–124v). Also famously making use of cryptography as a tool of bewilderment, in the first half of the volume, are *The Ascension* and *The Passion of Saint Juliana*, two texts ascribed to Cynewulf on the basis of the runic signatures they embed.

Either seven or eight of the enigmas, depending on one's count, encode their answers through one or another form of cryptic writing, most often involving runes. The hermeneutic strategies employed here tend to be complex, original and hard to keep in mind, even when one knows what they are.[3]

The first of these is Riddle 19. After decades of despair among the critics, this has been solved ingeniously by Mark S. Griffith (1992) as *snac(c)* 'small sailing ship'. The poem is worth quoting in full:

> Ic on siþe seah   · ᚺ ᚱ ᚠ
> ᚾ · hygewloncne,   heafodbeorhtne,
> swiftne ofer sælwong   swiþe þrægan.
> Hæfde him on hrycge   hildeþryþe

---

3   For discussion of the modes of cryptography employed in the Exeter enigmas, see Dewa 1995; Page 1999: 187–91; Fell 2002; DiNapoli 2005; Niles 2006a: 85–105 and 222–24; Bitterli 2009, esp. chaps. 4–6 (pp. 83–131); and Orton 2014: 149–65. Williamson (1977) offers a well-informed riddle-by-riddle commentary. The numeration of the enigmas differs slightly from edition to edition or critic to critic; I follow Muir's numbering.

·ᛏᚠᛗ· nægledne rad
·ᚠᛉᛗᛈ· Widlast ferede
rynestrong on rade   rofne ·ᚴᚠ
ᚠᚠᚠᚾ· For wæs þy beorhtre,
swylcra siþfæt.   Saga hwæt ic hatte.

(I saw a proud, shiny-headed SROH prancing swiftly along over the fertile plain. On its back it bore warlike valour, a NOM; an AGEW rode the nail-studded one. The long track, mighty in its movements, bore the keen COFOAH on its bridle path. The voyage, the journey of these men, was thereby the brighter. Say what I am called.)[4]

While this riddle's generic solution, 'ship', is not in doubt, the specifics that pertain to that answer are highly elusive. To begin with the easy part: the runes that comprise each mystery word are written in reverse order, as is the usual scribal practice when groups of runes are used to spell out words. When one converts the runes into roman letters and reverses their order so that they read from left to right, what is arrived at are the four words HORS 'steed'; MON (normally spelled *monn*) meaning 'man'; WEGA (normally spelled *wiga*) meaning 'man' again; and HAOFOC (normally spelled *hafoc*) meaning 'hawk'). But this strategy does not yet yield the riddle's solution. This is only arrived at when one abstracts the first letter of each runic cluster (that is, the first letter of the cluster as written out left to right) and then strings those letters together. This yields the riddle's answer, **snac**. This loan word from Old Norse, normally spelled *snacc* in Old English, denotes a type of swift sailing ship. One can now see that the horse of the riddle's first lines is a metaphor for 'ship', known elsewhere in Old English verse as a *brim-hengest* or *sǣ-hengest* 'sea-stallion' or similar terms.[5] The man is presumably the ship's master; the *sǣl-wong* 'fertile plain' is the sea over which the 'horse' advances; and the hawk too is a metaphor for the ship, which flies over the ocean like a bird.[6] Anyone who doubts the applicability of the term 'hyperliterary' to certain parts of the Exeter Anthology should take a good look at Riddle 19.

---

4   Riddle 19, cited from Krapp and Dobbie 1936: 189–90. For other handlings of the text see Muir 1: 298; Williamson 1977: 78, 186–92. Like other Exeter enigmas involving runic characters, Riddle 19 is best consulted either in Krapp and Dobbie (1936) or in Williamson (1977), where the runes are represented as such. In Muir's edition they are transliterated into their roman equivalents, thus minimizing their cryptographic effect.

5   At verses 423b–24a [862b–63a] of *The Ascension*, for example, Cynewulf refers to ships as *sund-hengestas* 'surf-stallions' and *ȳð-mēaras* 'steeds of the waves'.

6   Compare *Beowulf* 217–18: 'Gewāt þā ofer wǣg-holm winde gefȳsed/flota fāmī-heals fugle gelīcost' ('The foamy-necked vessel then departed over the high seas impelled by the wind, most like a bird'); *Klaeber's Beowulf*, p. 10. This same set of associations helps to confirm the metaphorical value of verses 81b–82a of *The Wanderer*, a troublesome passage where

The situation is simpler in Riddle 23, fairly easily solved as *boga* 'bow'. Here the word that provides the answer is very nearly announced in the riddle's first line: 'Agof is min noma eft onhwyrfed' ('AGOF is my name, switched about'). No runes are introduced here. The main trick is that the letters of the mystery word are given in reverse order, as if they were runes rather than roman letters. To provide an additional wrinkle—an unfair one, it must be said—the letter **f** stands in for the letter **b**, so that the correct solution to the riddle is ***boga*** 'bow' rather than nonsensical ***foga**. Although some might see this switch of one letter for another as the result of a scribal mistake, I suspect that it is deliberate, as with the slightly miswritten words of Riddle 19. If so, one of an Anglo-Saxon riddler's potential strategies was to throw the reader off the track through the creative miswriting of *bōc-stafas* 'letters', whether or not such a practice seems fair to us today.

Riddle 24 is easily solved as *higoræ*—that is to say, as the Old English word that is elsewhere written *higera* or *higræ*, with variations on those spellings. This is taken to be the Anglo-Saxons' name for the bird we call 'magpie' or 'jay', for birds of this type provide a reasonably close match for the poet's description of the creature whose name is to be guessed. The double riddling strategy here is that the letters of which that Old English word consists are represented by their runic equivalents, and the runes are set down in scrambled order. What is required of solvers is that they know the roman equivalents to the letters of the runic alphabet, and that they then recognize that a string of characters that comes out looking like nonsensical GO-RÆ-HI is an acrostic to be deciphered as *higoræ*.

In Riddle 42, customarily solved as *hana ond hæn* 'cock and hen', the solution is spelled out not in runes proper, but rather via rune-names woven into the texture of the verse. What this means in practice is that the reader is informed that the solution to the riddle consists of two instances of *nȳd* 'necessity', one *æsc* 'ash tree', two *ācas* 'oaks' and a pair of *hægelas* 'hailstones'. Someone who recognizes that these four words are rune-names that can stand in for the four runic letters whose roman equivalents are N, Æ, A and H, respectively; who can keep count of the numbers of each character that are needed; and who is also good at acrostics, will then be in a position to spell out the two words *hana* 'cock' and *hæn* 'hen'. The second of these nouns is usually written *henn*.

reference is made to the fate of one of a number of corpses: 'Sumne fugel oþbær/ofer hēanne holm.' What this means literally is 'a bird took one away over the deep sea'. Since no bird is capable of carrying off a human corpse of adult size, the 'bird' is apparently to be construed metaphorically as a ship, a funerary vessel in this instance. See Muir 2: 512 for references to the critical literature on this point.

Riddle 58 is a hard nut to crack. The likely solution in an approximate form, at least, is *rād-rōd*, a postulated Old English compound noun meaning 'well sweep'. There is a nasty twist to the solution, however, for we are told to seek out the riddle's answer in the medium of runes (OE *rūn-stafas*) rather than roman letters. Moreover, in the riddle's last three verses, which are reproduced below, we are told that the first of these runes is the R-rune. The conventional Old English name for that rune is '*rād*', a noun meaning 'bridle path', although equestrianism is irrelevant here:

>   Þry sind in naman
> ryhte runstafas,   þara is Rad forma.
>
> (Three runes are properly comprised in the name, of which *rad* is the first.)[7]

The proper answer to the riddle is therefore not the word **rād-rōd*, but the runic equivalent R—RFM. If you count the number of different graphic symbols that comprise this typographically exact solution, you will find that there are three, not four or six, and that the rune named *rād* is the first, as the correct solution requires. What is especially wicked about this riddle is that in the first instance where it occurs, the rune-stave R needs to be voiced as the word *rād*, while in the second instance it functions as one of three letters spelling out the word *rōd*.

Riddle 64, another ship-riddle like Riddle 19, is probably best solved as the kenning *brim-hengest* 'sea-stallion'. It involves the figure of a metaphorical horse (OE *wicg*)—with the first two letters of that word, W and I, spelled out in runes—riding over a metaphorical meadow (OE *wong*, once again denoting the sea). Moreover, the ship carries a man (OE *beorn*), with the first two letters of that word, B and E, likewise spelled out in runes. An additional eleven runes interspersed among six lines of verse add to the complexity of the puzzle, whose details have never been solved in a satisfactory manner and may have been garbled during textual transmission. These additional runes are the equivalents of the roman letters H and A; TH and E; F and Æ; EA; and S and P. It is possible that the remaining words to be guessed on the basis of these clues are respectively *hafoc* 'hawk'; *þegn* 'thegn' or 'man'; **fælca*, a postulated OE word for 'falcon'; and **ēa-spor*, another postulated word, one that is thought to mean 'water-track' or 'ship's wake'. The details of this Anglo-Saxon linguistic game, however, would probably have eluded the grasp of anyone

---

7   Riddle 58, lines 14b–15; Muir 1: 326. The noun *rād* derives from the verb *rīdan* 'to ride', with reference normally to horse-riding.

but the riddler, who after revealing the full answer would probably have had to fend off his guessers' blows.

The last of the cryptographic enigmas is Riddle 75. A period-appropriate solution for this puzzle is the doublet *hund ond hīnd* 'hound and hind', though other answers have been proposed.[8] The word DNLH, meaningless in itself, is spelled out in runes between two lines of verse that most likely comprise a single riddle:[9]

> Ic swiftne geseah   on swaþe feran.
> ·ᛗ ᛏ ᛚ ᚾ·
> Ic ane geseah   idese sittan.

As is customary in the Exeter Anthology, the runic letters are to be read in reverse order. In addition, in a manner similar to what we see with the miswritten 'AGOF/AGOB' or 'bow' riddle, runic L, or ᛚ, must be read as runic U, or ᚢ. This is not such a stretch in runic characters as it is in roman ones since these two *rūn-stafas* resemble one another visually. The letters of the mystery word, when read in the right order, then yield the Old English word *hund* 'hound'. As for the 'hind' of my proposed solution, it can readily be procured through a change in the pronunciation of a single vowel or, if one prefer to think in terms of visible script, through the substitution of runic I, or ᛁ, for runic L, or ᛚ—two *rūn-stafas* that, again, are similar in appearance. As an alternative way of arriving at a meaningful solution, one can substitute the roman letter I for the roman letter U as if correcting a minim error. Through any of these strategies, with far less trouble than a real dog could be made into a real deer, the word *hund* is transformed into the word *hīnd* 'female deer'. The riddle can readily be construed via the figure of metaphor:

> Ic swiftne geseah   on swaþe feran: HUND.
> Ic ane geseah   idese sittan: HĪND.

What this means in modern English is, 'I saw a swift creature (male in gender) running on a track: a hound. I saw a lady sitting alone: a hind.' As with the riddle genre in general, however, the only way to ascertain the right answer

---

8   The solution offered by Williamson (1977: 352–56) is *hland* 'urine' or 'piss', to be understood with reference to a man standing and a woman squatting. Although others have endorsed this solution, I find it both contextually improbable and philologically impossible; for discussion see Niles 2006a: 96–100.

9   Text from Krapp and Dobbie (with a period added after the first line), though those editors treat the third line as a separate riddle that they term Riddle 76. I follow Williamson and Muir in treating the pair of lines, with their runic insertion, as a single puzzle.

without dispute is for an authorized person to declare what that answer is, then to explain with a smile why one was so dense as not to have guessed it.

The manner in which runes and alphabetical puzzles are used in the Exeter Anthology is then remarkably diverse.[10] Each of the following strategies is employed in the riddle collection alone:

1. Runic letters are sometimes substituted for roman ones. This point is self-evident.
2. The letters constituting a word (whether written in runes or in roman letters) can be read in reverse order.
3. The letters constituting a word can be read in scrambled order, as in acrostics.
4. The first letter of a word, when written alone in the form of a rune, can stand in for the word.
5. The first two letters of a word, written as runes, can stand in for the word.
6. A runic symbol can be written (or miswritten) in a manner that throws the reader off the track, as in the riddle solved as *boga* or the one solved (plausibly) as *hund ond hind*.
7. When an English word that happens to be a rune-name is embedded in the text (or when a series of such words are), then the reader must recognize it (or them) as such, and then must arrange the corresponding runic letter (or letters) so as to spell out a word.

A good deal of mental agility is therefore required on the part of the would-be solver: there is not just one string to the cryptographer's **foga*.

Moreover, it is not just the enigmas of the Exeter Anthology that depend on the reader's ability to decipher runes. Other poems and passages do so as well. The best-known examples are Cynewulf's runic signatures in *The Ascension* and *The Passion of Saint Juliana* and the lines towards the end of *The Husband's Message* where five runes embellish the text. One's success in deciphering these passages may rest on one's willingness to interpret only certain runes 'by the book'. For other runes one must hit upon a word of the requisite initial sound that makes sense within this particular context. Modern readers may not like the rules of this game, but modern readers are not entitled to make the rules. As I have argued elsewhere, the same hermeneutic principles apply to *The Rune Poem*, a text that asks for some ingenuity on the part of its readers. Despite what has sometimes been said about this poem's supposed antiquity, it too

---

10 In addition to the enigmas just discussed, Riddle 36 involves cryptography of some kind. This text is almost certainly corrupt, however, perhaps as the result of someone's incorporating a gloss into it by mistake, and I will omit discussion of it here.

is one that, to my mind, savours more of the scriptorium than of the forests of Germany, particularly since not all of its runes have an ancient pedigree.[11] As for the runic passage at the end of *The Husband's Message*, it spurs readers to entertain a fundamental question: namely, who is the 'speaker' of the runes, in this dramatic monologue? Although one proposed answer has been 'a personified rune-stick' (Old Norse *rúnakefl*), my own favoured solution (as mentioned before) is 'the ship's personified mast'. Either answer involves the rhetorical figure of prosopopoeia, a familiar one in the schools as well as being an occasional feature of material inscriptions.[12] Whether the device of prosopopoeia is Latinate in origin, Germanic in origin or both, it pervades the Exeter enigmas and finds artful use in *The Husband's Message* in conjunction with that poem's embedded runes.

Worth note is that when the runic passages of the Exeter Anthology are read out loud, the runes are not always to be voiced according to their names. In order to crack the code of Riddle 19, solved as *snac(c)* 'sailing ship', for example, there is no need to sound out the names of the runes that figure in the text. Rather, the runes serve as defamiliarized roman letters, as do the runes inserted into the CCCC MS 422 version of *Solomon and Saturn*. Only after the letters are put in an order that generates meaningful words—in Riddle 19, the words *hors*, *monn*, *wega* and *hafoc*, plus the word *snac(c)* itself—can they usefully be converted to sound. This observation reinforces the point that certain poems of the Exeter Anthology are eyepieces, in addition to their being available for oral delivery. They have something of the style of what is known in the hat trade as a 'fascinator' about them.

Poetic form

While the unrhymed four-stress alliterative line is the norm in Old English verse, certain poems of the Exeter Anthology experiment with this form in an original manner. This is true especially as regards refrain-effects and the use of end-rhyme or internal rhyme. Most examples of such experimentation are found in the last quarter or so of the codex. Taken together, they suggest that Old English verse of the second half of the tenth century was scarcely

---

11 R.I. Page (1999) offers a sound guide to all these passages. In Niles 2003b, 2006c and 2006d, I consider them from a somewhat different perspective.
12 Isidore defines prosopopoeia in book 2 of his *Etymologiae*, chap. 14 (Barney 2006: 74). A well-known material example from the Anglo-Saxon period is the Alfred Jewel, with its first-person inscription AELFRED MEC HEHT GEWYRCAN ('Alfred had me made'), for which see Hinton 2008.

'degenerate', as used to be said so tiresomely. Rather, it had become a medium for technical experiment involving techniques of composition that were then coming into vogue among members of a European intellectual elite.

Famously, *Deor* is divided into six clusters of lines separated from one another by the elliptical refrain-like line *Þæs oferēode, þisses swā mæg* ('he/she overcame that; he/she/I can this, too'), reiterated at lines 7, 13, 17, 20 and 27. The use of a regular refrain is otherwise unattested in the extant records of Old English verse. Since neither the referent of *þisses* nor the grammatical function of the ambiguous main verb *oferēode* or the ambiguous auxiliary verb *mæg* is immediately apparent, the refrain serves as a kind of internal enigma offering 'bewilderment effects' of a grammatical kind. A coherent way of construing the repeated line is only revealed when one reads all the way through to the poem's end, then returns to the poem's start to reread its content in the light of one's more complete knowledge of what is being talked about.[13] In the end one can understand the refrain as meaning, in essence, 'Just as he (or she or they) overcame that trouble'—or 'just as that trouble passed away'—'I can overcome this one too.' This hermeneutic procedure provides a model for how to read any other enigmatic poem in the collection.

In like manner, *Wulf and Eadwacer*, the poem that immediately follows *Deor*, includes the repeated half-line *Ungelīc is ūs* 'things are not so with us' (3, reiterated at line 7 with an insignificant change of spelling). Although this refrain-like statement might be thought to be metrically defective since it sounds like an *a*-verse but no *b*-verse follows, it is clearly meant to stand alone. Another line from that poem that might be thought to be metrically defective reads: 'Wulf is on īege, ic on ōþerre' ('Wulf is on an island, I on another', line 4). Although, as a rule, alliteration is avoided on the fourth stressed syllable of an Old English line, this line with its alliteration on *ōþerre* breaks that rule in what is evidently a deliberate way. Moreover, two of the last three lines of this same poem consist of half-lines. These are lines 17, 'bireð wulf tō wuda', and 19, 'uncer giedd geador'. While each line has only two metrical pulses rather than the usual four, in neither one can a breakdown of sense or syntax be discerned. Each one features prominent alliteration. The fact that there are two such lines leads one to suspect that they result from poetic adventurism rather than some kind of error. It is partly on account of their abruptness that they make an impact on the reader as they stand, and Muir rightly resists the temptation to emend them.[14]

---

13 I offer more sustained discussion in Niles 2007b.
14 Thomas Shippey (1976: 131 n. 5), building on the work of Bliss (1971), endorses the editorial practice of leaving unemended what may seem to be anomalous isolated half-lines in Old English wisdom poetry, given the likelihood that they were never thought to be defective.

Other poems in this section of the Anthology display similar freedom as regards the rules of versification. Verses 24–25a of *The Wife's Lament* read as follows if left unemended: 'Is nū swa hit nō wære,/frēondscipe uncer' ('It is now as if it had never been, the love that we two once had'). Since the first line quoted here is defective in terms of normative four-stress metre, Muir, following the lead of other editors, emends the text to read: 'Is nū [fornumen] swa hit nō wære,/frēondscipe uncer' ('It is now *swept away* as if it had never been, the love that we two once had').[15] The emended text is less forceful than the scribal one. If line 24 is allowed to stand as written in the manuscript, then the two stressed words of which its *a*-verse consists—'Is nū'—are arguably the most effective two-syllable verse in the corpus of Old English literature. Granted, there is scant competition for the honour.

Rhyme is another unusual feature of certain of these poems, *The Rhyming Poem* in particular. While end-rhyme, or what in the schools was termed *homeoteleuton* 'like endings', is attested here and there in Old Germanic poetry, it is a more common feature of the Latin poetry of the Middle Ages, whether used incidentally in either prose or poetry or as a structural principle in verse. This is a fairly late development, however, one that post-dates the Exeter Anthology for the most part, though exceptions can be traced in the works of Aldhelm, which provided models for the polished composition of Latin verse in the monastic centres of ninth- and tenth-century Wessex. Precedents in Hiberno-Latin sources have been identified, as well. Still, *The Rhyming Poem* is strikingly unusual in its use of rhyme as a structural principle in what is basically the usual Old English metre conjoined with customary alliteration linking verse to verse.[16] Some of its diction too is unprecedented elsewhere. As James W. Earl (1987) has suggested, sustained use of rhyme in the eighty-seven lines of *The Rhyming Poem* points to an Anglo-Saxon poet's interest in exploring the potential of a radically new poetics incorporating elements of a hisperic or hermeneutic character. A chosen rhyme may be carried over for two, three or even four successive lines, as in the following technical tour de force. The poem's imagined speaker, the Convert, here speaks of the reasons why he has abandoned a life of privilege in order to prepare for his death in a penitential manner:

> Werig winneð,   widsið onginneð,
> sar ne sinniþ,   sorgum cinnið,
> blæd his blinnið,   blisse linnið,
> listum linneð,   lustum ne tinneð.[17]

---

15 Muir 1: 329. The square brackets are his.
16 O.D. Macrae-Gibson (1983: 21–25) provides an overview of the use of rhyme in Old English literature, devoting close attention to possible Irish influences.
17 *The Rhyming Poem*, 51–54; Muir 1: 264.

Teaching the Tools of the Poet's Trade   155

While the meaning of these grammatically parallel verses is scarcely self-evident, their gist is clear enough. The passage tells of a long journey undertaken by a person's spirit or soul through death to the afterlife. The following paraphrase represents a stab at what these lines mean phrase by phrase:

> Worn out, he will struggle on; he will set out on his long journey, his pain will be ceaseless, it will gape [?] with sorrows, his renown will come to an end, he will part from worldly joy, he will lose his skills, he will have no delight [?] in pleasurable things.

To judge from the difficulty one has in construing such lines as these, one can understand why sustained rhyme was generally shunned by poets composing in the Old English alliterative form.

A different kind of experiment with rhyme is assayed in Riddle 28, an enigma traditionally solved as 'John Barleycorn' with an anachronistic nod to Robert Burns's poem of that title composed in celebration of whisky. A culturally specific answer posed in the language of the Anglo-Saxons is the doublet *bere ond ealu* 'barley and ale'. Once the barley is harvested, it is treated rather severely, as we learn in a series of rhyme-laden half-lines:[18]

> [Biþ] corfen, sworfen,   cyrred, þyrred,
> bunden, wunden,   blæced, wæced,
> frætwed, geatwed,   feorran læded
> to durum dryhta.
>
> ([It is] cut, scoured, turned, dried, bound up, rolled, bleached, deprived of its strength, and brought from afar to the doors of the companies of men.)

Nowhere else in the corpus of Old English writings is to be found a more striking example of leonine rhyme—that is to say, internal rhyme, here linking the two stressed words of a single verse to one another. The result is a distinctly hybrid form, Germanic in its four-stress metre and its structural alliteration and Latinate in inspiration in its use of juxtaposed disyllabic rhyming words, one pair after another.

In *The Ruin* too, leonine rhyme is used in an exceptional manner that might be termed hermeneutic. The last word in verse 3a of this text, *hrōfas sind gehrorene* ('the roofs have tumbled down'), is echoed with rhyming words at verse 5b (*scorene, gedrorene* 'scored and collapsed') and then again with another pair of similarly rhymed words at 7b (*forweorone, geleorene* 'decayed

---

18 Riddle 28, 4–7a; Muir 1: 305.

and gone'). No fewer than five words within a space of five lines are linked by what is essentially the same trisyllabic rhyme. This passage confirms that while a general reading context for *The Ruin* may be sought in the medieval Latin genre of the *excidium urbis* (an account of a ruined city), the more precious aspects of this poem's style, including its arcane vocabulary and its arresting patterns of rhyme, reflect Aldhelm's influence.[19]

While rhyme is used as an incidental ornament with some frequency in the Exeter Anthology just as elsewhere in the Old English poetic corpus, the examples given here should be enough to demonstrate that the volume is unusually venturesome in this regard.[20]

Tropes

The two chief tropes that are set out in the Latin rhetorical handbooks of the Middle Ages are metaphor and allegory, two terms that are not always elucidated in the same manner. Bede, a major authority in tenth-century Anglo-Saxon schools, defines a trope as 'a figure in which a word, either from need or for the purpose of embellishment, is shifted from its proper meaning to one similar but not proper to it'.[21] Although most people today would probably take this to be an adequate definition of metaphor, metaphor for Bede is only one of thirteen types of trope. Other medieval authorities classify certain of Bede's tropes as *schemata* or rhetorical 'figures'. From a present-day perspective, these distinctions of nomenclature can start to seem mandarin. As for allegory, Bede defines it as 'a trope in which a meaning other than the literal is indicated'.[22] Although this is not a brilliantly helpful definition, it helps to confirm that allegory can be viewed as a kind of sustained metaphor, one whose conceptual span extends beyond a single word.

Both metaphor and allegory play a significant role in the Exeter Anthology, especially in its last thirty folios or so. Although metaphor is a powerful generative force in language in general, its use is especially prominent in riddling, where answering a riddle correctly may involve nothing more strenuous than intuiting its governing system of metaphor. The most plausible solution for Exeter Riddle 51, for example, is 'quill pen'

---

19 Christopher Abram (2000) points out this line of influence. For richly detailed discussion of the language and versification of *The Ruin*, see Orchard 2008.
20 Orchard 1995a offers detailed observations on the use of rhyme in several poems of the Exeter Anthology, *The Phoenix* in particular.
21 'The Venerable Bede: Concerning Figures and Tropes', trans. Gussie Hecht Tannenhaus (Miller *et al.* 1973: 96–122), at 106.
22 Ibid., at 116.

(OE *feðer*). This answer is easy enough since what the poet is describing is evidently the act of writing, and the quill pen consists of a feather. Moreover, metaphor can be built upon metaphor, as when the quill pen, seen here as a 'warrior' engaged in spiritual combat, metaphorically 'flies aloft' and then dives beneath the 'ocean wave' (the pot of ink), leaving 'black tracks' behind—that is, black letters—as if it were a bird seen first flying aloft, then diving below the surface, then walking on earth.

As this example suggests, an enigma can function as a small allegory, especially when a continuous action such as writing is described. Indeed, when Bede distinguishes seven subtypes of allegory, the third among them is 'enigma'. The huge popularity of allegory among medieval writers can be attributed in part to its capacity to combine high seriousness with entertainment of a kind that delights the intellect. Calvin B. Kendall identifies allegory as a master trope for Bede in his biblical commentaries, one that serves as 'a fundamental tool for uncovering the hidden meanings that underlie the letter of the scriptural text' (2010: 108).

A comparable example from the Exeter Anthology is Riddle 7, the much-admired 'wild swan' riddle. Although one might be tempted to read this poem as if it were an example of nature writing, Riddle 7 is hardly that. While the creature whose identity is to be guessed is indeed the wild swan, the swan in turn signifies the ascending Christ; for in the strand of medieval learning that evidently underlies this poem, the wings of the wild swan produce a kind of celestial music.[23] The allegory here can be likened to that which sustains the much longer poem *The Phoenix*, which tells of a transcendent bird, a figure for both the risen Christ and the risen soul, whose song is more pleasing than any sound of an earthly nature (lines 131b–39).

Not all the allegories to be found in the Exeter Anthology are expressive of an exalted theme. Many riddles that are of an allegorical nature deal with low life, as is characteristic of a genre in which heroic values or expectations are regularly undermined.[24] The first-person speaker of Riddle 27, for example, presents himself as a ruffian who delights in binding and flogging others. He is a wrestler who easily casts a young man down to the ground, and sometimes an old man too, until his opponents lie dazed, powerless to stir hand or foot. The riddle's answer, *medu* 'mead', is sure to raise a smile.

The ethic of sobriety that informs Riddle 27 is confirmed in a number of the other enigmas. Riddle 11, for example, whose solution is 'cup of wine', is far from a carouser's or an epicure's guide to the subject. Rather, the riddle's

---

23 Williamson (1977: 151–53) explicates this theme and its Latin source.
24 Edward B. Irving (1994) writes persuasively on the subversion of heroic values in the Exeter riddle collection.

personified speaker makes no secret of his ability to corrupt the unwary: 'Ic dysge dwelle ond dole hwette/unræd-sīþas' ('I lead the foolish into error and incite the stupid behaviour of those whom drink has made witless').[25] Riddle 28, solved as 'ale', likewise ends with a warning that excessive indulgence in this beverage, which is not despised in itself, can lead the soul to damnation.[26] Riddle 46, solved as 'Lot and his daughters', links drunkenness to lechery and incest.

These are not the only poems of the Exeter Anthology that warn of the dangers of overindulgence in alcohol. As we have seen, the speaker featured in *A Father's Precepts* speaks plainly on the topics of excessive drink and witless conversation, two vices that have been known to keep company with one another: 'Druncen beorg þē ond dol-līc word' ('Guard yourself from drunkenness and foolish words', 34). Likewise *Vainglory* makes pointed reference to excessive drinking as a source of social discord: 'Siteþ symbel-wlonc, searwum lǣteð/wīne gewǣged word ūt faran' ('He [the vainglorious man] sits proud at the feast; besotted with wine, he blurts out words in a venomous fashion', 40–41). The poet of *Doomsday* likewise reminds his audience that the afterlife will offer potential terrors to those who are blind to the vice of overindulgence in food and drink:

> Lyt þæt geþenceð,
> se þe him wines glæd wilna bruceð,
> siteð him symbelgal, siþ ne bemurneð,
> hu him æfter þisse worulde weorðan mote.
>
> (Little does a man who has what he wants, happy in his wine, direct his thought to this. He sits feasting wantonly; little thought does he give to how his journey will turn out after this world is done.)[27]

The virtue of sobriety is likewise exemplified here and there in the saints' lives. In Felix's *Vita Guthlaci*, for example, the young Guthlac is said to abstain from alcoholic liquor after taking the tonsure.[28] Examples drawn from

---

25 Riddle 11, lines 3–4a; Muir 1: 293.
26 Elsewhere I have presented an analysis of this poem that sets forth the grounds for this interpretation (Niles 2006a: 114–17). Saint Benedict's views on the dangers of excessive drinking are expressed in chapter 40 of his Rule. While Benedict somewhat grudgingly allows for the drinking of wine in monasteries, he urges that 'we should not drink to excess but sparingly' ('non usque ad sacietatem bibamus sed parcius'): Venarde, *Rule of Benedict*, pp. 140–41. Censures of excessive drinking are firmly grounded in Scripture, including Proverbs 20.1.
27 *Doomsday* 77b–80; Muir 1: 334. Magennis (1996: 53–55, 1999: 104, 121–22) rightly emphasizes this aspect of Old English writings on the subject of the appetites.
28 *Vita Guthlaci*, chap. 20; Colgrave 1956: 84–85.

either the Latin or the Old English tradition could readily be multiplied. The idealized world of convivial drinking that is on display in *Beowulf*, with its scenes of decorous speeches and gift-giving in the gold-hall Heorot, seems far away indeed from the penitential morality of the Exeter Anthology, with its reiterated reminders of the dangers of drink.

The main point I am making here, however, has to do with monastic poetics rather than with ecclesiastical warnings about the dangers of drink, though the two subjects are intertwined. Through the poems of the Exeter Anthology, prospective poets are offered models of poetic technique that are consubstantial with models of human action meant to be either imitated or avoided. The mastery of tropes—of the use of tropes by poets composing on Christian themes in the vernacular, that is—can be learned at least as readily through study of such poems as the 'wild swan' riddle or the 'mead' riddle of the Exeter Anthology as from the pages of Bede's Latin treatise *De schematibus et tropis*, where each and every example is culled from the pages of Scripture. This is an insight that can plausibly be attributed to the unknown compiler who thought a volume like this worth making.

Rhetorical figures

The use of Latin-derived *schemata* in Old English verse has been charted by now in its essentials. Some few years ago, Jackson J. Campbell demonstrated the importance to Anglo-Saxon authors of such grammatical treatises as the standard ones by Donatus, Bede and Isidore of Seville, with their catalogues of rhetorical figures and tropes. While these influences are fairly obvious in the prose writings of Ælfric, Wulfstan and other late Anglo-Saxon ecclesiastical authors, they are less apparent in Old English verse, which is typically both anonymous and hard to date and which relies on native modes of rhetoric suited to the alliterative verse form. Still, Campbell made a persuasive case that with their textbook Latinate rhetorical figures, certain Old English poems must have been composed 'silently by erudite men in a scriptorium' (1978: 189) rather than by oral-traditional means.

Glosses help to tell the story of this debt, for certain books of Latin poetry that were used in the schools were glossed so as to promote instruction in rhetoric. Leofric's inventory of his donations to Exeter Cathedral includes mention of three books of this kind that survive.[29] These are Oxford, Bodleian

---

29 Campbell 1967: 13–20. A fourth codex of this kind that Leofric mentions does not survive, though other copies of this work do: this is a copy of Statius's *Thebaid* as glossed by Lactantius Placidus.

Library, MS Auct. F.3.6, containing the glossed works of Prudentius; Oxford, Bodleian Library, MS Auct. F.1.15, containing the glossed *Satires* of Persius; and a glossed copy of Boethius's *De consolatione philosophiae*, also preserved in that last-named manuscript though originally a separate book. As Campbell observes, however, the influences that lie behind an Old English poet's use of a rhetorical figure may be difficult to determine, for 'there is always the possibility that a given figure may equally well be the result of the poet's instinctive use of his native linguistic tradition as the product of his following learned precepts acquired during his education' (1978: 190).

The poems of the Exeter Anthology provide countless examples of how *schemata* of the same type used by poets composing in Latin could readily be generated in the Old English alliterative form.[30] Any learned person in possession of the Exeter Anthology could have used this resource to point out instances of such familiar figures of speech as antithesis, personification, paradox, litotes, prosopopoeia and paronomasia, as well as such additional figures as anaphora (the repetition of a phrase at the start of neighbouring clauses), synonimia (the calculated multiplication of synonymous words or phrases), polysyndeton (the repeated use of a conjunction) and zeugma (the use of a single word in grammatical relation to two different parts of a sentence). These are just ten of the more familiar figures. Campbell, indeed, takes on the role of such an instructor himself when citing a number of examples of recognized figures of speech that occur in Old English verse, calling attention to their presence in *The Phoenix*, *The Seafarer*, *The Wanderer* and other poems of the Anthology.[31] Any prospective authors to whom such poems as these were available could readily have integrated Old English versions of Latinate figures of rhetoric into their vernacular practice.

In like manner, Milton McC. Gatch has demonstrated in some detail how *Advent Lyric 5* of the Exeter Anthology was 'conceived within the general framework established by the teaching of grammar in the schools and the application of the exegetical method' (1971: 98). Gatch argues that a medieval student approaching this text with Bede's treatise on rhetoric at his side would have had no trouble identifying the workings here of such rhetorical features as verbal allegory, enigma, antonomasia (where an epithet or phrase takes the place of a proper name) and prolepsis (where the speaker poses a rhetorical question and then immediately answers it). Marie Nelson (1974)

---

30 Joshua H. Bonner (1976) perceives no essential difference between medieval Latin verse and Old English verse in this regard.
31 Campbell 1978: 192–95. Muir likewise comments on lines 14b–20 of *The Phoenix* that the poet here 'demonstrates his command of rhetorical figures' including anaphora, antithesis, rhyme (both initial, medial and end) and isocolon, not all of which are found in the Latin that was the poet's source (Muir 2: 469).

has called attention to similar examples from the Anthology's collection of riddles, leaving open the question of whether these *schemata* represent imitations of Latin examples or derive from unconscious use of a native rhetoric that was never codified. The researcher who has taken up this matter most recently, Janie Steen, takes as her particular subject the manner in which Latinate rhetorical figures were adapted for use in *The Phoenix*, in Cynewulf's signed poems *The Ascension* and *The Passion of Saint Juliana*, and in two enigmas (numbers 35 and 40) that are based on Aldhelm's 'Lorica' riddle and Aldhelm's 'Creation' riddle, respectively.[32] Steen argues that the influence of Latin rhetoric on Old English verse led to a remarkable synthesis of poetic styles in the poems of Cynewulf, whose poetry is not just 'apostolic in its zeal' (2008: 111) but also creative in its use of such Latinate devices as paronomasia, apostrophe, assonance, alliteration, etymological puns, echoic repetitions, and anaphora, alongside such native resources as compound diction and traditional formulaic diction. In its hybrid rhetoric, Cynewulf's work exemplifies a mature monastic poetics.

There is no doubt, then, that by the time that the Exeter Anthology was in circulation, Anglo-Saxon craft-poets who wished to compose eloquent verse in their native tongue could have mastered the figures of rhetoric not just through study of the grammatical treatises that were staples of the early medieval classroom, but also through a process of absorption based on imitation of the works of past masters. Although it is natural to think of this process in terms of a transfer of literary accomplishment from the world of medieval Latinity into Old English, this would be to oversimplify the matter; for by the later tenth century, authors composing in English were in a position to learn from their predecessors in the vernacular tradition as well as by studying Latin authorities.

An engagement with poetic form and linguistic challenges is signalled from early on in the Anthology. *The Phoenix*, in particular, is very much a poem about poetry. While its through-set allegory could serve as a textbook model for the exegetical mode of composition and criticism,[33] this poem also draws attention to the pleasing aural qualities of Old English verse, as exemplified for example by the use of end-rhyme at the level of the half-line:

> Ne mæg þær ren ne snaw,
> ne forstes fnæst,   ne fyres blæst,
> ne hægles hryre,   ne hrimes dryre ...
> wihte gewyrdan.

---

32 Steen 2008; cf. Steen 2009.
33 See the discussion by James Cross (1967).

(Not rain nor snow, nor icy blast, nor blaze of fire, nor storm of hail, nor fall of rime ... can do harm in the least.)[34]

As if to flaunt his learning and verbal dexterity, the *Phoenix* poet ends his poem with an eleven-line passage composed in macaronic verse of a high technical quality.[35] English-language phrases filling the *a*-verse are interwoven with Latin phrases filling the *b*-verse in a meditation on the light and peace that await those who gain a place in heaven. There the souls of the blessed will join with the angelic host in plain sight of the *sigora frēan* ('lord of victories', 675a), whom they will celebrate *sine fine* (Latin 'without end', 675b) by singing the Lord's eternal *lof*, an English keyword that in the next line is juxtaposed with Latin *laude perenne*. This bilingual tour de force can be compared to the fragmentary Old English and Latin macaronic poem known as *Aldhelm* that precedes Aldhelm's prose treatise *De virginitate* in the tenth-century copy of that work that is preserved in CCCC MS 326.[36] Dobbie suggests that this poem, which might have been composed in tenth-century Canterbury, is best characterized as 'an exercise in metrical and linguistic ingenuity' (1942: xcii). It too exemplifies the mature monastic poetics of the late Anglo-Saxon period.

Nearly as complex in the demands they place on the reader are the rhetorical strategies of *The Seafarer*, with its extended use of paronomasia in that passage (lines 72–80a) where there is wordplay on the four words *lof*, meaning either earthly or heavenly honour; *drēam*, referring either to earthly joys or to heavenly ones; *blǣd*, meaning 'glory' but also 'salvation'; and the plural noun *duguðe*, used with reference either to bands of warriors or to hosts of angels conceived of in military terms.[37] Through this wordplay, as Hugh Magennis has remarked, ideas and images that in heroic poetry have to do with the communal life of the hall are 'transformed, remade, in a context of the renunciatory recognition ... that life in this world is a dead life and that our true home is elsewhere' (2007: 304).

These examples, singled out from among very many that could be cited, should confirm the value that the poets of the Anthology set on rhetorical figures as a constitutive element of the craft of verse, where their presence sharpens readers' appreciation of the central tenets of the faith.

---

34 *The Phoenix* 14b–16, 19a; Muir 1: 164. Cynewulf uses rhyme (together with off-rhyme) in a similarly sustained way at lines 152–57 [591–96] of *The Ascension* (Muir 1: 68–69). Elsewhere he does so in an ad hoc way, as do other poets represented in the Anthology.
35 *The Phoenix* 667–77; Muir 1: 187.
36 For text and translation see Jones, *OE Shorter Poems*, pp. 126–27.
37 Stanley B. Greenfield (1966: 157–59, 1972: 88–90) offered influential analyses of the wordplay in this passage; see Niles 2016: 191–92 for discussion. Fell (1991: 174–78) builds on Greenfield's insights with characteristic acumen.

Conclusion: a poetics of and for the cloister?

Old English poetry is various and complex, then, nowhere more so than in the poems of the Exeter Anthology. These works ask for alert, learned readers, especially when poets experiment with the traditional Germanic verse form through the use of cryptographic characters, the experimental use of rhyme, macaronic versification or other special effects. The trope of metaphor abounds, especially among the enigmas, many of which are so densely packed with metaphor as to make up a miniature allegory. The rhetorical figures used in these poems were not just incidental adornments. They could have served as models for poets aspiring to replicate the sophisticated effects of Latin verse in works composed in the vernacular. Taken together, these tools of the poet's trade contribute to the making of a monastic poetics: that is to say, they help to convert the medium of English verse into an effective vehicle for the expression of Benedictine ideals within the broad compass of Christian teachings.

CHAPTER 6

The Enigmas—a Special Problem?

The Exeter Anthology was evidently planned as a literary miscellany. Why, still, did the compiler choose to include nearly a century of enigmas in the codex?

One approach to this question is through reference to early medieval educational practices, for collections of enigmas were viewed as a valuable pedagogical resource. As Martin Irvine has observed, enigmas were exercises in decoding that formed a part of the education of those initiates who knew more than just the basics of grammar: 'Students and readers were ... expected to join the ranks of the *sapientes*, the grammatically wise, by learning the literate skills demanded and promoted by the highly figurative riddle poems.'[1] A practical knowledge of the more formal or technical aspects of poetry was among the skills to be acquired through the study of enigmas. Aldhelm, for example, ostensibly wrote his *Enigmata* for the sake of its value for teaching Latin metrics, a subject on which he wrote two independent prose treatises, *De metris* and *De pedum regulis*.[2]

In addition, with their quasi-encyclopedic scope and their engagement with the particulars of the material world, riddle collections had the potential to illuminate aspects of the Christian view of the universe and all that it contains. Aldhelm's enigmas were not trifles; rather, as Lapidge has noted, they offered their readers 'glimpses ... into the hidden meanings of things'.[3] As surprising as this thought may be to us today, the task of either writing or reading riddles could therefore have served the regular clergy as an aspect of the Benedictine *opus dei*. Rafal Boryslawski has reinforced this point with

---

1 M. Irvine 1994: 364. Patrizia Lendinara (2013: 308-09) makes a similar point about the use of enigmas for teaching purposes, while Leslie Lockett provides details as to how, 'through the combined efforts of several Anglo-Saxon scholars of the late seventh and early eighth centuries, Latin riddles became a fixture of elementary education in England' (2011: 260-64, at 260).
2 Lapidge and Rosier 1985: 61. See pp. 183-219 of this same volume for Aldhelm's prose treatises on meter, as translated by Neil Wright.
3 Lapidge and Rosier 1985: 63.

The Enigmas—a Special Problem? 165

reference to wide scope of the Exeter Anthology riddle collection, which he sees as ranging from 'the most sublime religious concepts or objects' to 'the most tangible or even outwardly offensive actions and objects'. He concludes:

> Their main feature is the contemplation of the divine creation. In other words, nothing is either too magnificent nor too shameful for their authors—*every* aspect of the divine plan of things had been conceived by God and thus becomes worthy of inspection.[4]

A related approach to the question of why the Exeter Anthology contains a substantial riddle collection is through genre and precedent. As Andy Orchard has made clear, *enigmata* were understood as a distinct literary genre throughout the early Middle Ages. Orchard notes:

> The longevity and vigour of an Anglo-Saxon riddle-tradition [...] can be traced at home and abroad, in prose and in verse, in Latin and Old English, in written and oral forms, on secular and religious topics, in the classroom and the mead-hall, from the seventh century to the eleventh, which is to say throughout the entire period of Anglo-Saxon literature.[5]

As the leading example of the genre, Aldhelm's riddle collection was often copied out in Latin miscellanies, including ones that served an educational purpose.[6] The compiler of the Exeter Anthology may have wanted to form a poetic miscellany that, while consisting wholly of vernacular verse, was based on similar principles of inclusion.

Aldhelm's *Enigmata*, among other early medieval riddle collections, was surely known in Glastonbury and its affiliated houses. Noteworthy in this connection is Exeter Riddle 40, solved as 'God in the Creation', for this is a translation of Aldhelm's Enigma 100, which brought his collection to a celebratory close. As Katherine O'Brien O'Keeffe (1985) has shown, Exeter Riddle 40 was translated from a manuscript of Continental origin that came to England in the early tenth century and that bears 'Hand D' annotations—that is, annotations by a hand that has long been thought to be Dunstan's own. The compiler of the Exeter Anthology may well have thought that a poetic miscellany of this kind would not have been complete without including a set of vernacular enigmas, one that in size and sophistication could compare

---

4 Boryslawski 2002: 39. As Frederick Tupper remarked long before, 'Nothing human is deemed too high or low for treatment' in the Exeter riddle collection (1910: lxxxvi).
5 Orchard 2005: 299. Similarly, Mercedes Salvador Bello (2015) documents continuities in the evolution of the riddle genre from the early Latinate Middle Ages to the relatively late Exeter Anthology collection of vernacular riddles.
6 As Lapidge notes (Lapidge and Rosier 1985: 68–69).

favourably with the celebrated Latin riddle collections of the past. Indeed, in the view of Dieter Bitterli (2009: 135), the vernacular riddles of the Exeter Anthology do not just replicate those of the Latinate tradition. In terms of their length, complexity and rhetorical sophistication, they often echo and surpass their Latin models.

Composing riddles as a monastic pursuit

Intriguingly, reference to the art of composing enigmas may possibly be made within the pages of the Exeter Anthology itself. Towards the end of *God's Gifts to Humankind*, a poem that develops the paired notions that the gifts possessed by human beings are manifold and that all gifts come from God, the skills of three different ecclesiastical groups are distinguished. The gift of one group is to conduct the liturgy in a beautiful fashion while singing hymns and psalms in church. The gift of a second group is in bookmaking and pedagogy. The gift of a third group, if I may venture my personal understanding of this passage, is to compose enigmas, among other compositions of a deep or esoteric kind:

> Sum craft hafað   circnytta fela,
> mæg on lofsongum   lifes waldend
> hlude hergan,   hafað healice
> beorhte stefne;   sum bið boca gleaw,
> larum leoþufæst;   sum biþ listhendig
> to awritanne   wordgeryno.

> (One man has skill in many of the offices of the church; he can loudly praise the Lord of Life in songs of praise, he has a high clear voice. Another is wise through his knowledge of books and is thoroughly competent in lessons. Another is adept at writing verbal enigmas.)[7]

The three groups of clergy who are singled out for attention are thus cantors and their like, teachers and their like, and poets and their like.

My interpretation of the last word of this passage, *word-gerýno*, to denote 'verbal enigmas' or 'verbal mysteries' departs from Bradley's translation 'words in their literal form', for his construction of this passage seems to me to slight the sense of 'mystery' that is inherent in the simplex noun *gerýne*, used here in the plural form.[8] While *gerýne* could refer to any of what Edward

---

7 *God's Gifts to Humankind* 91–96; Muir 1: 223.
8 Bradley, p. 328. See Bosworth & Toller, s.v. *word-gerýne*, glossed as 'a mystery expressed in words, a deep saying'. See the same source s.v. *gerýne*, glossed in the 1898 volume as 'a

B. Irving has called 'the dynamic mysteries of the universe as they are shaped in the Christian imagination',[9] or to what Muir refers to as 'the most profound mysteries of Christianity' or simply 'the ineffable',[10] the compound noun *word-gerȳne*, with its emphasis on verbal phrasing, could also refer to the art of composing enigmas, among other writings expressive of the mysteries of the faith. From this perspective, the writing or solving of enigmas is not just a pastime. It is a means of challenging the intellect so as to foster a sense of awe at the wonders of Creation.

In any event, the phrase *list-hendig to āwrītanne word-gerȳno* in the inset passage just quoted must refer to members of the clergy with skills in literary composition. This group would have included initiates who were sufficiently advanced in their study of the technology of verse to appreciate the formal complexities of the poems included in the Exeter Anthology. The hope of some of these *sapientes* may have been to become skilled enough in the art of verse composition to create such poems themselves, following the lead of Cynewulf.

Correspondingly, as Lawrence Shook has made clear, the Exeter riddle collection includes a number of items that relate directly to the scriptorium.[11] Their presence in the Anthology confirms that this is a book in which members of the educated elite are celebrating both their ecclesiastical vocation and the tools of their trade. These tools included not just the arts of grammar and rhetoric, but also the material objects, implements and skills involved in the making of books. Among these riddles are those with the probable modern English solutions 'Gospel book' (#26), 'psalter and bookworm' (#47), 'quill pen' (#51, better solved in Old English as *feðer*), 'reed

---

mystery, a sacrament', and in Toller's 1921 *Supplement* as (sense I) 'what is kept from observation or knowledge, a secret, mystery', and (sense III) 'what is beyond ordinary knowledge, an obscure subject'.

9 Irving 1996: 134, with reference to *Advent Lyrics* in particular.
10 Muir 2: 384, again with primary reference to *Advent Lyrics*. Note the poet's use of the word *gerȳne* at verse 41b of *Advent Lyric 2* with reference to the pregnancy of the young Virgin Mary, and the reiterated use of that word in that same context at verse 74a of *Advent Lyric 4*. The compound noun *gæst-gerȳne* is used five times in the Exeter Anthology with reference to spiritual mysteries of one kind or another, while Cynewulf uses the related compound noun *word-gerȳne* at verse 24b of *The Ascension* to refer to the spiritual mysteries, or perhaps 'signs', revealed by Christ to the apostles after the Crucifixion.
11 Shook 1974; see also Lockett 2011: 262 and Niles 2006a: 117–22 and 126–27. In that last-cited book (at 141–44), as an appendix to the chapter 'Answering the Riddles in Their Own Tongue' (Niles 2006b), I list a full set of solutions for the riddles of the Exeter Anthology in the language of the riddler—that is, in Old English. As I argue there, the stratagem of seeking for a solution in the language native to the Anglo-Saxons is in certain instances either a useful or an imperative one. In the present book, with a few exceptions, riddle solutions are given in modern English for the sake of immediate transparency.

pen' (#60, better solved in Old English as *hrēod*), 'ink well' (#87 and #92), and, in a complex solution that also includes the beech tree and several objects made from it, 'book' (#91, better solved in Old English as *bōc*).¹²

Complementing the riddles of the scriptorium are the ones that relate either to the conduct of the liturgy or to the practice of daily life on what could be either a monastic or a layman's estate. The riddles of the liturgy are the ones apparently best solved as 'wine vessel' (#11), 'paten' (#48), 'chalice' (#59), 'church bell' (#69) and 'candle' (#70). Enigmas that pertain more generally to scenes of daily life, whether on a monastic estate or a secular one, include those with the probable solutions 'water bucket' (#4), 'bee-skep' (#17), 'plough' (#21), 'onion' (#25), 'rake' (#34), 'bellows' (#37), 'key and lock' (#44), 'bread and oven' (#49), 'flail' (#52), 'churn and butter' (#54), 'well sweep' (#58), 'shirt' (#61), 'augur' (#62), 'horn' (#78/79) and 'fish and river' (#84). This is in addition to riddles featuring such commonplaces as 'wood' (#30), 'water' (#41 and #83) and 'fire' (#50). Closely related are what might be called riddles of the farmyard. These include 'an ox and its hide' (#12), 'ten chickens' (#13) and 'bull calf' (#38). Enigmas of these domestic kinds would have encouraged readers of the Exeter Anthology to examine the whole practice of their lives, down to the breaking of a furrow or the hauling of water in a pail, in a manner that encouraged reflection on that practice as a potentially symbolic one, in accord with well-established teachings about the symbolic nature of the Creation.

One purpose of the foregoing remarks is to question whether or not modern critics are justified in calling attention to what they perceive to be obscene or titillating aspects of those riddles of the Exeter Anthology that have a sexual dimension. To be sure, an element of humour is involved in riddling across the board, seeing that its modus operandi is to trick readers or listeners into drawing false assumptions about a statement before springing on them an unanticipated way of construing it. We all laugh at riddles. The humour that is inherent in riddling as a genre can be stepped up a notch or two, as well, when comic reference is made to sexuality, as in the Exeter Anthology 'cock and hen' riddle with its 'proud, fair-haired' hen copulating in plain sight in a manner that would scarcely be expected of a proud, fair-haired lady:

---

12 Models for the writing of enigmas pertaining to the scriptorium can be found in Aldhelm's *Enigmata*, in particular his enigmas #30 ('the letters of the alphabet'), #32 ('writing tablets'), #59 ('quill pen', or better, Latin *penna*) and #89 ('book-cupboard'). Compared with the enigmas of the Exeter Anthology, however, Aldhelm's enigmas more often involve biblical or classical learning. They tend somewhat less often to feature either liturgical objects or domestic items that played a role in the maintenance of monastic or secular estates.

> Hwitloc anfeng
> wlanc under wædum,   gif þæs weorces speow,
> fæmne fyllo.
>
> (If he succeeded in that deed, the proud, fair-haired one took in under her garments a woman's fill.)[13]

When translated back into barnyard terms, what this means is that 'If the rooster mounted the hen, the hen was impregnated.' The riddler's mock-courtly language is as delightful as in Chaucer's 'Nun's Priest's Tale'. Where some modern readers see titillation or even scandal in enigmas of this kind, however, perhaps what is involved is no more than broad humour. Since the time of the ancient Greeks and Romans, sexual humour has generally been thought unobjectionable, within certain limits, in adult social groups of almost any kind, and the same principle very likely applies here. The inclusion of enigmas of a sexual kind within the Exeter Anthology is an instructive aspect of that book for modern readers, for it points to a spirit of anything but puritanism on the part of the book's makers and potential users. This factor is consistent with the book's having been produced in the south of England during the relatively tranquil years of the 960s, 970s or 980s rather than during the more traumatic periods of unrest either before or after those decades; though the quality of tolerance, thankfully, is not limited to any one time or place.

Before taking up at greater length the problem posed by riddles with a sexual dimension, however, I wish to return to the idea that one reason for the inclusion of a substantial collection of enigmas in the Exeter Anthology was literary precedent, for this reason may extend as well to two poems of an enigmatic kind whose placement in the codex falls immediately to either side of the first main block of riddles. These are the dramatic monologues *Wulf and Eadwacer* (at fols 100v–101r) and *The Wife's Lament* (at fols 115r–v).

The power of literary precedent

The reasons for including *Wulf and Eadwacer* and *The Wife's Lament* in a book of the character of the Exeter Anthology are scarcely self-evident. Each of these monologues is composed in the voice of an anguished woman. Either text could perhaps be read allegorically so as to yield a Christian message—as, indeed, almost anything can[14]—but in neither poem can one locate language

---

13 Riddle 42, lines 3b–5a; Muir 1: 317.
14 Bradley (at 365–66 and 382–84, respectively) suggests possible Christian allegorical approaches to these two poems, but without pressing the point. Michael Swanton's (1964)

that has an identifiable religious content. Reasons for the inclusion of these poems in the Anthology might be sought, however, in the literary tradition in which they stand, for there is a precedent for the use of ventriloquized speech in collections of early medieval poetry. Many of the riddles themselves are examples, with their speaking storm winds, water buckets, shields and so forth. In like manner, both *Wulf and Eadwacer* and *The Wife's Lament* exemplify the rhetorical figure of ethopoeia. The classic locus for this figure of speech in the writings of classical antiquity was Ovid's epistolary collection the *Heroides*, a work that consists almost entirely of one versified monologue after another, each one set in the mouth of an anguished woman.[15] The themes of exile, bereavement, danger and betrayal that animate *Wulf and Eadwacer* and *The Wife's Lament* would have been nothing new to readers of the *Heroides*, and the fact that the speaker's physical and mental torment has no happy resolution goes with the turf.

Like Ovid's other poems of exile, the *Heroides* were carefully studied in the medieval school curriculum and survive in multiple glossed copies.[16] It is plausible that whoever compiled the Exeter Anthology thought that this compilation would make for a closer match to the Latin miscellanies of its day if it included not just a number of vernacular enigmas, but also a pair of monologues of this kind, each one set in the voice of a woman suffering as a result of her forced separation from her loved one.

Another possible reason for the inclusion of this pair of poems in the Anthology relates to the book's comprehensiveness. If its compiler aimed to put on display a number of representative examples of the human condition, then the inclusion of one or more poems set in a woman's voice would have been a *sine qua non*. Such poems provide a fitting complement to *The Wanderer* and *The Seafarer*, two comparable tales of woe or hardship set in the mouths of men. According to a literary tradition that owes much to Ovid and that is rooted in earlier Greek and Roman precedent as well, poems or dramas

---

    proposal for a Christian allegorical reading of *The Wife's Lament* has not been embraced by others, as far as I know.

15 Although the *Heroides* is one of his earlier works, Ovid alludes to it in a self-reflective fashion in his later poems the *Tristia* and the *Epistulae ex Ponto*, written during the time of his own bitter exile from Rome to the Gothic-speaking frontier region of Tomis, close by the mouth of the Danube. In the course of time, the theme of exile thus came to permeate the reception of the *Heroides* as well as these other works.

16 Hexter 1986. Klinck (1992: 237-38) discusses the possible debt of *Wulf and Eadwacer* and *The Wife's Lament* to the *Heroides* and others of Ovid's poems of exile, pointing especially to *Heroides* 11 as an analogue to *Wulf and Eadwacer* although without venturing to call it a source. In the appendix to her edition (at 254-67) she prints texts and translations of *Heroides 11*, Ovid's *Tristia 3.4b* and Ovid's *Epistulae ex Ponto 3.7*.

featuring abandoned or isolated women have served as suitable vehicles for the expression of strong emotions. While the Wanderer bears his burden of grief with stoic fortitude and speaks of the need to keep one's thoughts to oneself, the speaker of *Wulf and Eadwacer* cries out to her absent loved one, 'Wulf, min Wulf!' (13a).

The riddles with erotic content as a special case?

The presence in the Exeter Anthology of a number of enigmas that have either an overt or an implied sexual content has attracted a good deal of critical attention.[17] For the most part these are 'catch' riddles: that is to say, they are enigmas that have an amusing double meaning, one of which is 'clean' (the 'right' solution, though not an obvious one) while the other is 'dirty' (the obvious solution, but also the socially awkward one).[18] The language of duplicity used in these riddles is a specialized instance of the double language used across the board in the riddle genre, as well as here and there elsewhere in the Anthology, though normally, elsewhere, the purpose of such duplicity is to oscillate between the heroic and the Christian domains rather than between the obscene and the domestic. In addition to the sexually allusive *double entendre* riddles, two other Exeter riddles deal with the theme of sex, doing so, however, in a straightforward manner. One of these is the 'cock and hen' riddle to which reference has just been made. The other is Riddle 46, one that readers of Genesis 19 will have no difficulty solving as 'the drunken Lot and his daughters'. The moral purpose of this latter riddle is scarcely to endorse sex, but rather to warn of the dangerous intersections of drunkenness and shameful sexual acts.

The Exeter enigmas that are generally thought to be catch riddles are those numbered 25 ('onion'), 37 ('bellows'), 44 ('key and lock'), 45 ('dough'),

---

17 Jonathan Wilcox (2005: 51–53) offers a brief account of this type of enigma in the course of his urbane overview of the Old English riddles as a genre. For extended discussion of the subgenre, see Gleissner 1984 and Murphy 2011: 175–234, with references. Particular studies are cited in the notes that follow. While some critics refer to these enigmas as 'sexual riddles' (e.g. Tanke 1994, Salvador Bello 2011), Murphy prefers to call them 'sex riddles', an equally adequate designation. Such labels as these, however, have the disadvantage of encouraging a view of these texts as little more than exercises in erotic humour when many additional factors may contribute to their interest.
18 See T. Green (1997: 1: 116–17), s.v. 'catch question'. In situations of social riddling, the point of posing a mock-obscene riddle is to catch someone out into giving the sexual solution, which can then be pronounced 'wrong', to everyone's amusement. The Anglo-Saxon *double entendre* riddles are literary examples of the type.

54 ('churn'), 61 ('shirt'), 62 (probably 'augur'), possibly 63 (a fragment whose solution is probably 'glass beaker') and possibly 90 ('key' again).[19] The prospective solutions named here are the clean ones. The corresponding trick solutions ('penis', 'sexual intercourse', 'sexual arousal' and the like) have struck critics as obvious enough as not to require much exegesis. A few additional enigmas might possibly, at the critic's discretion, be ascribed to this same category of 'catch' riddle. An example is Riddle 21, solved as 'plough' but with a hint of a sexual double meaning. A special case is Riddle 20, solved as 'sword' but with a play on the Old English noun *wæpen*, which can signify either 'weapon' or 'penis'. The paronomasia here, however, seems to be developed in a manner free from a 'catch' or any coy humour.[20]

Hermeneutic problems with this subgenre abound, however. Given how fecund the imagination can be in matters involving sexuality, it is not clear what the critical criteria are for distinguishing a riddle with a purely innocent solution from one that is sexually charged through *double entendre*. A close look at a single example, Riddle 12, will shed light on this slippery terrain and will show how easy it is for critics to lose their footing there.

The consensus solution to Riddle 12 is 'ox', or more precisely 'an ox or calf and assorted leather products made from its hide'. Although this riddle was not formerly considered to harbour a sexual *double entendre*, at least five critics have recently construed verses 7b–13a of this riddle to allude to female masturbation.[21] This interpretation has been endorsed despite what I believe to be its philological improbability, in addition to its obvious incongruity from a codicological perspective; for, on the face of the matter, one might not expect to find a topic as obscene as 'a drunk woman masturbating late at night next to a fire with a dildo'[22] worked into a handsome presentation manuscript like the Exeter Anthology—a book made up chiefly of religious poetry, some of which is as exalted in tone as any literature that comes down to us from the early medieval period.

---

19 Paull F. Baum (1963: 57–60) translates as a group eight enigmas that he labels 'obscene'. For the most part these are the ones just listed.
20 For more sustained discussion see Niles 2006a: 137–39.
21 Critics who adopt this stance include Tanke 1994: 32–38, Rulon-Miller 2000, Higley 2003, G. Davis 2006: 46–47 and Neville 2012. Michael Alexander provides a modern English mistranslation of this part of the riddle that ought to be lewd enough for most tastes: 'Fetched between breasts by her hot hand, while she heaves about I must stroke her swart part' (2007: 30). Craig Williamson remarks in his note to lines 7–13 of Riddle 12 (his Riddle #10) that 'though the riddle itself is not usually classified as "obscene", the double entendre of these lines should be clear' (1977: 167); but he does not state what *double entendre* he has in mind.
22 Jennifer Neville advances this reading of Riddle 12 while immediately qualifying it with a one-word proviso: 'Maybe' (2007: 144).

The lines of Riddle 12 that have been thought to involve double language involving female masturbation read as follows.

> Hwilum feorran broht
> wonfeax wale   wegeð ond þyð,
> dol druncmennen   deorcum nihtum,
> wæteð in wætre,   wyrmeð hwilum
> fægre to fyre;   me on fæðme sticaþ
> hygegalan hond,   hwyrfeð geneahe,
> swifeð me geond sweartne.[23]

Although any translation from a foreign language can unwittingly inject bias into the discussion, I will offer the following paraphrase of this passage as a stab at its literal meaning:

> Sometimes in the dark nights a dark-haired slave woman, brought from afar, carries me and presses me, that foolish drunken maidservant. She immerses me in water; sometimes she warms me gently at the fire; she sticks her wanton hand into my depths and repeatedly moves it about, she runs it through me [OE *mē geond*], black as I am.[24]

The passage refers to a female slave doing something at night by the fire: just what, one has to guess. The first lines of the riddle, which are not reproduced here, refer to leather bonds of the kind used to tie up *swearte wēalas*, meaning 'dark-skinned slaves' or perhaps 'Welshmen' (4a). These same initial lines tell of the serving of liquor from a container of some kind, evidently a leather mug or bottle (5-6a). The lines also refer to a *brȳd ... fela-wlonc* 'a very proud bride', or perhaps 'a bride in her finery', walking on something—surely on a pair of leather slippers or shoes (6b-7a). The passage that I have just quoted comes next. The poem ends immediately thereafter in a conventional manner: 'Say what I am called, who plunder the land while living and am of service to groups of noblemen after my death.'

---

23 Riddle 12, lines 7b-13a; Muir 1: 294. Murphy (2011: 195-98 and 200-01) is the only critic of whom I know who engages with the difficulties of this passage at the level of diction and image. While discerning sexual innuendoes here, he finds sexual imagery impossible to decipher in any consistent fashion. He also points out that 'nothing like this is found in the other Exeter bull-calf riddles, nor do the Latin texts imply any such innuendo' (ibid., 196).
24 This last clause, 'swīfeð mē geond sweartne', is sometimes translated differently, but without good philological justification. The accusative singular pronoun *mē* is the object of the postpositive preposition *geond*, while the masculine accusative singular form *sweartne* agrees grammatically with *mē*. Whatever the leather object is that *mē* refers to, its name must be a noun of masculine gender. The masculine noun *scōh* 'shoe' is one possibility.

The 'plunderer' of the last lines of Riddle 12, of course, is the living ox, which can be harnessed to various implements, including a plough, so as to till the fields and bring in the harvest. The phrase 'I am of service to groups of noblemen' (*dryhtum þēowige*, 15b) evidently alludes to the numerous ways in which leather goods, made from the hide of a bovine creature, could be put to use in the homes of well-to-do Anglo-Saxons. Such people routinely owned slaves of the kind mentioned here.

A hint as to how the inset passage is to be construed is provided by the closing phrase 'I am of service to groups of noblemen'. To speak frankly, I find it hard to see what useful service a householder of the Anglo-Saxon period would have thought to be performed by a servant girl masturbating by the fire. What is actually referred to here, most likely, is the cleaning or washing out of one or more dirty or sooty leather objects. These might be black shoes or boots, seeing that an allusion to footwear is made in the immediately preceding verses. Cleaning a pair of shoes or boots by the fire at night is an activity consistent with the riddle's other details, all of which have to do with leather goods. Alternatively, the object to be cleaned could be a leather vessel of some kind, black perhaps because it is old and sooty. The fact that the person charged with cleaning out the object is a dark-haired slave girl who is far from home, is inebriated and has a wanton hand adds a delightfully risqué flavour to this image of life on the old English manor; but that, I believe, is where the erotic element stops.

Those who find my interpretation of Riddle 12 plausible, and who also agree with me that a reading of the 'black boot' or 'black vessel' passage in terms of a coded allusion to masturbation is almost impossible to sustain at the level of language and image, ought to agree that this is not a catch riddle of the kind represented elsewhere in the Exeter Anthology. We should keep in mind that in social riddling, the 'dirty' answer to a catch riddle is the one that leaps out to listeners as the obvious one, while the 'clean' solution may only become evident once the riddler explains it, meanwhile chiding anyone who has offered the 'dirty' answer for having a dirty mind.

To generalize from this example, those critics who find coded references to female masturbation, anal intercourse[25] or similarly obscene topics in the Exeter enigmas seem to me to be reading a tenth-century monastic codex with twentieth- or twenty-first-century eyes. They are enthusiastic

---

25 Tanke (1994: 23) ventures this suggestion, which rests on taking the phrase *sūþerne secg* 'a southern man' in verse 9a of Riddle 62 as an allusion to 'sex from below'. There is no need to argue against this reading since Tanke offers no argument in its favour, but Muir (2: 707), paraphrasing Gleissner (1984: 387–92 and 449), notes that 'this phrase cannot be translated as "the man who works from below" since the medieval mind did not locate the South at the bottom of the map'.

passengers on the 'search for sex' train that so many critics have boarded in recent years. Truly, such obscene readings as have been proposed for Exeter Riddle 12, among others of these enigmas, are impossible to reconcile with the notion of even a broad-minded monastic poetics being operative in the Exeter Anthology. There can be no doubt, all the same, that certain of the authors of the Exeter enigmas enjoyed using the resources of double language so as to dramatize, in amusingly sexualized terms, the domestic life of things.

The Exeter Anthology *double entendre* riddles have sometimes been called 'obscene'. Paull F. Baum has suggested that those enigmas whose trick solutions are sexual in character must somehow have slipped past Anglo-Saxon ecclesiastical censors under the cover of 'the natural ambiguity of all riddles' (1963: 57). Patrick J. Murphy, however, in his close study of certain of these enigmas and their analogues in both learned and popular traditions, rightly questions whether, even when they seem scurrilous, 'there would be anything truly obscene about these texts from an Anglo-Saxon perspective'.[26] In general, the assumption that the place of sexual humour in medieval literature is a scandalous one may pertain not so much to medieval thinking as to modern attitudes towards sexuality shaped by post-Reformation attitudes towards sexuality.

Latin riddle collections that were in circulation when the Exeter Anthology was made tend to confirm this point. For example, Andy Orchard (2005: 287) has called attention to a coarse riddle from a tenth-century Anglo-Latin verse collection, the *Flores* of pseudo-Bede, that can be paraphrased, 'How do you make an anus see?' The answer is, 'You add an **o**.' Jokes often fall flat when translated from one language to another and this one is no exception, but it works well in Latin, for if you add an **o** to the front of the word *culus*, meaning 'tail' but also metaphorically 'anus', the result is *oculus* 'eye'. There is wit here, and there is some learning, but there is no obscenity. Likewise, after demonstrating that riddles employing an erotic *double entendre* are to be found among Aldhelm's *enigmata* in addition to having precedents elsewhere in Latin tradition, Mercedes Salvador Bello finds it likely that 'this riddle category had a literary status of its own in the second half of the tenth century, when the Exeter Book was compiled' (2011: 377). Whether or not this was so, the compiler of the Exeter Anthology does not seem to have had the notion that items with erotic *double entendres* need be excluded categorically

---

26 Murphy 2011: 181. Similarly, Hugh Magennis finds that the attitude underlying the sexual *double entendre* riddles 'is one of good-humoured impudence' rather than of the hostility to sexuality that is sometimes found in the ecclesiastical writings of this period. In his view, which I share, the riddles of this type 'are underlain by a reassuring social morality which does not deny or repudiate sexuality but gives it a place in everyday life' (1995: 17–18).

from the volume, as long as such texts could be admired for other reasons including their wit and their verbal dexterity.

In sum, while it would be facetious to remark that 'monks just want to have fun', it would also seem unfair to deny monks or other *literati* the right to be amused by clever word games that have erotic overtones or allude to ordinary bodily functions. The inclusion of 'catch' riddles in the collection, alongside other riddles that allude in good-humoured fashion to sex, drunkenness and other aspects of life in our fallen world, is a sign of the unusual cosmopolitanism of the religious communities where these poems were made, compiled and read.

The Exeter Anthology—a book of sex and marriage?

More than any other early medieval literary genre, enigmas deal with the workaday world with its chickens, churns, rakes, domestic beasts and kitchen gardens. References to human or animal sexuality are at home in this context. A reader of the Exeter Anthology who progresses through it folio by folio will recognize that sex is inseparable from the microcosm that unfolds between the two covers of the book. This observation should come as no surprise to readers of the Vulgate Bible, with its series of 'begots' and its accounts of the besotted Lot, of the philandering but still blessed prophet David, of the reformed prostitute Mary Magdalene, and other figures whose sexuality is a fact of their existence. In like manner, the topics of sex, marriage and virginity are treated with nearly biblical variety in the pages of the Exeter Anthology.[27]

As one should expect of this codex, the elements of human sexuality are presented not at random but rather in a roughly hierarchical manner. Highlighted in *Advent Lyrics* through the use of ornamental capitals are four lyrics in praise of the Blessed Virgin.[28] Mary is presented in the second of these as 'wīfa wynn, ... fǣmne frēolīcost ofer ealne foldan scēat' ('the joy of women, ... noblest virgin across the whole face of the earth').[29] Somewhat later in the volume we are introduced to the virgin martyr Juliana, an exemplar for nuns in that she steadfastly resists a forced marriage that would violate

---

27 As Magennis remarks, 'with regard to the treatment of sexuality, as in other respects', the Exeter Anthology is 'more heterogeneous in content than any other manuscript containing Old English' (1995: 18–19).

28 These are the lyrics numbered 2, 4, 7 and 9 in Muir's edition. Clayton, *Poems of Christ*, prints *Advent Lyrics* without internal divisions so as to bring out their essential unity and their continuous flow.

29 *Advent Lyric* 4, verse 71a and line 72; Muir 1: 47.

her religious convictions. Juliana's male counterpart Guthlac, the quintessential *miles Christi*, likewise spurns marriage and its domestic complications, preferring to lead a celibate life in the wilderness.

Marriage as a civil institution, however, receives respectful attention. In this regard the Exeter Anthology is in ideological alignment with chapter 19 of Aldhelm's prose treatise *De virginitate*, where pious men and women who marry and propagate children while living in a state of conjugality receive the bronze prize among the ranks of the praiseworthy. (The silver prize is the reward of those who are legally married but who pledge themselves to chastity, while the gold prize is reserved for unmarried persons who lead their lives in a continuing state of chastity out of a spontaneous desire for that condition.)[30] Correspondingly, a passage in *Exeter Maxims A* echoes the words of God in the Book of Genesis in its encouragement of both conjugal love and child-rearing: 'Tū bēoð gemæccan—/sceal wīf ond wer in woruld cennan/bearn mid gebyrdum' ('Two persons are help-meets: a man and wife shall engender children in accord with nature').[31] A passage in *Exeter Maxims B* likewise calls to mind a domestic scene featuring a loyal wife. This is a Frisian woman who welcomes home her seafaring husband, washes his weathered garments and yields to his desire: 'Liþ him on londe þæs his lufu bædeð' ('She grants him on land what his love urges').[32] This willing female figure is evidently to be viewed as an exemplar for married women living in a state of conjugality.[33]

As if to provide a painful reminder that all marriages are not equal, however, the author of this same poem straight away then speaks of unfaithful women who provoke scandal by embracing strangers when their husbands are away from home (*Exeter Maxims B*, 30–32). This is a favourite theme of literature both comic and tragic, although here the mode of address is straightforwardly didactic. In *The Soul's Address to the Body*, as well, the embittered soul berates its former body for having indulged in *firen-lustas* 'wicked desires' (41b), or sins of a carnal nature.[34]

---

30   Lapidge and Herren 1979: 51–132 (at 75–76). The three categories of chastity are *iugalitas*, *castitas* and *virginitas*, respectively. Carol Braun Pasternack (2004) offers close discussion of Aldhelm's treatise.
31   *Exeter Maxims A*, 23b–25a; Muir 1: 249.
32   *Exeter Maxims B*, 98; Muir 1: 253. Since the phrase *on londe* might carry sexual overtones, an alternative translation 'on the ground' could be entertained.
33   Elsewhere, as is discussed by Susan Deskis (1994), *Exeter Maxims* features a variety of themes pertaining to motherhood, childbirth, women's personal adornment, marriage as contract, women's domestic duties, sexual mores and the like.
34   See the *DOE*, s.v. 'firen-lust', sense a: 'specifically of sexual desire: lust, wantonness'.

Marriage, sex and child-rearing are topics that find expression in this same part of the codex in *The Wife's Lament* and *Wulf and Eadwacer*, the two monologues set in a woman's voice. As in those lines from *Deor* that tell of Beadohild's sorrow or that make cryptic allusion to the unhappy love affair of Geat and Mæðhild,[35] what is of interest here is the potential grief or longing associated with erotic relationships. This is as one might expect in a manuscript so deeply invested in monastic values. The speaker of *The Wife's Lament* speaks bitterly of having been abandoned by her husband and persecuted by her in-laws. Her sense of betrayal is heightened by a consciousness that she and her husband once exchanged vows of love—an apparent allusion to an oral marriage contract. The speaker of *Wulf and Eadwacer*, too, is clearly distraught, whatever the exact circumstances of her suffering are imagined to be. She and her beloved are unable to meet except at rare intervals. Moreover, she has evidently given birth to a son in a situation fraught with danger for both the child and his father. In none of these monologues is the relationship between lovers presented in terms likely to reassure a prospective bride that her happiness will be lasting. One is reminded of Aldhelm's distinction between three groups of women: those who marry, those who marry but choose to remain celibate, and—the most blessed group—those who remain lifelong virgins.

An unremarkable conclusion to be drawn from the representations of sex and marriage in the Exeter Anthology is that just as there has been strife on earth ever since Cain struck down Abel,[36] sex has raised its head—and couples have had domestic troubles—ever since Adam and Eve dwelt in the Garden of Eden. The fact that 'sex happens' in the Exeter enigmas is in keeping with the worldly interests that come into view throughout the later parts of the codex, providing it with hoes, flails, bullocks, bee-skeps, *double entendre* ovens, a randy barnyard cock and hen, and other unrefined furnishings. Although no one is likely to call for the Exeter Anthology to be renamed 'The Anglo-Saxon Book of Sex and Marriage', it remains true that far more frequent reference to these aspects of the human condition is made in this codex than in the other extant volumes of Old English verse.

---

35 Klinck (1992: 161–64) discusses the difficulties involved in interpreting these legendary allusions in *Deor*.
36 See *Exeter Maxims C*, 196b–98a: 'Slōg his brōðor swǣsne/Cain, þone cwealm serede; cūþ wæs wīde siþþan,/þæt ēce nīð ældum scōd' ('Cain struck down his own brother; he plotted that killing; after that it was manifest far and wide that chronic strife was afflicting humankind'). Muir 1: 257.

Taking stock of the Exeter enigmas

There is nothing anomalous, then, about the fact that nearly a hundred enigmas are included in a large verse collection, the Exeter Anthology, that was basically a monastic production. There was medieval precedent for including enigmas within a literary miscellany, where their educative role served to reinforce key aspects of the Benedictine way of life, including its emphasis on learning. No few Exeter riddles celebrate God's awesome powers or take delight in the beauties and wonders of the natural world, thus reinforcing the religious perspective that finds expression in *The Wonder of Creation* and other poems of the volume. Other enigmas relate to the works of the scriptorium, the daily conduct of the liturgy or the routine of manual labour on either a monastic estate or a secular one.

Neither is it anomalous that certain enigmas touch on erotic themes, for sex, along with its attendant anxieties and tensions, was part of the earthly realm that Anglo-Saxon monks and cloistered women inhabited. Any number of monastics had previously lived for a time—some of them for a long time—in the 'real world' of courtship, marriage and erotic relations. Some monks and nuns would have had not just an intellectual concept of sex, but also an experiential knowledge of it. Moreover, poems on erotic themes were amenable to didactic use. They could confirm the sanctity of marriage; they could castigate lust; they could dramatize the damage done by acts of infidelity; they could portray the emotional sufferings that result from worldly ties; or in a number of other ways they could reinforce the governing ethos of monastic communities. The riddles that deal with sex thus have something in common with those that touch on the consumption of alcohol, another commonplace of 'real life' and another potentially hazardous source of pleasure. Whoever compiled the Exeter Anthology seems to have been confident that an educated Christian will know how to read these texts, appreciating their play on words, their audacious use of metaphor, and other aspects of their literary artifice while smiling, perhaps, at their occasional reference to bodily functions that were perfectly well known to all.

A modern reader coming across the Exeter Anthology for the first time might ask the innocent question: 'Did monks write scurrilous riddles, then?' Perhaps the best answer to this question is another one: 'Did monks write anything but scurrilous riddles?' When one sees that the answer to both questions is 'Decidedly, yes', then what some critics have seen as a problem in a miscellany of this kind tends to dissolve away.

CHAPTER 7

Poetry and World-View

Study of the Exeter Anthology from cover to cover opens up the question of what world-view underlies the volume, if indeed one is justified in speaking of a single world-view in this context.

By its nature, world-view is a slippery concept. Like ideology, it tends to be invisible, for it chiefly pertains to the subterranean realm of unconscious assumptions rather than to the brightly lit one of creeds; though creeds too can be involved, especially where religion enters in. Like the term 'mentality' (or French *mentalité*, or *mentalités* in the plural), and somewhat in distinction from the more individualistic and philosophical mode of perception that German-speakers call *Weltanschauung*, world-view pertains to collectivities, to groups of people who share a common culture and who think and talk about that culture in ways that are socially sanctioned and mutually intelligible.

While it is impossible to say if the individual poets whose works are included in the Exeter Anthology were in communication with one another in such a manner as this (for who is to know if they were even alive concurrently?), surely the unknown persons involved in the Anthology's compilation and copying in southern England during the period *c*.960–75 were participants in a common culture. It is in this sense that one is justified in speaking of a single world-view that underlies the collection, even if one's understanding of just what constituted that collective world-view rests on close study of the book's constituent parts.[1]

The workings of amplification

The choice of English as the linguistic medium of the Exeter Anthology had implications. When poems based on Latin sources were composed in

---

1   My discussion of world-view should be distinguished from that offered by Daniel Anlezark (2013) in his chapter 'The Anglo-Saxon World View'. While Anlezark seeks to generalize about Anglo-Saxon concepts of cosmology and geography, my attention is focused on a particular late tenth-century book of vernacular poetry. While religious concepts lie outside the scope of his analysis, they are central to mine.

the English language, the almost universal practice of their authors was to paraphrase those sources with latitude, and almost always in a venturesome manner. Expansion upon a base text, or what was known among medieval rhetoricians as *amplificatio*, was the norm. This aspect of Old English poetry is in accord with the art of paraphrase as set forth in Quintilian's treatise *Institutio Oratoria*, a standard text for instruction in *grammatica*. The art of paraphrasis, or *conversio ex Latinis*, is here said to be 'specially valuable with regard to poetry ... for the inspiration of verse serves to elevate the orator's style'.[2] Quintilian makes clear, moreover, that paraphrasis (or periphrasis) is not at all the same thing as what today we would call translation:

> Neque ego paraphrasim esse interpretationem tantum volo, sed circa eosdem sensus certamen atque aemulationem.
>
> (But I would not have paraphrase restrict itself to the bare interpretation of the original: its duty is rather to rival and vie with the original in the expression of the same thoughts.)

In keeping with Quintilian's teachings, such poems of the Exeter Anthology as *Advent Lyrics*, the versified saints' lives featuring Guthlac and Juliana, *The Phoenix*, the allegorical poems of the Physiologus, the gnomic poems including *A Father's Precepts*, and the enigmas are therefore both like their Latinate sources and significantly unlike them, when one takes into account their vim and rhetorical flourish.

Since the Old English alliterative verse form, with its appositional grammar and its systems of redundant synonyms, lent itself so readily to the device of *amplificatio*, a poem composed in the vernacular was almost guaranteed to be both longer and more repetitive than any source text on which it was modelled. Stylistic pleonism is the rule. In addition, the widespread medieval habit of glossing texts, or of writing independent commentaries on them, encouraged Anglo-Saxon poets to expand upon a source by incorporating expository material into their paraphrases, always in a manner that involved creative transformations at the level of individual phrasing. These factors encouraged the production of a body of vernacular verse that was potentially innovative and that is best approached on its own terms, even as one remains alert to its sources and analogues. Educated readers of the Exeter Anthology would have understood that the authors of such poetry as this did not just aim to replicate Latinate sources. They apparently vied with one another so as to create a new hybrid medium, one that was yet more challenging

---

2   Translation by H.E. Butler (1922: 114–15). The following quotation of text and translation is from the same source.

intellectually and yet more arresting from a formal perspective than were its Latin precedents. As Ruth Wehlau has pointed out, the art of this poetry involves the reconstruction of source texts in the vocabulary of the native English verse medium so as to draw out their moral, theological or tropological significance. Wehlau demonstrates how the author of *The Wonder of Creation* 'plays with the language' of his chief source, Psalm 18, so as to create 'a whole new poem, not a translation, but a transformation, a reworking of the fundamental images found in the Latin psalm'.[3]

Amplificatio can thus be regarded as the chief engine of a monastic poetics. A glimpse into its workings is afforded by the three extant Old English verse paraphrases of the Pater Noster prayer. The first of these, the shortest version, is written out at folio 122r of the Exeter Anthology.[4] The text consists of an eleven-line paraphrase of a simple prayer that all clergy and many other persons in society would have known by heart. The poet expands upon his liturgical source in ways that suit the alliterative verse form, that heighten the prayer's devotional mood, and that bring out the text's theological significance. The straightforward Latin clause 'panem nostrum cotidianum da nobis hodie', for example, is paraphrased here as follows:

> Syle us to dæge   domfæstne blæd,
> hlaf userne,   helpend wera,
> þone singalan,   soðfæst meotod.
>
> (Helper of men, give us today a glorious abundance, O faithful Creator, our bread—bread that lasts forever.)[5]

Here an uncomplicated reference in the Latin text to 'our daily bread' is expanded into three full alliterative verses. Through use of the adjective *sin-gāl* 'eternal', allusion is made to the Eucharist, while a pair of whole-verse allusions to God as *helpend wera ... sōðfæst meotod* reinforce the prayer's devotional mood while reminding one of one's debts to the Lord as the creator and comforter of humankind.

---

3   Wehlau 1994: 72. Similarly, Ann Savage finds that in Old English verse in general, 'translation by definition involves expansion ... for the purpose of drawing a reader or audience more closely into the personal significance of the Latin base text' (1989: 134). Emphasizing that the process of translation always involves change and, often, the transformation of a source text, Robert Stanton argues that translation can serve as 'an overarching idea to explain Anglo-Saxon literary culture' (2002: 2).
4   The three paraphrases, which are conventionally known as *The Lord's Prayer (I)*, *The Lord's Prayer (II)* and *The Lord's Prayer (III)*, are edited as a group by Jones, *OE Shorter Poems*, pp. 66–81. The second version is written out in CCCC MS 201, a late eleventh-century miscellany, and the third in Oxford, Bodleian Library, MS Junius 121, another eleventh-century manuscript.
5   Text from Muir 1: 349 (lines 6–8); Latin text (Luke 11:3) from Kinney, *New Testament*, p. 372.

The other two extant Old English verse paraphrases of the Lord's Prayer are a good deal longer than this, totalling respectively 123 and 36 lines of verse. Although discussion of them falls outside the scope of the present study, worth note is that these two greatly expanded versions of the prayer represent far more than paraphrases of its content, for incorporated into each text are extended meditative glosses on the prayer's implications for those who aspire to a pious life. Other well-known liturgical texts, including the Apostles' Creed and the Gloria, were subject to similar amplification when paraphrased into Old English alliterative verse, for they too were treated freely at the verbal level while being augmented with gloss-like versified commentaries.[6]

Another illustration of the factors that could be involved in the reworking of a source text is the remaking of Aldhelm's Enigma 33, his 'Lorica' or 'mail coat' riddle, into the version of that enigma that is included as Riddle 35 of the Exeter Anthology. The enigma was first translated into the Northumbrian dialect of Old English as the poem known as *The Leiden Riddle* that is preserved in Leiden, University Library, MS Voss. Q. 106.[7] The unknown maker of this text systematically reworked Aldhelm's seven Latin hexameters into fourteen Old English long lines, drawing on the conventional syntax and diction of vernacular verse so as to satisfy the formal requirements of the alliterative line. When *The Leiden Riddle* was later reworked into the West Saxon dialect and preserved as Riddle 35 of the Exeter Anthology, two lines were substituted for the last two lines of the Northumbrian version. In a manner that is typical of this volume's participatory style, they challenge the reader to declare the riddle's answer:

> Saga soðcwidum,   searoþoncum gleaw,
> wordum wisfæst,   hwæt þis gewæde sy.
>
> (Say in true terms, you who are skilled in puzzles, wise in the use of language, what this garment is.)[8]

These lines have no place in the riddle's prior history. With their call to the reader to provide a solution, however, they are wholly conventional within the context of the Exeter riddle collection. Moreover, the lines make striking use of the conventional Old English poetic device of verbal compounding, for no fewer than three compound nouns or adjectives are introduced in just

---

6 For texts see Jones, *OE Shorter Poems*, pp. 82–95.
7 For the text see Dobbie 1942: 109. The Latin text of Aldhelm's riddle is included at p. cviii of that volume.
8 Riddle 35, lines 13–14; Muir 1: 310.

these two lines: *sōð-cwidum* 'in true terms', *searo-þoncum* 'in cunning thoughts' and *wīs-fæst* 'secure in wisdom'. The three compounds have to do with truth, mental ingenuity and wisdom, thus serving to highlight the system of values within which the person who rewrote this text was working. Here as with Riddle 30b (the one solved as *trēow*), one wonders if it was at the time when this text was prepared for inclusion in the Anthology that its phrasing was slightly altered.

By following the progression of Aldhelm's riddle first to its translation into the Northumbrian dialect of Old English and then to the West Saxon version included in the Exeter Anthology, one witnesses a mature monastic poetics in the process of being born. More than ornamentation was involved in this process, for the use of the conventional lexicon of Old English verse was a value-laden enterprise. Among the key terms introduced by the poets who were responsible for the versions of the Lord's Prayer and of Aldhelm's 'Lorica' enigma that are included in the Exeter Anthology, for example, are the simplexes *dōm* 'glory', *blǣd* 'glory', *sōþ* 'truth', *searo* 'artful contrivance' and *wīs* 'wise'. Study of the workings of amplification in such poems as these offers an entry point to the ethos that animates this volume, saturating its language with values that are at the same time heroic and religious and that had a particular bearing on the conduct of the cloistered life.

If one were to ask, 'Why is it that Old English verse was chosen as the medium for the expression of religious ideas in the Exeter Anthology when prose was readily available for the same purpose?', the answer may have to do with the fact that the alliterative verse form used by all poets composing in Old English was not a neutral medium. Rather, it encouraged use of a conventional poetic vocabulary, much of which was anchored in heroic values. Together with other pre-Conquest codices that include significant amounts of vernacular verse, the Exeter Anthology could speak to the mentality of Christians who both honoured their ancestral heritage and took their religion seriously. For the select few who had adopted the monastic way of life, this meant observing the tenets of the Benedictine Rule, with its insistent reminders of the need for humility, self-restraint and abstemiousness: three virtues that were complementary opposites of the traditional heroic virtues of pride, military prowess and delight in the conviviality of the mead-hall. The practice of either one of these two sets of virtues, whether the heroic or the monastic, required that one dedicate oneself to a well-defined disciplinary regime, one that was believed to be essential to the welfare of society.

One of the leading virtues cultivated by the Anglo-Saxon monastic elite was the pursuit of wisdom, seen as a worthy equivalent to the warrior's pursuit of fame. When the religious poets whose work is represented in the Exeter Anthology made use of the traditional vocabulary of Old English heroic poetry, they ensured that verse composed on Christian themes would perpetuate, to some degree, the ethos of the warrior class. At the same time, they redirected that ethos to the quest for wisdom that was the prelude to the soul's journey towards salvation.

The book's style in relation to its readership

Although questions of style are sometimes approached in an autonomous manner, they are often best posed in conjunction with questions of audience and reception. One of the theses of the present book is that while the poems of the Exeter Anthology could have been read by any literate persons with access to them, their style and thematic content, steeped in heroic associations as they were, would have made this verse an attractive means by which persons of high birth were acculturated to the ethos of monasticism. Even if such persons might have lived lives of relative ease and comfort, they had chosen Christ as their lord and other monks as their companions. Cloistered women had fellowships equivalent to those of the monks. Dunstan and Æthelwold were two such men, for each had been born into a family of wealth and standing, hence into a role of potential leadership in worldly society, before asserting a different kind of leadership as monks who became founders of the Benedictine Reform. Many of the poems included in the Exeter Anthology seem tailor-made to suit the background and tastes of persons of this type, or else of persons who could identify with such an elite even if they themselves were of humbler birth.

The heightened style that is characteristic of the poems of the Exeter Anthology was not the only option for their makers, for other authors might have chosen other stylistic strategies. Very different, for example, is the low-key alliterative prose style adopted by Ælfric in his saints' lives in particular. While Ælfric evidently wished to draw on the affective potential of the Old English alliterative verse form, he studiously avoided the vocabulary of heroism, with its richly elaborated systems of compound diction. Likewise he made little use of the device of grammatical apposition, a feature of classic Old English verse that encouraged a profuse display of poetic synonyms and figures of speech. Distrustful of fables and indifferent to the hermeneutic style that suited the taste of certain of his contemporaries, Ælfric composed his works either in lucid and flowing prose, or else in a limpid verse-like alliterative form that appears to have been largely his own invention. The advantage of this latter medium was that while it had some of the rhythmic and aural appeal of traditional alliterative verse, it did not call attention to itself as language composed in a heightened register.[9] With its lack of verbal pyrotechnics, its virtues are those of grace and intelligibility. There is little sense in calling Ælfric's verse-like prose the product of a monastic poetics. Rather, what it represents is an artfully fashioned discourse of a different type, one that was suited to straightforward narration combined with homiletic instruction.

Style and audience are two topics that are intertwined. Ælfric's use of an accessible verse-like style suited the broad audience for which he composed his works. While the relatively esoteric poems of the Exeter Anthology seem to anticipate a small readership of learned persons, Ælfric evidently composed his saints' lives and sermons for the potential benefit of any and all members of his society, whether to be heard by people in any walk of life or to be read by those with sufficient literary competence. This would have been in addition to the rare person with learning as deep as his own.[10]

Still, different scholars envision the narrower readership of the Exeter Anthology in different ways. Taking up a line of argument pursued by Robin Flower (1933: 87–90), for example, Michael Lapidge (1991: 37) has surmised that the Anthology was commissioned by a lay patron such as Æthelweard (d.998), the literate ealdorman who was Ælfric's chief patron, as part of an attempt to make book learning available to a wider segment of society including the laity. This is a plausible enough inference, even though advanced book learning was a defining attribute of the clergy. In somewhat the same manner, while thinking of *Widsith*, *Deor*, the so-called elegies and the enigmas in particular, Patrick W. Conner has envisioned certain poems of the Exeter Anthology as 'the poetry of people who had lives beyond the cloister wall', even if those persons were familiar with Christian doctrine and the liturgy (2001: 266). This could be true to some extent. My own sense of the matter, however, is that very few people living outside monastic communities would have had either the learning or the opportunity to read these poems on the page, thereby gaining a full understanding of them in their manuscript context. Moreover, only the rare member of the laity would have been competent in the modes of exegesis on which an understanding of

---

9   For two different recent perspectives on what was involved in Ælfric's cultivation of this verse-like style, see Magennis 2006 and Bredehoft 2009. Elsewhere (in Niles 2016: 189–90) I offer a brief review of scholarship on this point. While Bredehoft speculates that Ælfric thought of himself as a poet working as a continuator of an ancient Old English tradition, an alternative view, favoured by Magennis as well as myself, is that Ælfric appropriated only certain of the aural qualities of traditional verse so as to enhance the appeal of his devotional writings. The great homilist's mistrust of poetry, in the usual sense of that word, seems to have been profound.

10 Jonathan Wilcox (2006) discusses Ælfric's audience with attention to its complex and inclusive character, spanning clerical and lay domains as well as oral and written ones.

certain of these poems depends. Equally rare would have been the lay person capable of recognizing the allusions to learned sources that lend depth to such poems as *The Ascension, The Seafarer* or *Vainglory* or, on a smaller scale, that help one to understand the 'wild swan' riddle (Riddle 7) as Christological in content, to cite just a few examples.

Given its heightened style and its frequently esoteric contents, the Exeter Anthology is more likely to have been directed to a well-educated readership consisting chiefly of members of the regular clergy. In this scenario, the book's readers would have been beyond the stage of elementary book learning. Already schooled in the basics of Latin grammar and rhetoric, such persons would have been as literate in English letters as they were in Latin. Their probable exposure to *runica manuscripta* as well as other writing systems in the course of their prior studies would have accustomed them to alternate forms of the alphabet. As members of ecclesiastical communities, such persons would have been familiar with the role of verse as a tool for the dissemination of learning and the contemplation of divine mysteries. One likely aim of the compiler of the Exeter Anthology was to elevate English verse to a status like that of its Latin counterpart in the medieval system of higher education.

The place of *The Ruin* in the microcosm that is the book

Whether or not the Exeter Anthology was compiled with an eye to its possible instructional use, the regime of reading that codex today in a manner consistent with the way that it is likely to have been read most often in a monastic institutional setting—that is, folio by folio, starting from the beginning and proceeding to the end—will yield insights into the overall picture to which each part contributes. Correspondingly, this way of reading the book will enhance one's understanding of the world-view that sustains the book and all its parts.

While the contents of the Exeter Anthology are to some extent miscellaneous, its overall scheme is coherent enough. The book proceeds in a roughly hierarchical fashion from the one to the many, from the high to the low, from the exalted to the dejected, from timelessness to the transitory realms of history and ordinary experience.

Two moments in this trajectory stand out as a contrastive pair. Very near to the volume's start, in *Advent Lyric 3*, we encounter a hymn in praise of the Heavenly Jerusalem, the *visio pacis* or 'mystical vision of peace', as the city's name was thought to signify.[11] Jerusalem is praised here as 'Cristes burg-lond,

---

11 On this medieval etymology see Campbell 1959: 85.

engla ēþel-stōl ... burga betelīcast' ('Christ's citadel, the angels' patrimonial seat ... the most excellent of cities').[12] In contrast to this exalted vision, very near to the book's end (at fols 123v–124v) we encounter a city of the dead, the wasteland of *The Ruin*.

Different critics have reacted to this latter text in different ways depending on whether they dwell on the poet's evocation of a world of opulence and communal festivities or on his description of the ruins that remain in sight after that former world has perished. Although one is free to read *The Ruin* as chiefly an exercise in nostalgia, as for example Roy Liuzza (2003) has done, and while it is also possible to admire the poem for its aesthetic value without coming to any conclusion as to its 'meaning',[13] other critics have seen a darker side to it. While identifying the poem's main theme as *sic transit gloria mundi*, Anne Klinck (1992: 62–63) sees hints in it of a moral relating to God's destruction of a civilization as punishment for the sins of its people. Such a reading of the poem sets it into relation to a mode of thinking that is characteristic of the psalms, with their repeated allusions to God's just destruction of earthly civilizations. Other critics, noting that the Old Testament concept of a fearful deity took on an apocalyptic dimension in the Christian Middle Ages, have approached *The Ruin* in terms of the medieval genre of *excidium urbis*, or 'the ruination of a city'.[14] Taking that argument one step farther, Martin Green has found that the poem reinforces a large body of Old English literature on the theme of Doomsday, with its imagery of the sweeping away of the things of this world by the awesome power of God.[15]

My own reading of the poem is in accord with this tendency. From an Augustinian perspective, the decayed city portrayed in *The Ruin* has a double value. In addition to its character as an earthly site, the city illustrates the fate of works of human engineering that are technologically advanced, visually splendid and conducive to pleasure, but that are empty of spiritual value so that in the end they come to nothing. *The Ruin* thus serves as a suitable companion piece to those other Exeter Anthology poems that treat of the ruins of earth (*The Wanderer*, *The Seafarer*), each of which relies implicitly on the Augustinian antithesis of the City of Man versus the City of

---

12 *Advent Lyric 3*, verses 51b–52a, 66a; Muir 1: 46. With a direct bearing on the imagery of this poem is the architectural imagery of Christ as foundation stone and as master mason in *Advent Lyric 1*.
13 Alain Renoir (1983), for example, argues that the poem speaks eloquently to its readers even if they view it from contrary critical perspectives.
14 For example Doubleday 1972, Anne Lee 1973 and Wentersdorf 1977.
15 M. Green 1975. Kathryn Hume (1976), similarly, draws a pointed contrast between the imagery of earthly ruins in this poem and images of the earthly hall as celebrated in heroic poetry.

God.¹⁶ The situation depicted in *The Canticles of the Three Youths* and in that poem's close analogue in the Old English poem *Daniel* makes for another instructive parallel, for both these poems allude to the destruction of a city and a kingdom because of a people's failure to maintain spiritual integrity. The city in this instance is the Babylon ruled over by Nebuchadnezzar, a figure of overweening pride. Cogent in this regard are the remarks of Arnold V. Talentino (1978) regarding the workings of moral irony in *The Ruin*. In his reading of that poem, the ruined city became waste because of the wantonness and self-destructive violence of its former inhabitants. Although once the seat of 'many a mead-hall' (*meado-heall monig*, 23a) filled with gold-adorned men, its inhabitants were flawed in their moral character, for they were *wlonc ond wīn-gāl* (34a).

This Old English phrase merits close attention. Bradley's translation 'proud and flown with wine' captures the negative force of the phrase but is perhaps still not a strong enough equivalent to it, for the adjective *wlonc* ranges in meaning from 'proud' to 'insolent', while the primary meaning of *gāl* is 'wanton, lustful, lascivious'.¹⁷ The basic sense of the compound adjective *wīn-gāl*, correspondingly, must be 'drunken and wanton'. It is noteworthy that the same formula, *wlonc ond wīn-gāl*, is used at verse 29a of *The Seafarer* with dismissive reference to city-dwellers whose hedonistic lifestyle the speaker scorns. Bradley therefore rightly takes the phrase as used in *The Seafarer* to mean either 'insolent and flown with wine' or 'arrogant and wanton with wine',¹⁸ and the phrase as it occurs in verse 34a of *The Ruin* carries overtones of this same kind.

When considered in this light, the former inhabitants of the wasteland described in *The Ruin* are thus only partly deserving of the reader's sympathy, for they represent a past that has rightly been superseded. Significantly, this was a pagan past, not a Christian one. Anne Klinck directs attention to the pagan associations of the phrase *enta geweorc* 'works of giants' that is used at verse 2b of *The Ruin* (1992: 62). The identical phrase is used at verse 87a of *The Wanderer* with reference to an ancient pre-Christian civilization that was laid waste by God.¹⁹ Though once physically attractive, the uninhabited

---

16 This point is made by Bradley, p. 401, as well as by certain of the critics mentioned in the two notes that precede this one. Rafal Boryslawski (2009) develops a similar point with reference to the moralizing use of urban imagery in a wide range of Anglo-Saxon literary texts.
17 See the *DOE*, s.v. *gāl*, adj.
18 Bradley, pp. 332 and 331, respectively. Magennis offers a comparable translation: 'proud and wanton with wine' (1999: 127).
19 P.J. Frankis (1973) has written persuasively on the phrase *enta geweorc* and its thematic significance.

city of *The Ruin* was destroyed, we are told, either through the inexorable workings of destiny (*wyrd sēo swīþe* 'fate, the irresistible', 24b), or because of the scourge of warfare (*crungon walo wīde* 'the slain fell far and wide', 25a), or because of the onset of pestilence (*cwōmon wōl-dagas* 'there came days of pestilence', 25b), or on account of all three factors working together.

According to widespread medieval belief, civilizations were not afflicted in these ways by chance. Rather, they perished because divine wrath had descended on them in response to their moral degeneracy.[20] This belief was rooted in biblical authority, as attested by such events as the drowning of Pharaoh's army in the Red Sea—an event that is called to mind in the Exeter Anthology poem *Pharaoh*, which challenges the reader to guess how great were the losses of the tyrant Pharaoh when he had the temerity to persecute God's chosen people. The same belief that national disasters result from a people's moral failings animates Gildas's sixth-century history *De excidio et conquestu Britanniae*, which excoriates the inhabitants of late Roman Britain for their sinfulness. God's consequent wrath took on the form of ruthless Saxon invaders. A similar message was brought home to the English themselves some few centuries later in the homiletic writings of Wulfstan, who served as bishop of Worcester and archbishop of York during the second Viking Age (during the years 1002–16) and whose most famous sermon, the *Sermo Lupi ad Anglos*, excoriates the English people for their manifold sins. Wulfstan ascribes the disasters that England suffered during the reign of King Æthelred not just to the rapacity of the Danes, but also, and especially, to God's wrath falling on his countrymen on account of their moral turpitude.[21] As he writes midway through that sermon, 'They harry and they burn, they plunder and rob and carry their spoils to their ships; and indeed, what else can it be, with all these things that have happened, other than God's anger, clear and visible, towards this people?'[22]

The role of *The Ruin* in the design of the Exeter Anthology gains in clarity when the poem is read from this perspective. The antithetical mode of thought that is characteristic of the Anthology as a whole finds expression in opposed architectural images that frame most of the book's contents. The first of these sets of images, advanced in *Advent Lyric 3* in particular, features the immutable City of God, the celestial Jerusalem. The later set of images,

20 For discussion see Klinck (1992: 62–63). My understanding of the moral condition of the ancient city-dwellers differs somewhat from hers.
21 Godden (1994) offers a close analysis of this sermon, in its changing texts, as an evolving set of responses to the Danish invasions.
22 'Hȳ hergiað ond hȳ bærnað, rȳpaþ ond rēafiað ond tō scipe lædað; ond lā, hwæt is ǣnig ōðer on eallum þām gelimpum būtan Godes yrre ofer þās þēode, swutol ond gesǣne?' Bethurum 1957: 272; sermon 20, lines 126–28.

introduced in *The Ruin* and in others of the so-called elegies, represent human civilization as something that is splendid *in potentia* but that is always either in ruins or in the process of decay.[23] As Bernard Huppé (1959) among others has pointed out, this controlling idea rests on a large and influential body of writings in the Augustinian tradition, Augustine's *City of God* in particular. It is expressive of Christian orthodoxy to its core. Although Huppé's extension of this same critical perspective to the whole body of Old English verse can be discounted as reductive,[24] its explanatory power in regard to the poems of the Exeter Anthology remains considerable.

From the preceding paragraphs it should be evident that I am reluctant to embrace the conclusion, favoured by R.F. Leslie (1988: 22-28) among others, that *The Ruin* describes a specific city and that the city in question is Bath in Somerset. After all, there may be significance in the fact that the poet chooses not to give his city a name, thus leaving the way open for readers to approach this poem in terms of the trope of earthly mutability rather than as a lament for a specific ruined site. Although multiple possible models for the poet's city have been proposed, from Bath to ancient Babylon,[25] it is unnecessary to choose out a single one among them, in my view.

If one were to opt for a single leading model among many possible ones, all the same, then a strong candidate for this honour would be ancient Rome. Rome's great ruined monuments, which included famous baths and broken walls, were well known to educated Anglo-Saxons, whether through prestigious guides to the sites of that city or through the frequent journeys and pilgrimages to Rome that were undertaken by members of the clergy, including those who needed to be endowed with the pallium, along with their entourages.[26] Rome was renowned as the mother of cities and could therefore

---

23 As Muir (2: 384) observes, commenting on *Advent Lyrics*, 'The architectural imagery introduced here reappears sporadically in other texts in the manuscript, and may be considered one of the unifying strands in the anthology (consider especially in this respect *The Wanderer*, *The Seafarer*, and *The Ruin*).'
24 Nicholas Howe (1997: 82-85) is among the critics who have justifiably taken issue with the sweeping character of Huppé's claims.
25 See Muir 2: 699 for discussion and 2: 705 for an enumeration of possible sources or analogues. Other proposed candidates for the location, besides Bath and Babylon, are Romano-British Chester, Hadrian's Wall and the Temple of Jerusalem. Still other commentators propose 'both Bath and the Scriptures' or the 'temple' of the human body, while, with their customary good sense, Greenfield and Calder suggest that 'the scene may be an imaginative amalgam of various locales' (1986: 281).
26 As Stephen Matthews (2007: 16) observes in the course of a well-documented study of travel between England and Italy during the Anglo-Saxon period, an area close by Saint Peter's basilica known as the Saxon Burgh or the *Schola Saxonum* was a regular place of residence for English-speakers who visited Rome or took up residence there.

stand for them all. As John Doran (2007: 31) has observed, medieval authors writing on the sites of Rome established its reputation as *the* city, the model for them all, made great in ancient times by its military might but laid low because of its uncertain moral foundation. Writers therefore referred to the city simply as *urbs*, a word that became synonymous with Rome. Correspondingly, when Saint Augustine, one of the authors who helped to shape this tradition, wrote at the start of his treatise *De civitate Dei* on the justice of God's plan for humankind, he based his discussion on the sack of ancient Rome by Alaric and his Goths, an event that took place in AD 410, just three years before Augustine began writing this work.[27] Later in his great treatise, Augustine likewise makes clear that Rome was founded in violence: fratricidal violence that represented a resurgence of the violence that led to the founding of the first earthly city by the fugitive killer Cain.[28]

The same theme of Alaric's sack of Rome is taken up in the verse proem to the Old English version of Boethius's *De consolatione philosophiae*. According to the editors of an authoritative edition of this nativizing translation, its versified parts could have been completed at just about any time from the early to the mid-tenth century, hence this composite work of prose and verse may have been completed not long before the Exeter Anthology was written out in the fair copy that we read today.[29] The proem to *The Old English Boethius* makes prominent mention of the ruination of Rome, *burga cyst* 'finest of cities'.[30] When read together, *The City of God*, *The Old English Boethius*, *The Ruin* and others of the so-called elegies of the Exeter Anthology reiterate a question as to whether any earthly civilization can long remain unbroken by the effects of time, regardless of its material comforts or the splendour of its architecture. This same theme of mutability, whose association with Rome has long been practically inescapable among artists and writers in the West, lodges at the heart of arguments for Christian conversion.

---

27 *St Augustine: Concerning the City of God*, book 1, chaps 6–7 (trans. Bettenson 2003: 11–13).
28 *St Augustine: Concerning the City of God*, book 15, chap. 5 (trans. Bettenson 2003: 600–01).
29 Godden and Irvine 2009: 146–51. The earliest manuscript of this Old English work dates from c.950.
30 'Ðā wæs Rōmana rīce gewunnen,/abrocen burga cyst' ('Then the kingdom of the Romans was conquered, the finest of cities sacked'): *The Old English Boethius*, Meter 1, verses 17–18a (Irvine and Godden 2012: 6–7). Alaric's conquest of Rome is recounted as a prelude to an account of why Boethius was imprisoned by Theodoric. This is evidently the same Theodoric as is recalled in lines 18–20 of *Deor*, envisioned in that Exeter Anthology poem, as in *The Old English Boethius*, as a tyrant whose reign was a source of widespread suffering.

The book's inclusivity

One leading aspect of the world-view that permeates the Exeter Anthology is thus its pessimism about the possibility of one's finding lasting *drēamas* 'joys, lively communal happiness' on earth. Although easily recognizable as a Christian commonplace, this sentiment is developed in numerous poems and passages in a manner that is often arresting.

Another leading aspect of this same world-view may strike some readers as more surprising. This is the book's inclusivity. In particular, the Anthology is accepting of all the various *hādas*, or 'ranks and types', of people seeking to order their life in alignment with Christian ideals.

The word *hād* can be numbered among the keywords of Anglo-Saxon social thought.[31] Although it has no free-standing reflex in modern English, the suffix *-hood* is derived from it, as in the noun 'brotherhood', denoting a set of metaphorical brothers rather than biological ones. Another example is 'neighbourhood', a word whose etymological meaning, from the root forms *nēah* 'near' and *būan* 'to dwell', is not 'a group of nearby houses and the adjoining land', as that word is used today, but rather 'the set of people who dwell in one's vicinity'.

In order to understand the poems of the Exeter Anthology in their period-specific context, one must be accepting, if only for this purpose, in the notion of a ranked society consisting of different *hādas*. According to the Anglo-Saxon social system, members of each and every free social group, from fishermen or tradesmen to thegns or monks, had the right to a wergild. They were thus all expected to contribute to the common welfare through actions sanctioned by tradition and common law. Ælfric's *Colloquy*, dating from not more than a single generation after the Exeter Anthology was written out, consists of a semi-dramatic presentation of the imagined voices of persons representative of different *hādas*. This extended exercise in the rhetorical figure of ethopoeia makes for an attractive entry point to the theoretical foundations of Anglo-Saxon social thought.[32] The poems of the Exeter Anthology presuppose a similar set of ideas about the ideal workings

---

31 The *DOE* distinguishes a number of senses of this word. The relevant ones for my discussion are sense 3, 'condition', and sense 5, 'order or degree; mainly: order in society, rank, office'. Whitelock (1952: 83–114) offers a concise review of the chief ranks of Anglo-Saxon society.

32 Earl R. Anderson (1974) offers extended analysis of Ælfric's *Colloquy* and its intellectual foundations within the context of Benedictine monasticism; see Niles 2016: 55–56 for summary remarks on that topic. Taking a different but related approach, Katherine O'Brien O'Keeffe (2012: 94–150) offers close analysis of the *Colloquy* not as a map of an ordered society but as a tool for the creation of monastic identity among young oblates during the period of the Reform.

of society. Correspondingly, while in a material sense the Exeter Anthology is a product of the Benedictine Reform, readers who work their way through it folio by folio in the expectation that it will be partisan in tone, in keeping with any real or imagined ecclesiastical infighting of the tenth-century Reform period, will find their expectations contradicted. Since the Reform has sometimes been characterized as an attempt to impose on all clergy a single concept of the religious life,[33] this point is worth emphasis.

The theme of the legitimate role of all ranks and types of people in a Christian commonwealth is made explicit in *God's Gifts to Humankind*, a poem that develops the theme that God's gifts are manifold and are distributed widely among humankind, much as all people are eligible for God's grace. The social philosophy that corresponds to this theme is an inclusive one that acknowledges the contributions to society made by people in all *hādas*, from clerical vocations to hunting, fowling, harping or oratory. When read as a whole, the Exeter Anthology is like a great minster in this regard, with its sacred space inhabited by men and women of all sorts.[34] The same guiding notion of inclusivity finds expression at lines 225–43 [664–82] of Cynewulf's poem *The Ascension*, where the theme of God's gifts to humankind is first introduced. In neither of these poems is a distinction made between ecclesiastics and the laity as potential recipients of God's favours, nor, notably, is the regular clergy distinguished from the secular clergy. One sees no trace of disparagement of the latter group such as one finds in the writings of the learned late Anglo-Saxon author Byrhtferth of Ramsay (*c*.970–*c*.1020), who wrote his bilingual *Enchiridion* and other works approximately forty years after the Exeter Anthology was written out.[35]

Significantly in this light, when the author of *The Life of Saint Guthlac* berates those members of the clergy who are guilty of lax discipline, no one set of ecclesiastics, whether monks or clerics, is singled out for castigation. In a scene from that poem that is set during the period when Guthlac is living in the wilderness subject to demonic assaults and temptations, a pack of devils lifts him high into the air so as to grant him a vision of ecclesiastical corruption:

---

33 As John Blair remarks: 'A notable feature of the whole movement was its *dirigiste* tone: there was to be one acceptable mode of the religious life, and the king and his advisers were to decide it' (2005: 351).
34 Nicholas Orme draws the following conclusion after outlining the many uses and functions of Exeter Cathedral during the medieval period: 'In short, the cathedral drew in people of every sex, age, and wealth at one time or another, and almost every kind of activity went on inside its walls' (2009: 136).
35 Rebecca Stephenson (2010) calls attention to the more condemnatory tone of Byrhtferth's writings in this regard.

> Hy hine þa hofun   on þa hean lyft,
> sealdon him meahte   ofer monna cynn,
> þæt he fore eagum   eall sceawode
> under haligra hyrda   gewealdum   415
> in mynsterum   monna gebæru,
> þara þe hyra lifes   þurh lust brucan,
> idlum æhtum   ond oferwlencum,
> gierelum gielplicum ...
>
> (Then they lifted him high in the air and gave him powers exceeding those of humankind, so that before his eyes he saw all the actions of such people, living in minsters under the authority of holy pastors, as were enjoying their life according to their appetite for worthless possessions and superfluous vanities and ostentatious adornments ...)[36]

Although the point of their trial of the saint is not made explicit, the devils evidently hope to dissuade Guthlac from his religious calling by showing him the extent to which church discipline has been corroded by hypocrisy and moral corruption. Their temptation of the saint fails of its purpose, for Guthlac remains unshaken in his resolve to remain a dedicated servant of Christ. Of special interest in this passage is the ambiguity inherent in the phrase *in mynsterum* (416a), for the OE noun *mynster* can denote either 'monastery' or 'church'.[37] The word is an inclusive one. Likewise, the phrase *hāligra hyrda* 'of holy pastors' (415) can refer to any persons entrusted with responsibility over Christian 'flocks'.[38] The lapses in ecclesiastical discipline to which the devils call attention could potentially be ascribed to any of God's servants, whatever their *hād*.

My interpretation of these lines therefore differs from that of Patrick W. Conner (1993b: 404–07), for Conner reads the passage as referring specifically to the corrupt doings of monks and their abbots in unreformed houses, as opposed to houses founded or refounded during the Benedictine Reform. In my own reading of this scene, the author of *The Life of Saint Guthlac* has no more interest in making distinctions between reformed versus unreformed houses than the devils do. Although one might argue that the scene referred to here must pertain to 'unreconstructed' monasticism on the grounds that

---

36 *The Life of Saint Guthlac* 412–19a; Muir 1: 122–23.
37 See Bosworth & Toller, s.v. *mynster*, sense I, 'a monastery, a place where a body of monks or of nuns resided', and sense II, 'a church, minster'. Similarly, while a *mynster-monn* is a monk, a *mynster-prēost* is a priest who conducts services in a minster. While a *mynster-þēaw* is a monastic custom, a *mynster-stōw* is a place where there is a minster, hence 'a town'.
38 See the *DOE*, s.v. *hyrde*, sense 2.c: 'keeper of a flock, pastor', with frequent reference to the head of a Christian community, whether a church, a monastery or other.

the historical Guthlac of Crowland, to whom the dates 673–714 are ascribed, lived well before the tenth-century Reform, a more plausible reading of this passage is that it calls attention to the perennial issue of lax discipline among the clergy. What is held up for admiration is the saint's commitment to his monastic vocation despite his knowledge that not all clergy display comparable zeal or moral integrity. Guthlac is aware that it is a specious argument—indeed, a satanic temptation—to think that a good man should abandon virtue because his neighbour is corrupt. As we soon learn (at 494–507), Guthlac refutes the devils' accusations on the grounds that lapses in church discipline tend to result from youthful ignorance or high spirits, not from hardened sinfulness. After all, it was God who created youth and the joys of being human ('God scop geoguðe ond gumena drēam', 495). Such misbehaviour as he has been shown, Guthlac therefore replies, is subject to correction over time. The contrast that is drawn in this part of *The Life of Saint Guthlac* thus hinges on a distinction between mature members of the clergy and those who have not yet turned from the follies of youth. Although the passage embodies a lesson for oblates and their abbots, it has no direct bearing on the distinction between reformed versus unreformed monasticism.

Significantly in this regard, when Dunstan was serving as abbot of Glastonbury, both clerics and monks continued to live in close conjunction there under his rule, doing so amicably as far as one can tell. As Nicholas Brooks has pointed out, Dunstan's Glastonbury did not share the 'contempt for "clerks" that came to typify the reformed houses of Æthelwold's tradition' (1992: 13). In like manner, as Michael Winterbottom and Michael Lapidge have observed, 'there is very little evidence to suggest that Dunstan played an active role in founding or refounding monasteries on strict Benedictine lines'.[39] Correspondingly, when the poems of the Exeter Anthology speak specifically to the condition of monks, their perspective is inclusive: that is, it is consistent with the ideals that have motivated monasticism in any and all historical periods. Lines 381–92 of *The Phoenix*, for example, elucidate the allegorical meaning of the phoenix and its miraculous resurrection in terms that have a particular resonance for persons in monastic orders. The bird signifies the happy way of life and the blessed death and resurrection of *þām gecorenum Crīstes þegnum* 'the elect thegns of Christ' (388). While this phrase could be construed as referring to any persons who are stalwart in the faith, it has a particular application to monks and nuns living in dedicated religious communities. At a later point in *The Phoenix*, these same chosen ones are called *meotudes cempan* 'the Lord's warriors' (471b). The most direct reference

---

39 Winterbottom and Lapidge 2012, page l (the lower-case roman numeral for '50') of the book's front matter.

here is to the *miles Christi* of the prologue to the Rule of Saint Benedict: that is, to monks and nuns seen categorically as soldiers of Christ.

The *Seafarer* may at first seem to present an exception to this principle of inclusivity, for the hardy speaker of this poem embraces a life of solitude and rigorous physical austerities. His path of self-imposed exile calls to mind the eremitic life favoured by certain Irish seafaring monks, or by Guthlac living alone in the fens of East Anglia, rather than being in accord with the communitarian practices prescribed by Saint Benedict. Given the allegorical dimension of *The Seafarer*, however, one can see that what is being held up for emulation is any Christian's dedication to the path leading to salvation. While this quest is necessarily an individual one, it is also one that each Christian undertakes within the congregation of the church, with its nave, the same church that in typological terms was figured as the ark of salvation.

Nautical allegory of a corresponding kind is developed towards the end of *The Ascension*. Adapted to special allegorical purposes here is imagery drawn from Gregory the Great's Ascension sermon (his homily 29) and, more importantly, Gregory's preface to his *Dialogues*:

> Nu is þon gelicost swa we on laguflode
> ofer cald wæter ceolum liðan
> geond sidne sæ sundhengestum
> flodwudu fergen. Is þæt frecne stream
> yða ofermæta þe we her on lacað
> geond þas wacan woruld, windge holmas
> ofer deop gelad.

> (It is at present very much like this: as though we are sailing across chill water upon the ocean-flood in ships, over the wide sea in steeds of the deep, and navigating ocean-going boats of wood. The streaming sea is hazardous, inordinate the waves in which we pitch about through this frail world, and squally the oceans along the deep waterway.)[40]

The only safe port for our wave-tossed ships, Cynewulf goes on to state, is offered by our steersman Christ, who at the time of his Ascension pointed the way to heaven. This passage from *The Ascension* too, then, provides a thematic anchor for the Seafarer's monologue.

---

40 *The Ascension* 411–17a [850–56a]; Muir 1: 78; translation by Bradley, p. 228. Gatch (1971: 144) discusses Cynewulf's indebtedness in this poem to the writings of Gregory the Great, while Steen (2008: 134–37) discusses this passage with reference to the nautical metaphors that are a commonplace of medieval Latin literature. Orchard (2009: 302–07) discusses the same scene with attention to parallels in both Latin and the vernacular.

While the two Exeter Anthology poems on the holy life and death of Guthlac might seem to offer support to an eremitical monastic ideal rather than a cenobitic one, they do not actually do so. As Christopher A. Jones has pointed out, the author of *The Life of Saint Guthlac* does not sidestep Guthlac's choice to live as a hermit. Instead, the poet transforms that feature of the saint's life, endowing it, 'however subtly, with qualities of the regular life, with the images and vocabulary of the *cenobium*'. The poem thus allows its readers 'to see in Guthlac a good Benedictine like themselves'.[41] In a related study, Mary Clayton has noted that even though there is little evidence for hermits in tenth-century England, and though Ælfric evidently went out of his way to avoid celebrating hermit saints, 'the reform movement in general does not seem to have objected to the ideal of the eremitic life' (1996: 157). The two poems on the holy life and death of Guthlac, then, are exemplary for all Christians, including the English regular clergy during the years when the Reform was in progress.

Doctrine and conversion

To review some of the leading themes of this chapter: the Exeter Anthology as a whole is expressive of a world-view that is both Christian in scope and Benedictine in its particular applications. The appeal of this world-view, despite its inherent pessimism about the things of this world, would have been enhanced through its expression in the pleasurable medium of Old English alliterative verse. This is especially true seeing that the diction of loyalty, devotion, sacrifice, joyful conviviality and even fame (*dōm*; *lof*) that was traditionally associated with Old English heroic poetry could so readily be adapted for religious purposes, as long as it was redirected in accord with the teachings of the faith.

Even while sharing a common world-view, the poems of the Anthology display a striking degree of originality within the conventions of their respective genres. Although most of these poems have Latin sources, their authors often depart freely from those models, amplifying them considerably so as to draw out the moral application of a source or to enhance its affective power. A key resource in this regard was the common store of formulaic diction that would have been available to poets familiar with the prior vernacular verse-making tradition. An example is the set of epithets of the *dryhtnes cempa* ('warrior of the Lord') type that is used of Guthlac, the archetypal champion of Christ—a man born into the warrior aristocracy who,

---

41 Jones 1995: 262 and 291, respectively.

while still young, renounced both weapons and material comforts so as to take up a solitary life devoted to worship and prayer.

The erudite character and high style of many of the poems of the Exeter Anthology point to their being directed to a fairly elite readership of persons who were already well trained in *grammatica*. Certain members of that elite group may have been recruited into the monasteries of tenth-century England from wealthy households. The prominent place of Guthlac in the design of the Exeter Anthology is suggestive of someone's desire to reach out to persons of such a background as his, young men in particular. The Convert who is the imagined speaker of *The Rhyming Poem* is another figure with whom readers who were born into the higher ranks of society might have identified, though any reader could have done so vicariously. The need for English-language books that could reach out to pious men and women of a relatively privileged background is likely to have been felt with some force in mid- to late tenth-century England, for this was a time when the restoration and expansion of monastic life required a steady supply of neophytes, some of whom would have been groomed to take on a role of leadership in their respective communities.

When viewed as a whole, the Exeter Anthology has a reasonably coherent structure, one that progresses in a loosely hierarchical fashion from the sublimity of *Advent Lyrics* to the desolate wastes of *The Ruin*. Rather than taking a partisan stance as regards the religious controversies of its day, the Anthology reaches out to all members of a Christian society, for all Christians alike are figured as sojourners or seafarers, according to the Gregorian metaphor that was widely embraced at this time. This figure of speech had a particular bearing on the situation of the Anglo-Saxon regular clergy, for these men and women above all were the self-chosen exiles of God. More than all others, they were the warriors of Christ whose dedication to the quest for wisdom within the regime of the Benedictine *opus dei* enabled them to draw on both prayer and parchment to advance their cause.

The Ruin and the search for Anglo-Saxon secular humanism

Some readers of the present book may wish to ask how my sense of the Exeter Anthology and its underlying world-view relates to current trends in Old English literary criticism.

In his book *The Search for Anglo-Saxon Paganism*, published over forty years ago, E.G. Stanley drew attention to certain ideological biases that were characteristic of the work of many nineteenth- and early twentieth-century literary scholars.[42] He succeeded in deflating these critics' claims about the supposedly pagan character of much Anglo-Saxon verse through the simple and efficient stratagem of letting those critics speak for themselves. An example is a quotation that he culls from E.E. Wardale's 1935 book *Chapters on Old English Literature*. Wardale sums up as follows her view of seven of the so-called elegies of the Exeter Anthology:[43]

> All must be early, for all are essentially heathen in character. This is seen in the kind of fatalistic acquiescence which runs through *Deor's Lament*, in the belief in the irresistible power of Fate which pervades the *Wanderer*, and in the absence of any Christian thought in the others. A later scribe has occasionally substituted a Christian for a heathen term, and probably it is such a scribe who has added a long passage of didactic nature at the end of the *Seafarer*, but such words or passages betray their later date by being out of harmony with the rest of the matter.

Wardale's remarks concerning 'the absence of any Christian thought' in these 'essentially heathen' poems scarcely call for rebuttal today, seeing that they are so markedly out of step with more recent scholarship that has demonstrated the essentially Christian character of virtually all Anglo-Saxon literature, often with meticulous attention to its medieval Latin sources. Equally out of step with a post-New Critical consensus is Wardale's assumption that these originally 'heathen' poems of the Exeter Anthology were brought into their present textual form through the meddling of Christian scribes.

Still, each age has its critical biases, ones that are often unperceived except with the passing of time. When one reads at all widely in the criticism of Old English poetry published in the last twenty-five years or so, one is struck by how much of it is expressive not of the search for Anglo-Saxon paganism, but rather of the search for Anglo-Saxon secular humanism.[44] In her contribution to the 2013 *Cambridge History of Early Medieval English Literature*, for example, Kathleen Davis writes in some detail about the theme of temporality in Old English lyric poetry, especially as this theme finds expression in the Exeter Anthology poems *The Wanderer*, *The Seafarer*, *The Ruin* and others of the so-called elegies. Davis draws her discussion to a close by directing attention to the first line of *The Ruin*, 'Wrǣtlic is þes weal-stān—wyrde gebrǣcon', a clause that she translates 'Wondrous is this wall-stone, broken by *wyrd*.'[45]

---

42 Stanley (1975: 50–61) provides extracts from the early criticism of the elegiac poems of the Exeter Anthology.
43 Wardale 1935: 29–30; Stanley 1975: 61.
44 Stanley himself has commented on this phenomenon (2011: 83–84).
45 K. Davis 2012: 356; subsequent quotations are from the same page. Davis evidently reads *gebrǣcon* (*The Ruin* 1b) as a variant spelling of the past participle *gebrocen* rather than as the

Seeing here 'a past that is celebrated, not mourned', she views in a positive manner the state of transience that is the preoccupation of these poets. In the emphatic concluding sentence to her chapter she reflects on the whole of *The Ruin* in this light, for 'no other Old English poem captures quite so precisely the foundational nature of transience—to life, narrative, experience, history, and an open future'.

The notion that transience is foundational to life, an open future and much else that is good, rather than being a likely source of grief and regret, may have an appeal to many persons of the present day. A stumbling block in Davis's analysis, however, is the theological void in which it is offered. An alternative approach to the theme of transience in *The Ruin* and these other poems would take account of the role of this theme in the Exeter Anthology as a whole, with its versified prayers, saints' lives, homiletic addresses, precepts and other overtly religious verse. It would also take into account the verbal and thematic correspondences that knit these poems together, as when the transcendent *weal-stān* that is the Christ of *Advent Lyric 1* is seen to form a counterpart to the broken *weal-stān* of line 1 of *The Ruin*. The whole set of these poems could then be seen to express an attitude whereby the ultimate emptiness of earthly things is precisely the reason why one should focus one's mind on the eternal.

Ideally, in addition, a critic's approach to the theme of transience in *The Ruin* and these other poems would take medieval social reality into account. The world-view that underlies the poems of the Exeter Anthology would thereby be seen to correspond to the tenor of life in a tradition-bound society where change was slow to come, and when it did come often arrived in the form of raids, warfare, famine and other forms of disruption and suffering. If, through some miraculous bending of time, a person of our own era could address the makers and the original readers of the Exeter Anthology so as to speak to them of transience as a source of life and an open future, one wonders if such a message would speak to their experience or core values.

A second example of the current secularist vogue in Old English literary studies is Renée R. Trilling's 2009 book *The Aesthetics of Nostalgia*, which analyses a wide range of historical writings composed in Old English verse.[46] When her discussion turns to the Exeter Anthology poems *Widsith*, *Deor* and *The Ruin*, Trilling approaches these poems from current critical perspectives, bringing to bear on them Walter Benjamin's nuanced writings from the 1920s

---

third person indicative plural form of the verb *brecan*, though she does not adjust the OE text accordingly, as certain editors have done. See Klinck (1992: 209) for discussion of this philological point.

46 Trilling 2009a; cf. also Trilling 2009b, where she takes up similar themes.

and 1930s on the subject of historical consciousness while passing over in silence the Old English poems' relation to Christian doctrine. One reason why Trilling feels free to disregard the relations of these poems to other poems of the Exeter codex that are of a religious character is that she regards the Exeter Anthology as 'a collection of fragments assembled by chance rather than by design' (2009a: 63). Correspondingly, she reads *The Ruin* as an expression of the awe and wonder that attends the imagined speaker's contemplation of the ruins of an ancient civilization. Endorsing the view that a 'strangely uplifting tone' persists throughout *The Ruin*, dominating the poem's second half,[47] Trilling finds that the ancient remains that inspire the poet's wonder are resolved into a place not just of 'fallen glory' but also of 'wholeness and beauty'. She concludes her analysis on an upbeat note: 'As the piece stands, its final image is not one of destruction, decay, or ruin, but rather of the very full lives of the people who once inhabited this spot: it ends not in nostalgia but in redemption.'[48]

A different understanding of this poem will result if one takes seriously the poet's statement that the inhabitants of the ruined city were not just happy in their material comforts, but were also *wlonc ond wīn-gāl* 'proud and wanton with wine' (34a). This phrase implies that the city's former inhabitants, among whom were warriors who 'shone in their war-gear' (*wīg-hyrstum scān*, 34b), were to some degree complicit in their own destruction. By means of this trope—a familiar one in medieval historiography—*The Ruin* is linked to the openly didactic poems *The Seafarer* and *Vainglory*, each of which contrasts the person of strong religious commitment to 'weaker' persons (*þā wācran*, *The Seafarer* 87a; *þone wācran*, *Vainglory* 7b), whether the reference is to a group of seemingly innocuous hedonists or to an arrogant hell-bound carouser ranting in his cups. When one reads *The Ruin* closely in its manuscript context, one can readily locate its thematic basis in the orthodox Christian belief that the only source of lasting joy is to be found in the afterlife.

Trilling's analysis of *Widsith* and *Deor*, the two Exeter Anthology poems that most clearly highlight the matter of history, proceeds along comparable lines. *Widsith* is thus said to advance the notion 'that poetry ... offers immortality through imagination, and that the permanence of art endows its subjects with similar longevity' (2009a: 62). Trilling passes over in silence a crucial proviso that is made by the narrator, in the conclusion to this poem,

---

47 Trilling 2009a: 54, quoting with approval Dailey 2006: 185.
48 Trilling 2009a: 54-55. Lori Garner (2011: 162) explicitly endorses the last-quoted sentence. The references to Garner and Dailey in this and the preceding note are meant to confirm that what is at stake in the present discussion is a trend in Old English scholarship rather than the views of one critic alone.

to the effect that earthly fame, even if desirable according to the old heroic code, is something that lasts only for a time, 'oþþæt eal scæceð,/lēoht ond līf somod' ('until everything dissipates, light and life together', 141b–42a). In the Exeter Anthology as a whole, the concepts of redemption and immortality have only one field of reference. This is not the realm of art or of the human imagination, no matter how attractive that thought may be in today's environment of secular humanism.

I have singled out these studies by Davis and Trilling for discussion because they are representative of leading trends in Old English literary scholarship at the present time. Additional examples could readily be cited from inferior sources. These too would confirm the adage that when any of us look into the well of history, what we are likely to see are our own features reflected there.

CHAPTER 8

Keywords

As Edward Evans-Pritchard, one of the founders of the discipline of social anthropology, remarked many years ago, 'the most difficult task in anthropological fieldwork is to determine the meanings of a few keywords, upon an understanding of which the success of the whole investigation depends' (1951: 80). Much the same can be said of research into the literature of the past, that foreign country whose customs, manners, mental assumptions and beliefs can be studied from many different perspectives, but rarely more profitably than through close study of certain key terms in a people's lexicon.[1]

Keywords of the kind studied by Evans-Pritchard in the course of his fieldwork among the Nuer people of North Africa are more than isolated items. Upon inspection, they can be seen to resolve into elements of a system by which groups of human beings, whether large or small in number, make sense of their lives and join together in a society, doing so despite the idiosyncrasies, ambitions, ranks or rivalries that distinguish these same people from one another when considered as individuals. Keywords in a group's lexicon are expressive of common threads in the psychology of the people who make up that group: their typical hopes, fears, beliefs and aspirations. To the extent that the members of a group can be said to share a common ideology, then study of well-chosen keywords provides an entrance to that realm.

Keywords, then, are key to a scholarly project in more senses than one. Not only are they central to one's research, they are also tools that can open doors giving entry to realms of thought and behaviour that are normally the exclusive property of insiders. Since not all insiders necessarily have a rational understanding of the mental and social system into which they have been born, as opposed to having competence in it, the mediating role of the researcher can be a significant one.

When Raymond Williams chose 'keywords' as the short title of his justly celebrated book on eighteenth- and nineteenth-century British mentalities,

---

1   My allusion to 'the past as a foreign country' is to Loewenthal 1985, supplemented by Loewenthal 2015.

he is likely to have had both these dimensions of the word's meaning in mind.² Writing as a cultural historian about the impact of the Industrial Revolution in England, Williams identified as keywords a number of terms that, when traced over time through a wide range of texts, yielded insights into the evolving consciousness of a people. Among the words chosen out by Williams for study in this manner are 'art', 'family', 'labour', 'medieval', 'nature', 'sex' and 'violence', to cite a few examples.

Analysis of the semantic range of certain key terms that figure in the Exeter Anthology has the potential to yield comparable insights.³ Given the difficulty of ascribing dates to the original composition of the poems that make up the volume, a study along such lines can have no real evolutionary dimension. Nevertheless, a project of this kind can help to define the role of each part of that book in a single system of thought, feeling and potential action, one whose temporal parameters are those of the main period of the Benedictine Reform in England (c.950–75). In turn, this system of thought, feeling and potential action, to the extent that it can be ascertained, can be viewed as a kind of conceptual grammar by which key terms in the Old English lexicon were deployed in verse. Through the workings of this implicit grammar, all parts of the discourse that we call the 'Exeter Anthology' can be seen to make sense in relation to one another and to a set of common aims.⁴

This is true even if certain of these poems were originally composed independently of one another, as they almost surely were; for the concept of 'craft poetry' according to which this body of verse is best understood implies the existence of textual communities made up of like-minded persons who were in communication with one another, who shared certain commitments, and who strove for formal and technical competence in verse composition of a kind that was guided by well-known conventions.

Moreover, when we think of the Exeter Anthology, we should not neglect to take into account the potentially transformative power of the act of compilation

2   Williams 1976, along with the later editions of that book.
3   I should perhaps distinguish my approach from Allen J. Frantzen's in his book *Anglo-Saxon Keywords* (2012). His is methodologically the opposite of mine. That is to say, Frantzen chooses out a number of keywords in the vocabulary of current cultural studies (with its substantial debt to Raymond Williams) and uses those terms as entry points to the Anglo-Saxon world. My interest is in how study of certain key terms in the native vocabulary of Old English, as used in the Exeter Anthology, can help to clarify the system of thought that underlies the poetry of that volume and hence, by extension, the world that produced it.
4   I borrow the term 'conceptual grammar' from certain researchers in the environmental sciences who are searching for ways to describe the complex interactions of humanity and nature over time, e.g. Bonneuil and Fressoz 2016. This use of the term 'grammar' is a metaphorical one, of course.

itself. As any collector knows, the compilation of like items can create a new hermeneutic context for the understanding of any one of those items, seen now in relation to a system of thought rather than in an atomistic way. Such systems can be either implicit or overt. We might compare the change of perspective that results when stones of a similar kind are set into a circle, or into a labyrinthine spiral, or are arranged so as to form a cross. The stones are the same stones, but their 'meaning-in-use' differs in each instance.

Perhaps needless to say, the foundation of the system of thought that governs the contents of the Exeter Anthology was religious belief. For one to call that system simply 'Christian', however, risks seeing it compartmentalized, and hence possibly belittled or distorted, by persons of the present day who might view it on the basis of different values and assumptions. In the neutral spirit that is required of research undertaken along the lines of historical anthropology,[5] I therefore prefer to call it a human system. That is to say, while deeply inflected by Christian doctrine and moral instruction, the Exeter Anthology offers an encompassing vision of life and one's place in it. This vision permeates the volume, rendering it an effective tool for the conversion, in the sense of personal transformation, of the members of an educated elite.

What words are worth special attention?

In order to keep this chapter to a manageable length, I will single out just four Old English keywords for close discussion. One of these is *sīþ*, a noun that basically means 'journey'. Another is *ellen*, a noun whose basic sense is 'courage'.[6] A third is *bōt*, a noun whose core sense is 'redress' or 'recompense'. A fourth is *hām*, the etymon of our word 'home'. Study of these four nouns will help to reveal a conceptual system that, while operative in the Exeter Anthology as a whole, has a particular bearing on our understanding of *The Wanderer* and *The Seafarer*, two poems that are often taught in the classroom and are discussed with some frequency in the critical literature. While these four words could not be considered 'code words' in the sense of being deliberately coded so as to conceal a message, they are ones whose meaning, in particular contexts, would have been transparent to insiders while remaining partially opaque to persons from outside the culture.

---

5   Anthropologically oriented approaches to medieval studies are much indebted to the work of Aron Gurevich, especially Gurevich 1992.
6   I discuss this word in Chapter 1 above, in the section headed 'God's exiles and the heroic ethos'.

If space were not a concern, other words that figure with some frequency in the Exeter Anthology would repay close study. An example is *dryhten*, a noun that can denote a secular lord, with his potentially dread powers, and that by extension can denote the Lord who created the universe, who oversees the course of a pilgrim's journey, who comforts the needy, who must be faced in a final reckoning, who judges the damned to eternal torment, and who is adored by the angels and the souls of the blessed in heaven. The author of *The Seafarer* exploits this verbal ambiguity in a strategic way.[7] Another word that would reward close inspection, but that I will only touch on here, is the feminine noun *wyrd*, whose semantic range extends from 'fate' or 'fortune' (often in a dire sense, hence 'death') to 'God's will' or simply 'the course of events'.[8] The notion that fatalism was deeply engrained in the Anglo-Saxon imagination remains deeply engrained in the modern imagination. There is good reason to believe that Anglo-Saxon poets used this term to express ideas that are fairly commonplace in any era. These include the notion that human beings have only partial control over the future, or even over conditions that impact them at the present moment; that events that occurred in the past could not have happened otherwise (for that would be a logical impossibility); and that divine dispensation is involved in the whole course of events, whether for good or ill from our limited human perspective. The narrator who introduces the Wanderer's monologue draws on such commonplace notions as these, which are regularly reinforced by Christian teachings,[9] when he declares that 'Wyrd bið ful ā-rēd'.[10] While the literal meaning of this phrase is evidently 'Fate is completely determined' or, with a degree of personification, 'Fate is fully resolute', what it means in practical terms, I suspect, is that 'Life goes on, and one had best be resigned to it.' The current idiom 'It is what it is' amounts to much the same thing. The somewhat garrulous speaker of *The Penitent's Prayer* concludes his monologue with a similar sentiment, one that is offered up in homiletic terms rather than in the taut form of gnomic

---

7   See Chapter 5 above, in the section headed 'Rhetorical figures', with reference to Greenfield's reading of this poem.
8   There is a large literature on the semantics of *wyrd* and on the place of a belief in *wyrd* in the Anglo-Saxon world-view. Two important early essays are Phillpotts 1928 and Timmer 1941; more recent studies include Lochrie 1986 and Griffith 1996. E.G. Stanley (1975: 85–109) has assembled a number of excerpts from the earlier critical literature with a bearing on modern misconceptions regarding this word and its supposedly pagan associations.
9   Compare verse 14b of *The Fortunes of Mortals*, with its allusion to the harshness of adult life and to tragedies that are out of our control: 'Ne bið swylc monnes geweald' ('Such things are beyond human control').
10 *The Wanderer* 5b. On the form *ā-rēd* see the DOE, s.v. *ā-ræd*. The primary sense of the verb *ā-rǣdan* is 'to arrange, settle, determine'.

wisdom: 'Giet biþ þæt [sēlest] þonne mon him sylf ne mæg/wyrd onwendan, þæt hē þonne wel þolige' ('When a person cannot turn aside the course of events through his own powers, it is best that he endure his lot with patience' (48–49).

Two other key terms in the lexicon of the poets whose works are represented in the Anthology are *drēam* and *frōfor*, though again I will only touch on them here. The first of them primarily denotes the happy revelry of people gathered together at a lively social event. Famously, near the beginning of *Beowulf*, the demonic creature Grendel seethes at the loud *drēam* that he hears emanating from the newly built royal hall Heorot[11] for, as is well known, a man's joy is a monster's misery. Anglo-Saxon religious poets frequently used the same word *drēam* to refer to what the *Phoenix* poet speaks of as *drēama drēam* 'the joy of joys' (658a)—that is, the unending jubilation of angels and of the righteous in heaven. It is also true that Ælfric, always the sober one at a party, used the same base word in a negative sense several times to refer to persons afflicted *in wōdan drēame*, a phrase that denotes an unfortunate state of frenzy or delirium.[12] In the Exeter Anthology, however, the word *drēam* is used exclusively of either present or eternal happiness, with happiness typically called to mind as a communal experience rather than an individual one. As for *frōfor*, it is a synonym of *miltse* and *ār* (also spelled *āre*), a noun whose meaning ranges from 'earthly solace' to 'spiritual consolation'. In religious contexts the word is used of the comfort offered by God to his chosen ones in return for the afflictions they have suffered on earth. In *Advent Lyric 7* (at 207b) the phrase *frōfre gǣst* denotes the Holy Spirit. The word also has a material basis, serving on occasion to denote alms given to the poor.[13] The Wanderer, however, finds no *frōfor* for his wretchedness, even though he has learned to endure it well.

Another two words whose role in the Anthology is a crucial one, though I will treat them only in passing, are *egsa* and *hyht*. The first of these refers to 'fear' or 'terror' of any kind. Examples relating to daily life (or imaginative literature) are the horrors with which, in *The Life of Saint Guthlac*, the devil is said to regularly persecute anchorites, terrors that recall Grendel's ghastly persecution of the Danes.[14] When used elsewhere in religious contexts the word can denote 'the awful majesty of God', especially as God's power over

---

11 'Hē dogora gehwām drēam gehyrde,/hlūdne in healle' ('Day after day he heard loud merriment in the hall'), *Beowulf* 88–89a; *Klaeber's Beowulf*, p. 6.
12 See the *DOE*, s.v. *drēam*, sense 2.
13 See the *DOE*, s.v. *frōfor*, including sense 3.b, where *frōfor* glosses *refrigerium* in the sense 'help, support (for the poor)'.
14 See respectively *The Life of Saint Guthlac* 84b–86a and *Beowulf* 276, 783b–84a.

all Creation will be made manifest at the Day of Judgement.[15] By extension, the word denotes the fear that is rightly felt by every Christian who contemplates his Lord. Rather than implying a troubled and unhappy state, this kind of fear, or reverence, can be a source of inner stability and well-being. In the comforting words of the psalmist, 'Beatus vir qui timet Dominum' ('Blessed is the man that feareth the Lord').[16] The complementary noun *hyht*, signifying 'hope', can likewise be used with reference either to the things of this world or to the salvation awaiting the blessed. In *The Ascension*, *hyht* is used twice in apposition with or in conjunction with *blis* 'joy',[17] with reference to the joys of heaven. By extension, in both *The Phoenix* and *The Passion of Saint Juliana* the word is used of God,[18] whose supreme power rightly inspires both love and fear, in accord with the theocratic mode of thought that is characteristic of Anglo-Saxon writings during the period of the Benedictine Reform.

All the words mentioned in the preceding paragraphs have in common that they can function as components of a language of duplicity. While, in the poems of the Anthology, their religious sense is the one that is most often in play, their semantic range extends from the secular domain to the sacred. In the prehistory of the Germanic-speaking peoples, these same words had evidently been used by people who had never known of Christ. The everyday sense of these words did not cease to exist when poets used them in the heightened register of heroic verse composed along the lines of *Beowulf*, nor when religious poets used them in devotional poetry that was modelled in part on earlier heroic verse. These factors contribute to the complex semantics whereby words used in the Exeter Anthology can be construed in one way or another depending on whether their worldly sense or their spiritual sense is taken to be paramount. This creative duplicity, or 'calculated ambiguity' as Roy F. Leslie has discussed the matter,[19] can add a

---

15 See the discussion of *timor domini* in Chapter 3 above, in the section headed 'The Exeter Anthology, "Saint Dunstan's Classbook" and *timor domini*'.
16 Psalm 111:1; Edgar, *Poetical Books*, pp. 458–59. Cf. O'Neill 2016: 452–53: 'Ēadig byð sē wer sē þe him ege Drihtnes/on ferhð-clēofan fæste gestandeð ('Happy is the man who steadfastly maintains fear of the Lord in his heart'). Compare in turn the rhetoric of the closing parts of *The Seafarer* ('Ēadig bið ...', 107a and following) and of *The Wanderer* ('Wel bið ...', 114b and following).
17 *The Ascension* 90b–91a [529b–30a] and 311b [750b].
18 In *The Phoenix* 423a, God is described as *sē ānga hyht* 'the one and only hope'; in *The Passion of Saint Juliana* 642a, as *hāligra hyht* 'the hope of the saints'.
19 Leslie 1985: 1–25 (at 19). Writing along different but related grounds, Fred C. Robinson (1985) has used this potential for verbal ambiguity in the language of Old English poetry as the basis of a theory of the religious language of *Beowulf*. Elsewhere (Niles 2016: 158–61) I offer a critique of Robinson's methods, drawing on the work of others.

lively challenge to the passages in which the words occur, creating a kind of double language whose ambiguities are exploited for special effect.

Despite the interest of the half-dozen words just mentioned, however, the ensuing discussion will be restricted to the four keywords *sīþ*, *ellen*, *bōt* and *hām*, though with passing attention also to the noun *trēow*, with its wide potential of meanings.

Journeys out: the keyword *sīþ*

The masculine noun *sīþ* calls for attention from the start. When used with reference to ordinary experience, the word has the basic meaning 'a journey' or 'an expedition', though it can also refer more generally to a person's 'experience'.[20] The word's overtones, however, lift its field of reference away from ordinary reality in the direction of something more portentous or dramatic. This is only natural since a journey can involve hardship and suffering as well as joy and exultation, as was even more true of early medieval journeys than of ones undertaken today. When the Seafarer states that 'I can tell a true tale about myself, can recount my journeys' (*sīþas secgan*, 2a), it comes as no surprise to learn that his seafaring has been of an intense kind, bringing him hardship on solitary nights when he has known nothing but icy cold and the terrible tossing of waves (*atol ȳþa gewealc*, 6a).

In like manner, when the speaker of The Wife's Lament declares that she will tell a tale about her own grief-stricken self, 'my very own experience' (*mīnre sylfre sīð*, 2a), the reader can expect that her tale will involve high drama as well as deep suffering. The Wife proceeds to tell of a love affair, apparently a marriage, that started off with great promise but then went tragically wrong, so that she now leads a wretched life as an outcast forced to dwell on her own in a cave in a dreary if not hellish landscape. Her monologue ends, if my reading of its last lines is accepted, with a curse brought down on her former lover or husband. If the *sīþ* that the Wife relates can be said to represent a 'journey', then it is a life-journey rather than an expedition of some kind, and there is no sign that it will end well.

---

20 Bosworth & Toller gloss *sīþ* as having the following seven related meanings, all of which are attested in OE verse though not with equal frequency: I, 'going, journeying, travel'; II, 'a journey, voyage, course, expedition'; III, 'coming, arrival'; IV, 'a proceeding, course of action, way of doing, conduct'; V, 'the course of events, lot, condition, fate, experience'; VI, 'a path, way'; VII, 'a time'. The word is of common Germanic origin. It has no reflex in current English, having gone out of use in its various senses by the end of the sixteenth century.

This brings us to a crux in *The Seafarer*, one that comes approximately midway through that poem. The speaker calls attention to the quickening of nature in spring as a beautiful phenomenon, but one that for him is no more than an incitement and an admonition to set out again on one of his harrowing journeys:

> Bearwas blostmum nimað, byrig fægriað,
> wongas wlitigiað, woruld onetteð—
> ealle þa gemoniað modes fusne
> sefan to siþe, þam þe swa þenceð
> on flodwegas feor gewitan.

(Woodland groves are blossoming, the settlements grow lovely, the meadows are turning fair, the whole world quickens; all these things incite a person who contemplates such a thing—a person of keen spirit—to set out on a journey far onto the sea paths.)[21]

Leaving certain grammatical complexities aside, the chief difficulty in interpreting this passage has to do with the implausibility of the Seafarer's resolve when viewed from a normal psychological perspective. Why on earth, in full knowledge of the dreadful sufferings that his previous sea-voyaging has entailed, would a sane man want to set out on such a voyage again, for no other reason than that the earth is turning beautiful again in spring?

Dorothy Whitelock was the first to offer a convincing response to this question by calling attention to early medieval practices of penitential pilgrimage.[22] The validity of such an approach to the poem is confirmed when one takes into account other passages in the Exeter Anthology where the word *sīþ* is used. There is a common thread here that should be evident from the following examples. At verse 440b of *The Phoenix* the word *sīþ* is used of the grievous journey of Adam and Eve into the world of mutability and death after being expelled from Eden. At verse 558b of *The Passion of Saint Juliana*, the same word is used of the devil's wretched journey back to his minions in hell after he has been rebuffed and humiliated by the heroine of that poem. In *The Soul's Address to the Body*, the narrator of the initial 'framing' part of that poem speaks of the need for each person to examine his *sāwle sīð* 'soul's journey' (2a), when death will come and will sever the company of the two 'kinsmen' that formerly dwelt together, the body and the soul. In *Doomsday* 79b, similarly, reference is made to the ill-fated *sīþ* of a sinner's soul after death.[23] At verse 27a of *Christ's*

---

21 *The Seafarer* 48–52; Muir 1: 231.
22 Whitelock 1950; see Chapter 4 above, in the section headed 'Voices of wisdom: *The Wanderer* and related poems'.
23 I quote this passage from *Doomsday* in Chapter 5 above, in the section headed 'Tropes'.

Descent into Hell the word refers to John the Baptist's prior journey into the nether realm to await the coming of Christ. What all these passages refer to is a painful or harrowing journey between worlds.

In other poems of the Exeter Anthology, moreover, the same word carries either eschatological or penitential associations. As the narrator of *Doomsday* declares, a time will come when all people who have inhabited the earth since the time of Adam and Eve will be summoned to judgement. Their souls and bodies will then be reunited as a prelude 'to that journey' (*tō þām sīþe*, 103a). The journey referred to here is that of the resurrected person, now made whole again, to its final destination, whether hellfire or eternal bliss. Just as significant for our understanding of the crux at lines 48–52 of *The Seafarer* is the penitential language of *The Penitent's Prayer*. The Penitent who is the imagined speaker of this poem declares his readiness for the journey that he will now undertake (see *tō þām sīþe*, 4a; *tō þām sīð-fate*, 34a). In a mood of acceptance of whatever hardship or suffering is in store for him—'for the sake of God, enduring it all with a cheerful spirit' ('þæt eal for Gode þolian/ blīþe mōde', 5b–6a)—he is now firm in his courage (his *ellen*, 1b) and, despite hints of self-pity, his spirit is now fixed in its resolve: 'ic gebunden eom/fæste in mīnum ferþe' (6b–7a).

When one contemplates the crux at lines 48–52 of *The Seafarer* with these other passages in mind, one cannot doubt what choice the speaker of that poem is making. What he is resolved to undertake is not an ordinary journey out to sea, or not only that. Rather, he is setting out on an ascetic's arduous and potentially dreadful journey through life to death and from death to final judgement.[24] The Seafarer's journey is a penitential yet hopeful one, like the sea journey that the speaker of *The Penitent's Prayer* has in mind to undertake. The Seafarer makes clear that he will not flinch from pursuing his journey to its final destination even when the earth's beauties offer such pleasant diversions. Neither will he be distracted by nights of wine-fuelled conviviality. The remainder of the Seafarer's monologue, with its gnomic and homiletic reflections on the demise of former civilizations and the inevitability of death, provides intellectual justification for the speaker's resolve; while the poem's last lines speak of the joy (*hyht*, 122a) that awaits those blessed ones who will see their Lord (their *dryhten*, 121b) face to face in their true home, heaven.[25]

---

24 Helena Znojemská (2005) offers a nuanced study of how the Seafarer's spirit is quickened to embark upon the soul's journey to God, crossing tempestuous seas associated with the uncertainties of life on earth.

25 Jennifer Neville (2009) presents an alternative approach to the theme of the soul's journey as it figures in the Exeter Anthology, one that engages only peripherally with the theological considerations that are my main concern here.

Courage and grace: the keywords *ellen* and *bōt*

Readers of Anglo-Saxon poetry will be aware of how much emphasis the makers of heroic verse put on the word and the concept of *ellen*, a noun whose basic meaning is 'courage' or 'fearlessness'.[26] The word comes in for prominent use, for example, in a gnomic passage where the hero of *Beowulf* generalizes about what can save a man's life in circumstances that might be fatal to others:

> Wyrd oft nereð
> unfægne eorl,   þonne his ellen deah!
>
> (Fortune often spares a warrior who is not preordained to die, as long as his courage proves strong!)[27]

There is no doubt what kind of courage is implied in this remark. At this moment in the narrative, the young hero is reflecting back on his own courage during a prior adventure on the high seas when, as a boy, he was harried by serpents and was pulled down to the ocean floor by a sea-monster of some kind. In the main action of the poem, in like manner, Beowulf proves himself to be the sole person brave enough to await and withstand Grendel's nocturnal assault on Heorot, just as he is the only man in Denmark brave enough to plunge into serpent-infested waters to seek out Grendel's terrible mother.

In the very last lines of *The Wanderer*, still, one cannot be sure just what kind of courage is alluded to when we are told that a good man is one who keeps his word (his *trēow*), keeps his feelings to himself, and acts *mid elne*, a phrase that would normally mean 'courageously' or 'vigorously':

> Til biþ se þe his treowe gehealdeþ,   ne sceal næfre his torn to rycene
> beorn of his breostum acyþan,   nemþe he ær þa bote cunne,
> eorl mid elne gefremman.   Wel bið þam þe him are seceð,
> frofre to fæder on heofonum,   þær us eal seo fæstnung stondeð.
>
> (Good are those who keep their faith. They are never too quick to complain of their afflictions unless they know beforehand what the remedy for them is: to act with good zeal in the world. Well

---

26 Definitions offered by the *DOE* when the word is used mainly in verse are 1: 'courage, strength' and 1.b: 'courageous deed, act of strength'. Of common Germanic origin, the word has no modern English reflex, having gone out of use by the middle of the thirteenth century; see Kurath and Kuhn 1952–2001, s.v. *elne*.
27 *Beowulf* 572b–73; *Klaeber's Beowulf*, p. 21.

shall they be who seek for grace, for consolation from the Father in heaven, where the immutable abides for us all.)[28]

Not just the phrase *mid elne* in the third line of this excerpt, meaning 'courageously', 'fearlessly' or 'zealously', but other words of this passage recall the heroic ethos of *Beowulf*.[29] The 'good man' referred to at the start is subsequently referred to by the terms *beorn* (113a) and *eorl* (114a), two nouns that in heroic poetry typically denote 'warrior'.[30] But *The Wanderer* is not a heroic poem, nor is its main speaker characterized as someone actively engaged in martial activities. Rather, he is portrayed as a person of some standing in his society who is in a state of grief as a result of the loss of his former lord and homeland. He has no need for the kind of courage that helps Beowulf overcome a pair of hellish ogres and a dragon. It might therefore seem that the gnomic statement with which *The Wanderer* comes to an end, with its injunction to 'act in the world courageously', has only a glancing relation to the main speaker's monologue.

Another phrase in this same passage, however, alerts the reader that reference is being made to something other than the heroic ethos that animates *Beowulf*. This is *þā bōte*, in the second line. Although 'redress' is a plausible translation of that phrase, the feminine noun *bōt* has a wide spectrum of possible meanings. These extend from the general sense 'a making good' (*DOE* sense A.1), to the more specific meaning 'relief, deliverance' (sense A.1.b), to the yet more specialized senses 'cure' (in medical contexts) or 'compensation' (in legal contexts), to cite just four aspects of the word's semantics.[31]

Of interest is the sense of the word *bōt* when used in penitential contexts. This is 'atonement, penance, repentance for sin' (*DOE* sense B) or, by extension, 'forgiveness, absolution' (sense B.1). This dimension of the word's meaning is worth pursuing. If the redress for the Wanderer's sufferings has to do somehow with penance or absolution, then the phrase *mid elne*

---

28 *The Wanderer* 112–14a; Muir 1: 218–19.
29 When the young warrior Wiglaf proves to be a pattern of courage during the hero's fight against the dragon, for example, he acts *elne* 'courageously' (*Beowulf* 2676a). On the meaning of *mid elne*, see the *DOE*, s.v. *ellen*, sense 1.a. Here I have found it apt to translate the phrase *mid elne gefremman* as 'to act with good zeal in the world', thereby echoing a phrase from the final chapter of the *Rule of Saint Benedict*, with its focus on the 'good zeal' (*zelus bonus*) that monks should have. See Chapter 1 above, n. 11.
30 See the *DOE*, s.v. *beorn*, sense 1.a: 'with emphasis on martial vigor: noble, hero, warrior'; and s.v. *eorl*, sense 1: 'nobleman' and sense 1.b: 'in poetry: warrior, man'. The two words function here in part as metrical fillers, though their aristocratic tenor is significant.
31 See the *DOE*, s.v. *bōt*. This word, which is of common Germanic origin, has a long later history of use; see *The Oxford English Dictionary*, 2nd edn, s.v. *boot*, sb.[1]

should be understood in the same sense in which it is used in any of the overtly religious poems of the Exeter Anthology, where it is best translated 'zealously'. This is the sense of that phrase in *A Father's Precepts*, for example, where the wise Father exhorts his son to avoid all reprehensible behaviour: 'heald elne þis—ne freme firene' ('keep zealously to this precept: commit no sins', 16b-17a). In *The Life of Saint Guthlac*, similarly, the narrator comments on what a demanding task it is to tell, with each point mentioned in due order, what the saintly hero of that poem experienced *on elne* 'in his good zeal' (532b). So the 'good man' of whom the Christian narrator speaks in the closing lines of *The Wanderer* is a person of both courage and the good kind of zeal, with penitential zeal in the faith being strongly implied.

Another instance of creative ambiguity can be observed at the start of this same passage. The clause 'sē þe his trēowe gehealdeþ' (112a) could potentially refer to anyone who stands by his word, a crucial virtue in Anglo-Saxon society. This is the sense of the word in *Cotton Maxims*, for example, in the gnomic statement 'Trēow sceal on eorle' ('Truth shall be in a man', 32b).[32] In the Exeter Anthology poem *The Husband's Message*, likewise, the unidentified messenger whose monologue is the substance of that poem affirms the truth and faith (the 'troth') of the man who sends the message to his beloved of former years: 'Ic gehātan dear/þæt þū þǣr tīr-fæste trēowe findest' ('I dare assert that you will find irreproachable faith there', 11b-12). In a religious context, however, *trēow* can refer to a person who is stalwart in the faith. This religious dimension comes into play in *The Life of Saint Guthlac* when we are told that Guthlac 'never felt doubt concerning his faith'—his *trēow*—'on account of the terror aroused by wretched outcast spirits' ('fore egsan/ earmra gǣsta', 339-40a). Later in this same poem, the narrator states of Guthlac that 'the faith in his heart never faltered' ('him ne getwēode trēow in brēostum', 543). In *The Ascension*, similarly, the risen Christ pledges a holy covenant between God and man ('gǣst-hālig trēow', 145b [584b]), much as in *The Passion of Saint Juliana* the heroine of that poem is said to hold firm to Christ as her chosen bridegroom: 'Hīo in gǣste bær/hālge trēowe' ('In her soul she bore the sacred faith', 28b-29a).

It is in this religious sense, I suggest, that the word *trēow* is used in the last lines of *The Wanderer*. Those who keep their faith are not just 'good' (OE *til*) in a moral sense, though goodness naturally follows. Rather, they are among the dedicated few who devote themselves with exceptional zeal to a life lived in accord with Christian teachings. As a true *beorn* and *eorl*—two nouns drawn

---

32 Like all these short *sceal* clauses, this one can be construed in several different ways depending on one's perspective. In a moral sense, what the verse means is 'a man should keep his word'.

from the language of heroic poetry, either of which can denote 'warrior' in a spiritual sense—the person who keeps his faith with undeviating devotion is a *miles Christi*, or 'warrior of Christ'.

The import of these remarks is that the 'good' person referred to in the closing lines of *The Wanderer* cannot be the Wanderer himself, even if our hearts go out to him. Rather, the 'good' person is one who has renounced the world and its vain comforts so as to seek out, through a dedicated penitential regime, the final *bōt* of eternal bliss.[33]

As readers of the whole of the Exeter Anthology will be aware, no few examples of 'good' people of this kind are featured in this compilation. Guthlac comes straight to mind, as does Juliana, the Seafarer, the Convert of *The Rhyming Poem* and—though his zeal is less than perfect—the Penitent of *The Penitent's Prayer*. At the end of *The Wanderer* we are invited to contemplate such examples of piety as these. In the larger religious context in which this monologue is to be understood, the grace and divine mercy to which the narrator alludes in the poem's first and last lines (*āre*, 1b, 114b; *miltse*, 2a; *frōfre*, 115a) are shown to be efficacious.

Instead of being approached as a secular lament, then, *The Wanderer* is best read as reinforcing the religious tenor of the Exeter Anthology as a whole. The narrator's closing reference to *þā bōt* (113b)—that is, to salvation, God's grace seen as a remedy for earthly afflictions—recalls the longing for union with the divine that finds poignant expression in *Advent Lyrics*, the songs of praise that are strategically placed at the Anthology's head. There, in *Advent Lyric 10*, in a prayer of thanksgiving offered to *ēce dryhten* 'the eternal Lord', reference is made to *sēo bōt*—that is, to the deliverance—that is 'gelong eall æt þē ānum' ('wholly dependent on you [Christ] alone', 365b-66a). Both passages likewise echo the prayer that in *Advent Lyric 6* is offered up to the Lord Christ by the Old Testament patriarchs who await Christ's harrowing of hell: 'Is sēo bōt gelong/eal æt þē ānum for ofer-þearfum.' The meaning of this statement is 'We who are in dire need are dependent on you alone for our deliverance' (152b-53).[34] Nearly identical phrasing is used towards the end of *The Penitent's Prayer* in that passage where the speaker cries out to God for forgiveness for his sins, for which he shows due contrition:

> Eala, dryhten min,
> meahtig mundbora, þæt ic eom mode [s]eoc,
> bittre abolgen. Is seo bot æt þe
> gelong after [li]fe.

---

33 See the *DOE*, s.v. *bōt*, sense C.2.a, 'reward of eternal life', with citations from the OE version of the psalms and the beginning of the poem *Exodus* from the Junius Manuscript.

34 Clayton, *Poems of Christ*, pp. 12–13.

(Alas, my Lord, my mighty protector, that I am troubled in spirit, cruelly vexed.[35] The remedy for this, after my life is done, depends on you.)[36]

The Penitent thus expresses in heartfelt personal terms a sentiment much like what is implied in the gnomic statement with which *The Wanderer* comes to an end.

By making the foregoing connections among different poems of the Exeter Anthology, I have no intention of levelling out the differences of genre, form and style that distinguish these individual texts from one another when considered from a literary perspective. The distinctions by which these poems are individualized extend to substantive matters as well. The stoic Wanderer is not to be confused with the cheerful, stalwart Guthlac, nor does either of these figures much resemble the Penitent—a man who knows he must answer to God for his sins and does his best, in these trying circumstances, to buoy up his spirits. On the contrary, the Wanderer may know of God, but he evidently has no hope of salvation. From bitter experience as well as deep philosophical reflection, he may have come to know much about the workings of mutability here *under hēofonum* 'under the heavens' (107b);[37] but as for receiving the grace of which the narrator speaks in the poem's coda, he appears to have no clear idea where to look or even what to look for.

Still, as readers of the Bible, the Anglo-Saxons knew God's grace to be infinite and to be at work in the world in mysterious ways throughout time. It is worth recalling that there is mystery of a hopeful kind in that passage from *Beowulf* that tells of the destiny awaiting the soul of the unbaptized hero of that poem at the moment of his death: 'Him of hræþre gewāt/sāwol sēcean sōð-fæstra dōm' ('From his breast his soul departed to seek out the judgement of the righteous').[38] The implication here, though it could only be made explicit at the risk of heresy, is that this great and magnanimous man is saved. Turning back to *The Wanderer*, it is of interest that, at the end of his monologue, the imagined speaker of this poem is said to 'sit apart' so as to

---

35 The reasons why the speaker is 'cruelly vexed' must be inferred from his monologue as a whole. Evidently as an act of penance for unspecified misdeeds (or else chiefly on account of the archetypal sin of Adam?), he has been required to leave his homeland and undertake a pilgrimage so as to expiate his sins. In my reading of the poem, he manifests contrition for his sins and yet still finds his required penance harsh. His spirit is unsettled on that account.
36 *The Penitent's Prayer* 39b–42a; Muir 1: 340.
37 This significant phrase is echoed, nine folios later, in the next-to-last verse of *Widsith*, another poem set in the voice of a speaker from the pre-Christian past.
38 *Beowulf* 2819b–20; *Klaeber's Beowulf*, p. 96. See the note on 2820b (*Klaeber's Beowulf*, p. 257) for critical controversies attendant on these verses, with references.

contemplate the world in superior wisdom. Robert E. Bjork has plausibly seen his isolation as the crucial first step in his conversion from the 'world-bound, essentially hopeless exile track of the Germanic world' into the 'hope-filled exile track of the Christian faith'.[39] The Anglo-Saxons clearly had an interest in the fate of the souls of virtuous pagans, and those of their poems that are set in the ancestral past gave them food for thought in this regard.

The journey home: the keyword *hām*

The Old English word *hām*, meaning 'home', might not seem to be a profitable one to single out for attention since it has a reflex in modern English whose meaning seems transparent. Home is home, is it not? Is it not where one dwells? And yet the matter is not so simple. When the woman who is the speaker of *The Wife's Lament* tells of her present dwelling place, for example, it is decidedly not the same place as her home. That difference is precisely the source of her grief: she lives as an exile in a miserable den where she is forced to remain as a result of her husband's evident abandonment of her. She has no close companions in the *locus horribilis* where she lives, and her days are filled with weeping. Her true home is elsewhere, whether it is one that she recalls with nostalgia or imagines with longing.

The basic meaning of the noun *hām* as defined by the DOE is 'dwelling, abode'.[40] The word is often used with that literal meaning in Old English prose and sometimes in verse as well. A leading synonym is *ēðel*, a noun that resembles Latin *patria* in that it calls to mind a place of some geographical extent, not just a dwelling. In a number of instances, almost all of them in verse, *hām* denotes an absent object of longing. This is the situation depicted in *The Wife's Lament*, although that specific word is not found there. It is the usual situation as well in Old English religious verse, where *hām* or its synonym *ēðel* is used most often with reference to heaven conceived of as the true home of human beings—a species whose life on earth, according to Gregorian teachings, is a kind of exile-pilgrimage.[41] According to this medieval commonplace, heaven is the home that makes up for the loss of Eden. During

---

39 Bjork 1989: 126. Similarly, E.G. Stanley (2008: 4–5) takes the word *dōm-georn* in line 17 of *The Wanderer* to refer to the hopes and fears of the solitary exile who is 'eager for Judgment', as if this speaker were aware of the possibility of redemption.
40 See the DOE, s.v. *hām* (noun), sense 2.
41 See the DOE, s.v. *hām* (noun), sense 2.b: 'dwelling, abode not on earth' and 3.b: 'an inhabited place or region not on earth'. Under these headings the DOE groups together references to either heaven as the true *hām* of Christ, the angels and humanity, or hell as the *hām* of devils. Dee Dyas (2001: 67–124) discusses the Gregorian trope of the journey of humankind

the interim period before Guthlac attains his home in the heights (*hāmes in hēahþu*, *The Life of Saint Guthlac* 796a), the hill that he occupies in his quest for solitude is called his *eorðlīc ēþel* only (261a)—that is, his earthly home as opposed to his heavenly one.

As Nicholas Howe has discussed in the course of a study of homes both real and imagined in Anglo-Saxon England, 'the linked tropes of the earthly home as temporary and the heavenly home as eternal' find recurrent expression in the religious poetry of the period.[42] A noteworthy instance of the use of *hām* in a spiritual sense occurs towards the end of the Vercelli Book poem *The Dream of the Rood*. At this point in the poem, the Dreamer, now comforted by knowledge of the meaning of his terrifying nocturnal vision, praises Christ for having redeemed humankind and for giving us both life and a heavenly home (*hēofonlīcne hām*).[43] This home, it is implied, can be attained both in futurity and, to some extent, through present contemplation. Rather than being a place of rest or stasis, this heavenly home is a site of music, light and resplendent movement, as is made clear in that part of the Exeter Anthology poem *The Phoenix* where reference is made to the flocks of heavenly birds that gather about in Christ's heavenly mansion, clothed in light and singing aloud *in þām gladan hām* 'in that joyous home' (593a). In this poem's transparent allegory, the heavenly birds represent the souls of all those who have been steadfast in the faith (*sōþ-fæstum sāwlum*, 589) and are now united with God.

Significantly, the word *hām* is used in this same sense towards the end of *The Seafarer* in that passage where the speaker of that poem, now taking on the role of an evangelist, calls on his audience to strive to gain salvation:

> Uton we hycgan   hwær we ham agen,
> ond þonne geþencan   hu we þider cumen,
> ond we þonne eac tilien,   þæt we to moten
> in þa ecan   eadignesse,
> þær is lif gelong   in lufan dryhtnes,
> hyht in heofonum.

---

through life to the heavenly home as one aspect of the broad theme of pilgrimage in medieval English literature.

42 Howe 2004: 151. As Anita R. Riedinger has remarked as well, an 'omnipresent tension between what is—a separation from home—and what is desired—a return to home—enhances the subliminal drama of much Old English poetry' (1995: 53).

43 *The Dream of the Rood* 148a; Clayton, *Poems of Christ*, p. 170. Other keywords or keyword phrases that occur in the final thirty-five lines of *The Dream of the Rood*, where the narrator speaks of his hope for salvation, include *elne micle* (123a); *hyht* (126b and 148b); *drēam* (with reference first to worldly pleasures and then to heavenly bliss, 133a, 140a and 144a); *sīþ* (in the form of the compound *sīð-fæt*, 150b, with reference to Christ's Ascension); and, as a synonym for *hām* in the poem's very last verse, *ēðel* (156b).

> (Let us consider where we have a home, and let us then consider how we might get there, and let us then also dedicate our efforts so that we may proceed into that everlasting state of bliss where life is inseparable from the Lord's love, where bliss is in the heavens.)[44]

Somewhat curiously, the editors of the DOE provide a separate subentry for *hām* ('sense 4') chiefly so as to account for this very passage, which is cited as one of two supporting quotations for the meaning 'place where refuge, rest or satisfaction is found'.[45] As a result of this choice, readers of *The Seafarer* who consult the DOE about the meaning of this passage may fail to recognize that here, as in *The Dream of the Rood* and *The Phoenix*, the word *hām* refers not to an ordinary refuge, but rather to heaven envisioned as a place of everlasting joy. Although the editors of the DOE were surely aware of the theological sense that the word bears in this context, they apparently wished to salvage the fiction that, even at this late stage in the poem, the Seafarer is still speaking as if he were a sailor setting out on a real-world journey rather than as a Christian pilgrim and evangelist.

The final instance of the use of the word *hām* to which I will call attention brings us back to the figure of the *miles Christi*. Towards the end of *The Life of Saint Guthlac*, we are told of righteous persons who, like the saint, will be granted redemption. This passage is worth quoting despite its length, for nowhere else in the Exeter Anthology is such a clear statement made concerning the place of the regular clergy in the scheme of salvation. Seldom elsewhere, that is, is the term 'monastic poetics' to be taken quite so literally. Among the key terms introduced here by the author of this poem (whom many suspect to be Cynewulf) are *hām* in the sense 'heaven', *cempa* in the sense 'warrior of Christ', *hyht* in the sense 'heaven' again, *ēðel* in the sense 'homeland' and hence yet again 'heaven', and *sōð-fæste* in the sense 'those who are steadfast in the faith', hence 'the righteous'. The passage tells of the bliss that awaits those who are ardent in their fulfilment of Christ's teachings:

> Swa soðfæstra   sawla motun   790
> in ecne geard   up gestigan
> rodera rice,   þa þe ræfnað her

---

44 *The Seafarer* 117–22a; Muir 1: 233.
45 The other illustrative quotation is from verse 35 of Psalm 106 of the *Paris Psalter*, where the psalmist sings of God's power to turn a parched land into a fruitful one: 'Þǣr hē hungrium hām staðelude ... þǣr hī eard nāmon āwā syþþan ('There he established a home for the hungry ... where they took up residence forever after'); O'Neill 2016: 434–35. There is no need to establish a new category of meaning for the word *hām* so as to account for this passage, however, for any *hām* is a potential refuge.

> wordum ond weorcum   wuldorcyninges
> lare longsume,   on hyra lifes tid
> earniað on eorðan   ecan lifes,   795
> hames in heahþu.   Þæt beoð husulweras,
> cempan gecorene,   Criste leofe,
> berað in breostum   beorhtne geleafan,
> haligne hyht,   heortan clæne
> weorðiað waldend,   habbað wisne geþoht,   800
> fusne on forðweg   to fæder eðle,
> gearwaþ gæstes hus,   ond mid gleawnesse
> feond oferfeohtað   ond firenlustas
> forberað in breostum,   broþorsibbe
> georne bigongað,   in Godes willan   805
> swencað hi sylfe   sawle frætwað
> halgum gehygdum,   heofoncyninges bibod
> fremmað on foldan.   Fæsten lufiað,
> beorgað him bealoniþ   ond gebedu secað,
> swincað wið synnum,   healdað soð ond ryht.   810

(Thus the souls of those steadfast in truth will be granted leave to ascend into an everlasting abode in the kingdom of the skies, those who here carry out in words and deeds the abiding precepts of the King of Glory and who in their lifetimes earn eternal life and a home in the heights. These are men of the sacrament, the chosen warriors beloved of Christ. In their breasts they bear shining faith and divine hope. Pure at heart, they worship the Ruler. They cultivate wisdom, a keen sense of purpose directing them on their way forth to the Father's homeland. They make ready the house of the soul and with diligence outfight the fiend, and they abstain from wicked desires in their breasts. Brotherly love they eagerly profess; they put themselves to trouble in the will of God; they beautify their souls with holy thoughts and fulfil on earth the heavenly King's command. They delight in fasting, they avoid wickedness, and they turn to prayer; they struggle against sins and uphold truth and right.)[46]

While this passage affirms that all those who strive in such a manner for salvation can gain it, its phrasing applies above all to the clergy, and in particular to persons in monastic orders. These people are the *hūsul-weras* of verse 796b, a noun that is compounded from the simplex *hūsl* 'the Eucharist' plus the simplex *weras* 'men'. Although the DOE defines *hūsul-wer* as meaning 'communicant', the word occurs only here, so that its meaning must chiefly be inferred from this context. It is an apt term to use with reference not just to

---

46   *The Life of Saint Guthlac*, 790–810; Muir 1: 135–36; translation based on Bradley, p. 268.

anyone who participates in communion, but also, more particularly, to those dedicated members of the clergy who take the Eucharist regularly, including those priests who administer it. The similarly formed compound noun *hūsel-bearn*, another hapax legomenon, is used at verse 559a of this same poem (spelled there '*hūsul-bearn*') with reference to Guthlac when he is harried by devils. Although the *DOE* again offers the neutral definition 'communicant' for that word, Bradley is justified in taking its meaning in this context to be 'saintly child of the eucharist'.[47] The sense of *hūsul-weras* in the long passage just quoted, likewise, is suitably expressed by the phrase 'men of the sacrament'.[48]

In any event, the phrase 'cempan gecorene, Crīste lēofe' that fills the next line (797) evidently refers above all to those 'chosen warriors, beloved of Christ' who have adopted a monastic vocation, even though this same phrase too can refer to either the clergy as a whole or to any zealous Christian. The phrases that follow this line all reinforce the same point, with their reference to the wisdom of such elect persons, their keen sense of purpose, their ability to outfight the fiend, their spirit of brotherly love, and their delight in fasting and prayer. This point is that a special place in heaven is reserved for those who have renounced earthly comforts and ambitions so as to devote their lives to the service of God.

Towards a conceptual grammar of the Exeter Anthology

To sum up my main point in the present chapter: the keywords that run through the Exeter Anthology help to transform what might have been no more than a miscellany of verse texts into a single coherent discourse, one that extends from the Anthology's start to its finish. To put this same matter another way: study of how certain keywords are deployed in the Exeter Anthology helps to identify the conceptual grammar that governed the composition of devotional verse in the vernacular in late tenth-century England, as witnessed by the poems included in this volume. By focusing our attention on a small number of keywords, we are well situated to understand the system of thought, feeling and potential action that informs each poem of the Exeter Anthology, in addition to other remarkable religious poetry of the late Old English period including *The Dream of the Rood*. This is a system to which each of these poems contributes, in turn, its own measure of art and devotion.

---

47 See the *DOE*, s.v. *hūsel-bearn*; Bradley, p. 263.
48 Bradley, p. 268. Likewise John Damon (2003: 145–46) favours the translation 'men of the sacrament', while taking this term to refer broadly to *oratores* 'members of the clergy' as opposed to *bellatores* 'men of the warrior class'.

CHAPTER 9

Intratextual Hermeneutics

What reading context for the poems of the Exeter Anthology is most likely to yield productive insights?

Somewhat paradoxically, as I have argued in the preceding chapters, the best reading context for these poems may be the Exeter Anthology itself. While study of their sources and analogues is likewise crucial to their understanding, the first place to which one should look for elucidation of a poem or passage from this codex is the rest of the contents of this same book. While the meaning of a poem or passage cannot be *determined* in this way (for each poem or passage must be granted its separate integrity), such a strategy may well help to confirm a viable interpretation. Sometimes, indeed, whole chains of interpretive nodes can be seen to run through the Exeter Anthology. An awareness of such nodes, together with an alertness to their relation to a prior tradition of thought and imagery, can strengthen one's confidence that one is reading these poems in a manner that is both philologically sound and consistent with the book's period-specific character.

This is not a wholly new argument, although my formulation of it with specific regard to the Exeter Anthology has no precedent of which I know. T.A. Shippey's groundbreaking 1972 book *Old English Verse* is based on a similar premise with regard to the whole corpus of Old English poetry. Much of what Shippey does in that study is to show the extent to which the corpus of Old English verse is interlaced with conventional elements that give it the effect of being all of a kind. 'Old English poetry gains from being read in large blocks', Shippey writes. 'The most valuable commentary on one poem may well be another poem.'[1]

An example to which Shippey directs attention is the Vercelli Book poem *Andreas*. Even though it is translated directly from Greek via Latin, this poem, Shippey claims, 'is still in its poetic effect much more like the rest of Old

---

1 Shippey 1972: 14. In his 1976 book *Poems of Wisdom and Learning* as well, Shippey calls attention to affinities between the gnomic poems recorded in the Exeter Anthology and those recorded in other codices, arguing that this body of verse is best understood when these poems (and others like them) are read together.

English verse than it is like anything else, including its original' (1972: 14). More to my purpose in the present study, Shippey cites a network of verbal cross references linking the so-called elegies of the Exeter Anthology not just with one another, but also with the 'wisdom' poems of that same codex (1972: 53–79). Worth emphasis is that these resemblances are specific to the Exeter Anthology rather having to do with the conventional language of Old English poetry in general.

Similarly, in an authoritative survey of Old English wisdom poetry, David Ashurst observes that the so-called elegies of the Exeter Anthology can perhaps best be viewed 'as extensions of the wisdom-poetry genre' (2010: 136). Just as a large body of Old English verse of the 'wisdom' type is nested in this codex, so are the ten poems identified by Anne Klinck (1992) as pertaining to the genre of the elegies. Some of the resemblances in language, theme and imagery between these two groups of poems can be traced as well in the riddles, as Rafal Boryslawski has argued while pointing out that the riddles of the Exeter Anthology do not refer to themselves using a form of the word *rædels*, but rather the word *giedd* (also spelled *gydd*, etc.), an encompassing term whose semantic range extends from 'poem' or 'song' to 'wise speech', 'parable' or 'riddle'.[2]

The Christian sojourner and the two cities

It will be helpful to turn to two examples of the kinds of interconnectivity to which I refer.

One chain of interpretive nodes within the Exeter Anthology links the five poems *The Ascension, The Seafarer, Vainglory, Widsith* and *The Ruin* as elements of a single discourse. In order to clarify how this is so, I will take up these poems in a sequence that is almost the reverse of their manuscript order. Although these poems are often classified into different genres and are therefore studied atomistically, often via separate editions, with *The Seafarer* and *The Ruin* approached as 'elegies', *Vainglory* as an example of 'wisdom literature', *Widsith* as a 'heroic' or 'encomiastic' poem, and *The Ascension* as a poem of a Christological and homiletic character that is part of the Cynewulfian corpus, there are points of resemblance between them that transcend these generic distinctions.

When a reader of *The Ruin* is told that the former inhabitants of the desolate cityscape described in this poem were not just *glæd-mōd ond*

---

2   Boryslawski 2002. Elsewhere (Niles 1999a: 16–19 and 30) I offer an integrative discussion of this super-generic term *giedd*. The *DOE*, s.v. *gydd*, lists the various senses of the word seriatim.

gold-beorht 'happy and brilliantly adorned with gold' (33a) but also *wlonc ond wīn-gāl* 'proud and wanton with wine' (34a), then that latter phrase ought to set off a small alarm in one's mind, for it calls to mind the arrogant, inebriated quarreller whose misconduct at the feast has been depicted in *Vainglory*. Such a carouser, we have been told, is headed for damnation. When construing *The Ruin* we can infer that a whole civilization characterized by similar moral failings is likely to have had within it the seeds of its own destruction, however impressive it was in its visual splendour and material wealth. Moreover, an alert reader of *The Ruin* will remember that the same phrase *wlonc ond wīn-gāl* was earlier used to refer to the town-dwellers mentioned in *The Seafarer*—people whose comfortable but self-indulgent way of life is scorned by the Seafarer himself.

The Seafarer's monologue in turn is linked to *Widsith* by wordplay on the keyword *lof*. In the last line of *Widsith*, the narrator of that poem (who should be distinguished from the imagined Scop) speaks of legendary kings who won *lof* 'an undying reputation' under the heavens. An alert reader will recall that the same word *lof* is used twice in *The Seafarer*, first (at 73a) with reference to good repute on earth and then (at 78a) with reference to salvation in heaven. This instance of calculated duplicity directs attention to the lack of the possibility of salvation in the world inhabited by the pagan kings whose names are recited in *Widsith*. While, like Alexander the Great, who is mentioned prominently at the start of that poem (at lines 15–17),[3] those kings may have gloried in their wealth and their wide domains, the only *lof* for which they strove was the earthly kind, for even the pious ones among them had no effective knowledge of Christ.

If any doubt remains as to what the Seafarer's austere life on the sea signifies, then that question is resolved when one recalls the passage at the end of *The Ascension* where seafaring serves as an extended metaphor for the journey of a Christian sojourner.[4] Even though his 'ship' is battered by the 'storms' of life, a Christian who keeps his faith still seeks the 'harbour' of heaven. This imagery drawn from *The Ascension* anchors the Exeter Anthology to the writings of Gregory the Great, thus also setting it in alignment with

---

3 From the text of *Widsith* alone, it is impossible to determine how the author of this poem regarded Alexander's moral character. Alexander is a profoundly ambivalent figure in medieval historiography, admired by some writers but hardly so by others. Andy Orchard has observed that in the Orosian tradition that is well represented in Anglo-Saxon England, Alexander was portrayed as 'a megalomaniac, a tyrannical mass-murderer, a figure of extreme Pride' (1995b: 117). In general, from the medieval Christian perspective, Alexander was an example to earthly kings of 'how their powers and glory must ultimately perish' (1995b: 139).

4 See lines 411–17a [850–56a]; Muir 1: 78.

a large body of other early medieval writings that make use of this same nautical metaphor.⁵

These five poems of the Exeter Anthology can thus be seen to play an interconnected part in a discourse on a single theme: the right conduct of the Christian life in a world whose pleasures and triumphs, even when they have the semblance of reality, are empty when seen with unclouded eyes. While a commonplace of early Christian literature, this theme is developed here in English, the language of the people, in a quasi-dramatic manner that is unparalleled elsewhere in the recorded literature of the Middle Ages.

A second example of this same phenomenon of interconnectivity can be traced in the recurrent imagery of walls, stones and storm-swept citadels that constitutes one of the leitmotifs of the Anthology. This thread of imagery is a complex one that begins with *Advent Lyrics* and continues with *The Passion of Saint Juliana* and *The Wanderer* (two adjoining poems that function in some ways as a pair). It too concludes with *The Ruin*, though there are ramifications in other poems of the Anthology as well. Among these other poems is *The Seafarer*, with its brooding meditation on the transience of earthly things. Again it will be helpful to take up these poems in reverse order.⁶

Readers of *The Ruin* will recall the poet's account of a *weal-stān* 'wall-stone' (1a) whose surface is beautifully fashioned (*wrǣtlīc*), but that in the course of time came to be broken and exposed to the elements so that it now lies useless. This imagery of a useless stone in a ruined city recalls the storm-beaten walls of the ruined city described towards the end of *The Wanderer*, regardless of the fact that *The Wanderer* is written out some forty-five folios earlier in the codex:

> Stondeð nu on laste   leofre duguþe
> weal wundrum heah,   wyrmlicum fah.
> Eorlas fornomon   asca þryþe,
> wæpen wælgifru,   wyrd seo mære,
> ond þas stanhleoþu   stormas cnyssað,
> hrið hreosende   hrusan bindeð,
> wintres woma ...
>
> (Now a wall wondrously high, adorned with serpentine patterning, stands where the beloved group of companions once walked. The might of spears has swept the warriors away—weapons hungry

---

5   I quote the passage from *The Ascension* in Chapter 7 above, in the section headed 'The book's inclusivity'.
6   The following account can be compared with the discussions of architectural imagery in the Exeter Anthology offered by Salvador Bello 2006, Kramer 2007 and Garner 2011, esp. at 115–21, and with Greenfield's analysis of the 'ruined wall' imagery of *The Wanderer* (1966: 150).

for slaughter, fate the far-famed one—and storms batter the ramparts; a swirling snowstorm binds the earth, the howling of winter ...)⁷

An alert reader of either of these poems will recall as well that imagery of a related kind, though of a sharply contrastive nature, is featured in *The Passion of Saint Juliana*, the poem that directly precedes *The Wanderer*. In this story of the triumphant martyrdom of one of God's virgin saints, much is made of the image of a walled citadel where those who are firm in their faith and who live by the law (that is, who are *ǣ-fremmende*, 648a) can stand secure, with their metaphorical house (*hūs*, 648b) unbroken by the metaphorical storms that batter it:

> Weal sceal þy trumra
> strong wiþstondan   storma scurum,
> leahtra gehygdum.
>
> (A wall that is strong withstands all the more firmly the blasts of storms—the promptings of sin.)⁸

A person who resists temptation is thus likened to a stone fortress that remains steadfast in the midst of tempests. By a related medieval commonplace that informs this passage, God's churches are figured as fortresses that protect their congregations against the metaphorical or actual storms of life. Eleven lines later in the same poem, a similar metaphor comes into play in a passage where persons of faith are urged to keep watch 'against the battle-roar of enemies' (*wið hettendra hilde-wōman*, 663). The unusual noun *wōma* 'howl'—one that is used in *The Wanderer* with reference to the onset of foul weather (*wintres wōma*, 103a)—is used in *Juliana* with reference to the howling of devils or vices that assault the 'citadel' of the soul, or by extension the church, according to the familiar terms of Prudentian psychomachia.⁹ To cement these connections between *The Ruin*, *The Wanderer* and *The Passion of Saint Juliana*, the narrator of that latter poem urges his faithful readers or listeners to build the foundation (*staþol*) of their metaphorical fortress on the 'living stone' of Christ rather than on anything less stable:

---

7 *The Wanderer* 97–103a; Muir 1: 218.
8 *Juliana* 650b–52a; Muir 1: 211. Kenneth A. Bleeth (1969) discusses this key passage, its most immediate Latin source, and its literary tradition going back to a number of early medieval commentaries on Scripture. Muir provides additional references (2: 499, his note on *Juliana* 647–52), citing as well a parallel at *The Ascension* 317–38b.
9 James Doubleday (1970) offers a productive analysis of the use made of this allegory in Old English verse.

> Ge mid lufan sibbe,
> leohte geleafan,   to þam lifgendan
> stane stiðhydge   staþol fæstniað ...
>
> (In the spirit of loving peace, in your bright faith, with courageous hearts, go build your foundation on the living stone ...)[10]

The oxymoronic image of the 'living stone' that is introduced in this part of *The Passion of Saint Juliana* offers a counterpart to the oxymoronic 'dead life' on land that the Seafarer scorns.[11]

As for the source of the image of the 'living stone' as used by these poets, it is to be found in the first of the two New Testament epistles of Peter 'the apostle' to various churches in Asia Minor. Peter urges the members of these congregations to remain true servants of Christ despite the persecutions that are inflicted upon them:

> Ad quem accedentes lapidem vivum, ab hominibus quidem reprobatum, a Deo autem electum et honorificatum, et ipsi tamquam lapides vivi super-aedificamini, domus spiritalis, sacerdotium sanctum, offerre spiritales hostias acceptabiles Deo per Iesum Christum.
>
> (Unto whom coming as to a living stone, rejected indeed by men, but chosen and made honourable by God, be you also as living stones built up, a spiritual house, a holy priesthood, to offer up spiritual sacrifices acceptable to God by Jesus Christ.)[12]

The exhortation 'go build your foundation on the living stone' in the passage from *The Passion of Saint Juliana* is echoed when the narrator of *The Wanderer* brings that poem to a close with the gnomic reminder that—despite the transience of all things earthly—there is still hope for those who seek a place in heaven 'þær ūs eal sēo fæstnung stondeð' ('where for us all the immutable abides', 115b). The keyword *staþol* that in *Juliana* denotes the foundation on which a stable building rests is here echoed with a synonym, *fæstnung*, that sums up the qualities of fixedness, stability and protection. As Ælfric uses the word in the sixth of his first series of Catholic Homilies, modified here by the adjective *ēce* 'eternal', *fæstnung* denotes God's everlasting covenant with Abraham and Isaac.[13]

---

10 *Juliana* 652b–54; Muir 1: 211.
11 'Forþon mē hātran sind/dryhtnes drēamas þonne þis dēade līf,/lǣne on londe' ('wherefore the joys of the Lord are warmer to me than this dead life, loaned to me on land', *The Seafarer* 64b–66a; Muir 1: 227).
12 1 Peter 2:4–5; Kinney, *New Testament*, pp. 1242–43.
13 See the *DOE*, s.v. *fæstnung*, senses 1 and 8, and, for the passage from Ælfric (which is based on Genesis 17:19), sense 2.a.i.a.

Working back to the head of this series of interpretive nodes, the image of Christ as the 'living stone' is initially introduced in *Advent Lyric 1*, the first of the poems of longing and worship with which the Anthology begins. Christ, the Master Builder, is here urged to come to earth again in apocalyptic fashion so as to refashion our corrupted world in the image of the New Jerusalem. Since this passage from *Advent Lyrics* can be read in retrospect as a key that unlocks the meaning of each of these subsequent passages, it is worth quoting at some length:

> Ðu eart se weallstan   þe ða wyrhtan iu
> wiðwurpon to weorce.   Wel þe geriseð
> þæt þu heafod sie   healle mærre
> ond gesomnige   side weallas   5
> fæste gefoge,   flint unbræcne,
> þæt geond eorðb[yrg] eall   eagna gesihþe
> wundrien to worlde   wuldres ealdor.
> Gesweotula nu þurh searocræft   þin sylfes weorc,
> soðfæst, sigorbeorht,   ond sona forlet   10
> weall wið wealle.   Nu is þam weorce þearf
> þæt se cræftga cume,   ond se cyning sylfa,
> ond þonne gebete,   nu gebrosnad is,
> hus under hrofe.

(You are the wall-stone that the builders formerly rejected from the building.[14] Well it befits you that you are the head of the glorious Hall and that you conjoin the wide walls, the unbroken flint, with an unbreakable joint, so that people dwelling in all the cities of earth will be exalted in wonder when they see the Lord of glory with their own eyes. Make manifest now, through your masterful handiwork—you, steadfast in truth, bright with the light of victory—the work of your own hands, and straight away let wall be joined to wall. The building is now in need of it, that the Craftsman and King himself should come and restore the house beneath its roof, now that it has fallen to ruin.)[15]

---

14 The biblical source for the image is Psalm 117:22-23: 'Lapidem quem reprobaverunt aedificantes, hic factus est in caput anguli. A Domino factum est istud, et est mirabile in oculis nostris.' ('The stone which the builders rejected, the same is become the head of the corner. This is the Lord's doing, and it is wonderful in our eyes.') Edgar, *Poetical Books*, pp. 472-73. Cf. the Old English poetic paraphrase in the Paris Psalter: 'Þone sylfan stān þe hine swȳðe ǣr/wyrhtan āwurpan, nū sē geworden is/hwommona hēagost; ... þæt is ūrum ēagum eall wundorlīc' ('That same stone which the masons had rejected outright is now become the most important of the corners; ... that is absolutely marvellous in our eyes'). O'Neill 2016: 472-73.

15 *Advent Lyric 1*, 2-14a; Muir 1: 43-44. In verse 7a, following Clayton, *Poems of Christ*, p. 2, I adopt the reading *eorðb[yrg]* 'cities of earth' instead of *eorðb[old]* 'building of earth', the reading in Muir's edition. The last letters of the word are illegible.

If one turns one's attention back to the sequence of poems discussed throughout the preceding paragraphs, a sequence that runs from nearly the start of the Anthology to nearly its end, then extensive parts of *The Wanderer* and the whole of *The Ruin* can now be read as extended glosses on the last clause quoted here: 'now that it'—meaning the world that human beings inhabit—'has fallen to ruin'.

Although *The Wanderer* and *The Ruin* are linked to one another by similar architectural imagery as well as by their common debt to the book of Isaiah and the Book of Lamentations,[16] these two poems are scarcely to be reduced to a single template. Their relation to *Advent Lyrics* is that of antithesis, for the leading theme of those hymns of praise is not the decline and fall of earthly civilizations; rather, it is the joyful anticipation felt by Christians at the thought of the advent of the Redeemer, figured here as Christ the Workman, the maker and restorer of earth and all that the earth contains. In both *Advent Lyric 1* and *The Passion of Saint Juliana*, the Saviour is figured as the architect of heaven, the heavenly Jerusalem, seen as the only lasting shelter from earthly storms.

The motif of building one's house on a firm foundation is featured in texts, in additional to the psalms, that were themselves foundational for the Reform. One of these is Æthelwold's Old English translation of the Rule of Saint Benedict. In a conspicuous addition to the Latin text, the Old English version of the Rule includes the following paragraph, featured towards the end of the Prologue:

> Se hælend cwiþ on þæm halgan godspelle þus clypiende: 'Se þe gehyrð þas mine word and hi mid weorcum gefylð, ic hine gelicne læte wisom were, ðe ofer fæstum stane bytlode; flodas coman, windas bleowan and þæt hus swiðlice gespurnun, and hit no feol, forðy þe hit gestaþolod wæs ofer fæstum stane'.

> (The Saviour speaks in the holy Gospel, saying: 'He who hears my words and fulfils them with deeds, I compare him to a wise man who built his house upon immovable stone. Floods came, winds blew and subjected the house to mighty blasts, and it did not fall, for its foundation was on firm stone.')[17]

The Gospel text that is paraphrased here is the parable of the rock ascribed to Jesus in Matthew 7:24–27 and Luke 6:46–49, where it provides emphatic closure to the Sermon on the Mount. The chain of interpretive nodes that

---

16 Compare for example Isaiah 24:11–12: 'Deserta est omnis laetitia; translatum est gaudium terrrae. Relicta est in urbe solitudo, et calamitas opprimet portas.' ('All mirth is forsaken; the joy of the earth is gone away. Desolation is left in the city, and calamity shall oppress the gates.') Kinney 2012: 94–95.
17 Schröer 1885–88: 4, lines 9–14. See Riyeff 2017: 31–32 for a recent annotated translation of this work.

leads back from *The Ruin* to *Advent Lyrics* thus does not stop there, as if the Exeter Anthology were a self-contained artefact. Rather, it extends outward so as to encompass the words of Jesus himself as expressed in two keystone books of the tenth-century monastic Reform: the Rule of Saint Benedict and the Gospels.

One challenge facing readers of the Exeter Anthology, as I hope to have shown, is to keep in mind the threads of thought and imagery that knit the individual poems of the volume together into a single complex meditation on the tenets of the faith and the nature of a life lived in accord with Christian teachings. A second challenge, one that is equally demanding, is not to lose sight of the differences of genre, style, voice, tone and emphasis that make each of these poems a remarkable individual achievement, one that is never reducible to the coin of doctrine alone.

Intratextuality versus intertextuality

The hermeneutical methods that I have been advocating as an approach to the Exeter Anthology are in keeping with Fred C. Robinson's stance in his seminal 1980 essay 'Old English Literature in its Most Immediate Context'. In calling for attention to the place of a medieval literary work in the codex in which it is written, Robinson was at the vanguard of what has since become a major turn in medieval scholarship towards manuscript studies, 'materialist philology' and the new history of the book.[18] The thrust of his argument has been developed in a wide range of other criticism, from Keith Busby's call for a 'codicological imperative' in Old French literary studies, to Karl Reichl's codicologically based survey of the early Middle English lyric, to Tim William Machan's advocacy of an approach to the textual criticism of Middle English literature that is deeply informed by knowledge of a work's codicological context, among other recent studies along similar lines.[19]

Still my remarks are specific to Exeter, Cathedral Library, MS 3501. They should not be extended to other literary records without a great deal of circumspection. They do not apply to a true miscellany, for example, as opposed to a focused verse collection such as the Exeter Anthology.[20] The coherence of this codex, which is palaeographically self-evident, is enhanced through the use of 'echo' words or phrases that serve to knit its contents

---

18 Ralph Hanna (2013) assesses the impact of the emergent field of manuscript studies on the shaping of literary conceptions and disciplines during recent decades.
19 Busby 2002: 1: 2; Reichl 2011; Machan 2011, respectively.
20 Andrew Taylor (2002) offers many insights into medieval miscellanies and their types.

together.²¹ Other factors that have the same effect are recurrent imagery, reiterated figures of speech and devotional commonplaces that are revisited from different points of view with different effects from poem to poem.

It should be clear as well that I do not advocate the intratextual reading of the poems of the Exeter Anthology at the expense of attention to source studies or other vertical relations. On the contrary, study of the sources of a poem or passage can provide invaluable insights into a text and its most plausible interpretation. It can also cast light on the intellectual milieu in which an author was working. On a grander scale, in Johanna Kramer's words, such research allows us 'to map more accurately and more completely the intellectual landscape of Anglo-Saxon England' (2010: 48). In earlier parts of the present book I have called attention to the manifold ways that the poems of the Exeter Anthology are dependent on Scripture, on scriptural exegesis or on the liturgy, or otherwise echo texts or clusters of imagery that were central to the Reform movement or to early medieval Christianity more generally. Examples of such indebtedness are now relatively easy to identify, for in the past half-century or so, passage after passage of the Exeter Anthology has been shown to have identifiable Latin sources or analogues.²² The twelve *Advent Lyrics* with which the Anthology begins, in particular, bristle with allusions to Latinate sources that would have been familiar to the learned persons of the era, as Robert B. Burlin and Bernard J. Muir have pointed out in their respective commentaries.²³

Parallels to certain poems of the Exeter Anthology can be traced as well in the literature of classical antiquity. The situation of the Wife in *The Wife's Lament* can be compared to that of certain female speakers in Ovid's *Heroides*, for example.²⁴ These parallels encourage one in the belief that the Wife, though destitute of help and ignorant of Christian consolation, is not therefore undeserving of sympathy. Ovid's *Heroides* was esteemed through much of the European Middle Ages, serving poets as a model of eloquence. Such outstanding works of ancient Latin literature as this were admired in the cosmopolitan circles in which Dunstan spent his adult life. The list of Bishop Leofric's donations to Saint Peter's monastic church at Exeter, correspondingly, includes the *Satires* of the first-century Roman poet Perseus and an annotated copy of Statius's *Thebaid*.

---

21 Many such echo effects are pinpointed by Bjork, *OE Shorter Poems*, in his 'Notes to the Translations' (pp. 241–61). Orchard (2010) presents a wealth of verbal correspondences among Old English poems recorded in the Exeter Anthology and elsewhere, providing evidence as well for Latinate sources and analogues for this phrasing.
22 The work of Thomas D. Hill, among others, has been of recurrent value in this regard. See Wright *et al.* (2007: 387–98) for a list of Hill's publications up to the year 2007.
23 Burlin 1968; Muir 2: 396–400.
24 I discuss this parallel in Chapter 6 above, in the section headed 'The power of literary precedent'.

The close relation of certain poems of the Exeter Anthology to Old English prose writings, particularly those of a homiletic character, has long been recognized and continues to repay close study. The rhetoric as well as the thematic content of the last part of *The Seafarer*, for example, is scarcely unique to that poem, but has much in common with a large body of homiletic literature.[25] As G.V. Smithers (1957) pointed out some while ago, the poet's representation of the state of exile in that elegiac poem, as well as in its companion piece *The Wanderer*, recalls the doctrinal content of any number of prose homilies in both the Latin tradition and the Old English. Striking among these parallels is a passage from Blickling homily 2 that explicates as follows the fundamental Christian paradox that the present life of humankind on earth is a form of exile (*wræc-sīþ*) from our true home:

> We send on þisse worlde ælþeodigness. We synd on þisse world ælþeodige, ond swa wæron siþþan se æresta ealdor þisses menniscan cynnes Godes bebodu abræc. Ond for þon gylte we wæron on þysne wræcsiþ sende, ond nu eft sceolon oþerne eþel secan, swa wite, swa wuldor, swa we nu geernian willaþ.

> (We are in a state of exile in this world. We are exiles in this world, and such have we been ever since the first forefather of this human race broke God's commandments. And for that offence we were sent into this exile-journey, and now in turn we are destined to seek out a second homeland, whether it be punishment or glory, just as we now wish to earn.)[26]

Nineteenth- and early twentieth-century readers of *The Seafarer*, lacking a knowledge of how that poem's treatment of the theme of exile is anchored in such homilies as this, went to some lengths to explicate this poem as an expression of a Germanic, or even 'pagan', spirit of endurance in the face of a hostile or indifferent fate. There is little need for critics to take that path today. In like manner, close textual and thematic affinities link *The Wanderer* to the anonymous Vercelli homily 10 in addition to that poem's well-known indebtedness to Blickling homily 8 and the Latin source of that same Blickling sermon.[27] Such parallels as these help to identify *The Wanderer* as a kind of 'heroic homily' that, in a highly original manner, takes on a semi-dramatic form through the device of ethopoeia.

---

25 Fulk and Cain provide specifics, speaking of the closing lines of *The Seafarer* as expressing 'ideas in general circulation' among the Anglo-Saxons in a manner that shows 'how deeply imbued the poem is with the intellectual temper of late Anglo-Saxon monastic life' (2013: 262).
26 Text from R. Kelly (2003: 14), with word division modified at one point. The same passage is quoted to good effect by Smithers (1957: 145) as well as by Cassidy and Ringler (1971: 330).
27 On these connections see Leslie 1985: 18–19 and Orchard 2002.

Given their originality and their confident manner of exposition, it is possible that by the late tenth century if not before, devotional writings composed in the vernacular in England had begun to take on an authority comparable to that of their Latin counterparts. Writing with reference to the vernacular homilies of this end-of-millennium period, Donald Scragg has pointed out that 'their authors are using English sources in the way that earlier writers used Latin, but whereas Latin had to be translated, English sermons were now used as source books verbatim'. Scragg adds: 'The fundamental principle of usage remains the same, but English had now become a language of authority, and texts written in it were seen as authoritative works' (2012: xiii). One reason why the poems of the Exeter Anthology were preserved so carefully could have been to make them available as models for other English verse compositions. As we have seen, Riddle 35 was modelled on a Northumbrian exemplar that was evidently thought to be authoritative, for it in turn was a translation of Aldhelm's 'Lorica' enigma.[28] It is not unreasonable to think that the whole contents of the Exeter Anthology, this high-end production, might have been meant for use in a similar manner. Its constituent poems might even have been granted a status superior to that of vernacular homilies, seeing that they are composed in the demanding and prestigious medium of verse. It is natural to think, as well, that these vernacular poems could have influenced the continuing evolution of Latin verse in Insular contexts.[29] Although these matters must remain speculative, they are worth contemplating.

In sum, all types of information with a bearing on the Exeter Anthology poems should be sifted judiciously if the book and its constituent parts are to be understood in period-specific terms. One last example, however, will strengthen the case for approaching the Exeter Anthology with due attention to the 'codicological imperative'.

Unanticipated pairings: *The Wife's Lament* and *The Penitent's Prayer*

Not all readers of the Exeter Anthology are aware that the bitter monologue of the female speaker of *The Wife's Lament* is followed just a few folios thereafter by a first-person-singular monologue of a complementary kind.

---

28 See the discussion of this point in Chapter 7 above, in the section headed 'The workings of amplification'.
29 Lapidge 1979 touches on this possibility of 'reverse influence' with reference to an earlier period of Insular literature.

I am referring not to *The Husband's Message*, which too forms a counterpart to *The Wife's Lament* though of a different kind,[30] but rather to *The Penitent's Prayer*. This verse monologue is set in the voice of a male speaker who portrays himself as a sinner, who is experiencing poverty and hardship while in a state of exile from his homeland, and who contemplates a difficult journey by sea to an unknown destination.[31] Though less than an exemplary character since he evidently carries some bitterness in his heart,[32] the Penitent still bears his afflictions with patience. With some self-pitying exaggeration, perhaps, he refers to his life as a form of *martirdōm* (12b). While in principle this term could be translated in neutral fashion as 'sufferings', it strongly recalls the martyrdoms of persecuted saints.[33] In any event, unlike the Wife, the Penitent prays devoutly to the Lord for succour in his present tribulations and in the life to come (41b–42a).

The likelihood is great that a deliberate contrast is being made between the despairing Wife and the troubled yet hopeful Penitent. This likelihood is increased when one takes into account the verbal and thematic echoes between these two poems. Just as the Wife identifies herself as a *winelēas wræcca* 'friendless outcast' (10a), so too does the Penitent, echoing the very same phrase *winelēas wræcca* at verse 22a. Likewise, much as the Wife declares that it is her own painful personal experience that qualifies her to speak her sad *giedd* 'lament'—'Ic þis giedd wrece be mē ful gēomorre,/mīnre sylfre sīð' ('I utter this poem about my own wretched self, my very own experience')—the Penitent declares in somewhat different wording that his *sār-spell* 'tale of pain' is based on his own bitter experience: 'Ic be mē tylgust/secge þis

---

30 For discussion from two different perspectives, compare Klinck 1992: 58–59 and Niles 2006a: 247–50. What is of interest here is not the question of whether the Husband and the Wife inhabit the same story, for they clearly do not. Rather, it is the question of whether there exists a conceptual symmetry drawing the two poems together as 'talking pieces'. In each poem, two lovers are long separated by circumstances beyond the woman's control. How does the woman respond emotionally to this situation? How does the man?

31 The sea journey is perhaps a metaphorical one, in keeping with the Gregorian allegory of seafaring, but a literal journey could also be meant. For discussion see Nelson 1983.

32 As Alvin A. Lee remarks, the Penitent is to some degree 'out of charity ... and therefore unable to thrive spiritually' (1972: 148), even though he remains a sympathetic character with whose frailties one can readily identify. It should be noted that Lee reads the poems that I call *Contrition* and *The Penitent's Prayer* as two parts of a single poem that he calls *Resignation*, following earlier scholarship in this regard.

33 Twice, in *The Life of Saint Guthlac* (at 472a and 514a), the loan word *martyr* or a derivative form is used of Guthlac, whose mortification of the flesh in his self-imposed exile would qualify him for that title. But the Penitent has not chosen such a militant path as this.

sār-spell ond ymb sīþ spræce' ('I most assuredly tell this tale of pain about myself and speak of my experience').[34]

These verbal echoes are neither fortuitous nor merely formulaic. One of their effects is to cast the Wife's response to her misfortunes in a more negative light, from a Benedictine perspective, than might be appropriate if her monologue were read in isolation from the rest of the manuscript. A medieval Christian reader proceeding from *The Wife's Lament* to *The Penitent's Prayer* is likely to have respected, as an expression of Christian fortitude, the Penitent's acceptance of his own state of sinfulness as well as his need for penance. From the same point of view, the persecuted and vindictive Wife might be seen as tragically lacking the knowledge that would allow her to integrate her experience into a religious perspective, one that alone might offer her consolation. In this regard, even though the analogy is only a loose one, the Wife is to the Penitent as the Wanderer is to the Seafarer.

The interpretation of *The Wife's Lament* is subject to dispute, of course, as is so much else in the criticism of Old English poetry. I have written elsewhere on the problem of the meaning of this poem's closing lines (Niles 2003a). Although certain critics have taken this passage to express the Wife's enduring love for a husband who has seemingly abandoned her, I myself view it as expressive of the bitterly vindictive mood into which her unjust sufferings have driven her. There is precedent in the classical Latin tradition for a poem expressing bitterness of this kind. In Ovid's *Heroides* 6, for example, Jason's abandoned wife Hypsipyle seethes with vindictive anger.[35] One factor that has a possible bearing on our interpretation of the closing lines of *The Wife's Lament* is that the speaker's monologue is apparently set in pre-Christian times, as are the neighbouring Exeter Anthology poems *Widsith* and *Deor* and as the Wanderer's monologue evidently is as well.

The inference that *The Wife's Lament* is set in a pre-Christian world rests in part on one's understanding of line 15 of the poem, 'Hēt mec hlāford mīn

---

34 *The Wife's Lament* 1–2a (Muir 1: 328); *The Penitent's Prayer* 27b–28 (Muir 1: 340). The beginning of *The Seafarer* and certain lines from *Deor*, too, are called to mind here, as Shippey (1972: 53–54) points out.

35 Hypsipyle curses Medea, her successor in Jason's bed, with particular vehemence (lines 80–83): 'May the woman who intrudes upon my marriage-bed suffer the woes in which Hypsipyle groans, and feel the lot she herself now brings on me ... Let her be an exile ... Let her wander, destitute, bereft of hope ... This fate do I, the daughter of Thoas, cheated of my wedded state, in prayer call down upon you' (Showerman 1977: 80–83). In the Old English poem, of course, there is no hint of a female rival to the embittered speaker. As with *Wulf and Eadwacer* (in the reading of that poem that I have advanced in Chapter 4 above, in the section headed 'Voices from the Germanic past'), the speaker's pain does not derive from a love triangle but rather from conflicts involving kin groups and in-law relations.

herh eard niman'. What this line most plausibly means, in my view, is 'My husband commanded me to take up my abode in the grounds of a *herh*'—that is to say, at a pagan sanctuary of some kind.³⁶ Seen from this perspective, the Wife's despair is not just personal, it is also existential, in that it is a natural response to misfortune on the part of someone ignorant of the consolation brought to humankind through Christ. Muir prefers a different reading of this line, adopting different word divisions and resolving the last three words as 'hēr heard niman' (Muir 1: 328). The line must then be translated, 'My husband, in his harsh spirit, commanded me to take here ...'). This handling of the text, however, entails the awkwardness of leaving no direct object for the verb *niman*. Since the phrase *eard niman* is used elsewhere in Old English to mean 'to take up one's abode',³⁷ there is reason to take the phrase in that same sense here. The Wife's abode is then best viewed as a pagan *herh*, whatever difficulties may be involved in reconstructing the other details of her story. If this interpretation is accepted, then the speaker is a woman of pre-Christian times who 'thinks like a pagan' in response to the injuries and humiliations she has suffered. The poem as a whole can be approached as 'a dystopian image of the pagan past' introduced 'for contrast with the Christian present', as Alaric Hall has phrased the matter.³⁸

The broad conclusion to which this comparison between *The Wife's Lament* and *The Penitent's Prayer* points is that these two neighbouring texts ask to be read as parts of a single conversation. Here as elsewhere, the Exeter Anthology is knit together by points of likeness and contrast tied to specific words, phrases and images. The full meaning of any one poem only emerges when one reads it in its manuscript context, remaining alert to such interconnections as these.

---

36 Wentersdorf (1981) offers an extended discussion of the physical setting of the woman's suffering, seeing it as a pagan sanctuary that was meant to serve her as a place of refuge.
37 Note verse 15 of the Old English verse paraphrase of Psalm 131: 'Þis is mīn rest, þe ic recene nū/on worulda woruld wunian þence,/þǣr ic eard nime' ('This is my resting place which I now plan to occupy at once, for ever and ever, where I will take up residence'). Text and translation from O'Neill 2016: 542–43.
38 A. Hall 2007: 229, with references to the critical literature on the poem's physical setting. See likewise A. Hall 2002: 5–8.

CHAPTER 10

Summary and Conclusions

The Exeter Anthology is not, then, a haphazard collection of whatever poetry of a relatively short kind, composed in English, happened to be available to the book's unknown compiler. Rather, it is a shaped collection, both in its broad contours and in the disposition of many of its details. That the Anthology includes poems of outstanding literary merit is a point that needs no labouring. The main thesis of the present book is that these poems belong together, contributing to a literary achievement that is greater than is apparent when these parts are read in isolation from one another. The Anthology's miscellaneous and yet still harmonious contents are in keeping with its uniformly attractive physical appearance and script, which exemplify the high standards that English bookmaking had achieved by the second half of the tenth century.

A correlative observation has to do with the volume's historical context and overriding purpose. Rather than being a timeless creation of the early medieval imagination, the Exeter Anthology is a product of a religious and literary movement that gained traction on southern English soil during the second half of the tenth century. The origins of this development can be traced back in several directions, whether one looks to Carolingian, Ottonian, Irish or Welsh precedents, to King Alfred the Great's encouragement of literacy in the vernacular, or to the work of poets composing religious verse in English ever since the time of the Abbess Hild and Cædmon. The underlying poetics of this movement are fittingly called 'monastic', seeing that what was involved was the redirection of the time-honoured medium of Old English verse so as to promote values consistent with the way of life of the regular clergy and, by extension, of any Christian of devout spirit. Essential to this project, in the learned circles in which this poetry was evidently composed and read, was the free and expansive reworking of Latin sources so as to naturalize them within the native idiom.

In principle, the Anthology could have spoken to many different *hādas*, or types and ranks of people, whether as a font of wisdom, as a vehicle for religious doctrine and moral guidance, or as a source of aesthetic pleasure. In practice, however, to judge from the rather sparse physical signs of its use, the manuscript is likely to have found only a small readership of educated persons up to the time when Bishop Leofric presented it to his new endowment at Exeter. After that bequest, too, it appears to have seen only minor use up to the time of its recovery by nineteenth-century scholars and critics. The reasons for this long period of neglect are probably best sought in the social and political upheavals of the eleventh century, when England was conquered by two different foreign powers in succession, with momentous effects on Insular literacy and learning. The wonderful thing is that the book survives, affording us knowledge about the culture of early medieval England that would otherwise be lost.

Today the Exeter Anthology is known to practically anyone who has even a passing acquaintance with Old English literature. Present-day readers are unlikely to be familiar with more than certain of the book's highlights, however. It is the rare person today who sets out to read the entire manuscript page by page, as it would have been read in Anglo-Saxon times if assigned to a cloistered person for study during Lent in accord with chapter 48 of the Benedictine Rule. The book's Christological, eschatological, moral and penitential dimensions would have stood out more clearly in that context than they do today, when, for the most part, only certain excerpts from the volume are read in isolation.

In its potential functions, the Exeter Anthology shares many of the characteristic features of medieval instructional miscellanies, differing from other books of its kind as regards its nearly exclusive use of the English language and its exclusive reliance on verse. These defining features of the book should not be misconstrued, however. Though written in the vernacular, the book was almost certainly made for the primary benefit of a bilingual educated elite whose regular regime of reading would have consisted chiefly of Latin prose. The Anthology was of an experimental character in this context, even of a risky character perhaps, given its wide range of subjects as well as the obscurity of some of its contents.

As for the chief reason why the Anthology contains only verse, we do not have to look farther than to the prestige and the practical value that were ascribed to poetry in early medieval education. Although prose was the default medium of literate communication, verse was a prized means of instruction in the schools, where it was admired as a source of wisdom and a model of rhetorical elegance. The affective value of poetry, too, made it a powerful tool of conversion or acculturation. The Exeter Anthology appears to embody a will, on the part of educated persons who were in communication with one another during the period of the Benedictine Reform, to elevate English poetry to a status like that of its Latin counterpart.

Since native English verse had long been a medium by which members of the Anglo-Saxon ruling class had cultivated a heroic ethos, the Anthology's heroic tenor is likely to have had a special appeal to oblates who had been born into society's upper ranks, as numbers of them evidently were. These heroic tones, grounded in time-honoured systems of formulaic diction, find forceful expression in passages that celebrate the fearless and zealous *miles Christi*. As has long been recognized, to turn from *Beowulf* to *The Life of Saint Guthlac* is a giant step in some ways but by no means in all.[1]

The book's interconnectedness

To reiterate a point: although each poem of the Exeter Anthology has its own integrity, each is also best understood when considered in relation to other texts included in the volume. Even with their obvious differences from one to another, these poems are comparable in style, just as they are compatible in theme. They are expressive of what is essentially a single world-view: that of orthodox Christianity, as that religion was finding expression in learned circles in the south of England during the tenth-century period that represents in some ways the high point of the Anglo-Saxon achievement in literacy and letters. One is tempted to identify this world-view with a Glastonbury school of vernacular poetics that flourished in a cluster of monasteries influenced by Dunstan, the leading intellectual of the Reform. That would be leaping ahead of the evidence, however, seeing that no other book quite like this one survives, whether one thinks in terms of its wide scope or its rhetorical sophistication. The Exeter Anthology is therefore rightly regarded as a unique treasure.

When thinking of the authors of these poems, there is no need to posit the existence of master poets, or *scopas*, of the kind that is implied by the text of *Beowulf*. Nor need we posit acts of dictation by which the words of an unlettered singer such as Cædmon were taken down by one or more scribes in an ecclesiastical setting. Instead, we can think more profitably in terms of multiple craft-poets working without much fanfare in a common learned tradition. Like any artisans, certain of those poets might have been highly regarded either during their lifetime or in subsequent generations, but not to the point that their names have survived. The sole exception is Cynewulf, who

---

1 Dorothy Whitelock has made thought-provoking comparisons between these two works of the Anglo-Saxon literary imagination (1951: 80–82). One point of likeness is that both the pagan hero Beowulf and the saintly hero Guthlac are to be numbered among the *sōð-fæste* or 'righteous ones' (see *The Life of Saint Guthlac* 22a, 567a and 790, and *Beowulf* 2820b).

made a point of seeing that his name would be remembered while leaving no solid trace of his identity. When, in the 'signature' passage of his poem *Elene* from the Vercelli Book, Cynewulf speaks of himself in the first-person-singular voice (at lines 1256b–70a), he portrays himself as a person born to a position of privilege who has turned his back on the world in his old age so as to embrace monastic discipline. In its conventionality, his capsule self-portrait reminds us of the Convert who is the speaker of *The Rhyming Poem*, so that one is free to suspect that it has hardly more real-world substance than the Convert does. Still, that 'signature' passage helps to establish a model of conversion that lies at the heart of the Anthology's whole enterprise.

As for the principles by which the Exeter Anthology is organized, I see them as fluent rather than obsessive. That is to say, coherence is achieved within an overall plan that probably allowed, to some extent, for the beneficent workings of chance as new poems or passages became available for use. Certain poems or passages may have been made or remade for the occasion. One favoured arrangement is a pairing of 'like with like', as with the oyster/crab riddle duo (Riddles 76 and 77) or the oak/ash pair (Riddles 74 and 73), or as with the paired *Guthlac* poems. Another is the device of trebling, as with the triad of the Christ cycle or the three juxtaposed sequences of gnomic verse that go by the names *Exeter Maxims A*, *Exeter Maxims B* and *Exeter Maxims C*. Somewhat less obvious than these collocations are pairings such as *The Seafarer* and *Vainglory*, two juxtaposed poems on topics that, while contrastive, are closely related in intellectual content. A reader who is inclined on internal grounds to read these two poems as companion pieces will note that they have an identical ending as written out by the same scribe who wrote out the rest of the contents of the manuscript, for each text ends with the extrametrical interjection 'Amen'.

Taking this point farther, it is fair to say that the whole of the Exeter Anthology is knit into a single fabric through a complex web of interrelations, only some of which involve the immediate juxtaposition of texts. When one strand is plucked, the whole web vibrates. Certain generic likenesses leap over a variable number of intervening folios, as with the two hagiographic poems *The Life of Saint Guthlac* and *The Passion of Saint Juliana* (separated by twenty folios), the two 'ancient singer' monologues *Widsith* and *Deor* (separated by twelve folios), the two 'marriage' poems *The Wife's Lament* and *The Husband's Message* (separated by seven folios), and the two main blocks of enigmas (separated by eight folios). While there is nothing mathematical about the relative placements of these texts, their relationships are clearly meaningful.

Moreover, the different parts of the book respond to one another at different levels of magnitude, from the structural to the lexical. Certain links are established through semantically charged echo-words or phrases that recur in the Anthology with noteworthy effect. The chief examples to which I have called attention are *sīþ* 'journey', *ellen* 'courage', *bōt* 'remedy', *hām* 'home', the plural noun *drēamas* 'joys', the phrase *Godes egsa* 'fear of God', and the compound words *sōð-fæste* 'the righteous', *gæst-gerȳne* 'spiritual mysteries' and *weal-stān* 'foundation stone'. Sometimes full-verse phrases, as well, are echoed with special thematic effect, as we see with *wlonc ond wīn-gāl* 'proud and wanton with wine' or with the phrase *winelēas wræcca* 'friendless outcast' that characterizes the speakers of both *The Wife's Lament* and *The Penitent's Prayer*. Then there are whole-line repetitions that are too specific to be the result of chance or convention, as with the precept 'Stȳran sceal mon strongum mōde' that is shared almost verbatim between *The Seafarer* and *Exeter Maxims A*. Other links take the form of images or image-clusters that have a symbolic value: a wall in need of repair, or a building and the storms that beat against it, or a storm-tossed ship, or the imagery of divine light. Yet others are established through controlling figures or themes: the ancient sage, or the uplifting power of verse, or the hazards of excessive drink.

While a sceptic is free to dismiss such connections as these as being practically inevitable in the literature of medieval Christianity, the specific ways in which passage answers to passage from folio to folio of the Exeter Anthology has the appearance of being, in large measure, the effects of a shared literary culture and an editor's shaping intelligence. The likelihood that the roles of anthologist, editor, scribe and poet were sometimes interchangeable complicates this picture in an intriguing way.

A revolution that never took hold?

In earlier chapters of this book I have suggested that whoever compiled the Exeter Anthology had a well-developed awareness of its potential uses in the bilingual English educational system of his day. One can go beyond this and surmise that the making of the Exeter Anthology was part of a revolution in English education that never took hold.

What I mean to suggest is that by the late tenth century, the English language was poised to take on a role in English schools that was in many ways parallel to that of Latin. The primacy of Latin would have remained unquestioned, seeing that Latin was the chief language of both Scripture and the liturgy, a status that it enjoyed in Western Europe throughout the Middle Ages. Still, as the production of a wide range of bilingual texts during the late tenth and early eleventh centuries attests, English was taking on an ever more significant place side by side with Latin. Easy to perceive is a florescence of native literature within the civilizing environment of Latinity.

This flowering of vernacular literature was evidently nipped in the bud, however. This was probably not because of any inherent weakness in that bilingual programme, but rather because of the force of external circumstances. It was the work of *wyrd sēo mǣre* 'fate, the far-famed one', as an Anglo-Saxon poet might have put it.

During the final decade of the tenth century, England was once again scourged by Viking attacks, as is well known to readers of *The Battle of Maldon*, the Anglo-Saxon Chronicle and other historical records dating from this era. In response to these rolling disasters, leading figures in both church and state adopted a besieged mentality. For two and a half decades, Viking raids and extortions threatened to impoverish the realm, including its monastic houses. The havoc continued until the years 1016–17, when King Swein of Denmark conquered the land and his son King Canute (r.1017–35) consolidated his father's victory.

Even though textual production in Latin prose continued without a halt during the reign of Canute, and even though texts of a legal, historical, devotional, scientific or medical kind continued to be produced for some while thereafter as well, the flood of verse texts recorded in the English language by about the year 1000 seems by this time to have fallen off to a trickle. In other words, the Normans should not be ascribed all the blame for cutting off the flower of native English poetry, even though it is true that William the Conqueror and his successors installed French-speaking abbots and bishops throughout the land in the aftermath of William's decisive victory at Hastings in 1066. Patronage for English verse had apparently dried up well before this time, especially with the expulsion of King Æthelred from the realm in 1016 and the subsequent consolidation of power in the hands of a Danish-speaking king and his court. The desperate situation of the upper ranks of society during decades of Viking raids, wars and extortions could scarcely have been conducive to the production of high-end poetic codices written in English.

The picture presented here in snapshot form is not the only way that experts have characterized this historical period. Joyce Hill (2001), for example, makes no mention of Viking incursions when speaking of the winding down of the Benedictine Reform during the period c.990–1015, perhaps taking the fact of that warfare for granted. On the other hand, David Knowles, whose history of medieval English religious establishments remains foundational, makes pointed reference to Viking raids in his account of those same decades, noting that their local impact at the time was sometimes devastating though they had little permanent effect.² There are evidently two models to choose from here: there is the clock that gradually winds down, and there is the clock that, while it gradually winds down, is also hammered by a Scandinavian-style axe.

Not all monastic foundations were so fortunate as to survive this period of destruction and impoverishment, though our knowledge of the exact conditions in any one time or place remains inexact. Exeter is a case in point. According to the C, D and E versions of the Chronicle, Exeter was stormed, razed and plundered by a Danish army in the year 1003.³ In Knowles's view, the monasteries at both Exeter and Bedford 'silently disappear from existence between 1000 and the Conquest' (1963: 69). On the other hand, Patrick W. Conner has argued persuasively for a measure of continuity at Exeter throughout the tenth century and extending beyond 1066 as well.⁴ It is possible that each of these perceptions has some validity, for a measure of continuity at Exeter could have coincided with a period of severe stress and dislocation.

In any event, the major extant collections of poetry written in Old English appear to date from no later than the first decade of the eleventh century, while several of them (including the Exeter Anthology) predate the period of late tenth-century Viking attacks. During none of the decades of the second Viking Age were conditions favourable for the recording or copying of non-mainstream English-language codices, especially ones consisting of such a kaleidoscope of verse as we see in the Exeter Anthology. Rather, the mood of the English clerical establishment shortly after the turn of the millennium finds expression in Wulfstan's rhetorically heightened prose, including his jeremiad the *Sermo Lupi ad Anglos*. This, the most famous of his sermons and the one that he took most care to rework during his lifetime, dates originally from about the year 1014.⁵ It is assuredly unfair to Wulfstan to suggest that his blistering tones in this homily displaced more gentle meditations on the Christian faith. He cannot be blamed for having silenced the voices of the Exeter Anthology birds, such as the heavenly voiced bird of *The Phoenix* as well as the wild swan, the nightingale and other musical birds of the riddle collection. The voices of these winged creatures provide a counterpart to the songs of the winged seraphim of *Advent Lyric 11*, who, 'in their multitudes, sing in a loud voice most exaltedly and sweetly, far and near':

2   Knowles 1963: 57, 69–70.
3   Whitelock 1979: 239.
4   Conner 1993a, esp. 21–32.
5   Bethurum 1957: 261–75 (Wulfstan's sermon 20). For an excerpt from it excoriating the English for their moral degeneracy, see Chapter 7 above, in the section headed 'The place of *The Ruin* in the microcosm that is the book'.

> þrymmum singað
> ful healice   hludan stefne,
> fægre feor ond neah.⁶

Indubitably, however, English writings took a turn away from books resembling the Exeter Anthology at all closely during the last decade of the long and unhappy reign of King Æthelred the Unready (978-1016).

To bring to a close this study of one of the great books of the medieval literary imagination, it is fitting to return to the figure of Dunstan, whose portrait in the manuscript known as 'Saint Dunstan's Classbook'—a page reproduced near the front of the present volume (Fig. 1)—could serve as a fitting emblem for the devotional spirit that motivates the Exeter Anthology as a whole.

It is tempting to imagine that in the period 965-75, just about a century before the Norman Conquest, if Dunstan had taken leave for a while from his archiepiscopal duties at Canterbury so as to attend to his continuing responsibilities as abbot of Glastonbury, he might at some point have held in his hands the very book that today we know of as the Exeter Anthology. What a fresh and invigorating collection the book must have seemed to speakers of English at that time! One likes to call up a picture of Dunstan, during one of the hours of the day set aside for private reading and devotion, trying to solve one of the book's more knotty or gritty enigmas, then reading aloud two or three of the sublime *Advent Lyrics*, then turning for a while to peruse his 'Classbook' (with its copy of at least part of Ovid's *Ars amatoria*) before joining the brethren of the minster to sing the Divine Office.

A picture of that kind is no more than a fantasy, or what a poet of the Restoration period might have called a green thought in a green shade. It is an image, however, that is by no means inconsistent with a period of history when—for a few years at least, in the south of Britain—classical Latin learning, mainstream Christian devotional literature and the enjoyment of English verse of a remarkably innovative kind were all features of one integrative educational system.

---

6   *Advent Lyric 11*, 388b-90a; Muir 1: 60. In *The Phoenix*, the souls of the blessed are likewise figured as *fuglas scȳne* ('beautiful birds', 591b) who sing praises to the Lord.

APPENDIX 1

A Translation of *The Wanderer*

Often the lone-dweller lives to experience grace, the Lord's merciful favour, even though for long, desolate at heart, he has had to traverse the ice-cold sea while following the paths of exile. What is fated cannot be turned aside.

So spoke the Wanderer, mindful of hardships, of cruel carnage in war, of the deaths of kinsmen:

'Often, each dawn, I have had to lament my sorrows alone. There is no one alive to whom I dare freely confide my thoughts. I know in truth that it is a good habit for a man to bind his feelings tight within his chest, to lock shut the treasure-coffer of his heart, let him think as he will. No one whose spirit is exhausted can withstand the course of events, nor does an agitated mood give help. Those who value the esteem of others therefore often confine a bleak spirit within their breast.

'Thus, often—disconsolate, cut off from my homeland, far from dear kindred—I have had to fasten my heart in fetters, ever since long ago I wrapped my gracious lord in the dark cover of earth and journeyed away from there downcast, plagued by winter, over the ice-bound waves. Desolate for lack of a hall, I sought out a generous gold-giver, someone far or near who might show affection for me in the mead-hall or welcome me at his table, destitute of friends as I was.

'Only he who has experienced it knows how cruel grief is as a comrade when one has lost one's closest friends. The path of exile is his lot, not twisted gold; a freezing body, not the earth's abundance. He recalls his hall companions and the exchange of gifts, how in his youth his gracious lord had entertained him at the feast. Those joys are gone. Those who have long been bereft of their dear lord's sagacious counsels know these things well.

'Often then grief and sleep, acting together, afflict the wretched lone-dweller. In his mind's eye he thinks he is embracing and kissing his liege lord, laying hands and head on his knee, just as he did in former days when receiving gifts at the benches. Then he wakes up again, that friendless man. He sees before him dusky waves, seabirds bathing and splaying their feathers, ice and snow swirling down, mingled with hail. Then the pain he feels for the dear departed one is yet harder to bear.

'His grief wells up anew when memories of kinsmen run through his mind. He greets them joyfully, those companions in the hall; he feasts his eyes on them. They swim away again. The spirit of seabirds, floating on the water, brings forth few songs with familiar words. Grief wells up yet again in one who must send his weary spirit again and again out over the ice-bound waves.

'Therefore I cannot think why in this world my heart does not darken when I contemplate the whole life of humankind, how they suddenly gave up their residence on earth, those brave men of old. Day after day, in this same manner, this whole earth decays and falls. No one can be considered wise, on that account, until he has lived a good number of years in the worldly realm.

'A wise man is patient. He is never too impetuous, nor is he too rash in speech, nor is he too compliant, nor too despairing, nor too fearful, nor too exultant, nor too greedy, nor ever too eager for praise, until his knowledge is fully formed. When uttering a vow, a man should curb his tongue until he knows with certainty where the promptings of his heart will lead.

'A wise man knows how appalling it will be when all the magnificence of this world lies waste, just as now, throughout this middle earth, walls are left standing that are windswept and shackled with ice, the buildings storm-blasted. Banquet halls have gone to waste; their erstwhile owners lie dead, cut off from revelry. A whole troop of retainers died by the wall, cut down in their pride. Warfare laid low no few, bearing them away on their journey forth. A ship—a sea-falcon—bore one off over the high seas; grey wolves shared out another as he lay dead; a tearful comrade hid away another in an earthen grave. Thus the Creator of humankind laid waste the kingdom of earth until the ancient works of giants stood empty, devoid of the revelry of their inhabitants.

'One who deeply contemplates these ruined foundations and this dark life—far hence, in his wise meditation—will call to mind many such acts of devastation. Grown wise through experience, he will speak these words:

'What has become of the horse? What has become of the warrior? What has become of the gift-giver? What has become of the settings of feasts? Where are the joys of the hall? Alas, the bright cup! Alas, the mailed warrior! Alas, the prince's majesty! How that time has passed, grown dark under the helm of night as if it had never been. Now a wall wondrously high, adorned with serpentine patterning, stands where the beloved band of retainers once dwelt. Spear-bearing warriors swept those men away—weapons hungry for slaughter, fate the far-famed one—and tempests now batter the ramparts; a swirling snowstorm, the howling of winter, locks the earth in ice as the shadow of night draws down. An advancing storm sends a blast of hail from the north as a torment to mortals. There is nothing but hardship in the kingdom of earth. An unswerving destiny alters the world under the heavens. Here wealth is fleeting; here friends are fleeting; here retainers are fleeting; here kinsfolk are fleeting; this whole framework of earth is turning to nothingness.'

So spoke the man in his wisdom; he sat apart in meditation.

Good are those who keep their faith. They are never too quick to complain of their afflictions unless they know beforehand what the remedy for them is: to act with good zeal in the world. Well shall they be who seek for grace, for consolation from the Father in heaven, where for us all the immutable abides.

APPENDIX 2

Folio-by-Folio Contents of the Exeter Anthology

8r–14r	*Advent Lyrics* also known as *Christ I* or *Christ I: The Advent Lyrics*
14r–20v	*The Ascension* also known as *Christ II* or *Christ II: The Ascension*
20v–32v	*Christ in Judgement* also known as *Christ III* or *Christ III: Christ in Judgement*
32v–44v	*The Life of Saint Guthlac* also known as *Guthlac A*
44v–52v	*The Holy Death of Saint Guthlac* also known as *Guthlac B*
53r–55v	*The Canticles of the Three Youths* also known as *Azarias*
55v–65v	*The Phoenix*
65v–76r	*The Passion of Saint Juliana* also called simply *Juliana*
76v–78r	*The Wanderer*
78r–80r	*God's Gifts to Humankind* also known as *The Gifts of Men* or *The Gifts of Mortals*
80r–81v	*A Father's Precepts* also called simply *Precepts*
81v–83r	*The Seafarer*
83r–84v	*Vainglory*
84v–87r	*Widsith*
87r–88v	*The Fortunes of Mortals* also known as *The Fortunes of Men*
88v–92v	*Exeter Maxims A, B and C* also known as *Maxims I (A), (B) and (C)*

92v–94r	*The Wonder of Creation* also known as *The Order of the World*
94r–95v	*The Rhyming Poem*
95v–96v	*The Panther*
96v–97v	*The Whale*
97v	*The Partridge* (a fragment)
98r	*Christ's Pledge of Grace* (a fragment) also known as *Homiletic Fragment III*
98r–100r	*The Soul's Address to the Body* also known as *Soul and Body II*
100r–v	*Deor*
100v–101r	*Wulf and Eadwacer*
101r–115r	*Enigmas 1–59*
115r–v	*The Wife's Lament*
115v–117v	*Doomsday* also known as *Judgement Day I*
117v–118v	*Contrition* also known as *Contrition (A)* or *Resignation (A)*
119r–v	*The Penitent's Prayer* also known as *Contrition (B)* or *Resignation (B): An Exile's Lament*
119v–121v	*Christ's Descent into Hell* also known as *The Descent into Hell* or *John the Baptist's Prayer*
121v–122r	*Almsgiving*
122r	*Pharaoh*
122r	*A Versified Lord's Prayer* also known as *The Lord's Prayer (I)*
122r–v	*One Faith One God* also known as *Homiletic Fragment II*
122v	Riddle 30b: *The Tree*
122v–123r	Riddle 60: *The Reed*
123r–v	*The Husband's Message*
123v–124v	*The Ruin*
124v–130v	*Enigmas 61–94*

APPENDIX 3

Latin Genre Terms and the Poems of the Exeter Anthology

Genres are slippery. They can overlap, and individual authors have been known to test their conventions to the limit. Moreover, genres are dynamic: new ones can sometimes be traced in the process of formation, especially when literary modes are translated from one language into another and are subject to the influence of a cultural substratum.

I make no claim that either the authors or the compiler of the poems included in the Exeter Anthology thought of them as instances of genres known to them from the Latin literature of the early Middle Ages. We cannot tell what those persons thought. Worth observing, still, is that the poems listed below display the formal characteristics of certain Latinate genres, doing so to an extent that the poems gain in sharpness of definition when considered in these terms. Each poem is also a unique artistic creation with its own character. Not every poem of the Exeter Anthology can readily be classified as to its genre, hence not all are listed below.

Advent Lyrics	**hymni**: songlike poems in praise of the divinity (here with reference to Christ's Incarnation)
The Ascension	**homilia**: a sermon (here versified, on many topics, but with central reference to the Ascension)
Christ in Judgement	**homilia**: a sermon (here versified, with Doomsday as its chief subject)
The Life of Saint Guthlac	**vita**: a saint's life (here versified, on the life of an English *miles Christi*)
The Holy Death of Saint Guthlac	**paraphrasis**: a paraphrase of a prior work (here, a versified paraphrase of the final part of Felix's *Vita Guthlaci*)

The Canticles of the Three Youths	**paraphrasis**: a paraphrase of a prior work (here, a versified paraphrase of liturgical elements based on part of the Book of Daniel)
The Phoenix	**paraphrasis** plus **allegoresis** (here, a versified paraphrase of the Latin poem *De ave phoenice*, followed by a versified exegesis of that poem's symbolism)
The Passion of Saint Juliana	**vita**: a saint's life (here, a versified paraphrase of a Latin *vita* telling of the martyrdom of a virgin of the early church)
The Wanderer	**planctus**: an imagined poetic lament spoken in the first person singular (here set in the voice of an exiled warrior-thegn of the Germanic past)
God's Gifts to Humankind	**carmen morale**: a didactic poem (here on the Pauline trope of God's gifts to human beings)
A Father's Precepts	**sententiae**: a collection of wise, pithy sayings (here versified and presented in the form of a father's address to his son)
The Seafarer	**carmen morale**: a didactic poem (here set in the voice of a man undertaking a *peregrinatio pro amore dei*)
Vainglory	**homilia**: a sermon (here versified, on the vice of arrogance versus the virtue of humility)
The Fortunes of Mortals	**carmen morale**: a didactic poem (here, on death seen in relation to God's gifts)
Exeter Maxims A, B and C	**sententiae**: a collection of wise, pithy sayings (here versified, rather loosely at certain points)
The Wonder of Creation	**carmen morale**: a didactic poem (here, on the psalmist's trope of the presence of God in his Creation)
The Panther, The Whale	**allegoresis**: an exposition of symbolism (here in the form of versified paraphrases of two chapters from the Latin *Physiologus*)

Appendix 3

Christ's Pledge of Grace	**paraphrasis**: a paraphrase of a prior work (here a versified paraphrase of an epistle by Saint Paul concerning Christ's faithful love for his followers)
The Soul's Address to the Body	**planctus**: an imagined poetic lament spoken in the first person singular (here set in the voice of a damned soul)
Wulf and Eadwacer	**planctus**: an imagined poetic lament spoken in the first person singular (here of an enigmatic nature, set in the voice of a woman of the Germanic past)
Enigmas 1–59	**enigmata**: riddles (here versified)
The Wife's Lament	**planctus**: an imagined poetic lament spoken in the first person singular (here set in the voice of a woman of the Germanic past)
Doomsday	**homilia**: a sermon (here versified, on the Day of Judgement)
The Penitent's Prayer	**planctus**: an imagined poetic lament spoken in the first person singular (here set in the voice of a Christian pilgrim)
Almsgiving	**carmen morale**: a didactic poem (here on the virtue of charity)
Pharaoh	**enigma**: a riddle (here versified, in dialogue form)
A Versified Lord's Prayer	**paraphrasis**: a paraphrase of a prior work (here versified, of the Pater Noster)
One Faith One God	**paraphrasis**: a paraphrase of a prior work (here versified, of the Creed)
Riddle 30b: *The Tree*	**enigma**: a riddle (here versified)
Riddle 60: *The Reed*	**enigma**: a riddle (here versified)
The Ruin	**excidium urbis**: a poem on the theme of a city that has been laid waste
Enigmas 61–94	**enigmata**: riddles (here versified)

Bibliography of Works Cited

Abraham, Lenore. 2011. 'Cynewulf's Recharacterization of the *Vita Sanctae Julianae* and the Tenth Century Benedictine Revival in England'. *American Benedictine Review* 62: 67–83.

Abram, Christopher. 2000. 'In Search of Lost Time: Aldhelm and *The Ruin*'. *Quaestio Insulares* 1: 23–44.

Abrams, Lesley. 2008. 'Germanic Christianities'. In *The Cambridge History of Christianity: Early Medieval Christianities, c.600-c.1100*, ed. Thomas F.X. Noble and Julia M.H. Smith. Cambridge: Cambridge University Press. pp. 107–29, 670–75.

Adair, Anya. 2011. 'The Unity and Authorship of the Old English *Advent Lyrics*'. *ES* 92 (2011): 823–48.

Aertsen, Henk. 1994. '*Wulf and Eadwacer*: A Woman's *Cri de Coeur*—For Whom? For What?' In *Companion to Old English Poetry*, ed. Henk Aertsen and Rolf H. Bremmer, Jr. Amsterdam: VU University Press. pp. 119–44.

Alexander, Michael. 2007. *Old English Riddles from the Exeter Book*. 2nd edn. London: Anvil Press.

Allen, Michael J.B. and Daniel G. Calder, trans. 1976. *Sources and Analogues of Old English Poetry: The Major Latin Texts in Translation*. Cambridge: D.S. Brewer.

Amodio, Mark C. 2014. *The Anglo-Saxon Literature Handbook*. Oxford: Wiley-Blackwell.

Anderson, Earl R. 1974. 'Social Idealism in Ælfric's *Colloquy*'. *ASE* 3: 153–62. Repr. in Liuzza 2002, pp. 204–14.

Anderson, James E. 1986. *Two Literary Riddles in the Exeter Book: A Critical Edition with Full Translations*. Norman: University of Oklahoma Press.

Anlezark, Daniel, ed. and trans. 2009. *The Old English Dialogues of Solomon and Saturn*. Cambridge: D.S. Brewer.

———, ed. and trans. 2011. *Old Testament Narratives*. DOML 7. Cambridge, MA: Harvard University Press.

———. 2013. 'The Anglo-Saxon World View'. In *The Cambridge Companion to Old English Literature*, ed. Malcolm Godden and Michael Lapidge. 2nd edn. Cambridge: Cambridge University Press. pp. 66–81.

Ashurst, David. 2010. 'Old English Wisdom Poetry'. In *A Companion to Medieval Poetry*, ed. Corinne Saunders. Oxford: Wiley-Blackwell. pp. 125–40.

Atherton, Mark. 2002. 'Saxon or Celt? Cædmon, *The Seafarer*, and the Irish Tradition'. In *Celts and Christians: New Approaches*, ed. Mark Atherton. Cardiff: University of Wales Press. pp. 79–99.

Bahr, Arthur W. 2014. 'Fear, Time, and Lack: The *Egesa* of *Beowulf*'. In *Essays on Aesthetics and Medieval Literature in Honor of Howell Chickering*, ed. John M. Hill,

Bonnie Wheeler and R.F. Yeager. Toronto: Pontifical Institute of Mediaeval Studies. pp. 53–66.
Baker, Peter S. 1981. 'The Ambiguity of *Wulf and Eadwacer*'. *Studies in Philology* 78: 39–51. Repr. in O'Brien O'Keeffe 1994, pp. 393–407.
Barney, Stephen A., et al. 2006. *The Etymologies of Isidore of Seville*. Cambridge: Cambridge University Press.
Barrow, Julia S. 2009. 'The Ideology of the Tenth-Century English Benedictine "Reform"'. In *Challenging the Boundaries of Medieval History: The Legacy of Timothy Reuter*, ed. Patricia Skinner. Turnhout: Brepols. pp. 141–54.
Baum, Paull F. 1963. *Anglo-Saxon Riddles of the Exeter Book*. Durham, NC: Duke University Press.
Beechy, Tiffany. 2010. *The Poetics of Old English*. Farnham: Ashgate.
Bethurum, Dorothy. 1957. *The Homilies of Wulfstan*. Oxford: Clarendon.
Bettenson, Henry, trans. 2003. *St Augustine: Concerning the City of God Against the Pagans*. With an introduction by G.R. Evans. Harmondsworth: Penguin.
Biggs, Frederick M. 1998. 'The Exeter *Exeter Book*? Some Linguistic Evidence'. In *The Dictionary of Old English: Retrospects and Prospects*, ed. M.J. Toswell. Old English Newsletter Subsidia 26. Kalamazoo, MI: Medieval Institute Publications. pp. 63–71.
Bitterli, Dieter. 2009. *Say What I Am Called: The Old English Riddles of the Exeter Book and the Anglo-Latin Riddle Tradition*. Toronto: University of Toronto Press.
Bjork, Robert E. 1985. *The Old English Verse Saints' Lives: A Study in Direct Discourse and the Iconography of Style*. Toronto: University of Toronto Press.
———. 1989. '*Sundor æt Rune*: The Voluntary Exile of the Wanderer'. *Neophilologus* 73: 119–26. Repr. in Liuzza 2002, pp. 315–27.
———. 2005. 'The Symbolic Use of Job in Ælfric's Homily on Job, *Christ II*, and the *Phoenix*'. In *Latin Learning and English Lore: Studies in Anglo-Saxon Literature for Michael Lapidge*, ed. Katherine O'Brien O'Keeffe and Andy Orchard. 2 vols. Toronto: University of Toronto Press. 2: 315–30.
———, ed. and trans. 2013. *The Old English Poems of Cynewulf*. DOML 23. Cambridge, MA: Harvard University Press.
———, ed. and trans. 2014. *Old English Shorter Poems, Volume II: Wisdom and Lyric*. DOML 32. Cambridge, MA: Harvard University Press.
Blair, John. 2005. *The Church in Anglo-Saxon Society*. Oxford: Oxford University Press.
Blake, N.F., ed. 1964. *The Phoenix*. Manchester: Manchester University Press. Revised edn, University of Exeter Press, 1990.
———. 1968. 'The Form of *The Phoenix*'. In *Old English Literature: Twenty-Two Analytical Essays*, ed. Martin Stevens and Jerome Mandel. Lincoln: University of Nebraska Press. pp. 268–78.
Blanton, Virginia and Helene Scheck, ed. 2008. *Intertexts: Studies in Anglo-Saxon Culture Presented to Paul E. Szarmach*. Tempe: ACMRS.
Bleeth, Kenneth A. 1969. '*Juliana* 647–652'. *Medium Ævum* 38: 119–22.
Bliss, A.J. 1971. 'Single Half-Lines in Old English Poetry'. *Notes & Queries* n.s. 18: 442–49.
Bloomfield, Morton W. 1968. 'Understanding Old English Poetry'. *Annuale Mediaevale* 9: 5–25. Repr. in his essay collection *Essays and Explorations: Studies in*

Ideas, Language, and Literature. Cambridge MA: Harvard University Press, 1970, pp. 59–80.

Bonner, Joshua H. 1976. 'Toward a Unified Critical Approach to Old English Poetic Composition'. *Modern Philology* 73: 219–28.

Bonneuil, Christophe and Jean-Baptiste Fressoz. 2016. *The Shock of the Anthropocene: The Earth, History and Us*, trans. David Fernbach. London: Verso.

Boryslawski, Rafal. 2002. 'The Elements of Anglo-Saxon Wisdom Poetry in the Exeter Book Riddles'. *Studia Anglica Posnaniensia* 38 (2002): 35–47.

———. 2009. 'Slash and Burn? The Rhetoric of the Conquered City in Anglo-Saxon Didactic Verse'. In *Images of the City*, ed. Agnieszka Rasmus and Magdalena Cieślak. Newcastle upon Tyne: Cambridge Scholars. pp. 38–49.

Bosworth, Joseph and T. Northcote Toller. 1898. *An Anglo-Saxon Dictionary*. Oxford: Oxford University Press. With *Supplement* by T. Northcote Toller (1921) and *Enlarged Addenda and Corrigenda* by Alistair Campbell (1972).

Bradley, S.A.J. 1982. *Anglo-Saxon Poetry*. London: Dent.

Brady, Lindy. 2016. 'An Analogue to *Wulf and Eadwacer* in the Life of St Bertellin of Stafford'. *RES* 67: 1–20.

Bragg, Lois. 1991. *The Lyric Speakers of Old English Poetry*. Rutherford, NJ: Fairleigh Dickinson University Press.

Bredehoft, Thomas A. 2009. *Authors, Audiences, and Old English Verse*. Toronto: University of Toronto Press.

Brooks, Nicholas P. 1992. 'The Career of St Dunstan'. In Ramsay *et al.* 1992, pp. 1–23.

Brown, George Hardin. 1984. 'The Anglo-Saxon Monastic Revival'. In *Renaissances before the Renaissance: Cultural Revivals of Late Antiquity and the Middle Ages*, ed. Warren Treadgold. Stanford: Stanford University Press. pp. 99–113.

———. 1995. 'The Dynamics of Literacy in Anglo-Saxon England'. *Bulletin of the John Rylands Library* 77: 109–42.

Brown, Michelle P. 2003. *The Lindisfarne Gospels: Society, Spirituality and the Scribe*. London: British Library.

———. 2007. *Manuscripts from the Anglo-Saxon Age*. Toronto: University of Toronto Press.

———. 2011. *The Book and the Transformation of Britain c.550–1050: A Study in Written and Visual Literacy and Orality*. London: British Library.

Budny, Mildred. 1992. '"St Dunstan's Classbook" and its Frontispiece: Dunstan's Portrait and Autograph'. In Ramsay *et al.* 1992, pp. 103–42.

Bullough, D.A. 1972. 'The Educational Tradition in England from Alfred to Ælfric: Teaching *utriusque linguae*'. In *La scuola nell'occidente latino dell'alto medioevo*, Settimane di studio del centro italiano di studi sull'alto medioevo 19. Spoleto. pp. 453–94. Repr. in a slightly revised version, with updated references, in his essay collection *Carolingian Renewal: Sources and Heritage*. Manchester: Manchester University Press, 1991. pp. 297–334.

Burlin, Robert B. 1968. *The Old English Advent: A Typological Commentary*. New Haven: Yale University Press.

Busby, Keith. 2002. *Codex and Context: Reading Old French Verse Narrative in Manuscript*. 2 vols. Amsterdam: Rodopi.

Butler, H.E., trans. 1922. *The Institutio Oratoria of Quintilian*, vol. 4. Cambridge, MA: Harvard University Press.

Butler, Robert M. 2004. 'Glastonbury and the Early History of the Exeter Book'. In *Old English Literature in its Manuscript Context*, ed. Joyce Tally Lionarons. Morgantown: West Virginia University Press. pp. 173–215.

Caie, Graham D. 1976. *The Judgment Day Theme in Old English Poetry*. Copenhagen: Nova.

Calder, Daniel G. 1972. 'Theme and Strategy in *Guthlac B*'. *Papers on Language and Literature* 8: 227–42.

Campbell, Jackson J., ed. 1959. *The Advent Lyrics of the Exeter Book*. Princeton: Princeton University Press.

———. 1967. 'Knowledge of Rhetorical Figures in Anglo-Saxon England'. *JEGP* 66: 1–20.

———. 1978. 'Adaptation of Classical Rhetoric in Old English Literature'. In *Medieval Eloquence: Studies in the Theory and Practice of Medieval Rhetoric*, ed. James J. Murphy. Berkeley: University of California Press. pp. 173–97.

Cassidy, Frederic G. and Richard N. Ringler, ed. 1971. *Bright's Old English Grammar and Reader*. 3rd edn. New York: Holt.

Cavill, Paul. 1999. *Maxims in Old English Poetry*. Cambridge: D.S. Brewer.

Chambers, R.W., with Max Förster and Robin Flower, ed. 1933a. *The Exeter Book of Old English Poetry*. London: Percy Lund.

———. 1933b. 'The Exeter Book and its Donor, Leofric'. In Chambers 1933a, pp. 1–9.

Chase, Colin. 1974. 'God's Presence through Grace as the Theme of Cynewulf's *Christ II* and the Relationship of this Theme to *Christ I* and *Christ III*'. *ASE* 3: 87–101.

Cherniss, Michael. 1972. *Ingeld and Christ: Heroic Concepts and Values in Old English Christian Poetry*. The Hague: Mouton.

Child, Francis J., ed. 1882–98. *The English and Scottish Popular Ballads*. 5 vols. Boston: Houghton Mifflin.

Clayton, Mary. 1996. 'Hermits and the Contemplative Life in Anglo-Saxon England'. In *Holy Men and Holy Women: Old English Prose Saints' Lives and their Contexts*, ed. Paul E. Szarmach. Albany: State University of New York Press. pp. 147–75.

———, ed. and trans. 2013. *Old English Poems of Christ and His Saints*. DOML 27. Cambridge, MA: Harvard University Press.

Colgrave, Bertram. 1956. *Felix's Life of Saint Guthlac: Introduction, Text, Translation and Notes*. Cambridge: Cambridge University Press.

Conner, Patrick W. 1980. 'The Liturgy and the Old English *Descent into Hell*'. *JEGP* 79 (1980): 179–91.

———. 1986. 'The Structure of the Exeter Book Codex (Exeter, Cathedral Library, MS. 3501)'. *Scriptorium* 40 (1986): 233–42.

———. 1993a. *Anglo-Saxon Exeter: A Tenth-Century Cultural History*. Woodbridge: Boydell.

———. 1993b. 'Source Studies, the Old English *Guthlac A* and the English Benedictine Reformation'. *Revue Bénédictine* 103: 380–413.

———. 1996. 'On Dating Cynewulf'. In *Cynewulf: Basic Readings*, ed. Robert E. Bjork. New York: Garland. pp. 23–55.

———. 2001. 'Religious Poetry'. In *A Companion to Anglo-Saxon Literature*, ed. Phillip Pulsiano and Elaine Treharne. Oxford: Blackwell. pp. 251–67.

———. 2005. 'The Old English Elegy: A Historicization'. In *Readings in Medieval Texts: Interpreting Old and Middle English Literature*, ed. David F. Johnson and Elaine Treharne. Oxford: Oxford University Press. pp. 30–45.

———. 2008. 'Parish Guilds and the Production of Old English Literature in the Public Sphere'. In Blanton and Scheck 2008, pp. 255–72.

———. 2011. 'Four Contiguous Poems in the Exeter Book: A Combined Reading of *Homiletic Fragment III*, *Soul and Body II*, *Deor*, and *Wulf and Eadwacer*'. In Hussey and Niles 2011, pp. 117–36.

Cook, Albert S., ed. 1900. *The Christ of Cynewulf: A Poem in Three Parts*. Boston: Ginn.

———, ed. 1919. *The Old English Elene, Phœnix, and Physiologus*. New Haven: Yale University Press.

Cross, James. 1956. '*Ubi Sunt* Passages in Old English—Sources and Relationships'. *Vetenskaps-Societeten i Lund Årsbok*, pp. 25–44.

———. 1963. 'Aspects of Microcosm and Macrocosm in Old English Literature'. In *Studies in Old English Literature in Honor of Arthur G. Brodeur*, ed. Stanley B. Greenfield. Eugene: University of Oregon Books. pp. 1–22.

———. 1967. 'The Conception of the Old English *Phoenix*'. In *Old English Poetry: Fifteen Essays*, ed. Robert P. Creed. Providence: Brown University Press. pp. 129–52.

Cubitt, Catherine. 1997. 'Review Article: The Tenth-Century Benedictine Reform in England'. *Early Medieval Europe* 6: 77–94.

Dailey, Patricia. 2006. 'Questions of Dwelling in Anglo-Saxon Poetry and Medieval Mysticism: Inhabiting Landscape, Body, and Mind'. *New Medieval Literatures* 8: 175–214.

Damon, John Edward. 2003. *Soldier Saints and Holy Warriors: Warfare and Sanctity in the Literature of Early England*. Aldershot: Ashgate.

Davies, Oliver, ed. 1999. *Celtic Spirituality*. New York: Paulist Press.

Davis, Glenn. 2006. 'The Exeter Book Riddles and the Place of Sexual Idiom in Old English Literature'. In *Medieval Obscenities*, ed. Nicola McDonald. York: York Medieval Press. pp. 39–54.

Davis, Kathleen. 2012. 'Old English Lyrics: A Poetics of Experience'. In *The Cambridge History of Early Medieval English Literature*, ed. Clare A. Lees. Cambridge: Cambridge University Press. pp. 332–56.

Deangelo, Jeremy. 2013. '*Discretio spirituum* and *The Whale*'. *ASE* 42: 271–89.

DeGregorio, Scott. 2005. 'Affective Spirituality: Theory and Practice in Bede and Alfred the Great'. *Essays in Medieval Studies* 22: 129–39.

Deshman, Robert. 1995. *The Benedictional of Æthelwold*. Princeton: Princeton University Press.

———. 2010a. '*Benedictus Monarcha et Monachus*: Early Medieval Ruler Theology and the Anglo-Saxon Reform'. In *Eye and Mind: Collected Essays in Anglo-Saxon and Early Medieval Art by Robert Deshman*, ed. Adam S. Cohen. Kalamazoo: Medieval Institute Publications. pp. 104–36. First published 1988.

———. 2010b. 'The Imagery of the Living Ecclesia and the English Monastic Reform'. In *Eye and Mind: Collected Essays in Anglo-Saxon and Early Medieval Art by Robert Deshman*, ed. Adam S. Cohen. Kalamazoo: Medieval Institute Publications. pp. 80–90. First published 1986.

Deskis, Susan. 1994. 'The Gnomic Woman in Old English Poetry'. *PQ* 73: 133–49.

Dewa, Roberta J. 1995. 'The Runic Riddles of the Exeter Book: Language Games and Anglo-Saxon Scholarship'. *Nottingham Medieval Studies* 39: 26–36.

———. 2002. 'Of Editors and the Old English Poetry of the Exeter Book: A Brief History of Progress'. In *'Lastworda Betst': Essays in Memory of Christine E. Fell with her Unpublished Writings*, ed. Carole Hough and Kathryn A. Lowe. Donington: Shaun Tyas. pp. 18–40.

Dictionary of Old English, ed. Angus Cameron et al. 1986–. Toronto: Pontifical Institute. Letters A through I currently available online by subscription at https://www.doe.utoronto.ca.

DiNapoli, Robert. 1998. 'The Heart of the Visionary Experience: *The Order of the World* and its Place in the Old English Canon'. *ES* 79: 97–108.

———. 2005. 'Odd Characters: Runes in Old English Poetry'. In *Verbal Encounters: Anglo-Saxon and Old Norse Studies for Roberta Frank*, ed. Antonina Harbus and Russell Poole. Toronto: University of Toronto Press. pp. 145–61.

Di Sciacca, Claudia. 2008. *Finding the Right Words: Isidore's Synonyma in Anglo-Saxon England*. Toronto: University of Toronto Press.

Dobbie, Elliott van Kirk, ed. 1942. *The Anglo-Saxon Minor Poems*. ASPR 6. New York: Columbia University Press.

Doran, John. 2007. 'Authority and Care: The Significance of Rome in Twelfth-Century Chester'. In *Roma Felix: Formation and Reflections of Medieval Rome*, ed. Éamonn Ó Carragáin and Carol Neuman de Vegvar. Aldershot: Ashgate. pp. 307–32.

Doubleday, James F. 1970. 'The Allegory of the Soul as Fortress in Old English Poetry'. *Anglia* 88: 503–08.

———. 1972. '*The Ruin*: Structure and Theme'. *JEGP* 71: 369–81.

Drout, Michael D.C. 2006. *How Tradition Works: A Meme-Based Cultural Poetics of the Anglo-Saxon Tenth Century*. Tempe: ACMRS.

———. 2007. 'Possible Instructional Effects of the Exeter Book "Wisdom Poems": A Benedictine Reform Context'. In *Form and Content of Instruction in Anglo-Saxon England in the Light of Contemporary Manuscript Evidence*, ed. Patrizia Lendinara, Loredana Lazzari and Maria Amalia D'Aronco. Turnhout: Brepols. pp. 447–66.

Drpić, Ivan. 2014. 'The Patron's "I": Art, Selfhood, and the Later Byzantine Dedicatory Epigram'. *Speculum* 89: 895–935.

Dyas, Dee. 2001. *Pilgrimage in Medieval English Literature, 700–1500*. Cambridge: D.S. Brewer.

Earl, James W. 1975. 'Typology and Iconographic Style in Early Medieval Hagiography'. *Studies in the Literary Imagination* 8: 15–46.

———. 1987. 'Hisperic Style in the Old English *Rhyming Poem*'. *PMLA* 102: 187–96.

Edgar, Swift, ed., with Angela M. Kinney. 2011. *The Vulgate Bible, Volume III: The Poetical Books*. DOML 8. Cambridge, MA: Harvard University Press.

Esser-Miles, Carolin. 2014. '"King of the Children of Pride": Symbolism, Physicality, and the Old English *Whale*'. In *The Maritime World of the Anglo-Saxons*, ed. Stacy S. Klein, William Schipper and Shannon Lewis-Simpson. Tempe: ACMRS. pp. 275–301.

Evans-Pritchard, E.E. 1951. *Social Anthropology*. London: Cohen & West.

Fell, Christine E. 1991. 'Patterns of Transience'. In *The Cambridge Companion to Old English Literature*, ed. Malcolm Godden and Michael Lapidge. Cambridge: Cambridge University Press. pp. 172-89.

———. 2002. 'Runes and Riddles in Anglo-Saxon England'. In *'Lastworda Betst': Essays in Memory of Christine E. Fell with Her Unpublished Writings*, ed. Carole Hough and Kathryn A. Lowe. Donington: Shaun Tyas. pp. 264-77.

Ferguson, Ron, ed. 1991. *Daily Readings with George MacLeod, Founder of the Iona Community*. London: Fount.

Flower, Robin. 1933. 'The Script of the Exeter Book'. In Chambers 1933a, pp. 83-90.

Foot, Sarah. 2006. *Monastic Life in Anglo-Saxon England, c.600-900*. Cambridge: Cambridge University Press.

Förster, Max. 1933. 'The Donations of Leofric to Exeter'. In Chambers 1933a, pp. 10-32.

Frank, Roberta. 1982. 'The *Beowulf* Poet's Sense of History'. In *The Wisdom of Poetry: Essays in Early English Literature in Honor of Morton W. Bloomfield*, ed. Larry D. Benson and Siegfried Wenzel. Kalamazoo: Medieval Institute Publications. pp. 53-65, 271-77.

Frankis, P.J. 1962. '*Deor* and *Wulf and Eadwacer*: Some Conjectures'. *Medium Ævum* 31: 161-75.

———. 1973. 'The Thematic Significance of *enta geweorc* and Related Imagery in *The Wanderer*'. *ASE* 2: 253-69.

Frantzen, Allen J. 1994. 'The Diverse Nature of Old English Poetry'. In *Companion to Old English Poetry*, ed. Henk Aertsen and Rolf H. Bremmer, Jr. Amsterdam: VU University Press. pp. 1-17.

———. 2007. 'Drama and Dialogue in Old English Poetry: The Scene of Cynewulf's *Juliana*'. *Theatre Survey* 48: 99-119.

———. 2012. *Anglo-Saxon Keywords*. Oxford: Wiley-Blackwell.

Frederick, Jill. 2005. 'Warring With Words: Cynewulf's *Juliana*'. In *Readings in Medieval Texts: Interpreting Old and Middle English Literature*, ed. David F. Johnson and Elaine Treharne. Oxford: Oxford University Press. pp. 60-74.

Frese, Dolores Warwick. 1975. 'The Art of Cynewulf's Runic Signatures'. In *Anglo-Saxon Poetry: Essays in Appreciation for John C. McGalliard*, ed. Lewis E. Nicholson and Dolores Warwick Frese. Notre Dame: University of Notre Dame Press. pp. 312-34.

Fry, Donald K. 1980. 'Two Voices in *Widsith*'. *Mediaevalia* 6: 37-56.

Fulk, R.D. 1996. 'Cynewulf: Canon, Dialect and Date'. In *Cynewulf: Basic Readings*, ed. Robert E. Bjork. New York: Garland. pp. 3-21.

Fulk, R.D. and Christopher M. Cain. 2013. *A History of Old English Literature*. 2nd edn. Chichester: Wiley-Blackwell. First published 2003.

Fulk, R.D., Robert E. Bjork and John D. Niles, ed. 2008. *Klaeber's Beowulf and The Fight at Finnsburg*. 4th edn. Toronto: University of Toronto Press.

Gameson, Fiona and Richard Gameson. 1995. Untitled review of Conner 1993a. *Notes & Queries* 42: 228.

Gameson, Richard. 1996. 'The Origin of the Exeter Book of Old English Poetry'. *ASE* 25: 135-85.

Garner, Lori Ann. 2011. *Structuring Spaces: Oral Poetics and Architecture in Early Medieval England*. Notre Dame: University of Notre Dame Press.

Gatch, Milton McC. 1971. *Loyalties and Traditions: Man and his World in Old English Literature.* New York: Pegasus.

Gleissner, Reinhard. 1984. *Die 'zweideutigen' altenglischen Rätsel des Exeter Book in ihrem zeitgenössischen Kontext.* Sprache und Literatur 23. Frankfurt am Main: Peter Lang.

Godden, Malcolm. 1994. 'Apocalypse and Invasion in Late Anglo-Saxon England'. In *From Anglo-Saxon to Early Middle English: Studies Presented to E.G. Stanley*, ed. Malcolm Godden, Douglas Gray and Terry Hoad. Oxford: Clarendon. pp. 130–62.

Godden, Malcolm and Susan Irvine, ed. 2009. *The Old English Boethius: An Edition of the Old English Versions of Boethius's De Consolatione Philosophiae.* 2 vols. Oxford: Oxford University Press.

Gollancz, Israel. 1893. 'Wulf and Eadwacer: An Anglo-Saxon Monodrama in Five Acts'. *Athenaeum* (23 December 1893), 883.

Gordon, I.L., ed. 1960. *The Seafarer.* London: Methuen. Reissued with a new bibliography by University of Exeter Press, 1996.

Gneuss, Helmut. 1996. *Books and Libraries in Early England.* Aldershot: Ashgate.

Green, D.H. 1998. *Language and History in the Early Germanic World.* Cambridge: Cambridge University Press.

Green, Eugene. 2001. *Anglo-Saxon Audiences.* New York: Peter Lang.

Green, Martin. 1975. 'Man, Time, and Apocalypse in *The Wanderer*, *The Seafarer*, and *Beowulf*'. *JEGP* 74: 502–18. Repr. in O'Brien O'Keeffe 1994, pp. 281–302.

Green, Thomas A., ed. 1997. *Folklore: An Encyclopedia of Beliefs, Customs, Tales, Music, and Art.* 2 vols. Santa Barbara: ABC-CLIO.

Greenfield, Stanley B. 1955. 'The Formulaic Expression of the Theme of "Exile" in Anglo-Saxon Poetry'. *Speculum* 30: 200–06.

———. 1966. 'The Old English Elegies'. In *Continuations and Beginnings: Studies in Old English Literature*, ed. E.G. Stanley. London: Nelson. pp. 142–75.

———. 1972. *The Interpretation of Old English Poems.* London: Routledge & Kegan Paul.

Greenfield, Stanley B. and Daniel G. Calder. 1986. *A New Critical History of Old English Literature.* New York: New York University Press.

Gretsch, Mechthild. 1999. *The Intellectual Foundations of the English Benedictine Reform.* Cambridge: Cambridge University Press.

———. 2013. 'Literacy and the Uses of the Vernacular'. In *The Cambridge Companion to Old English Literature*, ed. Malcolm Godden and Michael Lapidge. 2nd edn. Cambridge: Cambridge University Press. pp. 273–94.

Griffith, Mark S. 1992. 'Riddle 19 of the Exeter Book: SNAC, an Old English Acronym'. *Notes & Queries* n.s. 39: 15–16.

———. 1996. 'Does *wyrd bið ful aræd* Mean "Fate is Wholly Inexorable"?' In *Studies in English Language and Literature: 'Doubt Wisely': Papers in Honour of E.G. Stanley*, ed. M.J. Toswell and E.M. Tyler. London: Routledge. pp. 133–56.

Grosz, Oliver J.H. 1996. 'Man's Imitation of the Ascension: The Unity of *Christ II*'. In *Cynewulf: Basic Readings*, ed. Robert E. Bjork. New York: Garland, 1996. pp. 95–108. First published in *Neophilologus* 54 (1970): 398–408.

Gurevich, Aron. 1992. *Historical Anthropology of the Middle Ages*, ed. Jana Howlett. Chicago: University of Chicago Press.

Gwara, Scott, ed. 2001. *Aldhelmi Malmesbiriensis prosa De Virginitate cum glosa Latina atque Anglosaxonica*. 2 vols. Corpus Christianorum Series Latina, 124 and 124A. Turnhout: Brepols.

Hall, Alaric. 2002. 'The Images and Structure of *The Wife's Lament*'. *Leeds Studies in English* n.s. 33: 1–29.

———. 2007. 'Constructing Anglo-Saxon Sanctity: Tradition, Innovation and Saint Guthlac'. In *Images of Medieval Sanctity: Essays in Honour of Gary Dickson*, ed. Debra Higgs Strickland. Leiden: Brill. pp. 207–35.

Hall, Thomas N. 2008. 'The Armaments of John the Baptist in Blickling Homily 14 and the Exeter Book *Descent Into Hell*'. In Blanton and Scheck 2008, pp. 289–306.

Hanna, Ralph. 2013. *Introducing English Medieval Book History: Manuscripts, their Producers and their Readers*. Liverpool: Liverpool University Press.

Hansen, Elaine Tuttle. 1988. *The Solomon Complex: Reading Wisdom in Old English Poetry*. Toronto: University of Toronto Press.

Heighway, Carolyn M. 1984. 'Anglo-Saxon Gloucester to AD 1000'. In *Studies in Late Anglo-Saxon Settlement*, ed. Margaret L. Faull. Oxford: Oxford University Department for External Studies. pp. 35–53.

Hermann, John P. 1989. *Allegories of War: Language and Violence in Old English Poetry*. Ann Arbor: University of Michigan Press.

Hexter, Ralph J. 1986. *Ovid and Medieval Schooling: Studies in Medieval School Commentaries on Ovid's Ars Amatoria, Epistulae ex Ponto, and Epistulae Heroidum*. Munich: Arbeo-Gesellschaft.

Higley, Sarah L. 2003. 'The Wanton Hand: Reading and Reaching into Grammars and Bodies in Old English Riddle 12'. In *Naked Before God: Uncovering the Body in Anglo-Saxon England*, ed. Benjamin C. Withers and Jonathan Wilcox. Morgantown: West Virginia University Press. pp. 29–59.

Hill, John M. 1995. *The Cultural World in Beowulf*. Toronto: University of Toronto Press.

———. 2000. *The Anglo-Saxon Warrior Ethic: Reconstructing Lordship in Anglo-Saxon England*. Gainesville: University of Florida Press.

Hill, Joyce. 1981. 'The Soldier of Christ in Old English Prose and Poetry'. *Leeds Studies in English*, n.s. 12: 57–80.

———. 1984. '*Widsið* and the Tenth Century'. *Neuphilologische Mitteilungen* 85: 305–15. Repr. in O'Brien O'Keeffe 1994, pp. 319–33.

———. 2001. 'The Benedictine Reform and Beyond'. In *A Companion to Anglo-Saxon Literature*, ed. Phillip Pulsiano and Elaine Treharne. Oxford: Blackwell. pp. 151–69.

———. 2003. 'Learning Latin in Anglo-Saxon England: Traditions, Texts and Techniques'. In *Learning and Literacy in Medieval England and Abroad*, ed. Sarah Rees Jones. Turnhout: Brepols. pp. 7–29.

———. 2005. 'Leofric of Exeter and the Practical Politics of Book Collection'. In *Imagining the Book*, ed. Stephen Kelly and John J. Thompson. Turnhout: Brepols. pp. 77–98.

Hill, Thomas D. 1980. 'The *Virga* of Moses and the Old English *Exodus*'. In *Old English Literature in Context: Ten Essays*, ed. John D. Niles. Cambridge: D.S. Brewer. pp. 57–65, 165–67.

———. 2005. 'Wise Words: Old English Sapiential Poetry'. In *Readings in Medieval Texts: Interpreting Old and Middle English Literature*, ed. David F. Johnson and Elaine Treharne. Oxford: Oxford University Press. pp. 166–82.
Hinton, David. 2008. *The Alfred Jewel and Other Late Anglo-Saxon Decorated Metalwork*. Oxford: Ashmolean Museum.
Horner, Shari. 2001. *The Discourse of Enclosure: Representing Women in Old English Literature*. Albany: State University of New York Press.
Howe, Nicholas. 1985. *The Old English Catalogue Poems*. Anglistica 23. Copenhagen: Rosenkilde & Bagger.
———. 1993. 'The Cultural Construction of Reading in Anglo-Saxon England'. In *The Ethnography of Reading*, ed. Jonathan Boyarin. Berkeley: University of California Press. pp. 58–79. Repr. in Liuzza 2002, pp. 1–22.
———. 1997. 'Historicist Approaches'. In *Reading Old English Texts*, ed. Katherine O'Brien O'Keeffe. Cambridge: Cambridge University Press. pp. 79–100.
———. 2004. 'Looking for Home in Anglo-Saxon England'. In *Home and Homelessness in the Medieval and Renaissance World*, ed. Nicholas Howe. Notre Dame: University of Notre Dame Press. pp. 143–63.
Howlett, D.R. 1978. '*The Wife's Lament* and *The Husband's Message*'. *Neuphilologische Mitteilungen* 79: 7–10.
Hume, Kathryn. 1976. 'The "Ruin Motif" in Old English Poetry'. *Anglia* 94: 339–60.
Hunt, R.W., ed. 1961. *Saint Dunstan's Classbook from Glastonbury: Codex Biblioth. Bodleieanae Oxon. Auct. F.4./32*. Amsterdam: North-Holland Publishing Co.
Huppé, Bernard F. 1959. *Doctrine and Poetry: Augustine's Influence on Old English Poetry*. Albany: State University of New York Press.
———. 1970. *The Web of Words: Structural Analyses of the Old English Poems Vainglory, The Wonder of Creation, The Dream of the Rood, and Judith*. Albany: State University of New York Press.
Hussey, Matthew T. 2009. 'Dunstan, Æthelwold, and Isidorean Exegesis in Old English Glosses: Oxford, Bodleian Library Bodley 319'. *RES* n.s. 60: 681–704.
———, ed. 2014. *Exeter Manuscripts*. Anglo-Saxon Manuscripts in Microfiche Facsimile 22. Tempe: ACMRS.
Hussey, Matthew T. and John D. Niles, ed. 2011. *The Genesis of Books: Studies in the Scribal Culture of Medieval England in Honour of A.N. Doane*. Turnhout: Brepols.
Ireland, Colin A. 1991. 'Some Analogues of the O.E. *Seafarer* from Hiberno-Latin Sources'. *Neuphilologische Mitteilungen* 92: 1–14.
Irvine, Martin. 1994. *The Making of Textual Culture: Grammatica and Literary Theory, 350-1100*. Cambridge: Cambridge University Press.
Irvine, Susan and Malcolm R. Godden, ed. and trans. 2012. *The Old English Boethius*. DOML 19. Cambridge, MA: Harvard University Press.
Irving, Edward B., Jr. 1994. 'Heroic Experience in the Old English Riddles'. In O'Brien O'Keeffe 1994, pp. 199–212.
———. 1996. 'The Advent of Poetry: *Christ I*'. *ASE* 25: 123–34.
Jacobs, Christina. 2001. '*Precepts* and the Exeter Book of Vernacular Instructive Poetry'. In *Varieties and Consequences of Literacy and Orality/Formen und Folgen von Schriftlichkeit und Mündlichkeit: Franz H. Bäuml zum 75. Geburtstag*, ed. Ursula Schaefer and Edda Spielmann. Tübingen: Gunter Narr. pp. 33–48.

Johnson, David F. 2008. 'Spiritual Combat and the Land of Canaan in *Guthlac A*'. In Blanton and Scheck 2008, pp. 307–18.

Jones, Christopher A. 1995. 'Envisioning the *Cenobium* in the Old English *Guthlac A*'. *Mediaeval Studies* 57: 259–91.

———. 2009. 'Ælfric and the Limits of "Benedictine Reform"'. In *A Companion to Ælfric*, ed. Hugh Magennis and Mary Swan. Leiden: Brill. pp. 67–108.

———, ed. and trans. 2012. *Old English Shorter Poems, Volume I: Religious and Didactic*. DOML 15. Cambridge, MA: Harvard University Press.

Jurasinski, Stefan. 2007. 'Caring for the Dead in *The Fortunes of Men*'. *PQ* 86: 343–63.

Karkov, Catherine E. 2008. 'The Frontispiece to the New Minster Charter and the King's Two Bodies'. In *Edgar, King of the English 959–975*, ed. Donald Scragg. Woodbridge: Boydell. pp. 224–41.

Kelly, Richard J., ed. and trans. 2003. *The Blickling Homilies*. London: Continuum.

Kelly, Susan. 1990. 'Anglo-Saxon Lay Society and the Written Word'. In *The Uses of Literacy in Early Mediaeval Europe*, ed. Rosamond McKitterick. Cambridge: Cambridge University Press. pp. 36–62. Repr. in Liuzza 2002, pp. 23–50.

Kendall, Calvin B. 2010. 'Bede and Education'. In *The Cambridge Companion to Bede*, ed. Scott DeGregorio. Cambridge: Cambridge University Press. pp. 99–112.

Ker, N.R. 1957. *Catalogue of Manuscripts Containing Anglo-Saxon*. Oxford: Clarendon.

Keynes, Simon. 1990. 'Royal Government and the Written Word in Late Anglo-Saxon England'. In *The Uses of Literacy in Early Mediaeval Europe*, ed. Rosamond McKitterick. Cambridge: Cambridge University Press. pp. 226–57.

———. 1999. 'England, c.900–1016'. In *The New Cambridge Medieval History, Volume 3, c.900–c.1024*, ed. Timothy Reuter. Cambridge: Cambridge University Press. pp. 456–84.

———. 2008. 'Edgar, *rex admirabilis*'. In *Edgar, King of the English 959–975*, ed. Donald Scragg. Woodbridge: Boydell. pp. 3–58.

Kinney, Angela M., ed. 2012. *The Vulgate Bible, Volume IV: The Major Prophetical Books*. DOML 13. Cambridge, MA: Harvard University Press.

———, ed. 2013. *The Vulgate Bible, Volume VI: The New Testament*. DOML 21. Cambridge, MA: Harvard University Press.

Klein, Stacy S. 2006. 'Gender and the Nature of Exile in Old English Elegies'. In *A Place to Believe In: Locating Medieval Landscapes*, ed. Clare A. Lees and Gillian R. Overing. University Park: Pennsylvania State University Press. pp. 113–31.

Klinck, Anne L. 1992. *The Old English Elegies: A Critical Edition and Genre Study*. Montreal: McGill-Queens University Press. Repr. with a supplementary bibliography, 2001.

Knowles, David. 1963. *The Monastic Order in England*. 2nd edn. Cambridge: Cambridge University Press.

Kramer, Johanna. 2007. '*Ðu Eart se Weallstan*: Architectural Metaphor and Christological Imagery in the Old English *Christ I* and the Book of Kells'. In Wright et al. 2007, pp. 90–112.

———. 2010. 'Mapping the Anglo-Saxon Intellectual Landscape: The Old English *Maxims I* and Terence's Proverb "Quot homines, tot Sententiae"'. *Anglia* 128: 48–74.

Krapp, George Philip and Elliott Van Kirk Dobbie, ed. 1936. *The Exeter Book*. ASPR 3. New York: Columbia University Press.

Kurath, Hans and Sherman M. Kuhn, ed. 1952–2001. *Middle English Dictionary*. Ann Arbor: University of Michigan Press.
Laistner, M.L.W. 1957. *Thought and Letters in Western Europe AD 500 to 900*. 2nd edn. Ithaca: Cornell University Press.
Langenfelt, Gösta. 1959. 'Studies on *Widsith*'. *Namn och Bygd* 47: 70–111.
Lapidge, Michael. 1975. 'The Hermeneutic Style in Tenth-Century Anglo-Latin Literature'. *ASE* 4: 67–111.
———. 1979. 'Aldhelm's Latin Poetry and Old English Verse'. *Comparative Literature* 31: 209–31.
———. 1980. 'St Dunstan's Latin Poetry'. *Anglia* 98: 101–06.
———. 1985. 'Surviving Booklists from Anglo-Saxon England'. In *Learning and Literature in Anglo-Saxon England: Studies Presented to Peter Clemoes*, ed. Michael Lapidge and Helmut Gneuss. Cambridge: Cambridge University Press. pp. 33–89.
———. 1991. 'Schools, Learning and Literature in Tenth-Century England'. In *Il secolo di ferro: mito e realtà del secolo X*, Settimane de studio del centro italiano di studi sull'alto medioevo 38. Spoleto. 951–98. Repr. in his essay collection *Anglo-Latin Literature 900-1066*. London: Hambledon, 1993, pp. 1–48.
———. 2003. 'Cynewulf and the *Passio S. Iulianae*'. In *Unlocking the Wordhord: Anglo-Saxon Studies in Memory of Edward B. Irving, Jr*, ed. Mark C. Amodio and Katherine O'Brien O'Keeffe. Toronto: University of Toronto Press. pp. 147–71.
———. 2005. 'Poeticism in Pre-Conquest Anglo-Latin Prose'. *Proceedings of the British Academy* 129: 321–37.
———. 2006a. *The Anglo-Saxon Library*. Oxford: Oxford University Press.
———. 2006b. 'Versifying the Bible in the Middle Ages'. In *The Text in the Community: Essays on Medieval Works, Manuscripts, Authors, and Readers*, ed. Jill Mann and Maura Nolan. Notre Dame: University of Notre Dame Press. pp. 11–40.
———. 2007. 'The Career of Aldhelm'. *ASE* 36: 15–69.
Lapidge, Michael and Michael Herren, ed. 1979. *Aldhelm: The Prose Works*. Cambridge: D.S. Brewer.
Lapidge, Michael and James L. Rosier, trans. 1985. *Aldhelm: The Poetic Works*. Cambridge: D.S. Brewer.
Lapidge, Michael and Michael Winterbottom, ed. and trans. 1991. *Wulfstan of Winchester: The Life of St Æthelwold*. Oxford: Clarendon.
Lapidge, Michael, John Blair, Simon Keynes and Donald Scragg, ed. 2014. *The Wiley-Blackwell Encyclopedia of Anglo-Saxon England*. 2nd edn. Chichester: Wiley-Blackwell.
Law, Vivien. 1997. *Grammar and Grammarians in the Early Middle Ages*. London: Longman.
Leahy, Kevin. 2003. *Anglo-Saxon Crafts*. Stroud, Gloucestershire: Tempus.
Lee, Alvin A. 1972. *The Guest-Hall of Eden: Four Essays on the Design of Old English Poetry*. New Haven: Yale University Press.
Lee, Anne Thompson. 1973. '*The Ruin*: Bath or Babylon? A Non-Archaeological Investigation'. *Neuphilologische Mitteilungen* 74: 443–55.
Lees, Clare A. and G.R. Overing. 2011. 'Women and the Origins of English Literature'. In *The History of British Women's Writing, Volume 1: 700-1500*, ed. Liz Herbert McAvoy and Diane Watt. Basingstoke and New York: Palgrave MacMillan. pp. 31–40.

Lehmann, Ruth P.M. 1969. 'The Metrics and Structure of *Wulf and Eadwacer*'. *PQ* 48: 151–65.

Lehmberg, Stanford. 2000. 'Cathedral Priories (England)'. In *Encyclopedia of Monasticism*, ed. William M. Johnston. 2 vols. Chicago: Fitzroy Dearborn Publishers. 1: 253–54.

Lendinara, Patrizia. 2007. 'Instructional Manuscripts in England: The Tenth- and Eleventh-Century Codices and the Early Norman Ones'. In *Form and Content of Instruction in Anglo-Saxon England in the Light of Contemporary Manuscript Evidence*, ed. Patrizia Lendinara, Loredana Lazzari and Maria Amalia D'Aronco. Turnhout: Brepols. pp. 59–113.

———. 2013. 'The World of Anglo-Saxon Learning'. In *The Cambridge Companion to Old English Literature*, ed. Malcolm Godden and Michael Lapidge. 2nd edn. Cambridge: Cambridge University Press. pp. 295–312.

Lerer, Seth. 1991. *Literacy and Power in Anglo-Saxon Literature*. Lincoln: University of Nebraska Press.

Leslie, Roy F., ed. 1985. *The Wanderer*. 2nd edn. University of Exeter Press. First published 1966.

———, ed. 1988. *Three Old English Elegies*. 2nd edn. University of Exeter Press. First published 1961.

Liuzza, Roy M. 1988. 'The Texts of the Old English *Riddle 30*'. *JEGP* 87: 1–15.

———. 1990. 'The Old English *Christ* and *Guthlac*: Texts, Manuscripts, and Critics'. *RES* n.s. 41: 1–11.

———, ed. 2002. *Old English Literature: Critical Essays*. New Haven: Yale University Press.

———. 2003. 'The Tower of Babel: *The Wanderer* and the Ruins of History'. *Studies in the Literary Imagination* 36: 1–35.

———. 2006. 'Scribes of the Mind: Editing Old English, in Theory and in Practice'. In *The Power of Words: Anglo-Saxon Studies Presented to Donald G. Scragg*, ed. Hugh Magennis and Jonathan Wilcox. Morgantown: West Virginia University Press. pp. 243–77.

———. 2012. 'Literacy'. In *A Handbook of Anglo-Saxon Studies*, ed. Jacqueline Stodnick and Renée R. Trilling. Chichester: Wiley-Blackwell. pp. 99–114.

Lochrie, Karma. 1986. '*Wyrd* and the Limits of Human Understanding: A Thematic Sequence in the Exeter Book'. *JEGP* 85: 323–31.

Lockett, Leslie. 2011. *Anglo-Saxon Psychologies in the Vernacular and Latin Traditions*. Toronto: University of Toronto Press.

Loewenthal, David. 1985. *The Past Is a Foreign Country*. Cambridge: Cambridge University Press.

———. 2015. *The Past Is a Foreign Country—Revisited*. Cambridge: Cambridge University Press.

Lucy, Sam. 2000. *The Anglo-Saxon Way of Death: Burial Rites in Early England*. Thrupp, Gloucester: Sutton Publishing.

Luecke, Jane-Marie. 1983. '*Wulf and Eadwacer*: Hints for Reading from *Beowulf* and Anthropology'. In *The Old English Elegies: New Essays in Criticism and Research*, ed. Martin Green. Rutherford, NJ: Fairleigh Dickinson University Press. pp. 190–203.

Machan, Tim William. 2011. 'Editorial Certainty and the Editor's Choice'. In Hussey and Niles 2011, pp. 285–304.

Macrae-Gibson, O.D., ed. 1983. *The Old English Riming Poem*. Cambridge: D.S. Brewer.
Magennis, Hugh. 1995. '"No Sex Please, We're Anglo-Saxons"? Attitudes to Sexuality in Old English Prose and Poetry'. *Leeds Studies in English* 26: 1–27.
———. 1996. *Images of Community in Old English Poetry*. Cambridge: Cambridge University Press.
———. 1998. '*Godes þeow* and Related Expressions in Old English: Contexts and Uses of a Traditional Literary Figure'. *Anglia* 116: 139–70.
———. 1999. *Anglo-Saxon Appetites: Food and Drink and their Consumption in Old English and Related Literature*. Dublin: Four Courts Press.
———. 2004. 'Approaches to Saints' Lives'. In *The Christian Tradition in Anglo-Saxon England: Approaches to Current Scholarship and Teaching*, ed. Paul Cavill. Cambridge: D.S. Brewer. pp. 163–83.
———. 2006. 'Ælfric and Heroic Literature'. In *The Power of Words: Anglo-Saxon Studies Presented to Donald G. Scragg*, ed. Hugh Magennis and Jonathan Wilcox. Morgantown: West Virginia University Press. pp. 31–60.
———. 2007. 'The Solitary Journey: Aloneness and Community in *The Seafarer*'. In *Text, Image, Interpretation: Studies in Anglo-Saxon Literature and its Insular Context in Honour of Éamonn Ó Carragáin*, ed. Alastair Minnis and Jane Roberts. Turnhout: Brepols. pp. 303–18.
———. 2010. 'Germanic Legend and Old English Heroic Poetry'. In *A Companion to Medieval Poetry*, ed. Corinne Saunders. Oxford: Wiley-Blackwell. pp. 85–100.
———. 2011. *The Cambridge Introduction to Anglo-Saxon Literature*. Cambridge: Cambridge University Press.
Malmberg, Lars, ed. 1979. *Resignation*. Durham: Durham and St Andrews Medieval Texts.
Mann, Jill. 2006. '"He Knew Nat Catoun": Medieval School-Texts and Middle English Literature'. In *The Text in the Community: Essays on Medieval Works, Manuscripts, Authors, and Readers*, ed. Jill Mann and Maura Nolan. Notre Dame: University of Notre Dame Press. pp. 41–74.
Marafioti, Nicole. 2014. *The King's Body: Burial and Succession in Late Anglo-Saxon England*. Toronto: University of Toronto Press.
Maring, Heather. 2017. *Signs that Sing: Hybrid Poetics in Old English Verse*. Gainesville: University Press of Florida.
Matthews, Stephen. 2007. *The Road to Rome: Travel and Travellers Between England and Italy in the Anglo-Saxon Centuries*. BAR International Series 1680. Oxford: Archaeopress.
McCormack, Frances. 2015. 'Those Bloody Trees: The Affectivity of *Christ*'. In *Anglo-Saxon Emotions: Reading the Heart in Old English Language, Literature and Culture*, ed. Alice Jorgensen, Frances McCormack and Jonathan Wilcox. Farnham: Ashgate. pp. 143–61.
McEntyre, Sandra. 1990. 'The Monastic Context of Old English *Precepts*'. *Neuphilologische Mitteilungen* 91: 243–49.
Miller, Joseph M., Michael H. Prosser and Thomas W. Benson, ed. 1973. *Readings in Medieval Rhetoric*. Bloomington: Indiana University Press.
Moffat, Douglas, ed. and trans. 1990. *The Old English Soul and Body*. Woodbridge: Boydell & Brewer.

Morrison, Stephen. 1979. 'OE *cempa* in Cynewulf's *Juliana* and the Figure of the *Miles Christi*'. *English Language Notes* 17 (1979): 81–84.
Muir, Bernard J. 1991. 'Watching the Exeter Book Scribe Copy Old English and Latin Texts'. *Manuscripta* 35: 3–22.
———, ed. 2000. *The Exeter Anthology of Old English Poetry*. 2nd edn. 2 vols. Exeter: University of Exeter Press.
———. 2005. 'Anthologists, Poets and Scribes in Anglo-Saxon England'. *Journal of the Australian Early Medieval Association* 1: 99–118.
———. 2006. *The Exeter Anthology of Old English Poetry*. Electronic edition featuring a facsimile of the manuscript. Exeter: University of Exeter Press.
Mullins, Juliet. 2014. '*Hermium in Mari*: Anglo-Saxon Attitudes towards *Peregrinatio* and the Ideal of a Desert in the Sea'. In *The Maritime World of the Anglo-Saxons*, ed. Stacy S. Klein, William Schipper and Shannon Lewis-Simpson. Tempe: ACMRS. pp. 59–73.
Murphy, Patrick J. 2011. *Unriddling the Exeter Riddles*. University Park: Pennsylvania State University Press.
Neidorf, Leonard. 2013. 'The Dating of *Widsið* and the Study of Germanic Antiquity'. *Neophilologus* 97: 165–83.
Nelson, Marie. 1974. 'The Rhetoric of the Exeter Book Riddles'. *Speculum* 49: 421–40.
———. 1983. 'On *Resignation*'. In *The Old English Elegies: New Essays in Criticism and Research*, ed. Martin Green. Rutherford, NJ: Fairleigh Dickinson University Press. pp. 133–47.
Neville, Jennifer. 2007. 'What Else Is There? Joyous Play and Bitter Tears: The Riddles and the Elegies'. In *Beowulf and Other Stories: A New Introduction to Old English, Old Icelandic and Anglo-Norman Literatures*, ed. Richard North and Joe Allard. Harlow: Pearson Longman. pp. 130–59.
———. 2009. 'Pondering the Soul's Journey in Exeter Book *Riddle 43*'. In *The World of Travellers: Exploration and Imagination*, ed. Kees Dekker, Karin Olsen and Tette Hofstra. Leuven: Peeters. pp. 147–62.
———. 2012. 'Speaking the Unspeakable: Appetite for Deconstruction in Exeter Book *Riddle 12*'. *English Studies* 93: 519–28.
Nichols, Stephen G. and Siegfried Wenzel, ed. 1996. *The Whole Book: Cultural Perspectives on the Medieval Miscellany*. Ann Arbor: University of Michigan Press.
Niles, John D. 1983. *Beowulf: The Poem and its Tradition*. Cambridge, MA: Harvard University Press.
———. 1992. 'Sign and Psyche in Old English Poetry'. *American Journal of Semiotics* 9: 11–25.
———. 1999a. *Homo Narrans: The Poetics and Anthropology of Oral Literature*. Philadelphia: University of Pennsylvania Press, 1999.
———. 1999b. '*Widsith* and the Anthropology of the Past'. *PQ* 78: 171–213. Revised as chapter 2, '*Widsith*, the Goths, and the Anthropology of the Past' (pp. 73–109), of Niles 2007a.
———. 2003a. 'The Problem of the Ending of the *Wife's Lament*'. *Speculum* 78: 1107–50. Revised as chapter 5 (pp. 149–207) of Niles 2006a.
———. 2003b. 'The Trick of the Runes in *The Husband's Message*'. *ASE* 32: 189–223. Repr. as chapter 6 (pp. 213–50) of Niles 2006a.
———. 2006a. *Old English Enigmatic Poems and the Play of the Texts*. Turnhout: Brepols.

———. 2006b. 'Answering the Riddles in their Own Tongue'. In Niles 2006a, pp. 101–48.

———. 2006c. 'Cynewulf's Use of Initialisms in his Runic Signatures'. In Niles 2006a, pp. 285–306.

———. 2006d. 'Runic Hermeneutics in *The Rune Poem*'. In Niles 2006a, pp. 251–79.

———. 2007a. *Old English Heroic Poems and the Social Life of Texts*. Turnhout: Brepols.

———. 2007b. 'The Refrain in *Deor*'. In Niles 2007a, pp. 189–93.

———. 2016. *Old English Literature: A Guide to Criticism with Selected Readings*. Oxford: Wiley-Blackwell.

O'Brien O'Keeffe, Katherine. 1985. 'The Text of Aldhelm's Enigma no. C in Oxford, Bodleian Library, Rawlinson C. 697 and Exeter Riddle 40'. *ASE* 14: 61–73.

———, ed. 1994. *Old English Shorter Poems: Basic Readings*. New York: Garland.

———. 2012. *Stealing Obedience: Narratives of Agency and Identity in Later Anglo-Saxon England*. Toronto: University of Toronto Press.

———. 2017. 'Anglo-Saxon Vernacular Literary Culture'. In *Oxford Research Encyclopedias: Literature*. Oxford: Oxford University Press. <http://literature.oxfordre.com> [accessed 24 October 2018].

O'Camb, Brian. 2009. 'Bishop Æthelwold and the Shaping of the Old English *Exeter Maxims*'. *English Studies* 90: 253–73.

———. 2011. 'The Inscribed Form of *Exeter Maxims* and the Layout of Quire XI of the Exeter Book'. In Hussey and Niles 2011, pp. 137–59.

———. 2014. '*Exeter Maxims*, *The Order of the World*, and the Exeter Book of Old English Poetry'. *PQ* 93: 409–33.

———. 2016. 'Toward a Monastic Poetics: Envisioning King Edgar's Privilege for New Minster, Winchester, and *Advent Lyric 11*'. In *Anglo-Saxon England and the Visual Imagination*, ed. John D. Niles, Stacy S. Klein and Jonathan Wilcox. Tempe: ACMRS. pp. 167–98.

O'Neill, Patrick P., ed. and trans. 2016. *Old English Psalms*. DOML 42. Cambridge, MA: Harvard University Press.

Opland, Jeff. 1980. *Anglo-Saxon Oral Poetry: A Study of the Traditions*. New Haven: Yale University Press.

Orchard, Andy. 1994. *The Poetic Art of Aldhelm*. Cambridge: Cambridge University Press.

———. 1995a. 'Artful Alliteration in Anglo-Saxon Song and Story'. *Anglia* 113: 429–63.

———. 1995b. *Pride and Prodigies: Studies in the Monsters of the Beowulf-Manuscript*. Cambridge: D.S. Brewer.

———. 2002. 'Re-Reading *The Wanderer*: The Value of Cross-References'. In *Via Crucis: Essays on Early Medieval Sources and Ideas in Memory of J.E. Cross*, ed. Thomas N. Hall. Morgantown: West Virginia University Press. pp. 1–26.

———. 2005. 'Enigma Variations: The Anglo-Saxon Riddle-Tradition'. In *Latin Learning and English Lore: Studies in Anglo-Saxon Literature for Michael Lapidge*, ed. Katherine O'Brien O'Keeffe and Andy Orchard. 2 vols. Toronto: University of Toronto Press. 1: 284–304.

———. 2008. 'Reconstructing *The Ruin*'. In Blanton and Scheck 2008, pp. 45–68.

———. 2009. 'The Word Made Flesh: Christianity and Oral Culture in Anglo-Saxon Verse'. *Oral Tradition* 24: 293–318.

———. 2010. 'Old English and Latin Poetic Traditions'. In *A Companion to Medieval Poetry*, ed. Corinne Saunders. Oxford: Wiley-Blackwell. pp. 65–82.
Orme, Nicholas. 1991. 'Glastonbury Abbey and Education'. In *The Archaeology and History of Glastonbury Abbey*, ed. Lesley Abrams and James P. Carley. Woodbridge: Boydell. pp. 287–99.
———. 2006. *Medieval Schools: From Roman Britain to Renaissance England*. New Haven: Yale University Press.
———. 2009. *Exeter Cathedral: The First Thousand Years, 400–1550*. Exeter: Impress.
Orton, Peter (P.R.). 1979a. 'Disunity in the Vercelli Book *Soul and Body*'. *Neophilologus* 63: 450–60.
———. 1979b. 'The OE *Soul and Body*: A Further Examination'. *Medium Ævum* 48: 173–97.
———. 2001. 'To Be a Pilgrim: The Old English *Seafarer* and its Irish Affinities'. In *Lexis and Texts in Early English: Studies Presented to Jane Roberts*, ed. Christian J. Kay and Louise M. Sylvester. Amsterdam: Rodopi. pp. 213–23.
———. 2014. *Writing in a Speaking World: The Pragmatics of Literacy in Anglo-Saxon Inscriptions and Old English Poetry*. Tempe: ACMRS.
Page, R.I. 1982. 'The Study of Latin Texts in Late Anglo-Saxon England, 2: The Evidence of English Glosses'. In *Latin and the Vernacular Languages in Early Medieval Britain*, ed. Nicholas Brooks. Leicester: Leicester University Press. pp. 141–65.
———. 1999. *An Introduction to English Runes*. 2nd edn. Woodbridge: Boydell.
Parkes, M.B. 1997. '*Rædan, areccan, smeagan*: How the Anglo-Saxons Read'. *ASE* 26: 1–22.
———. 2008. *Their Hands Before our Eyes: A Closer Look at Scribes*. Aldershot: Ashgate.
Pasternack, Carol Braun. 1995. *The Textuality of Old English Poetry*. Cambridge: Cambridge University Press.
———. 2004. 'The Sexual Practices of Virginity and Chastity in Aldhelm's *De Virginitate*'. In *Sex and Sexuality in Anglo-Saxon England*, ed. Carol Braun Pasternack and Lisa M.C. Weston. Tempe: ACMRS. pp. 93–120.
Phillpotts, Bertha S. 1928. 'Wyrd and Providence in Anglo-Saxon Thought'. *Essays and Studies* 13: 7–27.
Powell, Stephen D. 1998. 'The Journey Forth: Elegiac Consolation in *Guthlac B*'. *ES* 79: 489–500.
Prosopography of Anglo-Saxon England. <http://www.pase.ac.uk> [accessed 24 October 2018].
Ralby, Aaron. 2010. 'The *Pœnitentiale Pseudo-Ecgberti* and the Old English *Precepts*'. *Notes & Queries* n.s. 57: 6–10.
Rambaran-Olm, M.R. 2014. *John the Baptist's Prayer or The Descent into Hell from the Exeter Book: Text, Translation and Critical Study*. Cambridge: D.S. Brewer.
Ramsay, Nigel, Margaret Sparks and Tim Tatton-Brown, ed. 1992. *St Dunstan: His Life, Times and Cult*. Woodbridge: Boydell.
Rankin, Susan. 1985. 'The Liturgical Background of the Old English Advent Lyrics: A Reappraisal'. In *Learning and Literature in Anglo-Saxon England: Studies Presented to Peter Clemoes*, ed. Michael Lapidge and Helmut Gneuss. Cambridge: Cambridge University Press. pp. 317–40.

Raw, Barbara. 2004. 'Pictures: The Books of the Unlearned?' In *The Christian Tradition in Anglo-Saxon England: Approaches to Current Scholarship and Teaching*, ed. Paul Cavill. Cambridge: D.S. Brewer. pp. 103–19.

Regan, Catharine A. 1970. 'Patristic Psychology in the Old English *Vainglory*'. *Traditio* 26: 324–35.

Reichl, Karl. 2011. 'The Beginnings of the Middle English Secular Lyric: Texts, Music, Manuscript Context'. In Hussey and Niles 2011, pp. 196–243.

Remley, Paul G. 2002. '*Daniel*, the *Three Youths* Fragment and the Transmission of Old English Verse'. *ASE* 31: 81–140.

Renoir, Alain. 1983. 'The Old English *Ruin*: Contrastive Structure and Affective Impact'. In *The Old English Elegies: New Essays in Criticism and Research*, ed. Martin Green. Rutherford, NJ: Fairleigh Dickinson University Press. pp. 148–73.

Reynolds, Robert L. and Robert S. Lopez. 1946. 'Odoacer: German or Hun?' *American Historical Review* 52: 36–53.

Richman, Gerald. 1982. 'Speaker and Speech Boundaries in *The Wanderer*'. *JEGP* 81: 469–79. Repr. in O'Brien O'Keeffe 1994, pp. 303–18.

Riedinger, Anita R. 1995. '"Home" in Old English Poetry'. *Neuphilologische Mitteilungen* 96: 51–59.

Rigg, A.G. and G.R. Wieland. 1975. 'A Canterbury Classbook of the Mid-Eleventh Century (the "Cambridge Songs" Manuscript)'. *ASE* 4: 113–30.

Riyeff, Jacob. 2015. '*Homo Contemplans*: *The Order of the World*, Gregorian Contemplative Anthropology, and Old English Poetics'. *Viator* 46: 1–20.

———, trans. 2017. *The Old English Rule of Saint Benedict, with Related Old English Texts*. Collegeville, MN: Liturgical Press.

Roberts, Jane, ed. 1979. *The Guthlac Poems of the Exeter Book*. Oxford: Clarendon.

———. 2005. *Guide to Scripts Used in English Writings up to 1500*. London: British Library.

———. 2008. 'A Man *boca gleaw* and his Musings'. In Blanton and Scheck 2008, pp. 119–37.

Robertson, A.J. 1939. *Anglo-Saxon Charters*. Cambridge: Cambridge University Press.

Robinson, Fred C. 1980. 'Old English Literature in its Most Immediate Context'. In *Old English Literature in Context: Ten Essays*, ed. John D. Niles. Cambridge: D.S. Brewer. pp. 11–29, 157–61. Repr. in O'Brien O'Keeffe 1994, pp. 3–29.

———. 1985. *Beowulf and the Appositive Style*. Knoxville: University of Tennessee Press.

———. 2001. 'Secular Poetry'. In *A Companion to Anglo-Saxon Literature*, ed. Phillip Pulsiano and Elaine Treharne. Oxford: Blackwell. pp. 281–95.

Ruggerini, Maria Elena. 2011. 'A Just and Riding God: Christ's Movement in *The Descent into Hell*'. In *Myths, Legends, and Heroes: Essays on Old Norse and Old English Literature in Honour of John McKinnell*, ed. Daniel Anlezark. Toronto: University of Toronto Press. pp. 206–24.

Rulon-Miller, Nina. 2000. 'Sexual Humor and Fettered Desire in Exeter Book Riddle 12'. In *Humour in Anglo-Saxon Literature*, ed. Jonathan Wilcox. Cambridge: D.S. Brewer. pp. 99–126.

Rumble, Alexander. 1998. 'Exeter Book'. In *Medieval England: An Encyclopedia*, ed. Paul E. Szarmach, M. Teresa Tavormina and Joel T. Rosenthal. New York: Garland. p. 285, col. 2.

———. 2008. 'The Laity and the Monastic Reform in the Reign of Edgar'. In *Edgar, King of the English 959-975*, ed. Donald Scragg. Woodbridge: Boydell. pp. 242–51.

Salvador Bello, Mercedes (Mercedes Salvador, Mercedes Salvador-Bello). 2004. 'The Oyster and the Crab: A Riddle Duo (nos. 77 and 78) in the Exeter Book'. *Modern Philology* 101: 400–19.

———. 2006. 'Architectural Metaphors and Christological Imagery in the *Advent Lyrics*: Benedictine Propaganda in the Exeter Book?' In *Conversion and Colonization in Anglo-Saxon England*, ed. Catherine E. Karkov and Nicholas Howe. Tempe: ACMRS. pp. 169–211.

———. 2008. 'The Edgar Panegyrics in *The Anglo-Saxon Chronicle*'. In *Edgar, King of the English 959-975*, ed. Donald Scragg. Woodbridge: Boydell. pp. 252–72.

———. 2011. 'The Sexual Riddle Type in Aldhelm's Enigmata, the Exeter Book, and Early Medieval Latin'. *PQ* 90: 357–85.

———. 2015. *Isidorean Perceptions of Order: The Exeter Book Riddles and Medieval Latin Enigmata*. Morgantown: West Virginia University Press.

Sánchez de Nieva, María José. 2009. 'The Significance of Mary's Role in the Exeter Book *Advent Lyrics*'. *Selim* 16: 47–63.

Savage, Ann. 1989. 'Translation as Expansion: Poetic Practice in the Old English *Phoenix* and Some Other Poems'. In *The Medieval Translator: The Theory and Practice of Translation in the Middle Ages*, ed. Roger Ellis. Cambridge: D.S. Brewer. pp. 123–34.

Schaefer, Ursula. 1991. 'Hearing from Books: The Rise of Fictionality in Old English Poetry'. In *Vox Intexta: Orality and Textuality in the Middle Ages*, ed. A.N. Doane and Carol Braun Pasternack. Madison: University of Wisconsin Press. pp. 117–36.

Schneider, Claude. 1978. 'Cynewulf's Devaluation of Heroic Tradition in *Juliana*'. *ASE* 7: 107–18.

Schröer, Arnold, ed. 1885-88. *Die angelsächsischen Prosabearbeitungen der Benediktinerregel*. Bibliothek der angelsächsischen Prosa, vol. 2, parts 1 and 2. Kassel: Wiegend.

Scragg, Donald. 2012. *A Conspectus of Scribal Hands Writing English, 960-1100*. Cambridge: D.S. Brewer.

Shippey, T.A. 1972. *Old English Verse*. London: Hutchinson.

———. 1976. *Poems of Wisdom and Learning in Old English*. Cambridge: D.S. Brewer.

———. 1994. '*The Wanderer* and *The Seafarer* as Wisdom Poetry'. In *Companion to Old English Poetry*, ed. Henk Aertsen and Rolf H. Bremmer, Jr. Amsterdam: VU University Press. pp. 145–58.

Shook, Lawrence. 1974. 'Riddles Relating to the Anglo-Saxon Scriptorium'. In *Essays in Honour of Anton Charles Pegis*, ed. J. Reginald O'Donnell. Toronto: Pontifical Institute of Mediaeval Studies. pp. 215–36.

Showerman, Grant, trans. 1977. *Ovid: Heroides and Amores*. 2nd edn, revised by G.P. Goold. Cambridge, MA: Harvard University Press.

Sisam, Kenneth. 1953. *Studies in the History of Old English Literature*. Oxford: Clarendon.

Smith, Scott Thompson. 2011. 'The Edgar Poems and the Poetics of Failure in the Anglo-Saxon Chronicle'. *ASE* 39: 105–37.

Smithers, G.V. 1957. 'The Meaning of *The Seafarer* and *The Wanderer*'. *Medium Ævum* 26: 137–53.

Squires, Ann, ed. 1988. *The Old English Physiologus*. Durham: Durham Medieval Texts.

Stafford, P.A. 1978. 'Church and Society in the Age of Aelfric'. In *The Old English Homily and its Backgrounds*, ed. Paul E. Szarmach and Bernard F. Huppé. Albany: State University of New York Press. pp. 11–42.

Stancliffe, Clare. 1983. 'Kings Who Opted Out'. In *Ideal and Reality in Frankish and Anglo-Saxon Society: Studies Presented to J.M. Wallace-Hadrill*, ed. Patrick Wormald. Oxford: Blackwell, 1983. pp. 154–76.

Stanley, E.G. (Eric G.). 1955. 'Old English Poetic Diction and the Interpretation of *The Wanderer*, *The Seafarer*, and *The Penitent's Prayer*'. *Anglia* 73 (1955): 413–66.

———. 1975. *The Search for Anglo-Saxon Paganism*. Cambridge: D.S. Brewer. Reissued as the first half of his book *Imagining the Anglo-Saxon Past: The Search for Anglo-Saxon Paganism and Anglo-Saxon Trial by Jury*. Cambridge: D.S. Brewer. 2000.

———. 2006. 'Fear, Chiefly in Old and Middle English'. *Poetica* (Tokyo) 66: 73–114.

———. 2008. 'Judgment Day: Hopes, Joys, and Sorrows in Medieval England'. *Studies in Medieval and Renaissance History*, 3rd series 5: 1–53.

———. 2009. 'Fear, Mainly in Old English'. In *The Kemble Lectures on Anglo-Saxon Studies 2005-2008*, ed. Jane Annette Roberts. Dublin: School of English, Trinity College. pp. 46–63.

———. 2011. 'Juliana Laid to Rest with Songs of Praise, and the Glories of Cynewulf's Poetic Art'. *Poetica* (Tokyo) 75: 83–101.

———. 2012. 'Idle Lustas'. *ES* 93: 509–18.

———. 2015. '*The Gifts of Men*: A Favourable Appraisal, with Some New Understandings'. *Anglia* 133: 330–77.

Stanton, Robert. 2002. *The Culture of Translation in Anglo-Saxon England*. Cambridge: D.S. Brewer.

Steen, Janie. 2008. *Verse and Virtuosity: The Adaptation of Latin Rhetoric in Old English Poetry*. Toronto: University of Toronto Press.

———. 2009. 'Translation or Transformation? Aldhelm's *Enigmata* and Exeter Book Riddles 35 and 40'. In *The World of Travellers: Exploration and Imagination*, ed. Kees Dekker, Karin E. Olsen and Tette Hofstra. Leuven: Peeters. pp. 133–45.

Stenton, Frank. 1971. *Anglo-Saxon England*. 3rd edn. Oxford: Clarendon.

Stephenson, Rebecca. 2010. 'Scapegoating the Secular Clergy: The Hermeneutic Style as a Form of Monastic Self-Definition'. *ASE* 38: 101–35.

Stevenson, William Henry, ed. 1904. *Asser's Life of King Alfred*. Oxford: Clarendon.

Swanton, Michael. 1964. '*The Wife's Lament* and *The Husband's Message*: A Reconsideration'. *Anglia* 82: 269–90.

Symons, Thomas, trans. 1953. *Regularis Concordia: The Monastic Agreement of the Monks and Nuns of the English Nation*. London: Nelson.

Talentino, Arnold V. 1978. 'Moral Irony in *The Ruin*'. *Papers on Language and Literature* 14: 3–10.

———. 1981. 'Riddle 30: The Vehicle of the Cross'. *Neophilologus* 65: 129–36.

Tamburr, Karl. 2007. *The Harrowing of Hell in Medieval England*. Cambridge: D.S. Brewer.

Tanke, John W. 1994. '*Wonfeax wale*: Ideology and Figuration in the Sexual Riddles of the Exeter Book'. In *Class and Gender in Early English Literature: Intersections*, ed. Britton J. Harwood and Gillian R. Overing. Bloomington: Indiana University Press. pp. 21–42.

Taylor, Andrew. 2002. *Textual Situations: Three Medieval Manuscripts and their Readers*. Philadelphia: University of Pennsylvania Press.
Thornbury, Emily V. 2014a. *Becoming a Poet in Anglo-Saxon England*. Cambridge: Cambridge University Press.
———. 2014b. 'Lyric Form, Subjectivity, and Consciousness'. In *A Companion to British Literature, Volume I: Medieval Literature 700-1450*, ed. Robert DeMaria, Jr., Heesok Chang and Samantha Zachar. Oxford: Wiley-Blackwell. pp. 30–47.
Thorpe, Benjamin. 1842. *Codex Exoniensis*. London: Society of Antiquaries of London.
Timmer, B.J. 1941. 'Wyrd in Anglo-Saxon Prose and Poetry'. *Neophilologus* 26 (1941): 24–33, 213–28.
Timofeeva, Olga. 2010. 'Anglo-Latin Bilingualism before 1066: Prospects and Limitations'. In *Interfaces Between Language and Culture in Medieval England: A Festschrift for Matti Kilpiö*, ed. Alaric Hall et al. Leiden: Brill. pp. 1–36.
Trahern, Joseph B., Jr. 1970-71. 'The *Ioca Monachorum* and the OE *Pharaoh*', *English Language Notes* 7: 165–68.
———. 1975. 'Caesarius, Chrodegang, and the Old English *Vainglory*'. In *Gesellschaft, Kultur, Literatur: Rezeption und Originalität im Wachsen einer europäischen Literatur und Geistigkeit*, ed. Karl Bosl. Stuttgart: Anton Hiersemann. pp. 167–78.
Treharne, Elaine. 2009. 'The Exeter Book'. In *Working with Manuscripts*, ed. Gale R. Owen-Crocker. Exeter: University of Exeter Press. pp. 99–101.
Trilling, Renée R. 2009a. *The Aesthetics of Nostalgia: Historical Representation in Old English Verse*. Toronto: University of Toronto Press.
———. 2009b. 'Ruins in the Realm of Thoughts: Reading as Constellation in Anglo-Saxon Poetry'. *JEGP* 108: 141–67.
Tupper, Frederick, Jr., ed. 1910. *The Riddles of the Exeter Book*. Boston, MA: Ginn.
Tyler, Elizabeth M. 2006. *Old English Poetics: The Aesthetics of the Familiar in Anglo-Saxon England*. York: York Medieval Press.
———. 2016. 'German Imperial Bishops and Anglo-Saxon Literary Culture on the Eve of the Conquest: *The Cambridge Songs* and Leofric's Exeter Book'. In *Latinity and Identity in Anglo-Saxon Literature*, ed. Rebecca Stephenson and Emily V. Thornbury. Toronto: University of Toronto Press. pp. 177–201.
Venarde, Bruce L., ed. and trans. 2011. *The Rule of Saint Benedict*. DOML 6. Cambridge, MA: Harvard University Press.
Wardale, E.E. 1935. *Chapters on Old English Literature*. London: K. Paul.
Wehlau, Ruth. 1994. 'Rumination and Re-Creation: Poetic Instruction in *The Order of the World*'. *Florilegium* 13: 65–77.
Weiskott, Eric. 2015. 'The Meter of *Widsith* and the Distant Past'. *Neophilologus* 99: 143–50.
Wentersdorf, Karl P. 1977. 'Observations on *The Ruin*'. *Medium Ævum* 46: 171–80.
———. 1981. 'The Situation of the Narrator in the Old English *Wife's Lament*'. *Speculum* 56: 492–516. Repr. in O'Brien O'Keeffe 1994, pp. 357–92.
———. 1985. 'The Old English *Rhyming Poem*: A Ruler's Lament'. *Studies in Philology* 82: 265–94.
Weston, Lisa. 2012. 'Saintly Lives: Friendship, Kinship, Gender and Sexuality'. In *The Cambridge History of Early Medieval English Literature*, ed. Clare A. Lees. Cambridge: Cambridge University Press. pp. 381–405.

Whitelock, Dorothy. 1950. 'The Interpretation of *The Seafarer*'. In *The Early Cultures of Northwest Europe*, ed. Cyril Fox and Bruce Dickins. Cambridge: Cambridge University Press. pp. 198–211.

———. 1951. *The Audience of Beowulf*. Oxford: Clarendon.

———. 1952. *The Beginnings of English Society*. Harmondsworth: Penguin. With subsequent reprinted editions incorporating minor revisions.

———, ed. 1979. *English Historical Documents, Volume 1: c.500–1042*. 2nd edn. London: Eyre Methuen.

———, ed. 1981. *Councils and Synods, with Other Documents Relating to the English Church, Volume 1: AD 871–1204*. Oxford: Clarendon.

Wieland, Gernot Rudolf. 2011. 'Bilingual Education in Anglo-Saxon England: Alfred to Æthelweard'. In *Mehrsprachigkeit im Mittelalter*, ed. Michael Baldzuhn and Christine Putzo. Berlin: de Gruyter. pp. 35–57.

Wilcox, Jonathan. 2005. '"Tell Me What I Am": The Old English Riddles'. In *Readings in Medieval Texts: Interpreting Old and Middle English Literature*, ed. David F. Johnson and Elaine Treharne. Oxford: Oxford University Press. pp. 46–59.

———. 2006. 'The Audience of Ælfric's *Lives of Saints* and the Face of Cotton Caligua A.xiv, fols. 93–130'. In *Beatus Vir: Studies in Early English and Norse Manuscripts in Memory of Phillip Pulsiano*, ed. A.N. Doane and Kirsten Wolf. Tempe: ACMRS. pp. 228–63.

Williams, Raymond. 1976. *Keywords: A Vocabulary of Culture and Society*. London: Fontana. 2nd edn, 1983. New edn with introduction by Colin MacCabe, 2015.

Williamson, Craig, ed. 1977. *The Old English Riddles of the Exeter Book*. Chapel Hill: University of North Carolina Press.

Winterbottom, Michael and Michael Lapidge, ed. and trans. 2012. *The Early Lives of St Dunstan*. Oxford: Clarendon.

Woolf, Rosemary. 1975. '*The Wanderer*, *The Seafarer*, and the Genre of *Planctus*'. In *Anglo-Saxon Poetry: Essays in Appreciation for John C. McGalliard*, ed. Lewis E. Nicholson and Dolores Warwick Frese. Notre Dame: University of Notre Dame Press. pp. 192–207.

Wormald, Patrick (C.P. Wormald). 1977. 'The Uses of Literacy in Anglo-Saxon England and its Neighbours'. *Transactions of the Royal Historical Society*, 5th series 27: 95–114.

———. 1978. 'Bede, *Beowulf* and the Conversion of the Anglo-Saxon Aristocracy'. In *Bede and Anglo-Saxon England*, ed. Robert T. Farrell. British Archaeological Reports 46. Oxford: BAR. 32–95. Repr. with addenda in *The Times of Bede*, ed. Patrick Wormald and Stephen Baxter. Oxford: Blackwell, 2006. pp. 30–105.

Wright, Charles D., Frederick M. Biggs and Thomas N. Hall, ed. 2007. *Source of Wisdom: Old English and Early Medieval Latin Studies in Honour of Thomas D. Hill*. Toronto: University of Toronto Press.

Zimmermann, Gunhild. 1995. *The Four Old English Poetic Manuscripts*. Heidelberg: Carl Winter.

Ziolkowski, Jan M. 1994. *The Cambridge Songs (Carmina Cantabrigiensia)*. New York: Garland.

Znojemská, Helena. 2005. 'Sailing the Dangerous Waters: Images of Land and Sea in *The Seafarer*, *The Panther* and *The Whale*'. *Prague Studies in English* 24: 87–105.

Index of Modern Authors Cited

Authors are cited here only when substantive reference to their work is made in the present pages. Incidental references are generally disregarded, as are routine references to printed editions.

Abraham, Lenore 42
Abram, Christopher 156 n. 19
Abrams, Leslie 16 n. 24
Adair, Anya 22–23
Alexander, Michael 172 n. 21
Anderson, Earl R. 193 n. 32
Anderson, James E. 139 n. 162
Anlezark, Daniel 60–61, 180 n. 1
Ashurst, David 224
Atherton, Mark 60

Bahr, Arthur 57 n. 53
Barrow, Julia 44
Baum, Paull F. 172 n. 19, 175
Beechy, Tiffany 145
Bitterli, Dieter 25 n. 11, 107, 146 n. 3, 166
Bjork, Robert E. 83, 84 n. 36, 105 n. 88, 112 n. 106, 131, 133 n. 149, 218, 232 n. 21
Blair, John 194 n. 33
Blake, N.F. 65, 89 n. 49
Bleeth, Kenneth A. 227 n. 8
Bloomfield, Morton 77 n. 21
Bonner, Joshua 160 n. 30
Boryslawski, Rafal 33, 164–65, 189 n. 16, 224
Bradley, S.A.J. viii, 26, 29 n. 22, 66–67, 83, 97, 129, 134 n. 152, 166, 169 n. 14, 189, 222
Brady, Lindy 122 n. 125
Bragg, Lois 95 n. 65
Bredehoft, Thomas 186 n. 9
Brooks, Nicholas 55 n. 42, 196
Brown, George Hardin 28 n. 18
Brown, Michelle P. 21, 26 n. 15, 58 n. 56, 108 n. 94
Budny, Mildred 56 n. 49, 57
Bullough, Donald 45

Burlin, Robert B. 232
Busby, Keith 231
Butler, Robert M. 52–54, 59

Caie, Graham D. 83 n. 33
Calder, Daniel G. 86, 96 n. 66, 191 n. 25
Campbell, Jackson J. 53, 159–60
Cavill, Paul 103 n. 84
Chase, Colin 72 n. 10, 80 n. 29
Clayton, Mary 66, 76 n. 20, 77, 176 n. 28, 198
Conner, Patrick W. vii, 27 n. 17, 29 n. 23, 42, 49–52, 70, 81, 88, 94 n. 61, 127 n. 142, 186, 195–96, 244
Cook, Albert S. 78 n. 24, 81 n. 30
Cross, James 48, 161 n. 33

Dailey, Patricia 202 nn. 47–48
Damon, John 9 n. 9, 222 n. 48
Davis, Kathleen 200–03
Deangelo, Jeremy 137 n. 158
DeGregorio, Scott 135 n. 154
Deshman, Robert 44 n. 15
Deskis, Susan 177 n. 33
Dewa, Roberta 3 n. 2, 29 n. 20, 146 n. 3
Di Sciacca, Claudia 71 n. 9
DiNapoli, Robert 108, 146 n. 3
Doubleday, James 188 n. 14, 227 n. 9
Drout, Michael D.C. 38 n. 43, 42, 52, 98 (with n. 74)

Earl, James W. 111 n. 104, 154
Esser-Miles, Carolin 136 n. 156
Evans-Pritchard, Edward 204

Fell, Christine 100 nn. 78–79, 146 n. 3, 162 n. 37

Index of Modern Authors Cited

Flower, Robin   32, 186
Foot, Sarah   7–8 n. 7, 26 n. 16
Frank, Roberta   43
Frankis, P.J.   124 n. 128, 189 n. 19
Frantzen, Allen J.   133 (with n. 150), 145 n. 1, 205 n. 3
Frederick, Jill   133 n. 149
Frese, Dolores Warwick   80 n. 29
Fry, Donald K.   128
Fulk, R.D., and Christopher Cain   38, 65, 77 n. 21, 96 n. 66, 126, 233 n. 25

Gameson, Fiona and Richard   70
Gameson, Richard   49
Garner, Lori   202 n. 48, 226 n. 6
Gatch, Milton McC.   48, 160, 197 n. 40
Gleissner, Reinhard   171 n. 17, 174 n. 25
Gordon, Ida   60 n. 67
Green, D.H.   86 n. 41
Green, Eugene   97 n. 72
Green, Martin   188
Greenfield, Stanley B.   94 n. 62, 96 n. 66, 162 n. 37, 226 n. 6
   and Daniel G. Calder   77 n. 22, 96 n. 66, 191 n. 25
Gretsch, Mechthild   40 n. 3, 56
Grosz, Oliver J.H.   112
Gurevich, Aron   206 n. 5

Hall, Alaric   85, 237
Hall, Thomas N.   141 n. 164
Hanna, Ralph   231 n. 18
Hansen, Elaine Tuttle   30, 111 n. 103
Heighway, Carolyn M.   91 n. 52
Hermann, John P.   12 (with n. 14)
Hill, John   16 n. 22
Hill, Joyce   12 n. 14, 17, 49 n. 26, 56, 119 n. 117, 243
Hill, Thomas D.   57 n. 52, 232 n. 22
Howe, Nicholas   25 n. 10, 36 n. 38, 96 n. 67, 97 n. 70, 102 n. 83, 191 n. 24, 219
Howlett, David   142 n. 166
Hume, Kathryn   188 n. 15
Huppé, Bernard H.   31, 71, 72, 99, 107 n. 92, 108, 116 n. 113, 121, 191
Hussey, Matthew   3, 42

Ireland, Colin   60 n. 68
Irvine, Martin   47 n. 20, 164
Irving, Edward B.   78 n. 22, 157 n. 24, 166–67

Jacobs, Christina   25 n. 12, 47 n. 20

Johnson, David F.   86 n. 39
Jones, Christopher A.   41 n. 5, 58 n. 58, 198
Jurasinski, Stefan   101

Kendall, Calvin B.   157
Keynes, Simon   43 (with n. 11)
Klein, Stacy S.   94 n. 62, 124 n. 132
Klinck, Anne   65, 96 n. 66, 122 n. 125, 122 n. 126, 126, 142 n. 166, 170 n. 16, 178 n. 35, 224, 235 n. 30
Knowles, David   40 n. 3, 243–44
Kramer, Johanna   226 n. 6, 232

Laistner, M.L.W.   46 n. 19
Langenfelt, Gösta   14 n. 18, 119 n. 118, 126 n. 140
Lapidge, Michael   18–19 (with n. 30), 40 (with n. 3), 45, 46, 48–49, 50 n. 29, 55 (with n. 44), 56, 91 n. 53, 119, 164, 186, 196, 234 n. 29
Leahy, Kevin   25
Lee, Alvin A.   107, 235 n. 32
Lee, Anne   188 n. 14
Lehmann, Ruth P.M.   126 n. 139
Lehmberg, Stanford   28
Lendinara, Patrizia   34–35, 45, 68–69, 73, 164 n. 1
Lerer, Seth   47
Leslie, Roy F.   60 n. 66, 191, 209
Liuzza, Roy M.   37 n. 41, 45, 66, 72 n. 10, 75 n. 17, 138, 188
Lockett, Leslie   164 n. 1

Machan, Tim William   231
Macrae-Gibson, O.D.   154 n. 16
Magennis, Hugh   8, 12 n. 13, 16, 31 n. 28, 89 n. 48, 119, 123–24 n. 127, 126, 158 n. 27, 162, 175 n. 26, 176 n. 27, 186 n. 9, 189 n. 18
Mann, Jill   69 n. 6
Maring, Heather   5 n. 5, 19 n. 33, 101
Matthews, Stephen   191 n. 26
McCormack, Frances   66, 135 n. 154
McEntyre, Sandra   97 n. 71
Moffat, Douglas   137 n. 159
Muir, Bernard J.   vii, 26 n. 14, 37, 48 n. 23, 53, 65, 70, 73 n. 11, 76 n. 20, 89, 95, 96, 137, 153, 154, 160 n. 31, 167, 174 n. 25, 191 n. 23, 232, 237
Murphy, Patrick   171 n. 17, 173 n. 23, 175

Neidorf, Leonard   119 n. 118
Nelson, Marie   160–61, 235 n. 31

Neville, Jennifer   172 nn. 21–22, 212 n. 25

O'Brien O'Keeffe, Katherine   13 n. 17, 15 (with n. 20), 58 n. 56, 165, 193 n. 32
O'Camb, Brian   ix, 4 (with n. 4), 42, 72 n. 10, 104 n. 86, 106 n. 89
Orchard, Andy   156 nn. 19–20, 165, 175, 197 n. 40, 225 n. 3, 232 n. 21
Orme, Nicholas   23 n. 6, 26 n. 15, 49 n. 25, 59 n. 64, 194 n. 34
Orton, Peter   23 n. 5, 38 n. 42, 60 n. 68, 146 n. 3

Page, R.I.   35, 146 (with n. 3), 152 n. 11
Parkes, M.B.   32 n. 33, 36 n. 38
Pasternack, Carol Braun   95

Rambaran-Olm, M.R.   73 n. 12, 74 n. 13
Rankin, Susan   78 n. 24
Raw, Barbara   58 n. 56
Regan, Catharine A.   114–15
Reichl, Karl   231
Renoir, Alain   188 n. 13
Reynolds, Robert L., and Robert S. Lopez   125–26 (with n. 138)
Richman, Gerald   95 n. 65
Riedinger, Anita R.   219 n. 42
Riyeff, Jacob   108 n. 97, 230 n. 17
Roberts, Jane   32 (with n. 32), 85, 115
Robinson, Fred C.   93–94 n. 59, 209 n. 19, 231
Ruggerini, Maria Elena   140 n. 163
Rumble, Alexander   13, 52

Salvador Bello, Mercedes   42, 43 n. 10, 71 (with n. 9), 165 n. 5, 171 n. 17, 175, 226 n. 6
Sánchez de Nieva, María José   42
Savage, Ann   182 n. 3
Schaefer, Ursula   94 n. 62
Schneider, Claude   92 n. 57
Scragg, Donald   26–27 n. 16, 49 n. 26, 67, 234
Shippey, Thomas   32 n. 30, 77 n. 21, 95–96 n. 65, 98 n. 74, 153 n. 14, 223–24 (with n. 1), 238 n. 34

Shook, Lawrence   167
Sisam, Kenneth   65, 75 n. 16
Smithers, G.V.   59, 98, 233
Squires, Ann   137
Stanley, E.G.   57 n. 53, 73 n. 11, 96, 107 n. 92, 199–200 (with n. 44), 207 n. 8
Stanton, Robert   182 n. 3
Steen, Janie   161, 197 n. 40
Stephenson, Rebecca   194 n. 35
Swanton, Michael   169–70 n. 14
Symons, Thomas   113

Talentino, Arnold V.   74 n. 15, 189
Tamburr, Karl   81
Tanke, John W.   171 n. 17, 172 n. 21, 174 n. 25
Taylor, Andrew   231 n. 20
Thornbury, Emily V.   5 n. 5, 18, 22–23, 106 n. 90
Trahern, Joseph B.   30 n. 26, 115 n. 112
Treharne, Elaine   32, 66
Trilling, Renée R.   201–03
Tupper, Frederick   121 n. 123, 134 n. 151, 165 n. 4
Tyler, Elizabeth M.   48, 49 n. 26, 55 n. 44, 145 n. 1

Wardale, E.E.   200
Wehlau, Ruth   182
Weiskott, Eric   119 n. 118
Wentersdorf, Karl P.   110 n. 102, 188 n. 14, 237 n. 36
Weston, Lisa   12 n. 13
Whitelock, Dorothy   60 n. 68, 86 n. 40, 98, 124 n. 131, 125, 193 n. 31, 211, 240 n. 1
Wieland, Gernot   45, 55
Williamson, Craig   146 n. 3, 150 n. 8, 157 n. 23, 172 n. 21
Winterbottom, Michael, and Michael Lapidge   55 n. 41, 196
Woolf, Rosemary   94 n. 61
Wormald, Patrick   14 n. 18, 43

Zimmermann, Gunhild   41–42 n. 6
Znojemská, Helena   212 n. 24

Index of Old English Words Discussed

ān-haga 'lone-dweller'   94–95 (with n. 63), 130

beorn 'man', 'man of heroic stature'   213–14, 215–16
blǣd 'fame', 'glory'   162, 184
bōt 'redress', 'deliverance'   206, 214–15 (with n. 31), 216 (with n. 33), 242

cræft 'skill', 'art'   24–25

dōm 'fame', 'glory' or 'salvation'   128–29, 184, 198, 217–18 (with n. 39)
  dōm-hwæte 'those eager for salvation'   78
dōn 'to place'   50 n. 31
  gedōn 'put, placed'   50, 51–52
drēam 'joy'   162, 208, 219 n. 43
  drēamas 'joys'   138, 193, 242
  wuldres drēam 'joy of salvation'   116
dryhten 'lord', 'the Lord'   19, 207, 212
  ēce dryhten 'the eternal Lord'   216
duguþ 'band of retainers'   162

ēalā! 'ah!', 'alas!'   76–77, 95, 141
ēðel 'homeland'   78, 79, 131, 141, 219, 233
egsa 'fear', 'terror'   57 n. 53, 58, 59, 208–09, 242
ellen 'courage', 'zeal'   9, 75 n. 17, 132, 206, 212, 213, 219 n. 43, 242
  on elne, mid elne 'fearlessly'   9, 31, 213–14 (with n. 29), 215
eorl 'man', 'nobleman'   214, 215–16

fæstnung 'stability'   228
frōfor 'comfort', 'grace'   208, 216

gedryht   16 n. 23
gerȳne 'mystery'   79
  gǣst-gerȳne 'spiritual mysteries'   112
  gerȳnu 'mysteries'   86

word-gerȳno 'verbal enigmas'   166–67
giedd (*gydd*) 'song', 'speech in a heightened register'   25, 224, 235

hād 'rank', 'type' or 'vocation'   110, 193 (with n. 31), 195
  hādas 'ranks', 'types'   25, 193, 194, 238
hām 'home'   31, 206, 218–21
here-spel 'war song'   107–08
herh 'pagan sanctuary'   237
hūsel-weras 'men of the sacrament'   221–22
hyht 'hope', 'joy'   208–09, 212, 219 (with n. 43), 220

lof 'praiseworthy deeds' or 'glory'   99 (with n. 76), 128, 162, 198, 225

mynster 'monastery', 'church'   195

scop 'poet'   16, 24, 25, 118
sīþ 'journey', 'experience'   79, 87, 131, 206, 210–12 (with n. 20), 219 n. 43, 235–36, 242
  gesīþas 'companions (on a journey)'   31
  hin-sīþ 'journey forth', 'death'   140
  wil-sīþ '"longed-for journey'   79
  wræc-sīþ 'exile-journey'   233
sōþ 'truth'   184
  sōþ-fæst 'righteous'   11, 133, 134, 217, 219, 220, 240 n. 1, 242

trēow 'tree', 'wood', 'rood', 'faith'   74–75, 139, 213, 215

weall-stān 'foundation stone'   226, 229 (with n. 14), 242
winelēas wræcca 'friendless outcast'   235, 242
wlonc ond wīn-gāl 'arrogant and wanton with wine'   189, 202, 225, 242

wōð-bora 'visionary poet'   16, 107, 117, 132
   wōð-cræft 'art of lofty song'   24
wōma 'howl'   226–27
wyrd 'fate'   207–08

þegn, þegnas 'servant, servants'   89 (with
   n. 48), 196–97
þēow, þēowas 'servant, servants'   88–89
   (with n. 48)

General Index

Advent Lyrics 5 n. 5, 19, 37, 44, 53, 65, 69, 73, 76–79, 82, 95, 108, 141, 167 nn. 9 and 10, 176, 181, 191 n. 23, 199, 230, 231
   authorship (probably monastic) 22–23
   sources 53, 78, 232
   Advent Lyric 1 24, 229–30
   Advent Lyric 2 78, 141
   Advent Lyric 3 187–88, 190
   Advent Lyric 4 134, 176
   Advent Lyric 5 81, 87, 108
   Advent Lyric 6 216
   Advent Lyric 7 134, 140
   Advent Lyric 9 134
   Advent Lyric 10 216
   Advent Lyric 11 134, 244
   Advent Lyric 12 78, 141
Ælfric (homilist) 12 n. 13, 185, 198, 208, 228
   his alliterative style 185–86 (with n. 9)
   his broad audience 186 (with n. 10)
   his *Colloquy* 25, 193
   his *Grammar* 69
Æthelwold (bishop) 13, 14, 44, 56, 185, 230.
   See also Rule of Saint Benedict
Aldhelm (bishop) 18–19 (with n. 30), 156
   his *De virginitate* 12, 17, 108, 177, 178
   his *Enigmata* 119, 142, 161, 164, 165–66, 168 n. 12, 175, 183–84, 234
   and the school curriculum 46
Aldhelm (poem) 162
Alfred the Great 18, 40, 60, 238
amplificatio 'the art of expansion' 19, 88, 180–84, 198–99
   as engine of monastic poetics 182
Anglo-Saxon social history 10, 125
   agonistic tenor of life 17 (with n. 25)
   impact of Norman Conquest 243
   impact of Viking wars 243–44
   people of high rank 'opting out' 13–14
   social change as trauma 201
   See also Benedictine Reform; Edgar the Peaceable; literacy; monasticism (Anglo-Saxon)
Ascension 29, 45, 58, 71, 74, 75, 79–83, 102, 112, 117, 118, 134, 146, 194, 224
   allegorical dimension 136, 197
   chief sources 197, 225–26
   a compendium of doctrine 79–80
   intratextual elements 80–83
Augustine (saint) 71
   De civitate Dei 191, 192

Babylon 115 (with n. 112), 189, 191
Battle of Maldon 9, 243
Bede: his poem *Judgement Day II* 135 n. 152, 139–40
   his treatise *De schematibus et tropis* 159
Benedictine Reform 13, 27, 40–45, 54, 61, 114, 195–96, 209
   its alliance of church and state 42–44
   its hieratic iconography 44, 114
Benedictine Rule. *See* Rule of Saint Benedict
Beowulf 6, 9 (with n. 10), 93, 130, 147 n. 6, 159, 208, 209, 213, 214 (with n. 29), 240
   fate of the hero's soul 217
   manuscript 3 n. 1, 41
bilingualism (Anglo-Saxon) 7, 17–18 n. 28, 27, 32, 38, 41–47, 61, 162, 239
   bilingual education 7, 13, 34, 45–46, 48–49, 56, 162, 242
   bilingual textual production 5 n. 6, 40, 56, 61, 194, 242–43
Blickling homilies 233
Boethius 112
   Old English Boethius 41–42 n. 6, 47, 115 (with n. 110), 120, 192
Byrhtferth of Ramsay 194

Cædmon 6, 46, 238

Caesarius of Arles   115 n. 112
Cain   17 n. 25, 115 (with n. 111), 178 (with n. 36), 192
Cambridge Songs   35, 47–48
Canticles of the Three Youths   6, 17 n. 28, 87–89, 93, 189
Cassiodorus   107–08 (with n. 94)
catalogue poems   96 (with n. 67), 100
Cathach of Columcille   21 (with n. 2)
Celestial Jerusalem   78, 91 (with n. 52), 187–88, 190, 229, 230
Christ   12–13, 53–54, 57, 78–82, 99, 103, 111, 124, 136, 137, 157, 197, 216, 219, 221–22, 237
  as cornerstone of the faith   45, 77–79, 201, 227
  his Harrowing of Hell   81, 95, 140
  his Incarnation   73, 74, 75, 77–78, 79, 95, 141
  his 'leaps'   79, 81, 112, 134
  as the light that illumines all light   78, 107, 108–09
  in Majesty   44, 74, 83–84, 134, 138
  as Master Builder   24, 188 n. 12, 229, 230
  his Resurrection   73–74, 75–76
  as the true sun   87, 90
Christ in Judgement   45, 54, 58, 75, 79, 118, 138, 139
Christ's Descent into Hell   81, 82, 140, 141
Christ's Pledge of Grace   80, 137
Christian exegesis   48, 74, 82, 89, 112 (with n. 106), 136–37, 161, 186–87, 197
Columba (saint)   21
Contrition   73 (with n. 11), 140. *See also* *Penitent's Prayer*
Coronation of Edgar   42–43
craft-poets (Anglo-Saxon)   22–26, 106, 138–39, 161, 205, 240–41
  contrasted with the *scop*   25
  and Latin verse   23, 26
  and native tradition   23
crafts (Anglo-Saxon)   25 (with nn. 10–11), 97
criticism (literary)   31, 171–76, 191, 236–37
  codicologically-based   231, 234
  search for Anglo-Saxon paganism   199–200
  secular in orientation   10, 93–94 (with n. 59), 200–03
  See also Christian exegesis
cryptography   145–52. *See also* runes
Cynewulf (the poet)   18, 26, 29, 81, 82–83, 84 n. 36, 86, 161, 220, 240–41
  his runic signatures   6, 29 (with n. 22), 38 n. 42, 151–52
  his self-presentation as a monk   241
  See also Ascension; *Fates of the Apostles*; *Passion of Saint Juliana*

David (the psalmist)   109, 111, 176
Deor (the poet)   16, 129, 132, 136
Deor   118–21, 127, 129, 153, 178, 201, 202–03, 236, 241
  paired with *Widsith*   118, 141
  use of refrain   153
devil, devils   11, 97, 99, 108, 115, 135, 227
  assault on Guthlac   85 n. 37, 194–96
  repulsed by Juliana   92, 133, 211
  and *The Whale*   136–37
Disticha Catonis   69
Doomsday (the Apocalypse)   158
Doomsday   58, 59, 82, 89, 158, 209
Dream of the Rood   6, 23, 75, 84 (with n. 35), 219, 222
Dunstan (saint)   25, 55–56, 59, 61, 165, 185, 196, 232, 240, 245
  and the hermeneutic style   55

Eadui Psalter   58, 114
Earendel (the light of Christ)   81, 87, 108
Edgar the Peaceable (king)   44, 54
  as patron of the Reform   42–43
elegy, elegies   93 n. 59, 94 n. 62, 96 (with n. 66), 100 n. 78, 186, 191, 192, 200, 224
  elegiac   48, 77, 93 n. 59, 233
  as a genre term   96 (with n. 66)
ethopoeia   99–100, 130–35, 170, 193, 233
  likened to drama   134
  likened to prosopopoeia   100, 133–34
Exeter Anthology
  audience or readership   4, 10, 14, 19–20, 28, 37, 80, 103, 181–82, 185–87, 239
  bilingual   17 n. 28, 38, 239
  constructed by the texts   30–31
  learned   29 (with n. 20), 33–34, 133 n. 150, 141 n. 164, 144, 163, 186–87, 199, 239
  potentially diverse   35, 39, 238
  readers, not just listeners   27–30, 37–38 (with n. 42)
  as a textual community   31, 35–36, 38, 104, 144
  character as a miscellany   vii, 32, 33, 52, 65–67, 68–69, 71, 121, 136, 143–44, 165, 170, 194, 222, 231–32

General Index 283

encyclopedia-like   71, 143
intellectually challenging   3, 55, 61,
   72, 73, 99, 147-52, 157, 167
like a microcosm   130, 135, 143, 176
participatory   30, 103, 104-06, 117,
   183
Christian character   4-13, 20, 31, 33-34,
   53, 65, 79-118, 128-41, 143-45,
   198, 206
   Augustinian perspective   72, 109-10,
      121, 138, 188-89, 191
   Christological focus   78-79
   didacticism   10, 33-34, 47, 102, 179
   freedom from ecclesiastical
      infighting   41, 193-99
   homiletic cast   10, 31, 137, 139-40,
      233
   humour not excluded   168-69,
      171-72
   liturgical elements   5, 53, 73-74
      (with n. 13), 77-78 (with n. 24),
      80, 88, 140 (with n. 163), 141,
      168, 182-83
   monastic affinities   4-5, 9, 10-12, 21,
      22-23, 27, 28, 31, 38, 42, 59, 61,
      75 n. 17, 85, 89, 91, 97-98 (with
      nn. 70 and 74), 101-02, 111,
      114, 144, 163, 178, 179, 184-85,
      194-97, 198, 220-22, 233 n. 25
   penitential tenor   60, 73, 82, 93, 98,
      140, 159, 211-12, 214-15, 216,
      236
   pessimistic view   48 n. 23, 113, 128,
      192, 193, 201, 202-03
composition
   overlapping roles of scribe, compiler,
      and poet   26-27, 66, 72, 82-83
   questions as to date   vii-viii, 61, 83,
      119 (with n. 118), 200, 205
functions (postulated)
   acculturation   13-14, 20, 34, 42, 185
   contemplation   4, 31, 39, 107, 165,
      187
   conversion   5, 38, 84, 206, 239
   education   10, 15, 34-35, 38 (with
      n. 43), 47-48, 68-69, 72-73, 136,
      164, 179, 239, 242-43
   as offering models for poets   18,
      19-20, 34, 39, 46, 72-73, 132,
      159, 161, 163, 234
genres represented   94 (with n. 61),
   251-53
   excidium urbis   143, 156, 188

   paraphrasis   86, 91, 181, 251, 252,
      253
   planctus   94, 252, 253
   See also catalogue poems; elegy;
      Exeter enigmas; saints' lives;
      wisdom literature
imagery
   architectural   190-91, 226-31
   avian   58, 80, 90-91, 112, 132, 135,
      137, 147-48 n. 6, 157, 196, 219,
      244-45 (with n. 6)
   of light and the sun   81, 87, 89-90,
      107, 108-09, 242
   seafaring   60, 82, 136, 137, 177, 197,
      210, 225-26, 235
   of storms   91, 92, 225, 226-27,
      230-31, 242
   of walls and stones   44-45, 78,
      200-01, 226-31, 242
organization
   coherence   3-4, 10-11, 65-76,
      117-18, 139 n. 162, 143-44,
      187-88, 199, 222, 231-32, 238,
      241-42
   diversity within unity   3, 65, 68,
      129-30, 133, 135-36, 135-36,
      143, 151, 217, 231, 241
   hierarchical tendencies   71, 176,
      187, 199
   and the liturgical year   73-74, 139
   pairing   99, 118-19, 140, 169-71,
      187-88, 226, 231-32 (with
      n. 21), 234-37, 241
   trebling   132-33, 241
place of origin
   Exeter itself unlikely   49-52
   Glastonbury a possibility   52-57,
      60-61
   in a Reformed setting   42-45, 61,
      114, 238
sources, influences and analogues
   from Ireland and Wales   59-61, 154
   in the Latinate tradition   9, 48 (with
      n. 23), 72, 78, 85, 88-90, 136,
      137, 139-40, 181-82, 198, 227
      n. 8, 232, 238, 251-53
   in Rule of Saint Benedict   97-98,
      100-01, 103, 111, 114, 158 n. 26,
      184, 196-97, 230-31
   in Scripture. *See* David; Gospels;
      Isaiah; Job; psalms; Solomon
   in vernacular tradition   6, 29, 42, 47,
      60-61, 84 n. 35, 87-88, 115 with

n. 110, 146, 151-52, 183-84,
192, 219, 222, 230-31, 233, 241
style   4-5, 15, 19, 25, 33, 55, 77, 109, 140,
145, 153-54, 156, 161, 181
  hermeneutic qualities   61, 154,
155-56
  heroic diction   9, 128-29, 162, 185,
198, 213-14, 215-16, 240
  hybrid poetics (Latinate and native)
155, 161, 181-82
  pleonism   19, 89-90, 181
  technical adventurism   15, 147,
152-56, 161
  See also *amplificatio*; cryptography;
ethopoeia; paronomasia;
rhetorical figures; rhetorical
tropes
themes (leading ones)
  assaults of fiends   81-82, 91-92,
194-95, 208, 227
  celibacy or chastity   91, 102, 176-77
  conversion   38, 84-85, 101, 109-10,
117, 192, 198-99, 206, 218, 241
  damnation   99, 137-38, 158, 225
  dangers of drink   97, 101, 127, 138,
157-59, 242
  death   84, 86-87, 100, 102, 105, 110,
128, 132, 154-55, 211-12
  Doomsday   79, 82, 83-84, 89, 113,
139-40, 188
  exile   vi-vii, 8, 98-99, 132, 141, 143,
197, 199, 218-19 (with n. 41),
233
  fear of God   57-59, 105, 116, 140,
208-09, 242
  God's gifts to humankind   15-16,
80-81, 96-97, 130, 166-67, 194
  heaven as true home   78-79, 98, 116,
162, 212, 218-22
  journey of the soul after death   8,
31, 79, 87, 131, 136, 155, 158,
210-12, 225, 235
  joys of the hall   109-10
  joys of heaven   78, 116, 162, 208,
212, 219
  marriage and sexuality   122-25, 133,
168-69, 171-78, 179, 210, 236,
241
  mutability   100, 109-10, 113, 117,
128, 131, 143, 188-89, 191-92,
201, 217
  physical dismemberment   101-02,
110

salvation   8, 10, 31, 33, 37, 77, 78, 86,
89, 94, 99, 102, 107, 111, 116-17,
128-29, 135, 137, 185, 197, 216,
219-22
titles of individual poems (problem
cases)
  Canticles of the Three Youths   88 n. 46
  Christ's Descent into Hell   73-74 n. 12
  *Contrition, Resignation, The Penitent's
Prayer*   73 n. 11
  Riddle 30: The Tree   139
  Riddle 60: The Reed   141-42
  Wonder of Creation   107 n. 92
women's voices   94 n. 62, 132-33,
170-71. See also *Passion of Saint
Juliana; Wife's Lament; Wulf and
Eadwacer*
Exeter Cathedral   23 (with n. 6), 49-52, 194
n. 34
Exeter codex (Cathedral Library, MS 3501)
  beauty overall   3-4, 21, 32
  bilingual scribe   27 (with n. 17), 52-53
  booklet theory   70-71
  date of hand   vii, 32 n. 32
  mise en page   xiv-xv (Fig. 2), 37
  punctuation   xiv-xv (Fig. 2), 76 n. 19
  quality of hand   xiv-xv (Fig. 2), 21, 32
  state of preservation   35, 69-70 (with
n. 7)
Exeter enigmas   25, 29 n. 20, 30, 37, 38
n. 42, 47, 72-73, 134 (with n. 151),
138-39, 146-51, 152, 157-58, 164-79,
224, 244
  encyclopedic scope   71, 164-65
  and Latin riddle collections   119,
165-66, 170, 175
  place in a poetic miscellany   68, 164-66,
179
  religious perspective   157, 164-65, 168,
179
  resource for study of rhetoric   73, 163,
164
  riddles of daily life   168, 176-78
  riddles relating to the liturgy   168
  riddles of the scriptorium   167-68
  riddles with a sexual dimension
168-69, 171-76, 179
  Riddle 7 (wild swan)   157, 187
  Riddle 11 (cup of wine)   157-58
  Riddle 12 (ox and leather objects)
172-75
  Riddle 19 (*snacc* 'ship')   146-47, 152
  Riddle 20 ('sword')   172

General Index 285

Riddle 23 (*boga* 'bow')   148
Riddle 24 (*higera* 'magpie')   148
Riddle 27 (*medu* 'mead')   157
Riddle 28 (ale)   158
Riddle 28 (*bere ond ealu* 'barley and ale')   155
Riddle 30 (*trēow* 'tree')   74–75, 139, 142
Riddle 35 ('Lorica')   161, 183–84, 234
Riddle 40 (the Creation)   165
Riddle 42 (*hana ond henn* 'cock and hen')   148, 168–69
Riddle 46 (Lot and daughters)   158, 171
Riddle 51 (*feðer* 'quill pen')   156–57
Riddle 58 ('well sweep')   149
Riddle 60 (*hrēod* 'reed')   38 n. 42, 65–66, 141–42
Riddle 64 (*brim-hengest* 'sea-steed')   149–50
Riddle 75 (*hund ond hind* 'hound and hind')   150–51
Riddle 89   17 n. 28
Exeter Maxims   30, 102–06, 177 n. 33, 241
and the order of the world   103–04
and Rule of Saint Benedict   42 (with n. 8), 98, 103
verbal parallels with other poems   105–06
Maxims A   103, 105–06, 177
Maxims B   103–04, 105–06, 177
Maxims C   17 n. 25, 75, 104, 106, 178 n. 36

Fates of the Apostles   29, 31
Father's Precepts   30 n. 24, 33, 87, 97–98, 113–14, 115, 117, 158, 215
and Rule of Saint Benedict   97–98 (with nn. 73–74)
Felix's *Vita Guthlaci*   86 (with n. 40), 129, 158
Fortunes of Mortals   33, 100–02, 127, 207 n. 9

Gildas's *De excidio et conquestu Britanniae*   190
Glastonbury   52–61, 196
as cosmopolitan literary centre   56, 60–61, 165, 240, 245
and the Exeter codex   52–54, 60–61
God's Gifts to Humankind   15–16, 24–25, 81, 96–97, 110, 120–21, 130, 166–67, 194
Gospels   96, 107, 124, 230–31
grammatica   17 n. 27, 19, 34, 46 n. 19, 160, 199
Quintilian's *Institutio Oratoria*   181

Guthlac (the protagonist)   53, 84–87, 94–95, 129, 135, 177, 198, 199, 215, 216, 217, 235 n. 33, 240 (with n. 1)
characterized by his speeches   131–32
cheerful demeanour   132, 217
as exemplar of the *ars moriendi*   132
as lover of Christ   91–92 n. 54
significance of his name   85
as spiritual warrior   85–86, 198–99
See also Felix's *Vita Guthlaci*; *Holy Death of Saint Guthlac*; *Life of Saint Guthlac*

heroic ethos   9–10, 16, 130–31
directed to Christian ends   9, 10, 11, 14, 16, 17, 38, 43, 92, 129, 184–85, 198, 213–15, 215–16, 240
and 'heroic Christianity'   10, 17
and the higher social ranks   240
undermined   92–93, 119–20, 157, 162
Holy Death of Saint Guthlac   84 (with n. 36), 86–87, 108–09, 198
See also Felix's *Vita Guthlaci*; Guthlac; *Life of Saint Guthlac*
Husband's Message   60, 65–66, 118, 134, 142–43, 151–52
paired with *Wife's Lament*   142 (with n. 166)

iconography   44, 140
of King Edgar as vicar of Christ   44
of the Rood   75
of Saint Benedict   114
Isaiah   83, 112, 230 (with n. 16)
as a dramatic persona   134
Isidore of Seville   71 (with n. 9), 100 nn. 77–78, 121–22, 152 n. 12, 159
Isidorean view of universe   72, 130

Job   111, 112, 135
John the Baptist   140, 212
Juliana (the protagonist)   58–59, 91–92, 93, 176–77, 215, 216
characterized by her speeches   133
as *Godes cempa* 'God's warrior'   92
See also *Passion of Saint Juliana*
Junius Manuscript   6, 41, 46

keywords   162, 193, 204–22, 225
defined   204–05 (with n. 3)
King Alfred the Great   18, 40, 55 n. 43, 238

land of the living   78 (with n. 26), 91, 131

Latin language   15, 17–18, 22, 25, 28, 45, 53,
    56, 57, 76–77, 160, 161, 162, 180–81,
    238. *See also* bilingualism; verse
    (medieval Latin)
Leofric (bishop)   49, 54
    donations to Exeter Cathedral   49–52,
        53–54, 61, 159–60, 232, 239
libraries (Anglo-Saxon)   35–36
Life of Saint Guthlac   12 n. 13, 58, 84–86, 91,
    92, 135, 194–96, 198, 208, 215, 219–22,
    235 n. 33, 240
    possible authorship   84 (with n. 36)
    See also Felix's *Vita Guthlaci*; Guthlac; *Holy
        Death of Saint Guthlac*
literacy (medieval)   26 n. 15, 28 (with
    n. 18), 61, 238
    of the laity   28, 45–46
liturgical drama   34, 80 (with n. 28), 140
    (with n. 163)

matter of history   86, 118–21, 125–27, 129
    Alexander the Great   225 (with n. 3)
    Eadwacer   125–27
    Eormanric   119, 120 (with n. 120), 127
    Odoacer   126–27
    Theodoric   119–20, 126, 127, 192 n. 30
miles Christi 'warrior of Christ'   11–14,
    96–97, 107–08 (with n. 94), 115,
    196–97, 216, 220–22, 240
    Guthlac as model   85–86, 177
    sources in Latin tradition   11–13
miscellanies (medieval)   32, 56–57, 68–69,
    71, 72, 121, 165, 170, 179, 231, 239
monastic poetics   ix, 5–6, 89, 132, 159, 161,
    162, 182, 184, 186, 220, 238
    defined   4–5 (with n. 4)
    as a hybrid poetics   5, 155, 161
    as a tool for conversion   5, 13–20
monasticism   8, 9, 97, 114
    the abbot as spiritual father   113
    discipline of reading   36
    monks as the Lord's warriors   9, 11,
        12–13, 196–97
    and the *opus dei* 'work of God'   7, 36, 199
    the word 'monk'   130 n. 146
    See also monasticism (Anglo-Saxon); Rule
        of Saint Benedict
monasticism (Anglo-Saxon)   7–8 (with
    n. 7), 13–14, 20, 22–23, 48, 61, 75 n. 17,
    91, 114, 144, 168, 184, 185, 186, 193
    (with n. 32), 195–98, 222
    bilingual character   41–42, 45
    Continental connections   41

monastic cathedrals   28
royal patronage   14, 41, 42–43
tenth-century growth   40–41
and Viking assaults   243–44
See also Benedictine Reform
music   10, 15–16, 109–10, 157, 219, 244

New Minster Charter   44

oral poetry (in Anglo-Saxon context)
    16–18, 19 (with n. 32), 23, 25, 27, 38
    its traditional functions   16
Ovid's *Ars Amatoria*   57, 245
    his *Heroides*   170 (with nn. 15–16), 232,
        236 (with n. 35)

Panther   136, 137
paronomasia   73, 75, 160, 162 (with n. 37),
    172
    as a language of duplicity   115–16, 171,
        175–76, 209–10
Partridge   136–37
Passion of Saint Juliana   29, 58–59, 82, 86,
    91–93, 133 (with n. 150), 136, 144, 146,
    227–28, 230
    chief source   91 (with n. 53)
    subversion of heroic values   92–93, 99
Penitent's Prayer   73 (with n. 11), 94, 95, 140,
    143, 212
    character of the speaker   130, 131, 132,
        207–08, 216–17, 235–36 (with
        n. 32)
    compared to *Wife's Lament*   234–37
peregrinatio pro amore dei ('pilgrimage for the
    love of God')   60, 98
periphrasis   86, 91, 181
Pharaoh   30, 74, 190
Phoenix   58, 72, 80, 81, 86, 89–91, 108–09,
    112, 135, 157, 160 n. 31, 161, 196, 219,
    245 n. 6
    chief Latin source   72, 89–90
    and the earthly paradise   91
    and the heavenly paradise   208, 219
    macaronic close   17 n. 28, 162
    use of rhyme   161–62
Physiologus   136–37. *See also Panther*;
    Partridge; *Whale*
Prudentius's *Psychomachia*   11, 12, 17
psalms (book of)   viii, 5, 20, 109, 110, 188
    as foundation of literacy   28 (with n. 18)
    Psalm 18   182
    Psalm 23   94 (with n. 60)
    Psalm 33   57

General Index

Psalm 73   117 (with n. 114)
Psalm 106   220 n. 45
Psalm 110   59
Psalm 111   209 (with n. 16)
Psalm 117   229 n. 14
Psalm 131   237 n. 37

reading practices (medieval)   29–30, 36 (with n. 38), 239
   page by page   187
   as part of the *opus dei*   36, 164, 239
Regularis Concordia   5 n. 6, 40 n. 1, 80 n. 28, 101–02
rhetorical figures (Latinate)   15, 73, 156, 159–63
   adapted into the vernacular   160–62, 163
   homeoteleuton (end rhyme)   154, 161
   prosopopoeia   133–34, 152 (with n. 12)
   ubi sunt motif   48 (with n. 23), 71 n. 9, 113
   See also amplificatio; ethopoeia; paronomasia
rhetorical tropes   156, 159
   allegory   11, 72, 113, 136–37, 156–57, 161, 163, 169–70 n. 14, 196, 197, 219, 227
   metaphor   81, 156–57, 163, 227
Rhyming Poem   55, 61, 109–10, 116–18, 154–55
   character of the speaker   109–10, 199, 216, 241
   compared with *The Wanderer*   110, 116–17
riddles (of Exeter Anthology). *See* Exeter enigmas
riddles (medieval)
   as a distinct genre   165
   instructional role   164
   and medieval miscellanies   165
   See also Aldhelm; Exeter enigmas
Rood (the Cross)   75, 84, 85, 142, 219 (with n. 43), 222. *See also* Dream of the Rood; Exeter enigmas, Riddle 30
Ruin   143, 156 (with n. 19), 187–92, 200–01, 201–02, 224–25, 226–27, 230
   its genre   143, 188
   its hermeneutic qualities   155–56
   its localization (Bath or Rome)   191–92
   its placement in the Anthology   77, 187–91, 199
   riddle-like   142, 146
   set in pagan past   189–90

   and *The Wanderer* and *The Seafarer*   188–89
   and theme of divine wrath   188, 190
   and theme of mutability   188, 191–92
Rule of Saint Benedict   5 n. 6, 9 (with n. 11), 12–13, 34, 36, 56, 88–89, 97–98, 101, 103, 111, 144, 158 n. 26, 214 n. 29, 231, 239
   Æthelwold's Old English translation   13, 14, 42, 56, 230–31
   on dangers of drink   158 n. 26
   and fear of the Lord   58 (with n. 50)
   and virtue of obedience   13 (with n. 17)
Rune Poem   6, 146, 151–52
runes   142, 146, 151, 152
   in Anglo-Saxon manuscripts   35, 146
   in the Exeter riddles   146–52
   names of the runes   29 (with n. 22), 148, 149, 152

Saint Dunstan's Classbook   245
   eclectic contents   56–57
   frontispiece   xii–xiii (Fig. 1)
saints' lives. *See* Felix's *Vita Guthlaci*; *Life of Saint Guthlac*; *Passion of Saint Juliana*
scribes   21, 26 (with n. 15), 27, 32, 107–08
   hero scribes, master scribes   21
Scriptural paraphrase   6, 46, 47, 87–88, 112, 230–31
Seafarer   59, 82, 98–99, 105–06, 136, 162, 197, 206, 207, 210, 211–12, 225
   allegorical dimension   197, 225–30
   character of the speaker   98, 116, 131
   and ethos of monasticism   233 n. 25
   homiletic close   31 (with n. 28), 116, 128–29, 209 n. 16, 219–20
   Irish and Welsh affinities   60
   and theme of pilgrimage   60, 211, 212
   Vainglory as companion piece   99, 202, 241
   Wanderer as companion piece   99
seafaring   146–47 (with nn. 5–6), 149
   as religious trope   82, 136, 137, 197, 225
Solomon (the figure of wisdom)   112, 134
Solomon and Saturn   6, 60–61, 146, 152
Soul's Address to the Body   23, 94, 101, 135, 137–38, 211
   compared with *Vainglory*   137–38
spiritual warfare   9, 12 (with n. 14), 20, 21, 85, 86 (with n. 40), 91–92, 99, 107–08, 141, 220–22
   and the Epistles of Saint Paul   11, 13

the pen as weapon 107–08, 156–57
  See also miles Christi
style (of Old English verse)
  and devotional themes 18–20, 180–87
  See also Exeter Anthology, style

textual communities (Anglo-Saxon) 22–24, 38, 144, 187, 205
timor dei 'fear of God' 57–59, 105, 114, 209
translation 56, 180–82 (with n. 3), 183–84, 234
  The Wanderer translated 246–48
  See also periphrasis; Index of Old English Words Discussed

Vainglory 33, 93, 99, 114–16, 117, 135, 137–38, 158, 202, 241
  excoriation of sensuality and pride 99, 115
  homiletic source 115
Vercelli Book 6, 29, 41, 65, 233, 241
verse (medieval Latin) 17, 18, 38, 46, 55, 139–40, 175
  as providing models in schools 15, 23, 39, 46, 159, 164, 239, 251–53
  See also Aldhelm; Bede; Prudentius's *Psychomachia*
verse (Old English) 5–7, 15, 41–42, 47, 52, 72–73, 118, 133, 138–39, 152–53, 159, 163, 181–82, 243
  its affective power 5, 14, 15, 239
  its formulaic character 19 (with n. 32), 20, 90
  and heroic values 14, 16, 209–10, 213–14
  inseparable from the Latin tradition 48–49, 160, 161, 162, 165, 183, 187, 234, 238
  as medium for Christian doctrine 6–7, 14, 15–17, 19, 33–34, 38, 93–94, 107–09, 162, 163, 182, 238
  possible educational role 18–20, 34, 39, 46–49
  read silently at times 37–38, 159
  as a tool of conversion 15–17
  traditional uses 4, 6–7, 16, 240
versification (Old English) 152–56, 185–86
  as amenable to *amplificatio* 181–83
  as encouraging heroic diction 184–85
Versified Lord's Prayer 6, 74, 77, 182–83
Virgin Mary 44, 53, 141
  as a dramatic persona 134, 140
  her role in *Advent Lyrics* 53, 78, 176

Wanderer (the speaker)
  his character 94, 95, 99, 110, 113, 130, 132, 171, 208
  as a 'lone dweller' 94–95, 130–31
  as virtuous pagan 130–31, 217–18
Wanderer ix, 9, 48, 65, 93–96, 99, 100, 113, 116–17, 147–48 n. 6, 188–89, 209 n. 16, 213–18, 228, 230, 233
  and genre of *planctus* 94
  polyphonic effect 95, 113
  speech divisions 95 (with n. 65)
warrior aristocracy (Anglo-Saxon) 9, 13–14, 94, 198–99
  as connoisseurs of verse 18
  as monastic converts 13–14 (with n. 18)
Whale 136 (with n. 156), 137
Widsith (the bard) 16, 117, 118, 121, 127–29, 132
Widsith 100, 118–21, 127–29, 201, 202–03, 224–25
  date (disputed) 119 nn. 118–19
  suitably paired with *Deor* 118
  two voices in 100, 127, 128–29
Wife's Lament 20, 94, 121, 132–33, 154, 169–71, 178, 210
  bleak physical setting 218, 237
  Ovidian affinities 169–70, 232
  set in pre-Christian era 133, 236–37
  and *Husband's Message* 142, 235 n. 30
  and *Penitent's Prayer* 234–37
wisdom literature 6, 10, 69, 77 (with n. 21), 93–110, 111–12, 224
  Christ as source of all wisdom 111
  the figure of the sage 107, 111–18
  wisdom as a quest, not a thing 30–31, 111–12, 114, 184–85, 199
Wonder of Creation 4, 16, 30–31, 81, 107–09, 117, 132, 136, 179, 182
  character of the speaker 107, 117, 132
  chief source 182
  as manifesto for new kind of poetry 108–09
Wulf and Eadwacer 94, 121–27, 129, 133, 153, 171, 178, 236 n. 35
  name and role of Eadwacer 123–24, 125–27
  not about adultery 124–25
  Ovidian affinities 169–70 (with n. 15)
Wulfstan's *Sermo Lupi ad Anglos* 190, 244

zelus bonus 'good zeal' 9 (with n. 11), 10, 214 n. 29. *See also* heroic ethos

www.ingramcontent.com/pod-product-compliance
Lightning Source LLC
Chambersburg PA
CBHW021137230426

43667CB00005B/144